AF335053

PROFESSIONALISM AND PUBLIC SERVICE

**The Institute of Public Administration of Canada Series
in Public Management and Governance**

Editor: Luc Bernier

This series is sponsored by the Institute of Public Administration of Canada as part of its commitment to encourage research on issues in Canadian public administration, public sector management, and public policy. It also seeks to foster wider knowledge and understanding among practitioners, academics, and the general public.

For a list of books published in the Series, see page 343.

Professionalism and Public Service

Essays in Honour of Kenneth Kernaghan

Edited by David Siegel and Ken Rasmussen

IPAC — IAPC

The Institute of
Public Administration of Canada

L'Institut d'administration
publique du Canada

UNIVERSITY OF TORONTO PRESS

Toronto Buffalo London

© University of Toronto Press Incorporated 2008
Toronto Buffalo London
www.utppublishing.com
Printed in Canada

ISBN 978-0-8020-9349-3

Printed on acid-free paper

Library and Archives Canada Cataloguing in Publication

Professionalism and public service : essays in honour of Kenneth
  Kernaghan / edited by David Siegel and Ken Rasmussen.

(Institute of Public Administration of Canada series in public management
and governance)
Includes bibliographical references.
ISBN 978-0-8020-9349-3

1. Public administration – Canada.   2. Civil service – Canada.
I. Kernaghan, Kenneth, 1940–   II. Rasmussen, Ken A., 1957–   III. Siegel,
David   IV. Institute of Public Administration of Canada   V. Series.

JL75.P758 2008   351.71   C2008-901552-5

University of Toronto Press acknowledges the financial assistance to its
publishing program of the Canada Council for the Arts and the Ontario
Arts Council.

University of Toronto Press acknowledges the financial support for its
publishing activities of the Government of Canada through the Book
Publishing Industry Development Program (BPIDP).

Contents

Foreword

When we realized that Ken Kernaghan's retirement from teaching was imminent, we recognized that it was important to ensure that his career received the commemoration it deserved. He has been one of the brightest lights in the field of public administration for the past four decades. He has made a significant mark in the academic and practitioner communities. We thought it important to recognize such a significant career in a special manner.

We must draw attention to how the first sentence in the previous paragraph is worded. Ken retired from his position at Brock University as of 31 December 2007. However, he shows no signs of retiring in the broader sense. He remains highly active as a researcher and as an adviser to governments. It is always dangerous to assemble a Festschrift like this for someone who is still so active. However, we felt it important to recognize his contribution to the field, and the occasion of his retirement from his long-time university post was as good an occasion as any.

A great many people played a role in the development of this book. It says something about Ken that it was easy for us to assemble as authors virtually all the strongest scholars in the field of public administration. Ken's status is such that everyone was pleased and proud to be making a contribution. The contributors include peers, colleagues, former students, academics, and public servants, both Canadian and international. They are the best and brightest of their generation, and we thank them for the willing contribution they have made.

The production of the book went very smoothly. Patrice Dutil and the late Joe Galimberti of the Institute of Public Administration of Canada provided early encouragement and support. Wendy Feldman ably took up the work at the Institute at the time of publication. Virgil Duff provided expert support at University of Toronto Press. Matthew Kudelka did an excellent job of copy editing and bringing together a number of diverse writing styles. The editors are also grateful for the financial support of the Institute of Public Administration of Canada, Brock University, and the University of Regina.

Finally, the book is dedicated to Ken Kernaghan, one of the great scholars of his time.

Abbreviations

ADENAP	l'Association des diplômés de l'École nationale d'administration publique
CAB	Canadian Association of Broadcasters
CAPAM	Commonwealth Association for Public Administration and Management
CAPPA	Canadian Association of Programs in Public Administration
CCMD	Canadian Centre for Management Development
CIO	Chief Information Officer
CMT	Common Measurement Tool
CPO	Consultation Projects Office
CRA	Canada Revenue Agency
CRTC	Canadian Radio-television and Telecommunications Commission
CSPS	Canada School of Public Service
DFAIT	Department of Foreign Affairs and International Trade Canada
ENAP	École nationale d'administration publique
EROPA	Eastern Regional Organization for Public Administration
FCM	Federation of Canadian Municipalities
FMC	Falls Management Corporation
GMP	gross maximum price
GOL	Government Online
IIAS	International Institute of Administrative Sciences
IMA	Innovative Management Award
IPAC	Institute of Public Administration of Canada
IQEA	Institut Québécois d'Ethique Appliqué

IT	information technology
IVR	interactive voice response
MMAH	Ministry of Municipal Affairs and Housing
NGO	non-governmental organization
NPM	New Public Management
NSAIDs	non-steroidal anti-inflammatory drugs
OCC	Ontario Casino Corporation
OECD	Organisation for Economic Co-operation and Development
OLGC	Ontario Lottery and Gaming Corporation
OPS	Ontario Public Service
PCO	Privy Council Office
PPBS	Planning Programming and Budgeting System
PSC	Public Service Commission
PSCIOC	Public Sector Chief Information Officer Councils
PSSDC	Public Sector Service Delivery Council
PWGSC	Public Works and Government Services Canada
RFP	request for proposal
SAPs	structural adjustment programs
SSHRC	Social Sciences and Humanities Research Council
TQM	total quality management
VAC	Veteran Affairs Canada

Introduction
Kenneth Kernaghan: Values, Ethics, and Canadian Public Administration

KEN RASMUSSEN AND DAVID SIEGEL

The discipline of public administration in Canada has made tremendous strides in a few generations, and like most disciplines it has its legacy of individual intellectual achievements that act as markers of this progress. Beginning with R. McGregor Dawson and then through to J.E. Hodgetts we witness Canadian public administration developing a distinctive intellectual tradition based on an ever more nuanced view of the role of the public service as a political institution in society.

Dawson was the first scholar to examine the public service in a systematic way. He noted its growing power as well as its need for greater independence from politicians if it was to help articulate a national interest in public policy formulation and implementation. But he also recognized that because of this new power and influence, the public service needed to be subjected to rigorous scholarly inquiry. To this end, he pried the study of public administration away from its traditional position – that is, subordinate to philosophy, history, classics, and law – making it clear through his scholarship that the study of government, and specifically the public service, must move beyond the study of its historical and legal position.

J.E. Hodgetts was the natural successor to Dawson and was himself the subject of a Festschrift by the public administration community in Canada.[1] He introduced a highly influential functionalism into the study of Canadian bureaucracy; he is equally notable for his perception that the public service is an organic and dynamic part of the Canadian government that evolved in tandem with political institutions and the broader social environment. Hodgetts, like Dawson, recognized the power of the public service; thus he placed accountability at the core of his scholarship. Both men saw and welcomed the growing influence and power of the public service even while recognizing that it would need to develop new relationships to ensure that it remained accountable to rapidly evolving political institutions.

Kenneth Kernaghan is the obvious successor to these scholars. He is staunchly 'Canadian' in the sense that he views our public administration as distinctive because of the particular institutional dynamics associated with the Government of Canada. Like Dawson and Hodgetts before him, he sees the public service as a powerful actor within the government that needs to be examined not as an appendage to political institutions but rather as an independent organization, one that is made responsible to government in a myriad of relationships and not simply through hierarchy.[2] But he has moved beyond the study of political/bureaucratic structures – a study that for many years was at the heart of scholarship – in order to look much more closely at issues associated with what has come to be referred to as public management. Political concerns regarding power, responsibility, and accountability informed his earlier work; more recently he has explored questions surrounding the management of the Canadian public service.

Kernaghan is somewhat unique in that he has focused on the importance of values and ethics in reconciling the political with the managerial. He argues that values and ethics are key for the development of a professional public service as well as crucial to most administrative reforms, which, to succeed, must delegate authority to public servants. He has argued that the 'choice made now to pay continuous and systematic attention to public service ethics is likely to make a long-term difference to public servants' trust in one another and to public confidence in government.'[3] In the wake of the sponsorship scandal (among others), Kernaghan has continued to argue that simply applying more rules will never bring an end to such events. To achieve successful and ethical public management, the normative foundations of public service must be recognized and strengthened.

It follows that values and ethics are at the heart of public administration's approach to balancing its relationship with legitimate political authority while responding to the needs of Canadians. This balance requires a public service that is committed to ethical and values-based leadership. But for Kernaghan, this is never a case of one set of values trumping another; rather, it involves the coexistence of various values, including ethical values, democratic values, and professional values. An awareness of competing values and of the compromises they require is much more likely to produce positive administrative results, increased trust in government, and better service to Canadians, especially when compared to simply writing up detailed sets of guidelines.[4]

This tendency to seek out the complexities within emerging issues surrounding public administration is a hallmark of Kernaghan's scholarship. It has allowed him to navigate between the positive and the negative in administrative reform processes, and to do so without becoming a partisan for any particular academic camp. He often expresses his desire to balance these tensions and paradoxes in the subtitles of his articles. Some key examples: 'Conceptual and Practical Considerations,' 'Ethical, Political, and Managerial Considerations,' 'Finding the Balance Point,' 'Revolutionary Advance or Passing Fancy,' and 'Road to Renewal or Impractical Vision?' His attitude towards debate in the discipline of public administration is always to 'keep the pot boiling.' And no one is better at doing that than Ken Kernaghan.

A clear example of this attitude relates to the issue of public service reform in the 1990s based on the New Public Management (NPM) model. Kernaghan agreed with many of his colleagues that this reform model had been framed using an inappropriate market metaphor; yet he was reluctant to dismiss NPM out of hand. Rather, he wanted to learn what was useful from various experiences with this model – both its failures and its successes – and thereby find ways to incrementally improve the operations of governments. Indeed, throughout his career he has remained open to the idea of examining and improving the performance of public organizations by examining the private sector literature on organizational behavior and organizational theory, and he has done much to alert public administration scholars to the valuable work being done in associated disciplines.

In examining the subjects that Kernaghan has chosen to write about during his career, it is clear that he is aware of the legacy, traditions, and institutions surrounding Canadian public administration and that he also has his eye out for the 'next big thing' in his discipline that might be of real benefit to public servants, scholars, and Canadians more generally. Though he is always sensitive to the importance of key conventions such as ministerial responsibility and civil service neutrality – indeed, he gave these conventions their most rigorous modern articulation – he never overlooks the importance of management innovations, whether it is the arrival of electronic government or the use of public–private partnerships. His scholarship never focuses on determining which institutional arrangement is superior or which new practice threatens existing institutions and practices. Rather, he insists that we must remain open to the possibility of innovation and that we can learn much that is useful from various experiments with reform without doing harm to the important values and traditions associated with the existing public sector.

With his interest in how organizations actually work and in the possibilities associated with reform, Ken Kernaghan has long been a champion of the middle level of the public bureaucracy. He feels that the wisdom, restlessness, and intelligence of this group has been underutilized and must be tapped into by governments if they hope to overcome some of the problems inherent in large-scale organizations. Thus he has always encouraged public servants to develop and implement new approaches to public management and not worry about the scholarly debates swirling around NPM and other controversial issues. He also considers it important for scholars to involve themselves directly with individual reformers, for this can 'assist and encourage their efforts by a rigorous analysis of the political and managerial implications and the purposes, benefits and limitations of these new approaches.'[5] He hopes that academics and career public servants will find ways to develop bonds of mutual support and trust that in the end will improve the quality of service delivery and governance more generally. This is not just a useful suggestion for others, but something he has taken to heart, most recently as chair of the Federal Task Force on the Disclosure of Wrongdoing. He views the public service as much more than an organizational appendage of government; he has come to regard it as an organic entity that thrives on its connections with the world beyond government departments and institutions.

His interest in public management and the role of middle managers in public organizations is genuine, yet he has never overlooked the key role retained by politicians in successful reforms. Only politicians can launch major public administration reforms. However, Kernaghan reminds them that they have to defend those reforms in public and in Parliament if they are to have any chance of succeeding. He has been quick to urge politicians to support new initiatives such as empowerment and the Quality Service Initiative, not because they are going to lead by themselves to improved public service, but because they represent a genuine effort by many individuals to bring new ideas to the attention of decision makers – ideas with the potential to improve the quality of public administration in Canada.

Despite all the positive efforts from public servants, Kernaghan has observed with alarm a decline in the stature of the public service in the eyes of Canadians and, more crucially, a decline in morale among public servants. In his view, this dilemma can be resolved by developing a more values-based public service, one that operates with respect for Parliament and citizens but that remains aware of its own special role in democracy. Other groups in society need to play their part in halting this erosion of public service as an honourable profession; but the public service itself must further this effort to make public service again 'an honour to be coveted.'[6]

The key to reviving public service as a desirable career for the most talented Canadians is to focus on values. Kernaghan is well aware that without a meaningful regime of values and ethics, only bureaucratic regulations are left. An excessive reliance on rules leads to frustrated citizens, inertia in the public service, and politicians who rely on yet more rules and who are uninterested in or unaware of the negative consequences of a rules-based regime for the long-term prospects for the public service. Kernaghan makes a telling argument that ethical conduct by public officials is essential if the public's trust in government is to be enhanced. At a minimum this requires a written code of ethics, because only by establishing such a code can the debate move beyond arguing about the existence of various values. For Kernaghan, the lack of a written code of ethics signals a lack of commitment to values in general and sends all the wrong signals, both internally and externally.[7]

Written codes provide some certainty, and they narrow the scope for personal discretion, but they do not eliminate the importance of ethical choices. To ensure that personal ethical standards are harmonized with organizational ethics, and to improve ethical sensitivity and understanding, public servants must receive ethics training from the organization's leadership. In this sense, ethical leadership is, for Kernaghan, the single most important determinant of ethical behavior. He notes that 'public servants are more effectively motivated by concrete examples of values-based leadership than by lofty declarations of values.'[8] Of course, leadership is not the exclusive preserve of deputy ministers; it is also found in the middle ranks: 'While values-based leadership is especially important at the senior levels of public organizations, it can be found – and encouraged – at all levels.'[9]

Kernaghan is concerned about ethics because, like Dawson and Hodgetts, he recognizes that public servants exercise power in the Canadian political system. Indeed, this recognition is central to his scholarship. He realizes that public servants can be a negative or positive influence on policy making, and he has worked to ensure that they remain a positive influence. Again, he is committed to the idea of values as a means to ensure this. In the end, he believes that the cause of popular distrust of government is never the *expansion* of administrative power; rather, the cause is the irresponsible *exercise* of this power by public servants and politicians.

The question of how to address the growing power of the public service is never easy to answer, and Kernaghan has never been swayed by simple arguments. For example, when discussing representative bureaucracy, he acknowledges that this has great symbolic value but is adamant that it will not lead to a more responsive bureaucracy. Simply adding individuals from designated groups will not bring this about because these individuals, if they are to do their jobs effectively, will need to remain responsible in a hierarchal manner. The value of representative bureaucracy is that it signals powerfully that there are no barriers to individual success in society.

Ken Kernaghan has long contended that bureaucratic power can be controlled most effectively by subjective responsibility supported by a strong ethics regime informed by ethical leadership. He has consistently rejected calls for a more objective type of responsibility based on rules and procedures. He has been expanding on the notion of subjective responsibility for much of his career, especially with his idea that administrative power can be checked by rigorously examining public servants' values.

Kernaghan has always struck a delicate balance between the subjective and the objective, recognizing that both values and rules are needed in order to create and support change in the behaviour of public servants. He never promotes an unhealthy dogmatism. Public administration is never a place for absolutes; rather, it requires thoughtful examination and principled compromises. It can never function on the basis of strict legislative constraints, but neither can it function on the basis of appeals only to the conscience and morality of public servants.

Ken Kernaghan unequivocally supports the view that values are the key to an effective public service, but he also realizes that value conflicts are possible. Thus he notes that a value such as accountability naturally conflicts with responsiveness. Still, he has always felt that 'the way in which public servants use their power will be shaped by a mix of these values and the relative importance of the values will vary over time.'[10] For a democratic society to be healthy, it *must* create a regime of firm but flexible values.

Ken Kernaghan is, above all, a very precise scholar who is concerned about making certain that definitions and words were used correctly, especially in the world of public management, which is often influenced by fads. Much of his scholarship focuses on defining concepts such as political neutrality, whistleblowing, and ethics; as a consequence he has influenced the very terms used for discussing the discipline. Likewise, he has long made a point of treating with respect and understanding the ideas with which he engages. Unlike a number of public administration scholars, he never dismisses out of hand ideas such as empowerment and total quality management (TQM). Rather, he seriously examines those ideas in an attempt to uncover what is useful and familiar in them and how they can be made to work in the context of public administration. He is equally adamant about the need for government organizations to accommodate themselves to new trends if the public service is to cope with change while still attracting highly qualified employees who will serve the public interest. Finally, it is hardly a surprise to note that more often than not, his conclusions have been correct.

The essays in this book reflect Ken Kernaghan's enduring concerns. As editors, we have attempted to include an essay representing every field in which he has made a contribution. Not surprisingly, this has turned out to cover practically every aspect of Canadian public administration. It is our good fortune that we have succeeded in attracting some of the best minds in the field to this project; as a result we have been able to produce a book that covers all of the current and enduring issues in public administration and public management.

We have asked each contributor to write an essay that discusses how his or her area of the discipline has evolved in recent years and the role that Ken Kernaghan has played in that evolution. We have also asked each contributor to speculate on future developments in the field.

Part One focuses on how some of the traditional public service institutions have evolved. This is an appropriate first topic because Ken Kernaghan has been one of the main chroniclers of this evolution – and sometimes its leader.

In chapter 1, Peter Aucoin traces the development of NPM, which, as he points out, is no longer so new. He then identifies some tensions that he sees developing between traditional NPM and elements of empowerment and what he calls the New Public Governance.

In chapter 2, Paul Thomas wonders whether there is a need for yet another discussion of accountability, and then goes on to answer his own question in a brilliant fashion by summarizing the various uses (and misuses) of the term, analysing the current accountability regime (or lack thereof), and speculating on some interesting potential future developments in this field.

In chapter 3, on political neutrality, David Good draws on his many years of experience as a senior public servant. To illustrate the unworkability of the ideal model of political neutrality, he begins with a hypothetical discussion between a minister and a deputy minister. He goes on to review some of the working principles developed by Ken; then he fashions three new principles of his own that he feels can serve as practical guides to action in this dangerous minefield.

In chapter 4, Michael Duggett, the Executive Director of the International Institute of Administrative Sciences at the time of writing, reflects on Ken's fifteen years as editor of the *International Review of Administrative Sciences* by tracing how the journal, during his tenure, treated the important issue of privatization. This provides some significant insights into the ways in which the views of the academic community on an important issue changed over time.

Part Two focuses on the public service as an institution. This reflects Ken's respect for the quality of the public service. His concern that its position be protected and improved is well known.

Chapter 5, the first in this section, is Iain Gow's aptly titled 'Between Ideals and Obedience.' As this suggests, Gow grapples with the age-old but still highly topical issue of the extent to which public servants can allow their own ethical values to direct their activities – that is, instead of following the directions of their political masters.

In chapter 6, Evert Lindquist offers an overview of some of the shocks that have hit the public service in the past few years and discusses the extent to which the injection of more 'soul' or 'spirituality' into the public service might help mitigate some of the problems he identifies.

In chapter 7, Jacques Bourgault and Esther Parent discuss an old question: Is the public service a profession? They tie their discussion to the evolving role of pride and recognition as instruments for improving the quality of the public service. They then report on an interesting survey of how governments are using incentive systems to foster recognition and develop pride among public servants.

Part Three focuses on recent innovations in service delivery – the focus of Ken's current research. It says something about Ken that he could have rested on his laurels and stayed in comfortable territory; instead he developed an interest in these recent innovations. He always seems to be on the cutting edge.

Sandford Borins and David Brown are currently working on a major project with Ken relating to electronic means of delivering government services. In chapter 8 they present eight case studies illustrating the use of electronic consultation in the federal and Ontario governments. They then draw some conclusions and provide some advice about best practices.

In chapter 9, on public–private partnerships, Jennifer Berardi builds on Ken's widely used typology of partnerships to analyse the development of the Niagara Fallsview Casino. She concludes that partnerships can produce desirable results, but she also raises some questions about how the partnership form was implemented in this particular case.

In chapter 10, Brian Marson discusses Canada's position as a leader in the provision of citizen-centred services. First he tracks how Canadian governments have measured levels of citizen satisfaction and have identified the drivers of that satisfaction. Then he discusses how governments have used this basic information to improve quality of services.

Part Four focuses on an area that has long interested Ken. He has never been the sort of passive academic who writes for the sake of writing. He has always been active in disseminating new information, and he has directed his research and writing with the goal of developing the current and next generations of public servants. This is evident in his involvement in professional associations and his concern about education.

One of the groups in which Ken has long been active is the Institute of Public Administration of Canada (IPAC). In chapter 11, Patrice Dutil and Michael McConkey write about how IPAC has transformed itself from a membership-based learned organization into a strong non-governmental organization drawing significant amounts of funding from international contracts. This has been vital to the health of the organization and has had a highly beneficial impact on the state of public administration in Canada. This transformation has given Canada a window on the world and allowed many Canadians to obtain valuable experience working in international settings.

In chapter 12, Barbara Wake Carroll, the current editor of *Canadian Public Administration*, writes about the difficulties inherent in editing a journal that must span academic and practitioner interests. Ken was able to walk this tightrope with two different journals over a period of almost twenty-five years. Carroll praises him for the work that he did to bridge this gap but also suggests that there are still significant obstacles to be overcome in getting practitioners and academics to talk together.

Finally, in chapter 13, Carolyn Johns, editor of the Case Program in Canadian Public Administration at the time of writing, discusses the importance of case studies as tools for training and development. She also discusses the important role the Case Program has played in advancing the use of cases in university as well as public service settings. She then recounts the importance of Ken's pioneering role as the founding director of the Case Program.

As editors, we owe a debt of gratitude to the scholars who agreed to contribute to this book. Given Ken's status in the field, it did not surprise us that we were able to line up such an exceptionally strong group. Together they comprise a virtual Who's Who of public administration academics at the turn of the new century. All gave willingly of their limited time to contribute to this tribute to Ken.

The final word must be about the person to whom this book is dedicated. It is often said that all academics stand on the shoulders of those who came before them. This is certainly true about the debt of gratitude that future generations will owe to Ken Kernaghan. However, what is significant in Ken's case is how remarkably broad and supportive those shoulders are. Most academics would be happy if they were remembered for one or two truly great works that had a significant impact beyond their own generation. Ken's broad interest in all aspects of public administration and his ability to discern important issues as they emerge guarantee that his works will serve as an indispensable foundation for future generations of scholars across the entire discipline. This book is one small way of repaying the debt that so many of us and our successors will owe him.

NOTES

1 O.P. Dwivedi, *The Administrative State in Canada: Essays in Honour of J.E. Hodgetts* (Toronto: University of Toronto Press, 1982).
2 Kenneth Kernaghan, 'Changing Concepts of Power and Responsibility in the Canadian Public Service,' *Canadian Public Administration* 21 (1978): 389–406.
3 Kenneth Kernaghan, 'Toward a Public Service Code of Conduct – and Beyond,' *Canadian Public Adminsitration* 40 (1997): 40–5, 54.
4 Kenneth Kernaghan, 'The Post-Bureaucratic Organization and Public Service Values,' *International Review of Administrative Sciences* 66 (2000): 91–104, 102.

5 Kenneth Kernaghan. 'Keeping the New Public Management Pot Boiling,' *Canadian Public Administration* 38 (1995): 481–4.
6 Kenneth Kernaghan, 'An Honour to Be Coveted: Pride, Recognition, and Public Service,' *Canadian Public Administration* 44 (2001): 67–83.
7 Kenneth Kernaghan, 'Integrating Values into Public Service: The Values Statement as Centerpiece,' *Public Administration Review* 63, no. 6 (2003): 711–19.
8 Kernaghan, 'The Post-Bureaucratic Organization.'
9 Kernaghan, 'Integrating Values into Public Service,' 718.
10 Ibid., 712.

PART I

The Evolution of Traditional Institutions

Other disciplines have sometimes questioned the value of studying institutions and structures rather than values or the ultimate outcomes of public policies. Yet it is clear that the study of institutions and structural arrangements has always been one of the cornerstones of public administration studies. The four chapters in Part One of this book make it clear why those structures and institutions are important. In different ways, they all demonstrate how the changing nature of governance and the role of the state reflect the way in which organizations have been changing. In particular, all of the chapters examine the impact of various aspects of NPM on government organizations. They remind us that organizations are not static; they change – sometimes quite rapidly – to reflect changes in their environment, such as the latest trends in management. They even change to reflect crises such as the sponsorship scandal (which will be mentioned several times in this section).

Peter Aucoin is one of the most prolific and insightful commentators on NPM. In chapter 1, he begins by placing NPM in its historical context by focusing on its antecedents, which include the Glassco Commission and the general expansion of government in the 1960s and 1970s. Aucoin also helps us understand the Canadian approach to NPM by setting it in an international context. Clearly, a phenomenon like NPM can mean different things in different milieux.

Aucoin reminds us that NPM focuses on public servants as managers and not simply administrators. He cautions, however, that public servants are managing the public's business; thus there are constraints on their ability to make autonomous decisions. His concern is that NPM has emphasized efficient management but not necessarily political control over public servants. He argues that a reaction to this has led to what he calls New Public Governance (NPG), which emphasizes strong – Aucoin suggests excessive – political control of the bureaucracy. This has resulted in a bureaucracy that is too close to politicians and too willing to do their bidding. His example is the sponsorship scandal. In his prescription, he references Kernaghan's work to argue for greater empowerment of public servants so that they are properly subservient to their political masters without, however, being politicized.

In chapter 2, Paul Thomas tackles the important but elusive concept of accountability. He concedes that much has already been written about it, but he adds that the concept is continuing to change, as suggested by the use of the word 'swirling' in the chapter title. He addresses the paradox that governments have added more and more accountability mechanisms in the face of concerns by the opposition parties, the media, and the general public; yet whatever mechanisms are introduced, they are never enough to satisfy the growing demand for more accountability.

Thomas points out that accountability in Westminster systems of government has traditionally been based on ministerial responsibility; yet one of the responses to demands for more accountability has been to focus on the kind of managerial accountability that is a part of NPM. He suggests that managerial accountability is a good complement to ministerial accountability but cannot be a substitute for it.

He takes us back to basics to discuss what accountability means and what its main components are. He then raises the concern that governments keep responding to calls from the public and the media to introduce more accountability by adding more accountability mechanisms, but not necessarily in a thoughtful or systematic way. The result is certainly more accountability mechanisms, but not necessarily a better system of accountability (with the emphasis on 'system'). He laments what he calls 'multiple accountability disorder' (MAD).

In chapter 3, to illustrate the practical difficulty of separating policy and administration, David Good draws on his extensive experience as a senior public servant to construct a hypothetical discussion between a minister and a deputy minister.

He uses this to frame a discussion of the evolving nature of ministerial responsibility, public service anonymity, and political neutrality. He discusses how many of the changes discussed in the first two chapters have had a strong impact on these concepts. NPM has introduced greater transparency in the operations of government – transparency that now requires public servants to be more visible in public consultations, by appearing before Parliamentary committees, among other highly visible tasks. Furthermore, the emphasis on partnerships, citizen-centred service delivery, and horizontal coordination of policy making and delivery across several departments presents challenges to traditional ideas of ministerial responsibility.

These continual changes have required a constant rethinking of the concepts of ministerial responsibility, public service anonymity, and political neutrality. However, Good argues that it is important to reaffirm the following three tenets:

1 It is ministers, not public servants, who answer to Parliament for policy decisions and politically contentious matters, and they do so in a manner that safeguards the political neutrality and anonymity of public servants.
2 Public servants avoid activities (e.g., criticizing their minister in public) that harm or seem to harm their impartiality or the impartiality of the public service.
3 Public servants provide advice to ministers in confidence and avoid activities that involve them in public debate or political controversy.

The final chapter in this section is Michael Duggett's review of how one aspect of NPM has been implemented in a number of different countries. Drawing on articles that appeared in the *International Review of Administrative Sciences* while Ken Kernaghan was editor, he demonstrates that privatization is a global trend that has gone beyond any one ideology or the specific needs of any one government. He argues that privatization went from being a mere technical issue to a politically charged one and then back to a more technical one.

However, the wide adoption of privatization has not limited the controversy associated with it. It has sometimes been seen as positive, the belief being that emulating the private sector is bound to improve efficiency. Other times it has been seen as a method of 'human degradation via contractual employment, lower wages, harder and less permanent work; and in a society with ever more police and security machineries; a culture only of individual consumer-pursuit, public sector debt, and a decaying infrastructure.' In the end, Duggett concludes that privatization has clearly had an impact, though it has not resulted in the huge changes that were envisaged by some.

1 New Public Management and New Public Governance: Finding the Balance

PETER AUCOIN

The New Public Management (NPM) that emerged over the past twenty-five years in the Anglo-American systems, but especially in the four major Westminster systems of Australia, Britain, Canada, and New Zealand, was new in several respects, especially in the extent to which it emphasized the 'management' of resources and operations over the 'administration' of processes and procedures. Management was regarded as an active, even proactive, endeavour in the pursuit of economy, efficiency, and effectiveness; administration was seen as passive compliance with established and standardized procedures. The new was pitted against the old, the innovative against the traditional.

The rhetoric associated with NPM called into question the classic bureaucratic paradigm of a professional, non-partisan, and career public service. This classic paradigm assumed a public service that both advised ministers on matters of public policy and implemented the government's public policies through departments they directly administered. The links between ministers and their departmental public servants were thus close, even though the public service was neutral in terms of partisan politics. Public servants possessed great influence because they advised their political masters. But they were restrained in exercising personal discretion in the management and delivery of public services by centrally prescribed and monitored administrative rules and regulations that governed the deployment of financial and human resources. Public servants in this model administered systems, processes, and procedures; they did not manage much – at least, not on their own individual accord. They were administrators, not managers.

NPM promised to change all this.[1] A new paradigm of management would replace traditional public administration.[2]

NPM is hardly new any longer, but there has not emerged another ascendant paradigm in public administration.[3] In several respects, there are new iterations of public management reform, given that reform remains on the agenda as governments and their public services continue to pursue improvements in management performance, policy and program implementation, and outcomes or results. There is now, for instance, a greater recognition of the need to provide better service delivery to citizens, and not merely to secure greater economy and efficiency in government operations. Canada has emerged as a leader on this front. In Britain and New Zealand, where at the outset of NPM the focus was essentially on efforts to combat budgetary deficits and debt by streamlining the state, its programs, and the cost of their delivery, there is a new concern for achieving better services and outcomes that citizens demand. At the same time, NPM's agenda remains relevant because everywhere the effectiveness of the administration of the public's business constitutes a significant factor in a country's achievement of economic prosperity and social well-being. But in addition to NPM, there has emerged what I call a 'new public governance' (NPG) that has brought forth a new architecture for public administration that, in several respects, challenges NPM.

Ken Kernaghan has been a leading figure in what Don Kettl[4] has called the 'global public management revolution,' a revolution that encompasses NPM. Kernaghan is one of those few scholars in public administration who recognized long ago that public administration requires that public servants, as administrators, be able to manage. His early work prefigured NPM; his later work centred on the most critical management components of NPM. At the same time, he always acknowledged that public managers manage not just any kind of business but rather the *public's* business. As such, reforms that seek to improve the management dimension of public administration must always be balanced by attention to the values and ethics of the public service dimension of public administration. Not surprisingly, Kernaghan has never been an apostle of simply 'letting the managers manage'; he has always cautioned against an 'entrepreneurial' managerial style that ignores or runs roughshod over the fundamental public service character of public administration. And given his inclination to link theory to practice, he has been a leading figure in articulating the public service values and ethics that define what the public service character of public administration should mean in practice.

Before the New Public Management

More than four decades ago, in the early 1960s, just before Ken Kernaghan began his professorial career, the Canadian Royal Commission on Government Organization – the Glassco Commission – delivered a report that proposed a major reform agenda for public administration predicated on this fundamental prescription: 'Let the managers manage.' The private sector's influence in this prescription was obvious. In the private sector there are boards of directors and managers, each with different roles and responsibilities. The realm of management belongs to the latter. The Glassco Commission recognized that the public and private sectors are different; but when it came to management in the public service, it wanted the public sector to emulate the private sector as much as possible. Recall that by the 1960s, 'management' in the private sector had fully come into its own. The modern corporation, with its division of roles and responsibilities between a board of directors and managers, had become the dominant organizational form of private sector business. The MBA was the new academic credential for management in the modern corporation (notwithstanding the retention of the term 'administration' in the degree's title). And management consulting firms, as well as the accounting profession, were entering a new era of prosperity with increased status and influence as well as increased revenues.

The Glassco Commission had a strong impact on Canadian public administration, and a good deal of administrative deregulation and decentralization followed. Numerous modern management techniques were introduced by the central corporate-management agencies of government, especially by the newly established Treasury Board Secretariat (itself the creation of the Glassco Commission) and the greatly expanded (albeit independent) Public Service Commission. Many if not most of these techniques were drawn from private sector management experience. Similar developments occurred in the United States. Indeed, Canada and the United States moved to the forefront of public administration reforms internationally.

At the same time, the managerial prescriptions of the Glassco Commission did not always fit well with the Westminster system of public administration, characterized as it was by collective cabinet executive authority, responsibility, and accountability for the whole of government, on the one hand, and by individual ministerial authority, responsibility, and accountability for the separate departments of government, on the other. Public servants – even deputy ministers as the administrative heads of departments – had no recognized status separate from that of their political masters. There was no acceptance of a politics/administration dichotomy, as had long been a feature of American public administration. Furthermore, the government had a collective interest in applying standardized management rules, processes, and procedures across the entire government. For their part, ministers relied on these government-wide standards of management, established and policed by central corporate-management agencies, to ensure that their departmental public servants complied with established management practices and to relieve ministers of the need to pay ongoing attention to management issues.

Within this management context, even senior public administrators had not been called on to exercise much discretion (if any) in managing their financial and human resources, in leading their staff, or in delivering public services. While it cannot be said that the government operated on automatic pilot, the government-wide and standardized system of rules, processes, and procedures meant that managers were first and foremost administrators of 'systems.' As Hodgetts expressed it, deputy ministers had responsibilities without authority.[5] Most of these systems were designed at the centre of government and were meant to control for maladministration by departmental officials as much as they were meant to advance good management. Hence the notion of a 'command and control' structure and culture.

The growth and complexity of Western government bureaucracies after the Second World War had, paradoxically, both stimulated interest in government-wide standards to constrain public servants' discretion and diminished the likelihood that these standards would secure economy and efficiency. The drawback to a highly centralized and tightly controlled system – even assuming that it could reduce the incidence of maladministration and corrupt behaviour – was that it prevented managers from making the most economical and efficient use of resources. This was because it restricted the authority, and thus reduced the range of options, for managers to take decisions that could achieve economies and efficiencies in their particular operational settings. It also relieved managers of responsibility and accountability for managing in ways that pursued economy and efficiency. In short, it impoverished the theory and practice of management in the public service.

Emergence of the New Public Management

It is important to remember that NPM arose in the 1960s and 1970s, a time when postwar ambitions coincided with postwar affluence and when the Westminster model of impoverished management (as described above) confronted an expanding number and range of public services as state intervention in the socio-economic order increased significantly. The result was an increasing number of diversified public services, provided by an ever expanding public service bureaucracy and accompanied by growing annual government deficits and mounting national debt. By the late 1970s something had to give, and it did, with the election of several governments intent on 'rolling back the state.' Margaret Thatcher's Conservative government in Britain led the way.[6] Rolling back the state meant

1 privatizing state enterprises,
2 contracting out to the private sector the task of delivering those public services that had not been privatized,
3 eliminating some public services, and
4 reducing government spending (or at least slowing down the rate of its growth) through greater economies and efficiencies.

Privatization and contracting out were justified on two grounds: first, it would reduce budgetary requirements; and second, it would improve national economic productivity. Privatization transformed what had been public services provided by state bureaucracies into private services under private ownership and provided in the marketplace. Contracting out placed public services under private sector management.

Privatizations, of course, were one-off exercises. Once privatized, a service was no longer a public service.[7] Contracting out, on the other hand, did more than bring the private sector into public service delivery. It also introduced the idea that the 'market' – that is, competition between competing potential providers (public sector and/or private sector providers) over contracts to deliver public services – would secure greater economy and efficiency in the management of these services as opposed to having them provided by the public service as a monopoly provider. In Britain this idea constituted the foundation of a policy that went beyond the case of contracting out to the private sector whenever it was clear that increased efficiencies could be obtained. This new policy regime imposed 'compulsory market testing' that required public service managers to subject some portion of their services to market competition on an annual basis. At the same time, in the spirit of open competition, the government allowed its public service units that had formerly provided these services to compete against potential private sector providers for the contracts under tender.[8] This approach acknowledges that *competition* between potential providers is what spurs improvements in economy and efficiency; it is not the public or private status of the providers. So long as the public service provider does not have monopoly control over a service, and thus must compete periodically against private sector providers to maintain a 'contract,' it should have every incentive to achieve all possible economies and efficiencies. In this respect, it is no different from a private sector provider; its vested interest is in winning contracts to stay in business.

It did not take long, though, for public management reformers to realize that there would still be a lot left to manage once the bulk of privatization was accomplished and the contracting-out policy was in full effect.[9] NPM, in other words, also had to involve improving the management of those services which the public service would continue to provide directly – that is, those not privatized or contracted out.

The British approach to reform initially stressed achieving greater economies and efficiencies by conducting wide-ranging 'efficiency scrutinies' to search out those areas where efficiencies could be achieved and then by taking the necessary decisions to realize them. This was coupled with some streamlining of central corporate-management regulations and some decentralization of financial and human resources administrative authorities. By the end of the first decade of reform the British had also adopted a more contractual approach to public management by separating ministerial departments from what came to be called 'executive agencies.' The former retained responsibilities for setting policy and monitoring its implementation; the latter were given responsibilities for policy implementation through the delivery of public services. These executive agencies had at one time been the divisions or branches of ministerial departments that managed and delivered public services. This decoupling of 'policy' from 'operations' (often referred to as the 'Next Steps' program, because it followed on from the initial efforts to improve performance simply by devolving management authority), allowed for a full-blown, contractually based performance management structure and regime.

In New Zealand the major theoretical influence on reformers was agency theory. This resulted in a restructuring of the relationship between ministers and their chief executives so that it was grounded on a contractual basis, rather than merely a hierarchical basis. The aim was to make it much clearer what the ministers expected of their chief executives. Performance measures were established to ensure that these executives were subject to rigorous evaluation of their performance in meeting ministers' expectations. Also, a vigorous management accountability regime was put in place to keep chief executives on track and in check by their ministers. But there was more to agency theory: chief executives were now regarded as professional managers, and as such they were expected to act as the professional 'agents' of their ministers, who were their 'principals.' In this context, the managers had the authority, discretion, and flexibility to deploy and manage the resources that were provided to them by their ministers for the production ('output') of public services in the most economical and efficient manner. Ministers, in other words, would not intervene in management; that would be the realm of professional managers as agents under contract. Performance awards provided managers with incentives to be economical and efficient in their use of resources, including financial and human resources. In addition, New Zealand redesigned its departmental structures so that some advised ministers on policy while others delivered the services that ministers wanted delivered. The British terminology of 'executive agencies' was not used; but the organizational design was similar.[10]

Australia was an interesting case of NPM reform because it did not accept the policy/operations dichotomy as the basis for organizing governance and public management, as occurred in Britain and New Zealand, even though it was willing to use it in limited circumstances when there was little need for ongoing policy direction from ministers and their senior advisers. Moreover, a major reorganization of ministerial portfolios in 1987 streamlined the number of ministerial departments and made the capacity for ministerial direction even more important in the context of reform. At the same time, the government was willing to devolve management authority to senior departmental managers, in part by substantially deregulating administrative controls and redesigning the central corporate-management agencies, especially those involved in human resources. Finally, the Australian approach was interesting because the government succeeded in achieving its budgetary objectives, ending deficits, and substantially reducing its debt.[11]

Equally important, however, was that the Australian government, throughout this first decade of reform, did not lose sight of the requirement that the government achieve its agenda of intended policy 'outcomes.' In its view, managing 'inputs' (especially money and people) to produce 'outputs' (services, programs, operations) as economically and efficiently as possible was important. But so, too, was achieving effective outcomes – in other words, outputs had to have the intended effect or impact so that the desired changes in the socio-economic order actually occurred. This meant managing to outcomes. It also meant that policy design was critical: no matter how good the management of programs, if the policy design was faulty then the intended effects would not be realized. Australian reformers regarded themselves as having an approach to public management reform different from that of the British and New Zealanders, whom they saw as focused first and foremost on economy and efficiency, with too little attention paid to effectiveness.

In Canada the emergence of NPM was slow and cautious.[12] There was precious little ministerial interest until the Conservatives came to power in 1984 with a campaign platform that promised many things, including public management reform. The Mulroney government sought to emulate both Reagan and Thatcher in rolling back the state by way of a major 'program review,' headed by the deputy prime minister and assisted by teams with equal numbers of public servants and private sector managers. The result was supposed to be a major streamlining of government services and operations. This effort was a failure (as was the American effort), in contrast to the more realistic and more professional (and, ironically, more public service) conduct of efficiency scrutinies in Britain. The consequence in Canada was a decade of successive rounds of what were essentially across-the-board percentage cuts to government administrative budgets, but no major program reductions.

There was a modest effort at streamlining management regulations and delegating authority to departmental managers, but no significant restructuring to produce anything like the policy/operations organizational separations found in Britain and New Zealand. A handful of 'special operating agencies' were established, but these paled in comparison to the British and New Zealand organizational designs. They employed less than 5 per cent of the public service; equally important, they were subordinate to the deputy ministers of their 'parent' departments instead of having direct contractual relationships with ministers. Their administrative authority made them 'special' in comparison to departments, but these were modest delegations of power compared to what was happening elsewhere. As in Australia, the integrated policy and implementation ministerial department remained the norm.

In 1989, however, the federal public service, with the backing but not the enthusiastic interest of ministers, unveiled a Public Service 2000 reform program that, at least in its rhetoric and scope, sought to match developments elsewhere. It was not a success. As a public service–led reform, this program could not and did not achieve a sufficient degree of coherence. It tried to maintain traditions while promoting reforms, some of which contradicted one another. The result could not be other than a good deal of inconsistency between rhetoric and reality as well as a tendency for the various reform components to ride off in different directions.

By the mid-1990s, however, NPM had begun to give ground to reforms or initiatives that were not inspired primarily, or at all, by the theoretical or ideological underpinnings of NPM. In Australia the new conservative government aggressively pursued an NPM agenda of competition and contracting; in Britain the New Labour government did not give up on performance measurement and competition, but neither did it add anything new to the NPM paradigm. At the same time, several initiatives that drew inspiration from traditional public service ideals – or at least a mix of the new and traditional – began to make their mark in the late 1990s and into the first decade of the twenty-first century. For instance, efficient management gave ground as a priority to better service delivery, with the focus on 'citizen centred' as opposed to 'customer centred' service delivery. For its part, performance management turned away from a focus on management performance for economy and efficiency towards the effective achievement of the results or outcomes of government policies, programs, and services. And the managerial pursuit of producing an organization's contracted outputs gave way to the ideal of interorganizational (horizontal, joined up, or whole of government) collaboration in the pursuit of integrated or shared objectives. These three general initiatives – citizen-centred service delivery, results-based management, and horizontal collaboration – emerged in a period of significant public management reform. These initiatives did not contradict NPM reforms; indeed, in several respects they assumed that public service managers had sufficient authority to realize these new initiatives.

New Public Governance: Tensions with New Public Management

NPM encompassed an understanding that the relations between ministers and their public servants needed to be altered. Economies had to be achieved in order to reduce budgetary outlays, and ministers had to ensure that they controlled any budget-maximizing behaviour on the part of their bureaucrats. Ministers had to insist on better public service management in order to achieve efficiencies as a second means to reduce costs. What they wanted from NPM was improved management of resources and better delivery of public services.

At the same time, political leaders such as Thatcher, Reagan, and Mulroney were not the least bit enamoured by what they perceived to be their self-serving bureaucracies.[13] They had to ensure that they were not captured by their bureaucrats' policy preferences. Thus they had to end the bureaucracy's monopoly position in giving advice to ministers by bringing in political staff as alternative or competing sources of advice. In public choice theory, these political leaders found an academically respectable and increasingly popular theoretical justification for their position in addition to useful rhetoric with which to bash their bureaucracies.[14] The theory provided the rationale for extensive political interventions in the staffing of their respective senior public services well beyond what these two systems had previously experienced, even in the American case.[15]

In Australia, political interventions increased as well. The approach was influenced by the American experience, though the new Labor government in 1983, which was originally expected to politicize the upper echelons of the public service in the American style, on the assumption of office decided instead to significantly expand the number and roles of political staff (also an American influence). It did so in part because it was able to appoint a host of former public servants to political staff positions. Ministers continued to head departments. However, they were now advised not only by their departmental public servants but also by their political staff. This introduced a new dynamic of competition between policy advisers. As managed by successive Labor governments, nonetheless, this new style worked exceptionally well, in large part because ministers engaged their public servants instead of overriding them.[16] This style ended with the election of John Howard's Liberal-National government in 1996, when the new government decided to rely primarily on its political advisers and to appoint politically friendly public servants to senior posts in the public service.[17]

In New Zealand, a new regime for staffing the senior cadre of the public service was adopted in order to give ministers a greater say in the appointment and management of their 'chief executives' (as the former permanent heads of departments were now to be called). Given what ministers and reformers were hoping to accomplish in New Zealand by restructuring minister–chief executive relationships, the reformed regime for staffing the chief executive cadre turned out to be the most independent among the four Westminster systems.[18] Chief executives are appointed by Cabinet on the recommendation of the State Services Commissioner following an open competition for vacant positions. The Cabinet can reject a recommendation but must disclose any appointment that it makes without a recommendation from the commissioner. Not surprisingly, this has not happened. Indeed, only one recommendation has ever been rejected (which required another recommended candidate), and that was early on after the adoption of the process. Though the commissioner consults with ministers before competitions are held, ministers – including the prime minister – have little room to intervene in favour of particular candidates relative to the other Westminster systems. As a consequence, there has been less bureaucracy bashing in New Zealand than in the other Anglo-American systems now that the new chief executive staffing regime has been fully implemented.[19]

In Canada, Brian Mulroney, while on the election campaign trail in 1984, had issued a clear warning to deputy ministers that bureaucratic intransigence and obstruction would not be tolerated under a Conservative government.[20] His party had expressed interest (the same interest as had been expressed a year earlier in Australia) in the American style of political appointments to the upper echelons of the public service. As in Australia, however, the Mulroney Conservatives, once in office, opted to increase the number and strengthen the role of political staff in the prime minister's and ministers' offices.

In each of these cases, developments were emerging that could not but introduce tensions with NPM. These developments constituted what I will call the New Public Governance (NPG). This new dynamic is clearly the political element of governance, an element that cannot but affect public management reform as an integral part of governance. (Together, NPM and NPG might even be viewed as parts of a dialectic process, with NPM the thesis and NPG the antithesis but with the synthesis not yet clear.) NPG entails the following:

- The concentration of power under the prime minister and his or her 'court' of a few select ministers, political aides, and public servants.
- An increased number of political staff, and their enhanced roles and influence.
- Increased personal attention by the prime minister to the appointment of senior public servants (where the prime minister has the power to appoint).
- Increased pressure on the public service to provide a pro-government spin on government communications.
- The increased expectation that public servants will demonstrate enthusiasm for the government's agenda beyond the traditional requirement of loyal implementation of the government's program.

Under NPG, political leaders seek to reassert their democratic right to govern by taking control of the state apparatus.[21] The structures of government everywhere are thus subject to pressures that serve to concentrate power at the centre.[22]

The resulting pressures on government are myriad. At times of breaking news, political leaders find themselves having to attend to the politics of governance with virtually no time for contemplation. A revolution in communications has made government information widely available. New laws are extending to the citizenry, including the press, the right to access government information. A new coterie of external audit and review agencies are keeping government under constant scrutiny. An increasingly aggressive complex of parliamentary committees is conducting ongoing examinations of ministers and officials. Public opinion polls are constantly testing public reactions to government policies and leaders. Finally, citizens are less deferential than in the past and are demanding an accounting from government officials, be they elected or appointed.

Political systems vary in the extent to which power is concentrated, in part because of the effectiveness of formal and informal institutional arrangements that are meant to serve as checks on executive power, in part because of the capacity of political executives to assert control over their political colleagues as well as their public services. It is now sufficiently clear, however, that this phenomenon is not limited to particular individuals or even political systems: the pressures are universal and so, too, has been the increased concentration of power. Canada's experience has placed it at the forefront of the concentration of power, given the relative weakness of the checks and balances to prime ministerial power.[23]

All of this pressures governments to be more strategic in what they do and especially in what they say as well as the way they say it. Modern government communications, accordingly, have become perhaps the driving force behind the concentration of power, as the political leadership seeks to manage a constantly turbulent political environment, especially in relation to the mass media, which have vested interests in political turbulence. The growing numbers of political staff in virtually all governments cannot but exacerbate the situation, now that political popularity, as measured in the polls and by the media, is becoming the sole standard of good government. Internationally, the best-known illustration here was the tussle between Tony Blair's press secretary, Alastair Campbell, and the British public service's communications staff over Campbell's insistence that public servants be enthusiastic in communicating the government's agenda with the desired 'spin' – a tussle complicated after Blair gave Campbell, a political staff appointee and not a public servant, the unprecedented power to give orders to public servants.[24] A not dissimilar illustration was evident in a political debacle in Australia, when ministers and political staff pressured the public service to spin a story in a particular way.[25]

In the Canadian context, a number of recent debacles have provided more than sufficient evidence that NPG is a dominant feature of the Canadian regime. Canada's public service has become too subservient to the government of the day in various ways – some of these completely inappropriate, as in the sponsorship scandal. Clearly, that scandal was an extreme case. But it is not an isolated exception. There has been virtually no opposition to or criticism of Savoie's thesis that the 'bargain' between ministers and public servants – a bargain that once governed relations between ministers and public servants – has been broken.[26] As one of Canada's most respected former deputy ministers, Arthur Kroeger, put it, in the sponsorship scandal the public service 'got their marching orders and they marched.'[27] They failed to exercise their responsibilities when confronted by ministers and their political staffs: they said 'Yes, Minister' when they should have said 'No, Minister,' and they failed to tell political staff to respect the constitutional system. Little evidence has come to light since that they challenged the Liberal government's efforts to re-establish a 'command and control' structure over public administration.

Even more to the point, the Conservative government of Stephen Harper, elected in 2006 entirely as a consequence of the fallout from the sponsorship scandal, has governed as though NPG's script was written expressly for it. The prime minister has taken complete command of the government by governing from the centre – that is, from his own office rather than with the Cabinet – and with the strictest definition of party discipline for his party caucus. He has given primacy to the strategic advice of his political staff. He has appointed a new deputy minister to himself and expects him, as head of the non-partisan, professional public service, to direct the public service in ways that conform to the prime minister's preferences. And, more generally, he expects the public service to enthusiastically advance the agenda of his government (portrayed as 'Canada's New Government'). Finally, he has ignored the principal findings and recommendations of the Gomery Commission[28] on the very scandal that brought him to power – namely, the fundamental requirements (1) to constrain the power of the prime minister, (2) to limit the roles of political staff, (3) to secure the independence of the professional public service, and (4) to enhance the powers of Parliament vis-à-vis the prime minister and government.

Striking the Balance: Empowerment in Public Administration

NPM is not going to disappear any time soon, even if this term for public management reform becomes less frequently used or even disappears from the lexicon. Indeed, in some critical respects NPM no longer exists as a reform movement; it has become the status quo. Everywhere it is now recognized that improved public management requires a necessary degree of management capacity and that management capacity begins with the authority to manage. There are no major calls to return to past ways.

Empowerment – as devolution, delegation, and decentralization – was the major contribution of NPM to contemporary public administration. NPM sought to empower public service administrators so that they could better manage public money, public service staff, and the delivery of public services. In each of these respects, Ken Kernaghan's scholarly fingerprints are everywhere.

Empowerment, as he deployed the concept,[29] is an essential condition for improved management. It is necessary because managers need authority in order to use resources economically and efficiently, engage their subordinate managers and staff so that they pursue organizational missions, and coach and train them so that they can achieve desired results. And increasingly, they need authority in order to partner effectively with those who manage other organizations so as to realize those organizational objectives that cannot be achieved without the collaboration of others.[30] Empowerment, in this sense, encompasses the structural or organizational dimensions that provide the authority for managers to act as managers. This is the case even where there is a hierarchy of managers – the norm in all complex organizations, however much senior managers attempt to develop management teams and thereby 'flatten' their hierarchies. But empowerment, as he emphasizes, is more. It is more precisely because it acknowledges that improved management demands that power be shared with others in order to get things done well. Hierarchy may be necessary for certain purposes, such as accountability; but for other critical dimensions of management, including achieving results, hierarchy must give way to power sharing, both vertical and horizontal.

Ken Kernaghan is at his best in thinking through what empowerment means because he has always considered public management reform in the context of the intellectual traditions and practical experiences of Canadian and Anglo-American public administration. Empowerment *in* public administration may be a movement that came and went as a management fad, but as a concept in his analysis it represents the fundamental challenge of striking a balance between NPM and NPG. He sees that balance not simply as between 'letting the managers manage' and 'making the managers manage,' but as between 'letting the managers manage' and 'making the managers manage' *according to the constitutional, democratic, and professional values and ethics of the public service.*

Letting the managers manage in the public service means allowing them to exercise discretion as to how best to use resources, serve citizens, engage staff, delegate, motivate, and partner. It is not simply letting managers down the line do whatever they want – to ignore, let alone discard, the constitutional, democratic, and professional values and ethics of the public service. Rather, it is to insist that empowered managers in an empowered public service maintain the highest standards of a professional public service but do so in ways that require them to exercise professional judgment on how these values and ethics apply to a wide range of matters – as opposed to simply following prescribed rules – and then provide an account.[31] Rules will not disappear altogether, for precision is required on some matters. But an extensive elaboration of rules cannot but diminish management authority and hence disempower managers. Writing more than a decade ago, Ken Kernaghan was clear on the need to keep managers in check so that the norms of public administration would prevail. He was equally clear that 'more attention must be paid to those elements of political neutrality that can be preserved or reinforced.' He was prescient in seeing the tensions that would arise as NPM and NPG clashed. He argued that 'this will require not only limitations on politically partisan activity and public comment by public servants below the senior levels of government; it will also require careful management of the line between political partisanship and political sensitivity and the avoidance of patronage appointments at the senior levels.'[32]

His prescription stands: the Canadian federal public service in 2008 needs to pay greater attention to measures that will secure a neutral public service, reduce partisan political pressures on public servants, and strengthen the independence of the senior public service. His scholarship has served us faithfully and well.

NOTES

1 Peter Aucoin, *The New Public Management: Canada in Comparative Perspective* (Montreal: IRPP, 1995).

2 Kenneth Kernaghan, Brian Marson, and Sandford Borins, *The New Public Organization* (Toronto: IPAC, 2000).

3 Christopher Pollitt and Geert Bouchaert (2004) argue that an alternative 'Neo-Weberian State' model has emerged in the continental European states, although, as they construct it, it is an alternative essentially to the extreme marketization version of NPM. This alternative might be viewed as NPM infused with public service values and ethics!

4 Donald Kettl, *The Global Public Management Revolution*, 2nd ed. (Washington, D.C.: Brookings Institution, 2005).

5 J.E. Hodgetts, *The Canadian Public Service* (Toronto: University of Toronto Press, 1973).

6 Aucoin, *The New Public Management*.

7 In several cases of privatization in Britain and elsewhere, however, the government then proceeded to create regulatory agencies to provide a measure of public policy control over these newly privatized enterprises. This was especially the case where the enterprises were essentially public utilities.

For many European governments, independent regulatory agencies were a new development. In Canada and the United States, there had long been a tradition of using independent regulatory agencies for these purposes. In Canada they were used even to regulate state enterprises, such as Air Canada and the Canadian National Railway Company.

8   There were a few strategic areas where it wanted the private sector to provide public services, which were exempted from this policy.

9   This was particularly the case in Britain as public service providers quickly became fully competitive with the private sector and began to win a majority of the contracts subject to market testing.

10   Christopher Pollitt, Colin Talbot, Janice Caufield, and Amanda Smullen, *Agencies: How Governments Do Things through Semi-Autonomous Organizations* (Houndsmills: Palgrave Macmillan, 2004).

11   Various neoliberal economic policies may have contributed as much if not more to the budgetary success of the government, but the management reforms were generally given credit as well.

12   Kernaghan, 'Career Public Service 2000: Road to Renewal or Impractical Vision?' *Canadian Public Administration* 34, no. 4 (1991): 551–72.

13   Donald Savoie, *Thatcher, Reagan, and Mulroney: In Search of a New Bureaucracy* (Toronto: University of Toronto Press, 1994).

14   Sandford Borins, 'Public Choice: "Yes, Minister" Made It Popular, but Does Winning the Nobel Prize Make It True?' *Canadian Public Administration* 31 (1988): 12–26.

15   Colin Campbell and Graham Wilson, *The End of Whitehall: The Death of a Paradigm?* (Oxford: Basil Blackwell, 1995).

16   Campbell, 'Judging Inputs, Outputs, and Outcomes in the Search for Policy Competence: Recent Experience in Australia,' *Governance* 14, no. 2 (2001): 253–82.

17   John Halligan, 'The Australian Public Service: Redefining Boundaries,' in Halligan, ed., *Civil Service Systems in Anglo-American Countries* (Cheltenham: Edward Elgar, 2004), 70–111; Patrick Weller, *Australia's Mandarins: The Frank and the Fearless?* (Crows Nest, NSW: Allen and Unwin, 2001).

18   Jonathan Boston, John Martin, June Pallot, and Pat Walsh, *Public Management: The New Zealand Model* (Auckland: Oxford University Press, 1996); idem, eds., *Reshaping the State: New Zealand's Bureaucratic Revolution* (Auckland: Oxford University Press, 1991).

19   Richard Norman, *Obedient Servants? Management Freedoms and Accountabilities in the New Zealand Public Sector* (Wellington: Victoria University Press, 2003).

20   Savoie, *Thatcher, Reagan, and Mulroney.*

21 Evert Lindquist, ed., *Government Restructuring and Career Public Services* (Toronto: Institute of Public Administration of Canada, 2000).

22 Savoie, *Governing from the Centre* (Toronto: University of Toronto Press, 1999); Campbell, 'Judging Inputs, Outputs, and Outcomes'; Graham Wilson and Anthony Barker, 'Bureaucrats and Politicians in Britain,' *Governance* 16, no. 3 (2003): 349–72.

23 Peter Aucoin, Jennifer Smith, and Geoff Dinsdale, *Responsible Government* (Ottawa: Canadian Centre for Management Development, 2004). There are significant checks in the Canadian political system, including the federal distribution of power as well as the court-enforced Charter of Rights and Freedoms. But within the executive and legislative structures, the powers of the Canadian prime minister are subject to no significant checks and balances when the governing party is a majority in the House.

24 Wilson and Barker, 'Bureaucrats and Politicians in Britain.'

25 Patrick Weller, *Don't Tell the Prime Minister* (Melbourne: Scribe, 2002).

26 Savoie, *Breaking the Bargain* (Toronto: University of Toronto Press, 2003).

27 Norma Greenway, 'They Got Their Marching Orders and They Marched,' *Ottawa Citizen*, 12 February 2004.

28 Canada, Commission of Inquiry into the Sponsorship Program and Advertising Activities, *Restoring Accountability: Recommendations* (Ottawa, 2006).

29 Kernaghan, 'Empowerment and Public Administration: Revolutionary Advance or Passing Fad?' *Canadian Public Administration* 35, no. 2 (1992): 194–214.

30 Kernaghan, 'Partnership and Public Administration: Conceptual and Practical Considerations,' *Canadian Public Administration* 36, no. 1 (1993): 57–76.

31 Kernaghan, 'The Emerging Public Service Culture: Values, Ethics, and Reforms,' *Canadian Public Administration* 37, no. 4 (1994): 614, 631; Kernaghan, 'Towards a Public Service Code of Conduct – and Beyond,' *Canadian Public Administration* 40, no. 1 (1997): 40–54.

32 Kernaghan, 'Empowerment and Public Administration,' 214.

2 The Swirling Meanings and Practices of Accountability in Canadian Government

PAUL G. THOMAS

I Introduction

Why another article on accountability? Haven't whole forests already been sacrificed to produce books, government reports, and thousands of articles on the topic? Doesn't everyone agree on the importance of government accountability in a democratic society, and don't they often disagree on what it should mean in practice? Who would be foolhardy enough to think that another article would resolve the perennial debate over accountability or even add value to the already huge volume of writing on the topic?

In response to these rhetorical questions, this article offers three justifications. First, this volume of essays is written to honour Kenneth Kernaghan. Probably no one in Canada has done more to refine our theoretical understanding and to identify the practical implications of the key contested concepts involved with the study and practice of public administration. The promotion of responsibility, accountability, responsiveness, and integrity in public offices has been a central theme in Ken's scholarly and applied work over four decades. To state that his contribution has been insightful and valuable qualifies as a gigantic understatement. Therefore, a book in his honour without a chapter on accountability would be incomplete, even if there is the risk that nothing new can be said to resolve the perennial disagreements over the most appropriate definition and the best practices to uphold this fundamental requirement in a democratic society.

The second reason for yet another article on accountability is reflected in this chapter's title. The verb 'to swirl' means to move with an eddying motion and to pass in whirling confusion. Debates over both the theory and the practice of accountability have taken on these qualities. Accountability has become a chameleon-like concept with ever expanding and not always consistent meanings. Academic commentators have developed theoretical frameworks to describe and interpret the different types of accountability that exist or that are being sought by modern governments. In the world of practice, governments have responded, in almost a knee-jerk fashion, to scandals and to more general performance problems by adopting new accountability structures and procedures, as well as by claiming to be strengthening existing mechanisms. In Canada, the most recent example of this tendency was the passage by Parliament in December 2006 of the Federal Accountability Act. By my count that act creates eight new accountability mechanisms for regulating political and administrative behaviour and for strengthening the mandates of several existing oversight bodies.

Layering new accountability requirements on top of existing arrangements has produced a more complicated, confusing, and seemingly more demanding accountability environment for both politicians and public servants. Yet at the same time, there are almost daily complaints in legislatures and the media and from the public that accountability is missing or is being weakly enforced. Part of the disillusionment with existing accountability practices reflects the varied, elastic, and not always consistent way that the concept is used in public debates. In the tradition of the scholarship of Kenneth Kernaghan, this article seeks to clarify and to make more precise the use of the concept.

A third reason for another 'accountability piece' is to take stock of the cumulative impact of the proliferation of accountability approaches and devices. To suggest that Canada has a 'system of accountability' is inaccurate and misleading because contemporary structures and processes reflect more historical happenstance than logical planning. The foundation of the so-called system is supposedly the principles and practices of collective and individual ministerial responsibility, which are based more on constitutional conventions than on strictly legal requirements. The popular view is that ministerial responsibility no longer works. The dynamics of power within Parliament reflect the dominance of the prime minister and Cabinet – a dominance that leaves them free to interpret and apply the principles of ministerial responsibility based on short-term political calculations. Usually they are able to avoid the most serious penalty of resignation from office for serious wrongdoing or mistakes. In these circumstances no one seems to be accountable. There is also the concern that – for a variety of reasons discussed below – individual ministers are not well placed to render a full account of the use of public authority and public money by public servants working in departments and non-departmental bodies. Debates over the relevance and effectiveness of ministerial responsibility have diverted attention from the rise of other types of accountability affecting governments today. So this chapter asks the following question: Do newer managerial approaches to accountability derived from New Public Management (NPM) thinking compensate for the perceived deficiencies of parliamentary accountability based on ministerial responsibility? This chapter argues that managerial accountability can supplement and complement ministerial responsibility but that it is not an appropriate or complete substitute for the traditional model of accountability, which is based on responsible ministers being forced to either boast or confess before the public's elected representatives in Parliament.

The discussion proceeds through six sections. The next section seeks to clarify the elusive and highly contested concept of accountability for the purpose of encouraging more careful use of the term in public debates. A discussion of ministerial responsibility, the main requirements that apply today, and the parliamentary processes that enforce political accountability is presented in the third section. Newer types of managerial accountability are described and assessed in the fourth section. Finally, the paper returns to the broad questions posed in this introduction and speculates on future approaches to accountability. Since the concept of accountability is complex, multifaceted, and controversial, the discussion is necessarily general and incomplete. Its main purpose is to raise questions and suggest avenues for future research.

II What Is Accountability? What Is Not to Be Confused with Accountability?

Accountability is accepted as a central requirement in liberal democratic societies as a basis for preventing abuses of authority by public officials, for promoting responsiveness to the public, and for providing assurances to the public that they are receiving value for their tax dollars.[1] However, there is limited agreement on the precise meaning of accountability and the best means to achieve it. In fact, the term has become something of a cliché and in the process has lost much of its precision as a description of the relationships that ought to exist among different institutions and actors within the political system.[2]

Often accountability is used in the most general way to refer to an insistence that powerful institutions and their members behave responsibly and respond appropriately to the particular publics or other organizations they serve. Used loosely in this way, accountability becomes synonymous with other concepts such as responsibility, integrity, control, transparency, and responsiveness. This adds to the confusion and controversy surrounding the topic. Moreover, the accountability picture has become further blurred by the fact that over the years governments have strengthened existing accountability requirements or added new ones. Such 'reforms' can be more symbolic than real, but they add to the complexity of the accountability environment and raise questions about which type of accountability takes precedence in a particular situation.

This chapter argues for a back-to-basics approach to the use of the concept of accountability. Accountability should be restricted to situations where an authoritative relationship exists between a principal and an agent and that relationship is maintained by a process of interaction. The essence of an accountability relationship involves five process components:

- The delegation or negotiation of responsibilities, ideally based on agreed expectations/standards.
- The provision of authority, resources, and a reasonably supportive environment to allow for the fulfilment of responsibilities.
- The obligation on the accountable party to answer for the performance of responsibilities based on valid information.
- The duty of the authorizing party to monitor performance and to take corrective action when problems arise.
- The bestowal of rewards and penalties based on performance.[3]

The sources of accountability relationships within the political system are many and give rise to multiple types of accountability.

Various classification schemes or typologies have been put forward, using a variety of criteria, but no one scheme has gained anything close to universal acceptance. Some of the more popular groupings of accountability devices and processes based primarily on subject matter are the following: constitutional, legal/judicial, political, institutional/hierarchical, professional/managerial, contractual, financial, performance-based, and 'customer/client-focused.'[4] As Mulgan[5] notes, none of the typologies is sufficiently robust to be universally applicable and each works best within its own constitutional context.

To make the case for a less elastic and stretched meaning for accountability, we need to distinguish it from such related, highly prized political and administrative values as responsibility, control, answerability, transparency, and responsiveness. The brief commentaries that follow on these values are necessarily incomplete. Also, they are presented in full recognition that accountability has become a mantra in the public mind, one that serves as a rhetorical device in the adversarial processes of politics so that a campaign to restrict its meaning is likely bound to fail.

In cabinet-parliamentary systems such as Canada's, where the constitutional principles of ministerial *responsibility* provide the starting point of the search for *accountability*, it is easy to see how confusion over the two terms can arise. Debates over responsibility are longer standing and more philosophical than those over accountability. In his provocative book *Responsibility as Paradox*, Michael Harmon identified three key meanings of responsibility: agency, accountability, and obligation. These ideas exist in a paradoxical relationship in the sense that they can be supportive as well as opposed to one another. *Agency* refers to the idea of individual office holders acting on their own will based on their sense of right and wrong and the freedom/capacity to act ethically or morally. *Accountability* refers to external direction, scrutiny, and consequences attached to performance. *Obligation* locates responsibility externally to the individual; it involves a duty to follow the law and/or moral principles. These ideas lead Harmon to identify the following paradox of accountability. When public servants are accountable solely for the effective achievement of purposes mandated by political authority, they bear no personal responsibility. Yet if they participate actively in defining 'the public interest,' political authority can be undermined. Harmon's discussion[6] of the distinctions and tensions among the three conceptions of responsibility illustrated the deeper philosophical issues involved with the use of individual words and provoked a lively debate.[7]

Accountability is often equated with control for two reasons. First, there is the rationale that individuals and institutions cannot be fairly held accountable for actions and outcomes over which they have no or limited control. Seldom are there situations where someone could be described as completely in control in terms of having all the authority, resources, and knowledge to guarantee outcomes. Opposite to the positive idea of control as enabling is the restrictive concept of control, which refers to following the rules, and to being subject to direction as well as to penalties for abuses of authority or mistakes. Both restrictive and enabling approaches to control are necessary to achieve meaningful accountability. The balance between restricting and enabling will shift depending on the level of trust that those who hold public office will exercise discretion in a responsible way. Responsibility and accountability are in a sense two sides of the same coin. Or as John Uhr observes, 'we institutionalize distrust so we can enculturate trust.'[8]

Answerability is another word often used synonymously with accountability. Put simply, it refers to the duty to provide information as well as factual explanations for events. It is a means to achieving accountability, but from the standpoint of this chapter it does not represent the real thing because it omits the implication that there are consequences for mistakes or non-performance. In cabinet-parliamentary systems based on ministerial responsibility, ministers provide information and explanations to Parliament about the actions of appointed public officials; and public servants, especially deputy ministers, support the political accountability of ministers principally through appearances before committees and the factual information they provide regarding policy and administrative matters. Yet Parliament cannot punish or reward ministers or senior public servants, except in the sense of criticizing their behaviour and damaging their reputations. Clearly, for the individuals involved a loss of reputation represents a significant cost so that the neat theoretical distinction between accountability and answerability is not so easily maintained in 'the real world.'

Transparency or open government is a highly prized political value in a democracy; it is also a means to promote accountability. Much could be written on this dimension of accountability, but in the space available only several brief observations are possible. First, open government is a broader and more fundamental concept than the principle of the public's right to government records, a right that is enshrined in the Access to Information Act. Open dialogue about future policy directions represents a form of prospective accountability in that it allows Parliament and the public to hold ministers accountable for fulfilling their promises. Retrospective accountability is promoted by the opportunities to scrutinize government performance in Parliament, and for this purpose comprehensive, valid, and balanced information is needed. This dimension is discussed later in this chapter.

Open public discussions about government activities are meant to encourage responsiveness, a concept that is closely related to yet also different from accountability. In general terms, responsiveness refers to both the inclination and the capacity to meet the expectations, demands, and needs of others. In the case of governments, responsiveness can be demonstrated on four levels: policy, resource allocation, service provision, and symbolism in terms of acknowledging the claims of different segments of society. Elections as well as the constant pressure to maintain public support provide ministers and parliamentarians with an incentive to be responsive. Traditionally, the public service has been seen as loyal and responsive to the government of the day and its priorities. By implementing the policy and administrative directions of responsible ministers in an efficient and effective manner, the public service supports the process of parliamentary and public accountability.

More recently the idea that the public service's identity and role is defined entirely in terms of serving the current government has been challenged.[9] With public trust and confidence in the political process declining, and with the adoption of the language of consumerism in the public sector, there has been pressure on the public service to become more directly responsive to the clients it serves and to the public in general. In the context of the public administration community in the United States, the phrase 'customer accountability' has been used to describe this new orientation. More accurately, what is being proposed is enhanced responsiveness because the capacity to reward/punish public servants is not being granted to their clients.

Also, reflecting the anti-politics mood of the times and the growing public insistence on integrity and higher ethical standards in public office, the argument is being made that the public service must have a measure of independence from ministerial control in order for its members to 'speak truth to power' and to uphold the rights of the people it serves.[10] This argument almost makes the public service into a 'fourth branch' of government – along with Parliament, the political executive, and the judiciary. Identifying a separate constitutional role for the public service that goes beyond serving ministers has fundamental implications for accountability.

The equation of transparency and responsiveness with accountability reflects the central, albeit not always constructive, role played by the media in transmitting messages to the attentive public about the activities of government. The media do not simply serve as a communications channel; they also contribute to the agenda-setting process in government – for example, by highlighting issues for which ministers and public servants will be held accountable before Parliament and beyond. Ministers are the most likely actors to appear in the media.

However, the traditional anonymity of senior public servants is being eroded by the fact that they are appearing more regularly in public forums, where they lead consultation exercises and testify before parliamentary committees. They are also being quoted in newspapers and on television and radio. The media are well aware of the elaborate efforts that modern governments make to shape public opinion and to portray their own performance in the best possible light. For this reason, and because it is fashionable in journalism today, members of the media see themselves as critics of government. In the search for headlines and audiences, the media tend to amplify, simplify, personalize, and sensationalize the more dramatic abuses or failures of government even while neglecting the vast expanse of policies and programs that have a positive impact on society. Sustained media (especially television) coverage of policy and/or administrative blunders often forces governments on the defensive, yet the media seldom play any role in identifying the remedial actions that are required.

Most people gather their perceptions of government through the kaleidoscopic and largely negative images presented in the media. As a consequence there is a strong subjective and symbolic dimension to accountability debates. The negative stereotype that government fails at everything it tries becomes the basis for public perceptions and reinforces the insistence on greater accountability. Increasingly, the public sees accountability less in legal, political, and organizational terms and more in terms of integrity, ethics, and morality in public office. This trend towards equating accountability with ethical responsibility has been encouraged by governments themselves, which have recently moved into 'the ethics business' by adopting codes of conduct/ethics and by appointing commissioners/agencies to monitor their operations.

To summarize, accountability is a dynamic and controversial term that has acquired multiple meanings over time. My own preference is to restrict the term's use to situations where an authoritative relationship exists; where processes for reviewing performance operate; where there is a recognized obligation to take corrective action when untoward events occur; and where there is the potential for penalties and rewards to be applied depending on whether the outcomes achieved fell below, matched, or exceeded agreed-on expectations. Balancing rewards and penalties may be the theory, but in practice the emphasis is far more on blame and sanctions. Because accountability has become such an emotional rallying cry for the public to express its disappointment and frustration with government, as well as a weapon in the permanent election campaign that is the essence of the parliamentary process, there is little prospect that the term will be used in the more limited and balanced way that I am suggesting.

III The Constitutional Foundations of Accountability

In a democratic state the key accountability relationships are between citizens and holders of public office, be they elected or appointed, and between elected politicians and public servants. The gradual emergence of multiple meanings and approaches to accountability has somewhat diminished the crucial importance of these relationships. The degree of accountability that exists in any political system depends on a number of factors, including the constitution, the political and administrative cultures, the scope and nature of government activities, and the leadership philosophies and styles of public officials. Constitutional arrangements will be the focus of this section.

The Canadian Constitution is a blend of law and politics in that vitally important aspects of our public life are governed by unwritten conventions that have emerged from long-standing political practices.[11] These constitutional conventions vary in the extent to which they are seen as morally binding on ministers, parliamentarians, public servants, and others in public life. Given the informal, unwritten nature of conventions and the fact that we live in a highly cynical age, many people believe that neither politicians nor public servants can be trusted to play by the rules of the game. The broad, unwritten nature of our constitutional conventions means that they reflect as much as they shape political realities. The introduction of new organizational arrangements and new procedures may have constitutional impacts that are only dimly perceived, if at all, at the outset. As an evolutionary form of government, Canada's cabinet-parliamentary system has adapted over time, but changes must be consistent with the key principles of the constitution.

The principles of collective and individual ministerial responsibility represent the way Canadians have sought to achieve the democratic accountability of office holders to the public as well as to ensure the rule of law. Within the political system these principles represent a theory for the use of power and the structuring of authority. They present a statement of the relationships that ought to exist between cabinets and parliaments, between cabinet ministers and the public service, between the public service and parliaments (to a lesser extent), and between all office holders and the citizens they serve. The conventions of ministerial responsibility are largely unwritten and have only a limited basis in public law.

The convention of collective ministerial responsibility assigns the initiative for legislation, taxing, and spending to the Cabinet. Having concentrated authority in the hands of the prime minister and Cabinet, the cabinet-parliamentary system seeks to hold ministers accountable through a number of devices, most notably through the so-called confidence rule, which requires governments to maintain the support of a majority in the House of Commons. Apart from explicit votes of no confidence, exactly what constitutes a defeat of sufficient importance to require a government to resign and to request a dissolution of Parliament leading to a general election is somewhat unclear and controversial. In practice, owing to party loyalty and discipline, governments are rarely defeated; generally, they exercise control over Parliament. This creates the impression of a break in the accountability chain, since elected representatives no longer are able to hold governments continuously accountable. Even so, governments are still forced to explain and defend their activities on almost a daily basis through parliamentary events such as Question Period and the related media coverage.

Besides this collective responsibility, individual ministers are legally responsible for their departments and politically answerable before Parliament for all official actions of their departments. On the basis of these legal and political responsibilities, ministers are also expected to provide leadership, direction, and control in relation to the administrative activities of their departments. Exactly how ministers set agendas, provide direction, and enforce accountability within their departments is a little documented and understood process.

In terms of accountability, individual ministerial responsibility is often mistakenly taken to mean that ministers can be forced by Parliament to resign from Cabinet as a result of serious policy or administrative errors in their departments. In fact, only the prime minister, perhaps with the advice of Cabinet, can remove a minister. Ministers seldom resign for policy mistakes, in part because department policies have arisen from the cabinet processes of collective decision making. As for administrative mistakes, a study of resignations from federal cabinets during the period 1867 to 1991 could identify only two instances where ministers were prepared or required to give up their cabinet posts because of administrative problems.[12] The fact that ministers seldom feel compelled to resign leads many commentators to conclude that individual ministerial responsibility is a myth and therefore useless as a device for holding ministers directly and public servants indirectly accountable for their actions.

Typically, ministers now resign only for one of three reasons: (1) an inability to accept the policies of the government and thereby contribute to cabinet solidarity and collective responsibility; (2) knowingly misleading Parliament and failing to correct the error at the earliest opportunity; and (3) being guilty of a serious personal impropriety. It is increasingly accepted that ministers should not resign for administrative errors in which they were not involved and had no prior knowledge. In these instances the minister's duty is to explain the problem and fix it – what might be called 'remedial accountability' as opposed to 'sacrificial responsibility.' Most accountability debates place too much emphasis on the forced resignation of ministers and undervalue the contribution of Parliament to forcing corrections when things go wrong – a topic discussed later in this chapter.

One of the conventions related to ministerial responsibility is the concept of a politically neutral and anonymous public service. In the pure version of this model, ministers take all the credit or blame for policy and administrative initiatives and do not identify the public servants who are responsible for giving policy advice and for implementing departmental decisions. In a seminal article published in 1979, Kernaghan laid out the six components of the idealized model of public service neutrality and then commented as follows on how the conventions were being modified under the pressure of changing circumstances within the political system:

> Politics, policy and administration are intertwined; most public servants are selected and promoted on the basis of merit but some positions are filled by partisans of the governing party; most public servants may participate in partisan political activities; public servants may not express publicly their personal views on government actions but are involved in various forms of public comment in the normal course of their duties; public servants provide confidential advice to ministers; ministers protect the anonymity of public servants but this anonymity is gradually declining for other reasons; and public servants execute policy decisions loyally regardless of their personal views.[13]

Public service neutrality and anonymity have usually been seen as a corollary of ministerial responsibility. However, Lorne Sossin[14] has recently argued that the impartiality of public servants is a separate constitutional convention. He contends that the relationship between ministers and the public service involves both interdependence and independence and that bureaucratic independence arises from an amalgam of legislation, conventions, codes, and well-established practices. Independence exists to preserve impartiality in policy advice and in the administration of programs, but it also upholds such values as the rule of law, impartial staffing, and the capacity of the public service to speak truth to power. Just as on the political side of accountability, similarly on the administrative side there is today considerable flux and confusion about what it means to be a responsible and accountable public servant.

IV Parliament and Accountability

Within the political system, Parliament is expected both

- to support the existence of strong and responsive governments by processing and passing legislation and spending in a timely manner, and
- to hold the political and administrative executives accountable for the exercise of public power and to make them more responsive to the concerns of society.

There is both potential and actual tension involved with the performance of these two roles. How can Parliament – which operates on the basis of competitive, disciplined political parties, and which is largely under the control of the governing party for law-making purposes – maintain sufficient autonomy, especially when performing in the scrutiny role? This dilemma is most pronounced for MPs from the government caucus, who are not encouraged to poke and pry around looking for policy and administrative problems that would prove embarrassing to ministers and the prime minister.

In theory, parliamentary scrutiny serves a number of purposes:

- It holds ministers accountable.
- It ensures that laws are implemented as intended.
- It determines whether laws, policies, and programs need to be changed.

- It promotes economy, efficiency, and effectiveness in spending and uncovers waste and mismanagement.
- It prevents and corrects abuses of discretionary authority arising from delegated law-making powers.
- It allows parliamentarians to act as liaison agents with ministers and the bureaucracy on behalf of constituents, provinces, and regions.
- It promotes a subjective sense of responsibility among public servants and holds them indirectly accountable for the use of authority and resources.

In practice, Parliament's accountability effort focuses almost entirely on ministers, their policies, and occasionally the high-profile aspects of departmental performance. In short, Parliament deals with the 'tip of the iceberg' and leaves untouched in its scrutiny efforts the wide expanse of past policies and the huge, submerged lower levels of policy making by public servants based on delegated law-making authority.

Figure 2.1. Parliamentary techniques for accountability purposes

- Question Period
- Members' statements
- Debates of bills and periodic reviews of legislation
- Review and approval of spending
- The availability of performance plans and performance reports for more than eighty departments and agencies
- Creation of standing committees, which cover broad policy sectors and are somewhat independent of the executive
- The conduct of general inquiries by parliamentary committees and the requirement that ministers reply to reports
- Requirements that ministers present Parliament with information on a regular basis – for example, the annual report on the public service and the annual report on Crown corporations
- The provision of professional staff to committees and to individual parliamentarians
- The mandate of the Joint Committee on the Scrutiny of Regulations to review the exercise of delegated law-making authority
- The existence of an Access to Information Act to promote openness in government, and the appointment of an Information Commissioner who reports to Parliament

- The existence of a Privacy Act and the Personal Information and Protection of Electronic Documents Act, and the appointment of a Privacy Commissioner who reports to Parliament
- The existence of conflict-of-interest rules for parliamentarians and a Code of Ethics, and the appointment of an Ethics Commissioner
- The publication of Public Accounts, reliance on the Auditor General to review spending and financial management practices, and the operation of the Commons Public Accounts Committee chaired by an opposition MP

Figure 2.1 presents a list of the potential surveillance devices available to parliamentarians. The list is impressive in length; in practice, though, Parliament finds it impossible to provide anything close to comprehensive scrutiny and evaluation of the enormously wide-ranging and complicated activities of government.

The appointment over several decades of Officers of Parliament – such as the Auditor General, the Information and Privacy Commissioners, and the Commissioner of Official Languages – reflects Parliament's acknowledgment that it needs help in conducting surveillance of the bureaucracy. The Federal Accountability Act, passed in December 2006, has added to this list by requiring the creation of a Public Appointments Commission to review appointments to agencies, boards, and commissions; a Public Sector Integrity Commissioner to oversee a whistle-blower protection law; and a Parliamentary Budget Office to provide Parliament with objective evidence on the state of the economy and government finances.

Unfortunately, the opportunities and assistance available to parliamentarians to provide scrutiny are underutilized. For example, departments and agencies now present annual performance plans and performance reports, yet one careful study found scarcely any use of these documents by MPs reviewing estimates in standing committees.[15] The explanations for the limited use of the available accountability devices are both *political* (party discipline, government control over committees, the lack of media attention to scrutiny efforts, the concern for publicity by MPs to support re-election, the lack of knowledge among inexperienced MPs, etc.) and *practical* (inadequate time, restrictions on access to information, the shortage of professional staff, etc.).

As mentioned above, most of the accountability efforts by Parliament focus on ministers, who become in a very real sense the personification of their departments. In this way, parliamentarians have a real person whom they can embarrass politically and to whom they can address the grievances of their constituents. Moreover, parliamentarians can influence departments by challenging ministers, because ministers do not like negative publicity and will insist that departments take action to prevent a recurrence of problems. In this sense, loss of reputation rather than loss of office serves as an incentive for ministers to heed departmental matters and represents the real sanction underlying the concept of ministerial responsibility. When opposition parties sense that a particular minister and a department are exposed, they often embark on a siege campaign in Question Period and in committees designed to generate the maximum media coverage possible. This means that the most high-profile parliamentary activities relating to accountability are adversarial, blaming, and theatrical in content.

The largely negative nature of current approaches to parliamentary accountability, the fact that ministers refuse to resign for administrative foul-ups, and the recognition that ministers cannot possibly be in charge of everything that goes on in their departments have all contributed to growing interest in the concept of holding deputy ministers directly and personally accountable before parliamentary committees. This approach, it is claimed, would prevent senior public servants from hiding behind the doctrine of ministerial responsibility. Holding deputy ministers accountable is a popular idea, but not without its drawbacks. First, it is difficult to draw the line between policy (which would remain the responsibility of ministers) and administration (for which the deputy would answer). Accountability would still be sought in the parliamentary committees, which are highly partisan bodies, and deputies could find their neutrality compromised. If committees found deputies at fault or deficient in their performance, how could Parliament impose sanctions? And how could the prime minister, Cabinet, and individual ministers retain control over the public service if its senior leaders were accountable in a general way to another authority?

Despite the complications of defining and applying the concept of deputy ministerial accountability, the Harper government fulfilled its election promise and incorporated this feature into the Federal Accountability Act passed in December 2006. Under the act, deputy ministers have been designated accounting officers in a fashion similar to a long-standing practice in Britain. As officers, deputies are responsible for ensuring the prudent use of public funds and for the efficient management of their departments. The act sets forth a process to resolve disputes between ministers and their deputies over whether a proposed action constitutes a misuse of public funds. The Harper government is careful to insist that deputy ministerial accountability operates within the historical framework of ministerial responsibility. However, previous governments (and the Privy Council Office, which advises governments) had rejected the accounting officer concept on the ground that it would compromise ministerial responsibility because the line between policy and financial management could not be drawn precisely. The accounting officer concept requires deputy ministers to spend more time testifying before parliamentary committees on their own performance as stewards of the financial and human resources of their departments.

Most 'accountability' sessions for deputies take place before the Public Accounts Committee, which is chaired by an opposition MP. Unlike its British counterpart, the Canadian committee holds most of its sessions in public, and especially in recent years it has become highly partisan in its internal dynamics. The fact that parliamentary committees cannot reward or discipline deputies may encourage MPs to 'play to the grandstand' at the risk of unfair damage to the professional reputations of the deputy ministers who appear before them. However, experienced deputies have learned to navigate skilfully in the potentially dangerous shoals of parliamentary committees so that many are quite open to participating in such public sessions on their own leadership and management of departments.

The Senate is usually the object of political ridicule and calls for reform, yet it actually does more than the House of Commons in terms of surveillance of the bureaucracy and evaluation of existing programs.[16] Most of this work is conducted in Senate committees and goes unnoticed in the media. For example, the Standing Committee on National Finance was the only parliamentary body to track the progress of public service reform in the 1990s. Similarly, the senators on the Joint Committee on the Scrutiny of Regulations have done most of the work to ensure that the rules employed by public officials stay within the parameters of the authorizing legislation and conform to the Charter of Rights and Freedoms. Over the years many Senate committees have undertaken relatively in-depth evaluations of policies and programs in a wide range of fields, and when circumstances are fortuitous their reports have influenced government thinking and actions. Because senators do not face re-election, do not have constituency matters to deal with, are often experienced in other public offices, and serve for longer periods of time than the average MP, they have the knowledge and time to engage in worthwhile, more objective studies of topics that are not central to the partisan controversies of the day. Of course, the fact that the Senate is appointed, not elected, robs its work of some legitimacy, and its efforts at accountability rarely attract media coverage.

As the most democratic institution in the Canadian political system, Parliament should play a key role in holding ministers directly and public servants indirectly accountable for the exercise of public power. The implicit 'ideal' behind calls for greater parliamentary accountability is that Parliament should provide an ongoing, objective, and constructive dialogue on government performance and methods of improvement – almost like an evaluation seminar. In reality, however, the House of Commons mostly resembles a permanent election campaign with competitive, disciplined political parties dominating its proceedings and seeking to use the institution to gain ground politically.

Over the past decade a multiparty Parliament, with a fragmented opposition and a governing party led by a prime minister who insists on strict party discipline, has weakened the parliamentary accountability of ministers. Opposition parties have hurled charges, and the government has responded defensively – a dynamic that has led to little enlightenment or improvement. After the federal elections of June 2004 and January 2006 produced minority governments, Parliament and its committees obtained greater freedom to investigate problems and to force government responses. However, it remains the case that most MPs – and to a lesser extent senators – find the task of conducting scrutiny over the wide range of policies, programs, departments, and non-departmental bodies to be a daunting, difficult, and frustrating task. For the most part it is also politically unrewarding. Attacking ministers in Question Period, debating big policy issues, and looking after constituency concerns are higher priorities for most MPs than trying to make government work more efficiently and more effectively, regardless of what parliamentarians might say rhetorically to the contrary. Opinion polls suggest that Canadians want to see more constructive, and less negative and theatrical, approaches to holding governments accountable and improving their performance.

V Managerial Accountability as an Alternative?

If parliamentary accountability is deficient, this increases the significance of the newer approaches to managerial accountability based on the thinking of NPM. The leading ideas of NPM will be familiar to readers of this book and are covered to a certain extent in other chapters, so only brief references will be made to them here. Reflecting its origins in several disciplinary traditions and approaches, writing on NPM has exhibited an ambivalence in its approach to accountability. From the public choice school in economics, it has derived a suspicion of the self-interested behaviour of bureaucracies and the desire of those bureaucracies to assert political control. From the private management literature based on commercial firms, it has derived the idea of protecting management from political interference and increasing the power of 'customers' to make choices and to influence the provision of public sector services. Another ambivalence is that NPM has viewed accountability first as a goal in its own right (the aim being to prevent the abuse of power and to ensure fairness) and second as a means to promote efficiency and effectiveness in government, as well as to assure the public that they are receiving value for money. NPM has injected new perspectives and practices into the perennial debates over accountability, but it has fallen far short of resolving the so-called accountability problem.

Each tool in the NPM toolkit comes with its own implications for accountability. Different countries have been selective in their use of its tools; and the consequences for accountability have depended on their constitutional frameworks, the established structures, processes, and traditions of their governments, and the challenges faced at the time of adoption. The Canadian government's approach to applying NPM ideas can best be described as cautious and experimental. To its credit, the government has made some effort to foresee and address the potential impacts on parliamentary accountability arising from its managerial reforms.

Privatization of Crown corporations and other transfers of functions to the private sector represent a loss in terms of political accountability because responsible ministers are no longer obliged to answer before Parliament about the performance of the organizations involved. In some situations, government ownership replaces government regulation and a minister continues to serve as a communications channel to Parliament regarding how well the privatized entity is complying with regulatory requirements. If privatization does not simply substitute a private monopoly for a former public sector monopoly, then – supposedly – competitive market forces will oblige the new company to be responsive to the people it serves. As noted earlier, however, responsiveness is not the same as accountability.

Contracting out to the private sector the delivery of services previously provided by public agencies involves an extra link in the chain of accountability leading back to the minister and to Parliament.[17] Ministerial involvement is limited to setting the terms and conditions of the contract and conducting periodic reviews. To realize the efficiency and effectiveness gains of contracting, departments must become 'smart buyers,' able to specify what they want to purchase from the for-profit or not-for-profit organizations and having the capacity to monitor and evaluate the performance of contractors. Accountability becomes limited to the terms of the contract; and the more conditions imposed, the greater the risk of limiting the flexibility, creativity, and productivity that reliance on the private sector supposedly brings. In calculating the potential loss of accountability from contracting out, the appropriate comparison is to the realities of ministerial responsibility, not to the theoretical model in which the minister is supposedly answerable and liable for everything. By requiring departments to think harder about the objectives of their activities and by requiring them to develop indicators of success, methods of monitoring, and procedures for terminating unsatisfactory contractual relationships, the contracting process has the potential to enhance rather than diminish accountability. However, this presumes that contracting out works as intended, and there is plenty of evidence that problems can arise – problems such as poorly specified objectives and standards of performance, a lack of competitive tendering, inadequate monitoring of contractors, and nearly automatic renewals when contract periods expire.

Closely related to contracting out is the growing use of public–private partnerships. Long-term contractual relationships often amount to a partnership. What constitutes a partnership is, however, open to debate.[18] The alternative service delivery document put out by the federal Treasury Board Secretariat defines partnership as 'two or more parties working towards shared and/or compatible objectives with: shared authority and responsibility, joint investment of time and resources, sharing of risks and benefits and an explicit agreement, contract or other instrument that sets out terms.'[19] Compared to conventional contracting out, partnerships involve more substantial involvement by private sector actors in public decision making.

Governments can develop partnerships with a wide variety of organizations, including commercial firms, not-for-profit agencies, and sometimes trade unions. The popularity of the partnership approach reflects various desires: to encourage the private sector to share risks; to overcome the rigidities of bureaucracy; to benefit from the managerial approaches and techniques of the private sector; to enhance the quality and responsiveness of service delivery; and to allow the public sector and public managers to do more with less. These are the presumed benefits of partnerships, but there are also many questions to be raised, including some that relate to accountability:

- When elected politicians strongly endorse partnerships, can public servants be appropriately discriminating about the partners they select?
- Even when partnerships begin as balanced and equal, do they become unbalanced over time?
- Is there an asymmetrical quality to partnerships because the goals of the private partner are usually better defined and more concrete?
- Do partnerships lead to closed negotiations and collaborations between private and public officials?
- How are governments to monitor and evaluate partnerships? And does downsizing rob governments of the capacity to do these things?
- Does long-term collaboration dilute public sector values, including accountability?

There are many different types of partnership arrangements involving different fields of government activity, and the dynamics of a particular partnership relationship can change over time. Clearly, generalizing about partnerships being all good or all bad is inappropriate. To succeed, partnerships require a clear assignment of responsibilities, a proper evaluation of the risks and how they are to be shared, an appropriate measure of transparency, and proper accountability requirements, including an audit trail to safeguard public expenditures.

Under the influence of NPM thinking, there was much talk during the 1990s about the empowerment of public sector managers and front-line employees. In 1991 Ken Kernaghan observed that the concept evoked lyrical rhapsody from some, cynical dismissal from others, and mixed reactions from most.[20] These varied responses reflected in part the elusiveness of the concept, which called for more than the traditional debates over the appropriate delegation of authority. Partnerships had to involve making the best possible use of employees' knowledge and skills by encouraging them to work and to share knowledge in team structures. Leadership, authority, power, information, knowledge, and rewards were to be moved to the lowest feasible level in public bureaucracies in order to improve employees' confidence, commitment, creativity, and responsiveness.

Kernaghan recognized that introducing empowerment was a radical change – one that was especially difficult to accomplish in government organizations where the conventions of ministerial responsibility lead to limits on downward delegation of decision making and create more risk-averse cultures in which more sensitive decisions must be pushed up the line in the hierarchy to be checked for their political safety. Despite these fundamental constraints, there was a shift (more rhetorical than real, some suggest) away from central agency and hierarchical controls within departments, towards granting managers and employees more freedom. However, when controversies erupted over the so-called billion-dollar boondoggle at HRDC, misspending and abuses of staffing authority by the former Privacy Commissioner, and most recently the sponsorship scandal, the pendulum swung back towards tighter control. In a December 2003 report the Association of Public Service Financial Administrators attributed these breakdowns in control and accountability to three causes:

- Management reforms that took empowerment too far, too fast.
- Structural and process reforms that weakened financial oversight.
- Loss of financial management capability (resources, experience, and development) throughout the public service.

In response to the problems, the government adopted a series of measures: a Financial Information Strategy, the Modern Controllership initiative, the introduction of the Management Accountability Framework for deputy ministers, and a renewed commitment to evaluation. These initiatives followed a long series of past attempts under a bewildering array of labels (and snappy acronyms) to strike just the right balance between control and freedom for the purposes of internal accountability. In a period of turbulent change, the problem of how to maintain adequate control of accountability in public organizations that are exhorted to be flexible, creative, and innovative – while avoiding risks – is a huge challenge.

The main response to this challenge over the past decade has been to rely on what might be described as 'tight–loose' control. The clearest expression of this approach was the adoption of the requirement in the mid-1990s that all departments and agencies within the Government of

Canada annually produce performance plans and performance reports for tabling in Parliament. Plans are meant to set the direction, parameters, and standards for performance; reports are meant to provide a comprehensive and balanced review of results for purposes of both internal and external accountability. More than eighty entities now table annual performance reports with Parliament, and since 2000 the government has also published an annual report titled 'Canada's Performance,' which is officially described as a 'whole of government' view of results in key areas of responsibility for the national government. Canada is one of the few countries in the world to combine departmental, program-level reporting with a broad, social indicators approach.

The shift from accountability defined in procedural terms towards accountability for results has been a slow and difficult process, and there has been some reversal in the aftermath of recent scandals. The obstacles to the shift have been analytical, financial, institutional, and political.[21] Significant progress has been made, and it is easy to be hypercritical about the continuing shortcomings of the performance management system. For example, studies by the Office of the Auditor General suggest that departmental performance reports are not comprehensive and balanced and that planning, budgeting, program management, and performance appraisals of managers have yet to be thoroughly integrated. In terms of external accountability, the news is even more depressing: Parliament and its committees have made almost no use of departmental performance reports or of the social report card on the country's progress.

The trends described above have combined to challenge the traditional, vertical conception of accountability — the sort that leads back up the chain of command to the minister at the apex of the department. Reduced reliance on authority and hierarchy is a factor in the accountability challenge; so is the greater emphasis on decentralization and empowerment. The coordination challenge has also increased, owing to the fragmentation that is a consequence of public–private partnerships, contracting out, the use of semi-independent special operating agencies, and collaborative approaches to the design (and delivery) of joint federal–provincial policies (and programs). To achieve greater coherence and coordination, there has been a strong push recently for a 'whole of government' approach, one that would involve more horizontal policy making and horizontal program management to deal with problems of overlaps, contradictions, gaps, and weakly integrated services.

How do governments define, promote, measure, and enforce accountability in the emerging world of networked, interdependent organizations that share authority, power, risks, and rewards – and blame when something goes wrong? The idea that particular individuals (e.g., deputy ministers) or even organizations (e.g., departments) can state with certainty a set of expectations and demonstrate conclusively that results have been obtained through their efforts seems unrealistic in the 'flatter' world of 'joined up' government. What are the practical requirements for a more 'collective,' 'shared,' 'mutual,' or '360-degree' (choose your label) approach to accountability, when there is seldom a single individual or organization so completely in charge that he or she or it can deliver results singlehandedly? Useful work on this issue has been done by the Office of the Auditor General, but governments are a long way from developing effective accountability mechanisms to match new collaborative approaches to governance.[22]

VI Multiple Accountabilities Disorder?

It has been assumed by the public, legislatures, the courts, the media, and (somewhat grudgingly) by governments that accountability is a good thing and that therefore there can never be too much of it. Traditionally, the emphasis in the accountability literature has been on criticizing and punishing powerful institutions when they abuse authority or screw up in some way. More recently, there has been an attempt to balance this negative, blaming approach with claims that better accountability processes lead to better performance by promoting learning and improvement. As Melvin Dubnick[23] has recently observed, we should not assume a relationship between accountability and performance – which underpins most of the NPM agenda – for that relationship remains untested and there is available evidence that it does not work in the simplistic way intended.

Widespread agreement on the importance of accountability has masked underlying disagreements regarding its meaning. Loose use of the term has added to the confusion. Multiple conceptions and procedures of accountability have emerged, leading to a wide array of expectations, institutions, and procedures as well as multiple criteria for judging whether individuals and organizations are truly accountable. This chapter has focused on the changing meanings and practices of ministerial responsibility, parliamentary accountability, and managerial accountability within the bureaucracy. It has not discussed the growing importance of legal/judicial accountability through the courts and quasi-judicial tribunals under the Charter of Rights and Freedoms and the constantly evolving body of administrative law. There is also the role played by 'soft law' in the form of codes of conduct, guides to ministers and deputy ministers, ethics codes, values statements, and the forthcoming Charter of the Public Service promised by the Canadian government. How effective these mechanisms are or will be in promoting responsible and accountable behaviour by both politicians and public servants has not been investigated systematically.

Multiple conceptions and procedures of accountability can lead to the pathology of 'multiple accountabilities disorder' – MAD, for short.[24] This term refers to the loss of a useful concept for governance purposes owing to its rhetorical overuse and misuse. It refers to a blurring of the accountability picture when public office holders face multiple, and not always consistent, accountability requirements. It also refers to the weakening of organizational performance caused by requirements to comply with multiple accountability demands. No one can state authoritatively that there is too little, too much, or just the right amount of accountability. The appropriate degree and type of accountability is context dependent; it depends on the relationships among organizations and on what is at stake. Clarity in accountability relationships – in terms of who is accountable to whom, for what, how, and with what consequences – is obviously desirable but is often difficult to achieve under current conditions within government. To argue, as Robert Behn has done, that we should promote a culture of '360° accountability' in which everyone – politicians, public servants, organized groups, the media, and the public – is accountable to everyone else, is an intriguing notion but lacks a practical means of implementation.[25] It also ignores the public's insistence that an identifiable individual or institution pay a significant price when something goes wrong in government. It is not acceptable to state that a system failed and that everyone involved is blame free.

Some overlap and redundancy within an accountability system is not all bad because it involves different perspectives on the subjective, value-laden issue of what qualifies as responsible and accountable behaviour. For example, auditors general make a valuable contribution to the promotion of greater accountability from the disciplinary perspectives of accounting and management science, but accountability goes well beyond compliance with accounting rules and management principles. While accountability is important, it cannot trump other important public sector values such as representation, responsiveness, legitimacy, fairness, and public trust and confidence in governments. It is easy and popular to talk about balancing accountability with these other values; but more realistically and honestly, we must acknowledge that often trade-offs are involved. For example, how much efficiency and effectiveness has been sacrificed by the proliferation of accountability processes? Governments have raised accountability standards and toughened accountability demands even while restraining budgets and downsizing the public service. In other words, they have acted as if accountability is a 'free good.'

Cynicism about politics and pessimism about Parliament's capacity to enforce accountability have contributed to the introduction of numerous managerial forms of accountability based on NPM ideas. There is a sense in which reformers have sought to get accountability 'out of the swamps of politics' by emphasizing supposedly more rational, objective, and constructive managerial approaches. This type of thinking is both misguided and futile. It is misguided because the focus on efficiency and results popularized by the advocates of NPM does not satisfy the need for accountability to other democratic norms and values. That is not to say that focusing on results is unimportant; clearly, managerial techniques are valuable if they bring improvements and benefits to the public. However, the ultimate goal of accountability processes is to make governments, their agencies, and their officials answerable to *citizens*, not customers. In a democratic society, accountability depends ultimately on the political process; therefore, all accountability roads must lead back to Parliament. Managerial accountability can supplement and complement accountability to Parliament but is not an appropriate or adequate substitute.

As the single most representative institution in the political system, Parliament exists to promote and uphold the democratic requirement of accountability and other closely related values such as responsibility, representation, transparency, responsiveness, and integrity. Currently, Parliament performs its accountability role in an imperfect and incomplete manner. However, there must be realistic expectations attached to Parliament's role. It will always be dominated by political parties and partisanship. It is on this basis that the collective responsibility and accountability of prime ministers and cabinets to the public are maintained. Parties seek electoral mandates and are held to account for keeping their promises and for dealing with issues not discussed during election campaigns. Requiring individual ministers to explain and to deal with problems in their departments contributes to remedial accountability, even if it seldom reaches the stage of punitive accountability involving the forced resignation of a minister. Despite the obvious gap between the theory and the practice of Parliament's capacity to scrutinize the executive, ministers and public servants cannot ignore Parliament or approach it with imprudence. Parliamentary accountability processes may in fact make their most valuable and positive contribution by requiring public officials to practise 'anticipatory accountability' – that is, to be more carefully thoughtful and restrained in their exercise of public power. Questioning and challenging ministers and public servants can galvanize the norms of responsible behaviour. There is an important research project to be conducted on the impacts of accountability relationships among ministers, public servants, and Parliament.

Most Canadians and nearly all expert commentators find Parliament's accountability efforts to be excessively partisan, theatrical, shallow, and negative. In part, this reflects the fact that opposition parties, on whom accountability mainly depends, have a stake in embarrassing the government; the governing party often reacts defensively to this, refusing to acknowledge that anything is wrong. Obviously, this dynamic is not helpful in terms of learning and improving performance. However, the noise and heat generated by partisan clashes does produce media coverage, and it does bring issues to the attention of the interested public. At times the process also works in reverse, with Parliament reflecting and amplifying the issues raised initially in the media. The interaction between parliamentary and media processes in the achievement of accountability is another area for future research.

In terms of the practice of parliamentary accountability, there are obviously institutional, procedural, and organizational reforms that could be made to improve Parliament. More independent committees with more qualified staff is probably the most promising avenue of reform. However, for strengthened committee systems to work in the House of Commons (and to a lesser extent in the Senate) would require a change in the parliamentary culture involving an acceptance that not all issues should be seen and debated in partisan terms. There are already occasions in committees where parliamentarians approach issues more objectively, based on the available evidence, and achieve a cross-party consensus on what needs to be done. This needs to happen more often. Ministers need to accept that well-staffed parliamentary committees with the freedom to investigate the effectiveness of past policies and significant administrative issues can help them set policy directions and hold the bureaucracy accountable. This would mean giving MPs on the government side permission to conduct inquiries without being accused of disloyalty. For their part, opposition parties and their members must avoid the temptation to distort administrative concerns into partisan disagreements for the purpose of scoring political points. In somewhat abstract and altruistic terms, when parliamentarians are performing their scrutiny function they should be thinking in terms of what committees can contribute to 'good government,' defined as improved performance, and not in terms of what their efforts might do to the standing of their parties in the polls. There will always be a partisan dimension to MPs' behaviour, but Canadians are looking for a better quality of partisanship, one that sees accountability, not simply as blaming, but also as learning.

As Kenneth Kernaghan has recognized often in his writings on complex political and administrative concepts, there are seldom simple definitions and practices on which everyone can agree. This is true of accountability. The concept will always be debatable, and we will continue to experiment with different mechanisms to uphold the concept as circumstances in government change. Therefore, Ken's insistence that responsible authorities clarify how they define key terms and how they will apply them in practice will continue to serve practitioners and scholars in public administration well.

NOTES

1　Peter Aucoin and Ralph Heintzman, 'The Dialectics of Accountability for Performance in Public Management Reform,' in B. Guy Peters and Donald J. Savoie, eds., *Governance in the Twenty-first Century: Revitalizing the Public Service* (Montreal and Kingston: McGill-Queen's University Press, 2000), 244–80.

2　Robert D. Behn, *Rethinking Democratic Accountability* (Washington, D.C.: Brookings Institution, 2001).

3　Paul G. Thomas, 'Section 13: Accountability,' in B. Guy Peters and Jon Pierre, eds., *Handbook of Public Administration* (London: Sage, 2003), 549–57.

4　Patricia Day and Rudolf Klein, *Accountabilities: Five Public Services* (London: Tavistock, 1987); Melvin Dubnick, 'Accountability and the Promise of Performance: In Search of the Mechanisms,' *Public Performance and Management Review* 28, no. 3 (2005): 376–417; Matthew Flinders, *The Politics of Account-*

ability in the Modern State (Burlington: Ashgate, 2002); Kevin Kearns, 'Accountability in a Seamless Economy,' in B. Guy Peters and Jon Pierre, eds., *Handbook of Public Administration* (London: Sage, 2003), 581–90; Richard Mulgan, *Holding Power to Account: Accountability in Modern Democracies* (Houndsmills: Palgrave Macmillan, 2003); Barbara S. Romzek and Melvin J. Dubnik, 'Accountability in the Public Sector: Lessons from the *Challenger* Tragedy,' *Public Administration Review* 47, no. 3 (1987): 227–38; Bruce Stone, 'Administrative Accountability in the 'Westminster' Democracies: Towards a New Conceptual Framework,' *Governance* 8, no. 4 (1995): 505–526; Diane Woodhouse, *Ministers and Parliament: Accountability in Theory and Practice* (Oxford: Oxford University Press, 1994).

5 Mulgan, *Holding Power to Account,* 32–3.

6 Michael A. Harmon, *Responsibility as Paradox: A Critique of Rational Discourse on Government* (Thousand Oaks: Sage, 1995).

7 Jennifer Alexander, John P. Burke, Terry L. Cooper, and Michael Harmon, 'Spirited Dialogue: Michael Harmon's "Responsibility as Paradox?"' *Public Administration Review* 56, no. 6 (1996): 593–610.

8 John Uhr, *Terms of Trust: Arguments over Ethics in Australian Government* (Sydney: University of New South Wales Press, 2005), 60.

9 Linda de Leon, 'On Acting Responsibly in a Disorderly World: Individual Ethics and Administrative Accountability,' in Peters and Pierre, eds., *Handbook of Public Administration,* 569-80.

10 Lorne Sossin, 'Speaking Truth to Power? The Search for Bureaucratic Independence in Canada,' *University of Toronto Law Journal* 55 (2005): 1–59.

11 Andrew Heard, *Canadian Constitutional Conventions* (Toronto: Oxford University Press, 1991).

12 S.L. Sutherland, 'Responsible Government and Ministerial Responsibility: Every Reform Is Its Own Problem,' *Canadian Journal of Political Science* 24, no. 1 (1991): 91–120.

13 Kenneth Kernaghan, 'Power, Parliament, and Public Servants in Canada: Ministerial Responsibility Reexamined,' *Canadian Public Policy* 3 (1979): 392.

14 Sossin, 'Speaking Truth to Power?'

15 Peter Dobell and Martin Ulrich, 'Building Better Relations: Parliamentary Committees and Government Departments,' Occasional Paper no. 13 on Parliamentary Government, Ottawa, Parliamentary Centre, 2002.

16 Paul G. Thomas, 'Comparing the Law-Making Roles of the Senate and the House of Commons,' in Serge Joyal, ed., *Protecting Canadian Democracy: The Senate You Never Knew* (Montreal and Kingston: McGill-Queen's University Press, 2003), 189–228.

17 Paul G. Thomas, 'Contracting Out: Policy and Management Issues,' in Aucoin and Savoie, eds., *Managing Strategic Change: Learning from Program Review* (Ottawa: Canadian Centre for Management Development, 1998), 167–222.
18 Kenneth Kernaghan, 'Partnerships and Public Administration: Conceptual and Practical Considerations,' *Canadian Public Administration* 36, no. 1 (1993): 57–76.
19 Treasury Board Secretariat, "Stretching the Tax Dollar Series—The Federal Government as 'Partner': Six Steps to Successful Collaboration"(Ottawa, 1995), retrieved on 6 January 2008 from www.tbs_sct.gc.ca/pubs-pol/opepubs/TB_03/FGPE_e.asp.
20 Kenneth Kernaghan, 'Empowerment and Public Adminstration: Revolutionary Advance or Passing Fancy?' *Canadian Public Adminstration* 35 (1992): 194–214.
21 Paul G. Thomas, 'Performance Measurement, Reporting, and Accountability: Recent Trends and Future Directions,' Public Policy Paper no. 23, Saskatchewan Institute of Public Policy, 2004.
22 Office of the Auditor General of Canada, 'Involving Others in Governing: Accountability at Risk,' *Report of the Auditor General of Canada* (Ottawa: 1999), ch. 23.
23 Dubnick, 'Accountability and the Promise of Performance.'
24 Jonathan Koppell, 'Pathologies of Accountability: ICANN and the Challenge of "Multiple Accountabilities Disorder,"' *Public Administration Review* 65, no. 1 (2005): 94–7.
25 Behn, *Rethinking Democratic Accountability*, 120.

3 An Ideal Model in a Practical World: The Continuous Revisiting of Political Neutrality and Ministerial Responsibility

DAVID A. GOOD

More than a generation ago, Kenneth Kernaghan revisited two important and closely knit doctrines – political neutrality and ministerial responsibility – that have always been central to the relationship between public servants and politicians. In a 1976 article, 'Politics, Policy, and Public Servants: Political Neutrality Revisited,' he explained the traditional doctrine of political neutrality in terms of an idealized model that included six conditions:

1 Politics and policy are separated from administration. Thus, politicians make policy decisions; public servants execute these decisions.
2 Public servants are appointed and promoted on the basis of merit rather than on the basis of party affiliation and contribution.
3 Public servants do not engage in partisan political activities.
4 Public servants do not express publicly their personal views on government policy or administration.
5 Public servants provide forthright and objective advice to their political masters in private and in confidence. In turn, political executives protect the anonymity of public servants by publicly accepting responsibility for departmental decisions.
6 Public servants execute policy decisions loyally and zealously irrespective of the philosophy and programs of the party in power and regardless of their personal opinions. As a result, public servants enjoy security of tenure during good behaviour and satisfactory performance.[1]

He then noted the shortcomings of this model to describe accurately how political neutrality was actually practised in government.

Three years later, in 1979, Kernaghan revisited the related doctrine of ministerial responsibility in an article titled 'Power, Parliament, and Public Servants: Ministerial Responsibility Revisited.'[2] He reported 'widespread agreement' in the academic literature that individual ministerial responsibility had two components. First, 'the minister is answerable to Parliament for all the administrative errors of his departmental subordinates in the sense that he must resign in the event of a serious error by his department'; second, 'the minister is answerable to Parliament in that he must explain and defend the actions of his department before Parliament.' He noted, however, that the first component was often described as 'a myth' and that 'the importance' of the second was 'ignored or minimized by some Canadian commentators.'[3]

Throughout his many writings, Kernaghan has conceived of ministerial responsibility as 'tightly bounded up with the conventions of political neutrality and public service anonymity,' noting that 'their definition and usage shape to a large extent the pattern of interaction between public servants on the one hand and parliamentarians and ministers on the other.'[4] Once again, like Kernaghan did, this chapter revisits the idealized model of political neutrality, ministerial responsibility, and public service anonymity.[5] The focus here is on policy making as well as on administrative issues that in recent times have become a source of strong public controversy.[6] To suggest how the idealized model and its requirements actually operate in practice, this chapter begins by recounting a fictional meeting between a minister and a deputy minister. It then sets out the modifications to the idealized model that Kernaghan has identified in his writings and examines some of the new and emerging forces that are widening the gaps between the model and actual practice in the Canadian federal government. It concludes with a call for a continued debate and re-examination of the ideal model, its interpretations, and its application.

An Ideal Model in a Practical World

The ideal model of political neutrality, ministerial responsibility, and public service anonymity and the subsequent and ongoing interpretations of these by scholars cannot and must not be taken lightly. This is because the ideal model and its interpretations are what set the standards against which the behaviour of politicians and public servants is judged in the real world. Ultimately it is citizens who make these judgments. However, in a complex world of instantaneous information, the standards and the evidence on which these public judgments depend are shaped and determined by the political interplay between the government of the day and the opposition as they feed off the findings and recommendations of auditors, watchdogs, and independent inquiries. These in turn are refracted, interpreted, and distorted by the increasingly probing media, which are always hungry for political scandal.

To be sure, some governments to varying degrees have attempted to bring into practice some of the conditions of this ideal model. However, to my knowledge no government anywhere has been able to do so to an extent that ensures that these conditions govern the relationship between politicians and public servants. As we will see, there are good reasons why governments do not follow the ideal model. What would such an ideal government look like, and how would it operate in practice?

Come with me to a government that is run according to the ideal model of ministerial responsibility, political neutrality, and public service anonymity. We enter a darkened minister's office – blinds closed and curtains partly drawn. A small lamp illuminates two figures – a minister and his deputy minister, who are seated at a small oval table in front of a large oak desk. On one corner of the desk we see a huge, sprawling pile of documents and papers partly covering what appears to be an in-basket; on the other, we glimpse the dark oak bottom of an empty out-basket. We pick up their discussion in mid-sentence.

MINISTER: … yes, I'll handle all matters of policy and you make sure that the administration in the department gets done without any problems. It's the administrative errors, you know, that'll get me into trouble. That's what the opposition focuses on. And when it comes to administration we can't afford any mistakes. You do your job on administration and I'll be responsible and answerable to Parliament for both the policies of the government and the actions of the department. And you and your fellow public servants have my word that I will protect your anonymity.

DEPUTY MINISTER: Agreed. As objective, anonymous, and permanent administrators we will implement your decisions loyally and zealously. *(Pauses)* Now, about that new program you want set up in order to create jobs in areas of high unemployment. We've developed a plan on how departmental officials will implement it.

MINISTER: Good, take me through it.

DEPUTY MINISTER: (*Reaching down into his several briefcases he slowly places ten six-inch-thick binders, one after the other, on the table in front of the minister.*) These are the program manuals that our public administrators will use to implement the program. They provide the rules. We have rules for everything. But let me just focus on the highlights.

MINISTER: OK ... but ... you really have rules for everything?

DEPUTY MINISTER: For everything, Minister, and they are rules to be followed, not simply guidelines to be considered. Let me start with eligibility. To be eligible for funding the employment project must take place within a geographic area of the country of high unemployment – that is, in an area with an unemployment rate over 10 per cent as measured and reported the previous quarter by the government agency, Stats-Can-Talk. In total, there are sixty such geographic areas in the country and currently twelve have unemployment rates above 10 per cent. The annual cost per job (including contributions from all partners – public, private, and voluntary sector organizations) must be no more than $25,000. There are strict procedures for calculating 'in-kind' contributions. The total public subsidy per job from all levels of government must be no more than 50 per cent of the total cost per job in any one year and the federal subsidy from this program can be no more than 50 per cent of that. If the project involves other federal programs, such as those administered by our regional development agencies, then the total contribution from the new program must be no more than 50 per cent of the total federal contribution. (*Pauses*) Are you following me, Minister?

MINISTER: (*Hesitantly*) I think so ... (*Questioning*) But, all these requirements – they're simply matters of administration?

DEPUTY MINISTER: Yes, I believe they are, but let me continue so you can get the whole picture. The projects are for small businesses only, and this section of the manual includes the definitions of which types of businesses are eligible. (*Holds up a document; between his thumb and his index finger are sixty pages.*) To avoid any confusion, any business activity not included in the manual is not eligible. And, for most that are included, there are special conditions that must be met. For example, new or expanded fish plants that process wild fish are not eligible because we do not want to add to processing capacity and encourage overfishing of our depleting wild stocks. But expansions to plants that process farmed fish are eligible, but not new plants. No fish harvesting activity is eligible. No businesses with major debts outstanding to the government are eligible. Only established businesses with a five-year track record will be eligible. All applications will require a full business plan and we have a separate manual detailing the information we will need. And we …

MINISTER: (*Interrupting*) Hold it; hold it, just a minute. This is getting ridiculous. This program wouldn't create any new jobs in any of the areas of the country where unemployment is high. It's much, much too restrictive.

DEPUTY MINISTER: (*Pauses, reflects, and slowly responds.*) You may be right, Minister, but I can tell you, by doing it this way and being very specific and clear about everything, we can avoid administrative mistakes. If there is ever a question about what should be done, we just look up the answer here in the manual. Here, Minister, you try. Ask me any question and I'll give you the answer.

MINISTER: (*Firmly*) Deputy, I'm not going to play that game … Let me tell you how I want to proceed. These are, after all, matters of policy, not matters of administration. While you and your bureaucrats were 'beavering away' on these so-called 'administrative manuals,' I had my political staff in my office consult with several external think tanks on the policy issues surrounding this new program. Here is what the policy should be. I agree the program needs to be targeted to geographic areas of high unemployment – above 10 per cent. But when we find that within areas of low unemployment – that is, below 10 per cent – there are pockets or subareas of high unemployment, I want these small pockets included. Also, if there are groups with special employment needs, like aboriginals, low-income single women with children, or youth at risk, I want them to be eligible even if they happen to be living in geographic areas with unemployment rates less than 10 per cent. I will not be a slave to bureaucratically and artificially determined geographic boundaries for eligibility. We've got to think about the people – the unemployed people. We've got to be responsive to local needs and to local capacities. We need some human judgment here.

In addition, I want the local member of Parliament to be consulted on all projects taking place within his or her riding. Without their concurrence, projects should not proceed. Similarly, we will need the concurrence of provincial and territorial governments. I agree, we'll need financial partnerships with private sector firms and voluntary organizations, but I don't think their unwillingness or their inability to contribute financially should stand in the way of good projects. The jobs should be sustainable and they should be cost effective. I also want your departmental officials to be active in communities, to be visibly out there, using their knowledge and expertise to help groups and organizations develop and promote creative project submissions so that we can get good projects.

By the way, I've just talked to the Minister of Finance and explained to him that I need $200 million a year to run this program.

DEPUTY MINISTER: And … Did you get the money?

MINISTER: Well, no … at least, not yet. It's amazing how difficult it is to get money for a new policy initiative, even from an old friend and colleague. It's like we're in different political parties … But don't you worry about that. It's a matter of policy. I'll deal with Finance.

DEPUTY MINISTER: (*Expressing great worry.*) O … K … but as public servants we'll need much more explicit criteria and rules if we are to administer *your* program without problems. Your scheme leaves much too much discretion in the hands of departmental officials in the field. Without more explicit criteria and rules the department and its officials will be subjected to political pressure and will be vulnerable to criticism of not being objective and fair when it comes to these projects.

MINISTER: (*Pauses for a long time and then begins slowly.*) Yeah … I can see what you mean … But I need the flexibility to deal with the different employment needs of different communities and different groups. One size won't fit all. (*Pauses again.*) But don't worry, when it comes to making these decisions on individual projects we won't treat them as administrative matters, nor should we. In fact, because they involve judgment and discretion they are policy decisions. Therefore, as minister I will make these decisions myself.

DEPUTY MINISTER: (*Leaning forward in his chair.*) I really worry about formally involving MPs in the decision-making process on individual projects. I think it will confuse accountability between you and MPs. As public servants, it will erode our political neutrality, increase our public visibility, and make us much less anonymous. (*Speaking slowly and sternly.*) Minister, you said you would protect our anonymity, and I worry that you won't be able to do that. I'm very concerned that as administrators we will become politicized. This is not a good idea at all.

MINISTER: You just don't understand. This is a key part of our government's policy – to involve MPs more directly in what they know and represent best – their communities and their constituents. Public servants will not be making any of these decisions. They will simply be recording and compiling the views of MPs and providing them to me and to my office. That way, we can make informed decisions on the projects.

DEPUTY MINISTER: (*Timidly*) Minister, I know these are matters of policy and therefore it's not really my business … But I do have one question. Will you be handling government MPs and opposition MPs in the same manner?

MINISTER: You're right it's not your business. (*Pausing for a moment and then smiling slightly.*) Of course, we'll do our best to treat them all the same.

DEPUTY MINISTER: (*Glancing at the overflowing in-basket on the minister's desk.*) Right … but given the hundreds of project proposals that will result from the program, will you be able to make all these decisions in a timely manner?

MINISTER: (*Showing impatience*) The decisions will be timely. And if I need more political staff to help make the decisions, then I'll get them.

DEPUTY MINISTER: (*Sceptically*) And *you* will personally make all the decisions yourself, not members of your political staff? As you know your political staff is not accountable to you in the way that I am directly accountable to you for matters of administration. Also, by implementing the program the way I propose, I can hold my subordinates directly accountable to me through a well-defined chain of command within the department. That way, Minister, you can hold me and the department accountable and be publicly responsible for all the decisions.

MINISTER: I understand your point about political staff. You are right they are not accountable to me in the way you are. In fact, they are not accountable to me at all. Therefore, let me just say that I and I alone will make the decisions. I will be personally responsible for all the decisions and I will accept personal accountability, too.

DEPUTY MINISTER: I'm also concerned about having our departmental administrators operating as highly visible 'community organizers' in helping proponents develop and promote their projects. We can't be anonymous and neutral public servants like that. That will undercut our objectivity.

MINISTER: Well, if you're not prepared to have your officials do this important community development work then I'll have to hire external consultants to do it … In fact, that takes me to a related point – I want to have public consultations with stakeholders before I finalize and announce this new program. It's important that we get public input on the program. Now, I'm sure you would agree this is not a job for anonymous public servants. Public consultation is policy work, not administration. Consultation could well require staking out policy positions in public, which could undermine your anonymity and neutrality. Therefore, this is what I propose. Tom Smooth in my office is very skilled at these sorts of things and I want you to hire him into the department into a senior executive position so that he can conduct these public consultations from the neutral perspective of the department rather than, from what might be seen as, the politically partisan perspective of my office. In addition, to work with and support Tom, I'll be hiring 'Stratego,' the consulting firm that helped us on our last election campaign.

DEPUTY MINISTER: (*Taking a firm and cautionary tone.*) Minister, I must remind you that when it comes to matters of hiring into the public service there are specific authorities and responsibilities that have been assigned by law and delegated to me by the Public Service Staffing Commission. I am directly responsible and I am publicly accountable for these matters. I should also add that my responsibility and my accountability also apply to certain financial and other matters delegated or assigned to me by the Treasury.

MINISTER: (*Emphatically*) Now as you know, it's never my practice to make too fine a point, but I must say that when it comes to these matters I need to. You and I both know that under long-standing practice and convention, as explained most recently by the Clerk of the Privy Council at the Gumley Inquiry, as the minister, I am directly accountable to Parliament for all matters within the department. On these and on all matters you are directly accountable to me. Remember that while you are answerable to Parliament, you're not directly accountable to MPs. That is what the government's published guidelines on this matter say. (*Pauses*) Now I know that the new legislation, the Federal Surreal Accountability Act, currently under consideration, seems to be proposing that you as Deputy Minister could be accountable *before* (as opposed to *to*) parliamentary committees for certain responsibilities. But quite frankly I find all this business of *before* and *to* to be rather confusing, especially when it is not precisely clear which aspects of administration not affecting policy deputy ministers will be directly accountable for. Until it gets sorted out through real experience and practice, who knows what it actually means?

DEPUTY MINISTER: (*Sensing an impasse and stalling for time so that he can seek the advice of the Clerk of the Privy Council before definitively responding to his minister's request that the department hire Mr Smooth.*) I want to reflect on your specific request and get back to you in the morning. Now minister, we also need to come to the important matter of ...

The meeting is abruptly interrupted by the minister's executive assistant, who informs him that the prime minister is on the phone concerning the minister's failure to respond to the urgent letter he sent him last week about getting a new program up and running to help the unemployed. The minister bolts to his desk, reaches down, and picks up the receiver as two political aides, in search of the prime minister's letter, frantically sift through the endless piles of papers and notes overflowing the in-basket.

This is hardly an ideal model for the minister, the deputy minister, departmental officials, or the government. When the model is extrapolated fully, it is likely to lead to one of three outcomes. Under the first outcome, no new program is undertaken; this is because if the minister and deputy minister remain true to the principles and requirements of the ideal model, they cannot reach common ground and general agreement about the program, its design, and how it will be implemented. Public servants cannot administer the program as designed by the minister, and the minister cannot accept the administrative procedures as proposed by the deputy. Those who question the role of government in undertaking such programs might see this as a good outcome; however, it is hardly sustainable.

With the second outcome, the program is implemented according to the flexible policy design of the minister. The deputy minister and his public servants are unable to develop explicit rules for making decisions and for structuring responsibilities and accountabilities. At best they are only able to produce vague guidelines, which are variously interpreted by various public servants. Understandings are not holistic, explicit, and institutional; rather they are partial, implicit, and interpersonal. The minister and his office become overwhelmed with project requests. In an effort to cope, the minister hires more political staff and more outside consultants who are not accountable to him or to anyone else. Serious mistakes are made or appear to be made: opposition MPs complain about the lack of program guidelines; government MPs complain that they are not eligible for projects in the 'pocket' areas of unemployment; public servants who are highly visible in communities and in dealing with MPs are accused of compromising their political neutrality; hidden and unaccountable consultants are accused of 'pulling the strings behind the scenes'; and project approvals are painfully slow, with approvals being made only after intense lobbying and political pressure. All of this reinforces impressions of political interference and political favouritism, with the opposition and the media making allegations of corruption and political kickbacks. Public servants are openly criticized for not putting in place sound and transparent administrative procedures and guidelines. The minister makes an effort to assume full responsibility and accountability for all the projects. But if the opposition, media, and public attacks become too vigorous and sustained and if the prime minister, for whatever reasons, is no longer prepared to defend his minister, that minister is forced to resign.

In the third outcome, the program is designed and implemented according to a strict and rigid set of administrative rules, leaving little or no room for judgment by public servants. No administrative mistakes are made, but the program is completely ineffective. Only a few projects are approved because most of the proposals cannot meet the predetermined rules. Some promising projects are simply abandoned because the approval process is too lengthy, too cumbersome, and too expensive. Other projects never come forward because the small businesses and community organizations that serve as project proponents find the 'web of rules' in the decision-making process too costly and time consuming. The deputy minister is seen by some of his fellow colleagues as a model bureaucrat in the classical tradition, as someone who can develop a multiplicity of seemingly foolproof rules to implement flawlessly the rules that underlie the policy decisions that his minister has reluctantly and quietly come to accept. To his colleagues, however, the minister is far from the ideal politician. He places administration before policy and even before politics, produces programs that will not work for citizens, caves in to the demands of his bureaucrats, and is unprepared and unable to exercise political leadership. He is seen by his colleagues and by his constituents as weak and ineffective. Both he and his government are soundly defeated in the next election, and a new government, which had campaigned on a platform of decisive leadership and good government, of 'cutting through red tape and not being pushed around by faceless bureaucrats,' is elected.

As we can see, this government, which may have looked ideal in the abstract, turns out to be far from ideal in practice. Indeed, the ideal model establishes standards for government that in some instances cannot be met and that in most others can be achieved only at great cost to society, democracy, and the effective functioning of government. In the end, this 'model government' is a 'problem government.'

Because no government will be satisfied with any of the outcomes flowing from this ideal model, subsequent ministers, deputies, and governments will adapt and change their behaviours and practices in an effort to achieve more desirable outcomes. In short, they will adjust the model. Deputy ministers realize that the insistence that policy and administration be separated invariably leads to the creation of undesirable 'work-arounds' through the disregard of public servants and the inappropriate use of consultants and political staff in ministers' offices. All of this creates new and more significant problems. They see at first hand the results of the old adage of public policy and public administration: if there is a vacuum, someone will fill it. Ministers realize that this separation leads not only to extreme choices but also to a public service that does not provide 'forthright and objective advice' because its advice is sharply limited, focusing solely on matters of administration. Forbidding experienced public servants to make recommendations on policy leads easily to their subsequent avoidance of responsibility in the form of 'I would have told you so, had you only asked' when the inevitable problems in administration and implementation arise. In short, when it comes to policy and administration it seems that artificial conventions and ideal models cannot separate what nature and experience deem must go together and work together.

The ideal model, when strictly applied to the world of practice, produces significant problems for both politicians and public servants, problems that reduce both their individual and their collective performance. As a consequence, they have over time adjusted their behaviour based on what they have learned from their earthly experience rather than on what they have been taught about heavenly ideals.

Continuous Revisiting

In 1976, Kernaghan discussed the 'obvious' failure of this ideal model to depict accurately how political neutrality actually played out in parliamentary governments at the time. He concluded that 'the present operations of the Canadian public service are not in accord with the traditional doctrine of political neutrality' and that 'public servants are actively involved in the political process both by necessity in the areas of policy development and execution and by choice in the sphere of political partisanship.[7] He proposed a restatement of the convention of political neutrality along the following lines:

> Politics, policy and administration are intertwined; most public servants are selected and promoted on the basis of merit, but some positions are filled by partisans of the governing party; most public servants may participate in partisan political activities; public servants may not express publicly their personal views on government actions but are involved in various forms of public comment in the normal course of their duties; public servants provide confidential advice to ministers; ministers protect the anonymity of public servants, but this anonymity is gradually declining for other reasons; and public servants execute policy decisions loyally, regardless of their personal views.[8]

Concerning ministerial responsibility, in 1979 Kernaghan proposed softening the strict conditions of the ideal model, concluding that 'the minister is answerable to Parliament in that he must explain and defend the actions of his department before Parliament [but] is not answerable to Parliament for all the administrative errors of his department.'[9] He went on to emphasize that 'the essential condition' is that

> elected and appointed officials, or both, bear responsibility for all government actions ... if officials waste public funds, break the law or violate citizen's rights, the public expects that someone will be held accountable for these misdeeds. If ministers do not accept responsibility for departmental transgressions, the focus of blame shifts to public servants. But the conventions of ministerial responsibility and political accountability still protect the anonymity of public servants and restrict their answerability to Parliament.[10]

He recognized however, that this formulation did not resolve the matter, as there were 'major problems' in the way ministerial responsibility was actually practised:

> On those exceptional occasions when blame is publicly attributable to specific officials, disciplinary action is handled as an internal administrative matter with the result that the public rarely learns what penalties, if any, are imposed ... Moreover, successive Auditors General have documented the 'horrible stories' of a widespread and continuing absence of economy, efficiency, and effectiveness in the government's expenditure of public

funds. Consequently, it appears to the public that on some occasions a gap exists between ministerial and administrative responsibility because neither minister nor public servant seem to be held accountable for maladministration.[11]

Kernaghan revisited these doctrines because he understood their fundamental conceptual importance, how they were inextricably related, and perhaps most important, the changes and tensions in the actual practice of public administration and politics that required their continued re-examination.

Emerging Pressures and Reforms

Since these writings, broad societal, technological, and economic changes have continued at an accelerating pace and have placed further pressure on the idealized model and on the practice of political neutrality, ministerial responsibility, and public service anonymity. The response of governments to these pressures over the past several decades is perhaps best encapsulated in the public management reforms that have been undertaken. Some of the reforms that have accompanied the introduction of the so-called New Public Management (NPM) – most notably, the separation of politics and administration – actually originate in fundamentals of the idealized model.[12] It is not surprising, then, that some of the most recent and most highly lauded public management reforms have raised new challenges and problems for political neutrality, ministerial responsibility, and anonymity, as well as for the increasingly important issue of accountability.

For example, there have been periodic attempts to delegate decision-making authority to managers and front-line staff (some call this empowerment), with decisions being been pushed 'down and out' in an effort to increase efficiency, flexibility, and responsiveness. This has been done with the promise (in the hope?) that regular flows of timely and reliable information will be provided 'up and in' towards the centre and top of the organization so that ministerial responsibility and accountability can be maintained. It may seem easy in an idealized world to establish centralized information to control decentralized decision making; experience on the ground, though, indicates that this is difficult to accomplish on a sustained and regular basis.[13] Furthermore, the government's overreaction to the media, the opposition, and the public regarding the sponsorship scandal and the findings of the Gomery Report have led the Blue Ribbon Panel on Grants and Contributions to strongly recommend drastic cuts to the excessive administrative red tape that has unnecessarily entangled programs involving grants and contributions.

Compared to a generation ago there have been significant increases in the transparency of government decision making and the public availability of government information. Public administration is increasingly being conducted in a fish bowl: the news media have been probing persistently; the opposition parties have been scoring points by exposing and vigorously pursuing administrative and political scandals; access to government information has increased; and actions of public servants are constantly being exposed through parliamentary committees, media events, and policy processes. All of this has reduced the anonymity of public servants at all levels; in new ways it is challenging their efforts to maintain political neutrality.

The increased emphasis on public consultation and citizen engagement on nearly all matters and aspects of public policy has raised the profile and increased the exposure of public servants from deputy ministers to district directors. The potential for visible public conflict between public officials and stakeholders has increased as ministers have come to depend on public servants to handle these tricky issues instead of relying on independent 'facilitators' who are outside government. In addition, many stakeholders who have felt overconsulted and underpowered on issues that are often deeply divisive and ideological in origin have increased their pressure on senior public servants and not necessarily on ministers. Even for less senior, front-line public servants, the significant focus on citizen-centred service has meant that they have become less anonymous and more visible to those they serve. This has sometimes led to criticism that departments and officials have become 'unbalanced,' focusing too much on citizen service and too little on internal control and sound management.[14]

Initiatives to strengthen horizontal coordination and shared decision making across departments and agencies of government have become the mantra of modern governments in their efforts to take a comprehensive and coordinated approach to issues that go well beyond the boundaries of stovepiped organizations. The implicit assumption here is that the individual responsibilities and accountabilities of ministers and their public service agents can be clearly defined. In practice, this has proven to be difficult.

Finally, government departments and agencies are entering into partnership arrangements with private and voluntary sector organizations with the goal of improving efficiency, effectiveness, and responsiveness in program delivery and project management. The assumption is that in the process of transferring and sharing risk across these sectors, responsibilities and accountabilities will be sorted out and clearly defined. Again, this has proven to be more difficult in practice than it first seemed in theory.

It is not surprising, therefore, that Kernaghan, writing on his own and with collaborators, throughout his career has revisited and re-examined the practice of the conventions of political neutrality, ministerial responsibility, and public service anonymity.[15] Other scholars and practitioners, in Canada and elsewhere, have also examined these conventions.[16] In 2001, Kernaghan concluded that 'these three conventions, taken together, provide a framework for understanding and explaining relationships among politicians, public servants, and members of the public' and that 'significant change in the meaning or application of one of them is likely to have important implications for the others.'[17] More specifically, he set out three requirements for making the framework succeed:

- Ministers, not public servants, answer to Parliament, by way of explanation, for policy decisions and politically contentious matters in a manner that safeguards the political neutrality and anonymity of public servants.
- Public servants avoid activities that harm or seem to harm their impartiality or the impartiality of the public service (e.g., criticizing their minister in public).
- Public servants provide advice to ministers in confidence and avoid activities that involve them in public debate or political controversy.[18]

These are significant requirements. When taken together, they represent important adjustments to the ideal model and help make the model work in a real world. These requirements do, however, place significant and far-reaching obligations on both ministers and public servants. The key question is this: Is it reasonable to expect ministers and deputy ministers to uphold sufficiently these requirements in both the normal and the abnormal course of their work, which increasingly takes place in a world of 'gotcha journalism' and 'spin politics'? Let us explore briefly each requirement in turn.

It is conceivable that in matters of policy, ministers may be able to provide answers to Parliament in a manner that safeguards the political neutrality and anonymity of public servants. In that regard, it is increasingly appropriate for members of Parliament to hold ministers (and not officials) accountable for the outputs and for some of the outcomes of various government policies and programs, but to ensure that officials are responsible for the information and measurement systems that provide the necessary policy and program information.

When it comes to politically contentious matters, we are now finding that they are less often issues of policy and more often issues of administration. Problems in administration are bound to occur and will continue to occur. In modern government it cannot be otherwise. As problems of administration are publicly reported by auditors general or internal departmental auditors, the opposition and the media are often able to transform them into issues of 'lost money' or 'government mismanagement' – an approach that finds easy resonance among citizens and taxpayers. After all, when issues are encapsulated in this way, they come across as simple, dramatic, and personalized. And because such problems are administrative, public servants are naturally drawn into them. As a consequence, public servants are increasingly appearing in the media and before parliamentary committees and public inquiries. There is no evidence that this recent trend is moderating.

Indeed, it is now all too common for elected officials to acknowledge that responsibility rests with them, but then say in the next breath that they are not personally responsible or accountable for what went wrong. They confess to nothing of any significance. And perhaps more important, they place the spotlight on career public servants, who, under the conventions of accountability and ministerial responsibility, are less able to defend themselves in public, be it in a parliamentary committee or in front of the media. Unless ministers are prepared to accept personal responsibility for what went wrong, it seems unlikely that they will be able to safeguard the anonymity and political neutrality of public servants.

The second requirement for public servants – to avoid activities that harm or seem to harm their impartiality or the impartiality of the public service – raises some important issues for public servants at all levels. Despite the more activist role of Supreme Courts in matters of public policy,[19] governments are finding it difficult to avoid or sidestep issues that are deeply contentious and divisive. As a result, public servants are increasingly being asked to undertake various forms of public consultation and engagement in and around these difficult issues. More often than not these are 'zero sum' exercises where the gains to one group in the form of rights, allocations, programs, or benefits come at the expense of another group. Public servants have become 'front and centre' and highly visible in some of these consultations across competing stakeholders, whether it involves determining which programs to cut in order to fund a dominant priority such as health care, deciding in whose 'backyard' a federal prison will be located, or determining how many Fraser River–bound sockeye salmon should be taken from commercial and recreational fishermen to fulfil the ill-defined but constitutionally protected rights of Aboriginal fishermen.

Skilful public servants who are called on to engage diverse and competing stakeholders in a meaningful process of open consultation can usually avoid appearing to openly criticize their ministers. They can, however, run a real risk of eroding their appearance of impartiality as they undertake the important task of ensuring that all aspects of the public interest are represented and heard. This can occur, for example, when they support or facilitate minority views – views that if not encouraged might go unspoken and thus unheard. This can also occur when they attempt to channel or limit dominant, narrow, and highly vocal interests in an effort to ensure a balance of perspectives on a difficult and divisive issue.

Public servants are finding that meeting the third requirement – to provide advice to ministers in confidence and to avoid activities that involve them in public debate or political controversy – is also becoming more difficult. On both these scores, public servants are at risk. First, their advice to ministers is less confidential than it used to be as well as considerably more open to the scrutiny and reappraisal of others. Second, they are increasingly undertaking activities of public consultation and engagement that can lead them into public debate and political controversy. They are also being called on to explain and defend their departments, programs, and expenditures in parliamentary committees and in the media during times of political controversy and allegations of scandal.

The confidentiality of public service advice to ministers has been reduced significantly, in general through greater openness in government and in particular through access-to-information legislation.[20] Despite the various exemptions in the legislation for 'confidences of the Queen's Privy Council' and other items, senior officials are finding more and more that the contents of their memoranda, reports, emails, meetings, and conversations, which together form the basis for their ministerial policy advice, are making their way into the newspapers and into radio and television news. Indeed, there is a growing reluctance within the public service to commit certain sensitive things to paper.[21] This means there is increased risk that important decisions will get made without the benefit of thorough, in-depth documentation and analysis. It also compels deputy ministers and the most senior departmental officials to 'speak truth to power' on matters of complex public policy in the absence of a sophisticated, written policy analysis to inform internal discussion and debate.

Fulfilling the third requirement – providing confidential advice and avoiding political controversy – has become much more difficult and at the same time more risky. Verbal advice has always been an important ingredient in policy analysis, but traditionally its contribution has been strengthened and supported by solid and thorough policy analysis that has withstood the discipline of the thought and debate that comes from 'putting pen to paper.' If current trends continue, there is a chance that confidential advice will increasingly become verbal advice, detached from and uninformed by written analysis regarding the desirability, impacts, and feasibility of policy options.

Avoiding political controversy continues to be the desire of public servants, but succeeding at this has the potential to affect their behaviour in matters of both policy and administration. Public servants with responsibility for policy might reduce or curtail their visibility and personal role as they engage and consult stakeholders in the development and implementation of policy, relying on external consultants to do the work for them. Experience suggests that this arm's-length approach can create the impression among stakeholders that no one of importance is listening to what they have to say and that little or nothing will be done with the advice they offer. Public servants with operational responsibilities, fearing that they will be drawn into public and political controversy, might be increasingly inclined to leave ministers and their political staffs to deal with the fallout from administrative problems that have been transformed into crises, scandals, boondoggles, and the like. This would not serve ministers and governments well because the expertise, information, and knowledge that public servants can offer on these matters are critical not only for the minister in handling the crisis but also for the opposition and the media as they ask questions and make demands for information and explanation.

These three requirements entail significant adjustments to the ideal model, and as such they can help make the revised model work in the real world. But these requirements also restrict the interactions among public servants, ministers, parliamentarians, the media, and the public – and such restrictions are unlikely to ensure good government and good public administration. As always, drawing fine lines and making fine distinctions and adjustments will be required.

Reappraising the Doctrine

Upholding these three requirements in the actual practice of public administration will undoubtedly be difficult and increasingly challenging for both public servants and ministers. A host of new pressures are taking root with the old and are pushing up against the application of these requirements in the real world. Explicitly reinterpreting any long-standing doctrine and its requirements is no doubt risky business. But it is even riskier to let the doctrine slide on its own in various directions, with some practitioners and commentators taking a strict classical view, others a liberal interpretation, and others arguing that the doctrine has little or no relevance. This is because the expectations for the behaviour of public servants and politicians can increasingly diverge among various public servants, ministers, members of Parliament, the government of the day, the opposition, the auditor general, the media, academics, and the public.

The widening gap between the ideal model and actual practice is more than stretching the limits of those who are responsible for interpreting the doctrine. It also appears to be giving licence to some for the way in which they practise the doctrine and subsequently report on their practice. As the interpreters or enforcers of the doctrine struggle to provide meaningful guidance to public servants and politicians in a world that is changing in fundamental ways, their interpretations are finding less resonance. In addition, the increasing public exposure of the failures of some practitioners to live up to even the most rudimentary aspects of the doctrine indicates that there is confusion over what is ideal in theory and what is actually possible in practice. This suggests the need for a constant revisiting of the doctrine and, perhaps, for a more fundamental reappraisal.

Whatever reinterpretations of the doctrine might be made in the future, there are several criteria that should guide any reappraisal. Like any good public policy change, it should involve open and informed debate among the key interests – public servants, ministers, members of Parliament, auditors, the media, academics, and the public. Any adjustments or changes to the doctrine should be effective in the long term and feasible in the short term and should anticipate and minimize the negative and seemingly unintended consequences that will invariably emerge. Just as Kenneth Kernaghan has done so thoroughly and thoughtfully for more than a generation, we again need to constantly revisit this important doctrine.

NOTES

1 Kenneth Kernaghan, 'Politics, Policy, and Public Servants: Political Neutrality Revisited,' *Canadian Public Administration* 19, no. 3 (1976): 433. Reprinted in updated and expanded form in Ron S. Blair and Jack McLeod, eds., *Canadian Political Traditions: Basic Readings,* 2nd ed. (Scarborough: Nelson Canada, 1993), 447–71.
2 Kenneth Kernaghan, 'Power, Parliament, and Public Servants: Ministerial Responsibility Revisited,' *Canadian Public Policy* 3 (1979): 383–96. Reprinted in expanded form in Harold Clarke, Colin Campbell, F.Q. Quo, and Arthur Goddard, eds., *Parliament, Policy, and Representation* (Toronto: Methuen, 1980), 124–43.
3 Kenneth Kernaghan, 'Power, Parliament, and Public Servants,' 127.
4 Ibid., 125.
5 The model is described and discussed in many important public administration textbooks. See, for example, Kenneth Kernaghan and David Siegel, *Public Administration in Canada* (Toronto: International Nelson, 1987; 2nd ed. 1991; 3rd ed. 1995; 4th ed. 1999); and Kenneth Kernaghan and John Langford, *The Responsible Public Servant* (Toronto: IPAC and IRPP, 1990).
6 For a retrospective review of policy analysis and advice in Canadian governments, see Michael J. Prince, 'Soft Craft, Hard Choices, Altered Context: Reflections on Twenty-Five Years of Policy Advice in Canada,' in David Laycock, Laurent Dobuzinskis, and Michael Howlett, eds., *Policy Analysis in Canada* (Toronto: University of Toronto Press, 2007), 163–85.
7 Kernaghan, 'Politics, Policy, and Public Servants,' 456.
8 Ibid.
9 Kernaghan, 'Power, Parliament, and Public Servants,' 135–6.
10 Ibid.
11 Ibid., 137.
12 For a critique of the separation of policy and administration, see Donald Savoie, *Breaking the Bargain: Public Servants, Ministers, and Parliament* (Toronto: University of Toronto Press, 2003).

13 See, for example, David A. Good, *The Politics of Public Management: The HRDC Audit of Grants and Contributions* (Toronto: University of Toronto Press, 2003).

14 See, for example, the House of Commons Standing Committee on Human Resources Development and the Status of Persons with Disabilities, *Seeking a Balance: Final Report on Human Resources Development Grants and Contributions* (Ottawa, 2000).

15 Some of his most important collaborative work on these issues includes *The Responsible Public Servant* (with Langford) and *Public Administration in Canada* (with Siegel).

16 See, for example, A.W. Johnson, 'The Role of the Deputy Minister,' *Canadian Public Administration* 4, no. 4 (1961): 363–9; Darcy McKeough, 'The Relations of Ministers and Civil Servants,' *Canadian Public Administration* 12, no. 1 (1969): 1–8; Tim Plumptre, 'New Perspectives on the Role of the Deputy Minister,' *Canadian Public Administration* 30, no. 3 (1987): 376–98; and Oonagh Gay and Thomas Powell, 'Individual Ministerial Responsibility – Issues and Examples,' UK House of Commons, Research Paper 04/31, 5 April 2004.

17 Kernaghan, 'Ministerial Responsibility: Interpretations, Implications, and Information Access,' Access to Information Review Task Force, 2001. www.atirtf-geai.gc.ca/paper-ministerial-e.html.

18 Ibid.

19 Ran Hirschl, *Towards Juristocracy: The Origins and Consequences of the New Constitutionalism* (Cambridge, MA: Harvard University Press, 2004).

20 For an award-winning article on cabinet secrecy, a convention that is neither well understood nor particularly popular, see Nicholas d'Ombrain, 'Cabinet Secrecy,' *Canadian Public Administration* 47, no. 3 (2004): 332–59.

21 Savoie, *Breaking the Bargain*, 289–90. More recently confirmed by Ken Rubin in 'Putting Public Safety First – Some Access to Information Act Experiences,' a dialogue sponsored by the Department of Political Science and the School of Public Administration, University of Victoria, 28 November 2005.

4 Fifteen Years of Privatization: Kenneth Kernaghan as Editor of the *International Review of Administrative Sciences* (1990–2005)

MICHAEL DUGGETT[1]

Kenneth Kernaghan became the editor of the *International Review of Administrative Sciences* (hereafter the *Review*) in the autumn of 1989. The *Review* is the official journal of the International Institute of Administrative Sciences (IIAS) and appears four times a year. The IIAS is a government-funded NGO whose mission since 1930 has been to increase knowledge of public administration around the world and thereby help it get done better. It is governed by an executive committee, among whose number – and elected by them – is the editor of the *Review*. The *Review* is the flagship of the institute and its principal mouthpiece. Its editor has a special responsibility not only to reflect the breadth of debate around the world but also to provide a strategic focus on key issues. He or she must select what matters and at the same time allow many voices to be heard. The *Review* must be a global forum but must sometimes discuss just one subject. It must reflect different national traditions but also be aware of common themes. For the fifteen years from 1990 to 2005, the *Review* had a consummate editor in Ken Kernaghan.

The *Review* has a distinguished history. It first appeared in 1928, before the IIAS itself was founded. Naturally at the time for a journal based in Brussels, Belgium, it was published in French, the then-dominant international scientific and diplomatic language.[2] The *Revue Internationale des Sciences Administratives* ran uninterrupted from 1929 to 1939; its final issue under that name announced a future conference in June 1940 in Berlin, which did not happen for obvious reasons. It was relaunched in 1947 and has continued to the present day. The English edition (often referred to as the *IRAS* as opposed to the *RISA)* began publishing in 1958. From 1957 to 1979 there was also a Spanish edition, which recommenced publication in 2006.

Looking at Privatization: Kernaghan as Editor

In many ways, the fifteen years' worth of volumes that Ken Kernaghan edited cannot easily be summarized. An editor *selects*, he does not write. It would be a mistake to deduce from his selections any particular point of view. Nonetheless, one can judge the resonance of the *Review* and also gain a sense of Kernaghan's editorial style by looking briefly at how the journal covered a particular topic during his years at the helm. Privatization is an appropriate subject for this purpose because its rise, fall, and transformation neatly followed Kernaghan's years as editor. In addition, the very first edition he edited was a 'Symposium on the Progress, Benefits, and Costs of Privatization.' The topic would recur throughout the volumes he edited and thus provides a useful approach to judging his career and style as editor.

This is not the place to analyse yet again what the term privatization means or to recount its origins and relentless rise in the world. Not until 1983 did the word appear in *Webster's*,[3] but since then millions of words have been written about it, and by 1994 more than one thousand books.[4] When his editorship began in 1990, the phenomenon had already passed its zenith in Britain and the United States and was invading the rest of the world. It is worth remembering that the world in 1990 was a very different place. A volume of the *Review* produced just before Kernaghan took over the editorship included a lengthy account, by the German scholar Klaus König, of the likely prospects for privatization in 'West Germany.'[5]

The March 1990 Symposium featured discussions of privatization from various countries' perspectives. An introductory article by H.J. de Ru and Roger Wettenhall likened privatization to 'a bullet train speeding through the administrative systems of the world'[6] and noted that it had less to do with *what* government did than with *how* it did it – a view that prefigured the debate surrounding management-over-policy that has dominated recent years. At the time, the Soviet Union still existed, so at several points the symposium discussed *perestroika*. To succeed, argued Seidman, Russian civil servants would need 'talents in negotiating and bargaining and an awareness of the values and incentives which motivate those in the private sector.'[7]

The next appearance of 'privatization' in the *Review* was in 1993, in Curwen's account of its impact on the Italian state. One would not have expected Italy to be in the front ranks of countries adopting it as a strategy, but Curwen recorded the efforts of governments in the 1980s to trim the size of the Italian state – a state that was stereotypically viewed as bloated and wasteful ('In Calabria there are allegedly more forestry workers drawing pensions than trees'[8]) but that was unable to jump-start any privatization process even though no fewer than forty state-owned companies had been sold off between 1980 and 1987. The article ended with guarded optimism that the Amato government would have more success. For much of the early 1990s, Kernaghan's article selections feasted on a wealth of experiences of how the new panacea of privatization worked.

The developing world had high hopes in the 1990s. Reflecting this was a study of the Ivory Coast that appeared in the *Review* in 1993. N'Doli Ahoua reported that the privatization program launched in that country in December 1990 had six objectives:

1 To improve the management of state enterprises.
2 To attract foreign capital.
3 To win foreign currency.
4 To provide opportunities to local investors.
5 To eliminate government subsidies.
6 To raise revenue for the government.[9]

That study, however, said nothing about the results of privatization. But in March 1994 the *Review* carried an account of how Jamaica had handled the process. By 1981 the Jamaican government had established a Divestment Committee 'to reduce the role of the state in commercial activities.' By 1991, 90 per cent of state-owned enterprises had been sold off and the government had received $250 billion in proceeds. This triumph, however, was accompanied by an annual inflation rate of 70 per cent and by a drastic deterioration of the Jamaican currency, which required IMF intervention in the form of loans. In 1990–1 a more left-wing party was elected, which nonetheless continued the process of privatization and also shrank the role of the state (it is estimated that eight thousand officials were sacked). The study concluded that while privatization was no panacea, it could not be called a failure. This article amounted to a detailed study of the pros and cons of what the Jamaicans had done, with little of the ideological taint so often encountered in privatization research.

Kernaghan underscored the point that privatization is sometimes viewed as a technical matter rather than a right-wing ideology. In this vein, the December 1994 issue of the *Review* carried an interesting study: 'Privatization in China: The Case of Health-Care Management.' Here, Chunmei You pointed out that China was departing ideologically from the Marxist tradition and that from the time privatization 'as a political philosophy and managerial strategy' appeared in Britain in the 1980s, it had been adopted by many developing states. The People's Republic of China had been applying it 'on a grand scale' in the fields of housing, education, and health.

Prior to privatization, all Chinese citizens had had to pay state medical practitioners; those *employed* by the state, however, had free medical treatment. This led to skyrocketing costs for the rest of the population and to a bias in favour of urban areas, where more public employees lived. Under the privatized system, introduced in the 1980s, doctors were able to register as private practitioners; also, public employees no longer received free treatment and instead had to pay a portion of the cost of each visit to a doctor. Under this new system there was a huge increase in the number of private practitioners: from 3,100 in 1978 to 110,000 in 1985 and 160,000 in 1990. The result was much greater responsiveness to patients' needs: 'Private doctors were more flexible and responsive to the needs of the patients. They paid home visits and would come immediately if necessary. It was much more convenient for the elderly and young.'[10] Chunmei You noted a downside to this: Chinese doctors cared mainly about curative rather than preventative medicine since their income depended on patient turnover. Overall, however, he considered the new system an improvement: life expectancy in China had increased dramatically. The author's most interesting point was that the new system implied a different role for the state. It was no longer the 'direct manager'; rather, it was the 'regulator and coordinator' of health care in China. The leadership of the Chinese Communist Party had 'modified the socialist state, but did not dissolve it.' This was a worthwhile article for those states which retained (and some still do) – as a matter of almost theological certainty – a centrally managed (national) health system in which fees need never be paid at the point of delivery.

Under Kernaghan's stewardship the *Review* carried many articles on the often exceptional case of France.[11] This included an article in 1996 on shipbuilding which noted that against prevailing trends, France had begun nationalizing that industry. The French state's preference for intervening in sectors that many other governments abandon is still evident today. In this, France has long been an exception, yet studies of francophone Africa do not necessarily show the same patterns.

For example, the March 1996 issue of the *Review* published an article by Asfaw Kumssa: 'The Political Economy of Privatization in Sub-Saharan Africa,' which discussed the supposed benefits of privatization. Had development in that region been held back because there was *too much* privatization? Or was it because there had been too little? Kumssa noted that in the twenty years leading up to 1996 that part of the world had suffered a decline in living standards. Clearly, a complicated historical process was at work. Most of French-speaking Sub-Saharan Africa gained independence in 1960. After that year, many newly assertive states attempted to impose national control and thereby demonstrate the benefits of home government. Many foreign enterprises were brought under state control, and the ideology of the time saw this as the modern and appropriate thing to do. But after the 1980s the 'alternative development paradigm' built around privatization came into force, strengthened by the disappearance of the alternative socialist model after 1990. The World Bank and similar bodies had sold the new paradigm hard to this part of the world. According to the World Bank, between 1980 and 1996 no fewer than three thousand public enterprises existed in that region; but from the 1990s onward, in Guinea, Côte D'Ivoire, Niger, Uganda, Ghana, Nigeria, Senegal, and Togo (mainly francophone states), those enterprises began to be sold off, with 373 being privatized. Kumssa, a UN employee, was sceptical about this development: 'Indiscriminate and full-scale privatization is likely to have dire economic consequences'[12] for Sub-Saharan Africa.

On its face, this seems to be an obvious example of the negative consequences of privatization. But this is balanced by another article in the *Review*, from March 1997, in which Mouhamadou Rassoulou Deme also examined privatization in Sub-Saharan Africa. He, too, noted the impulse towards state control in the 1960s and 1970s, one purpose of which was to 'create a sort of clientele for the patronage of the only recently installed public authorities,' who wanted themselves to 'simultaneously incarnate political, economic, and financial power.' Deme in his article made it clear that in this region the regime of public enterprises had failed. The enterprises were often criticized for their inefficiency: their prices had been capped for political reasons, and the income they generated was used to support government finances. He noted that public enterprises in this region in 1988 had a debt that 'exceeded the total GNP of the continent and was growing by around 2% a year.'[13] In 1980 the total debt/GNP ratio of these countries was 28.1 per cent; by 1991 it had risen to 106.1 per cent! Deme reported that since public enterprises were often remote from economic realities, they faced no pressure to perform. Remember here that privatization was following a system that itself was plagued with systemic problems. Public enterprises were often, Deme argued, associated with black markets such as the Ugandan *magendo*. 'In African countries we are witnessing the failure of the growth model managed and controlled by the state.'[14]

Obviously, in these circumstances a new type of regime would be sought. In Africa a wave of privatizations was launched under the auspices of structural adjustment programs (SAPs), which were guided by international financial organizations. Deme described the typology of strategies followed by African states. First, they distinguished between strategic and non-strategic enterprises. The former were generally retained by the public sector, whatever their economic viability. The latter, if they were non-viable, were often liquidated, abolished, or closed down; if they were viable they were usually sold to private investors. The 'commanding heights' of the economies were often kept in the public sector. Other enterprises were sold outright, with shares being floated; that, or the enterprises were deregulated or leased. Deme noted that 550 companies once in the state sector (20 per cent of the total) had been disposed of in these ways.

Another study examined this issue in post-Soviet Central Asia. In June 1997 there appeared an article on 'The Influence of Institutional Arrangements on the Progress of Privatization: The Example of Kazakhstan,' by Waddah Saab and Mukul Kumar. Their subtle argument was that in countries such as Kazakhstan, whose privatization began with the Soviet Union's collapse, it was necessary to ensure that the state remained strong enough to enforce a workable privatization. Under a horizontally decentralized process, so many tensions might develop between the privatizing agency and other ministries or other social elements that privatization could not be done properly or well: 'In countries encountering strong political or social tensions, it may also be politically difficult to concentrate horizontally the decision-making power in the privatization agency. This requires strong political commitment from the highest level of the state.'[15] To 'roll back' the state, a strong leader is necessary – a lesson that even the 'Iron Lady,' Margaret Thatcher herself, had had to learn.

György Jenei of Hungary notes that Kernaghan took special pains to arrange contributions from the former socialist states: 'He opened up a worldwide window and timely opportunities for making active participants out of Central European academicians.' His editorial work covered a broad geographical range; it also brought in theoretical work from the general discipline of administrative science. In December 1998 the *Review* carried a piece by Silvia Dorado and Rick Molz from McGill and Concordia Universities in Montreal: 'Privatization: The Core Theories and Missing Links.' This was a thorough account of the two main theoretical schools in the field: neoclassical economics and public policy. They pointed out that the former focused on the sale of companies to the private sector, companies that manufactured or delivered direct tangible products, and they argued that where this had occurred, the newly privatized companies became more efficient, more market responsive, and more profitable. Examples given were Aero Mexico and British Airways. The latter school considered how the privatization of organizations delivering public services – prisons, schools, hospitals – had changed the bureaucratic culture and led to autonomous bodies delivering targets more effectively. They set out the different models in the following table:[16]

	Neoclassical economist	Public policy
Primary focus	State-owned enterprise	Public service delivery
Theoretical drivers	Property rights	Public choice
Analytical view	Ownership and markets	Competition, standards
Organizational goals	Profits to owners	Social welfare
Implementation mechanism	Agency theory	Responsive bureaucracy

After empirically testing the success of privatization across a range of states, they concluded that the truth was mixed. One clear result almost everywhere was that the number of employees was reduced. However, managerial behaviour and 'style' did not always change, nor was there clear evidence that the organizations were more responsive to the markets. In other words, they found the conventional wisdom regarding privatization's benefits to be highly questionable, although they stopped short of concluding that this finding was definitive.

The Theory and Globalization

As noted earlier, privatization policy has been presented by its proponents as a mere technique, as value free, and as inescapable at a political level. In some ways that argument has been won, given that many governments on the political left (Britain, New Zealand) have carried out such policies. But opponents of privatization have always denied that it is merely a technique; rather, they have seen it as an element in the broader process of globalization, a process that is deeply embedded in the neoliberal agenda.

In the *Review* in December 1999 and September 2002, Ali Farazmand discussed this issue in two hard-hitting critiques. He asked why privatization had become so pervasive, and he argued that it is 'a global ideological strategy of capitalism, pursued by concentrated corporate elites and designed to reverse the older strategy of state intervention in the economy pursued through much of the 20th century for reasons of social and economic justice.'[17] He pointed out that only a handful of states (here he listed Iran, Japan, Vietnam, Libya, Ireland, and Cuba) had actually resisted this trend. He explained that privatization had been brought forward because of local factors, such as a perception that the private sector was more efficient; but he also listed six other factors and then added a seventh, which he described as 'political economic.' For him, privatization also ought to be seen as 'globalization of surplus values pursued by transnational/transborder corporations to capture the realms of state functions … dismantle state capitalism and its associated administrative state.'[18]

His 2002 article focused in particular on globalization, arguing that privatization was a key part of a deliberate strategy followed by hegemonic capitalism. This ideology sees the free market as always superior to government action; thus it is only possible to reach 'the highest level of governing and managing the entire globe as a village where the market … operate[s] as the only acceptable institution.'[19] Furthermore, he argued that this ideology was supporting an expansion of the private sector into many functions that had been solely those of the state, such as health and policing, because it 'broadens and expands the fields of operation for corporate and corporate-led business enterprises with little or no regulation and control from government, it expands the fields of market for absolute rate of surplus accumulation worldwide. Privatization, therefore, takes away the governmental field and turns it into an exclusive realm for the globalizing corporate capitalists.' The results? Human degradation as a consequence of contractual employment, lower wages, and harder and less permanent work; a society with ever more security machineries; a decaying infrastructure; public sector debt; and a culture ruled by consumer self-gratification. Even the New Public Management (NPM) came into this analysis: 'The NPM has been wrapped up in deceptive gold-colored papers with the smell of money and sold to governments and non-governmental elites through seminars, workshops and conference presentations worldwide ... Its mission is to transform governance and public administration into a subservient agent of globalising corporate elites.'[20]

This was a vigorous – indeed, contentious – analysis of the kind one does not often read. Whether it persuaded many people or not, there is no doubt that in running two pieces of this kind, the *Review* was raising issues not often discussed and showing its eagerness to stimulate debate.

Since 2002 the *Review* has not published articles specifically on the issue of privatization, although the June 2004 issue looked in detail at public–private partnerships (PPPs). In the 1990s PPPs would have been treated as an element of privatization; by 2004, however, they were being viewed as a separate subject, and many governments were pursuing PPPs as an alternative to the more aggressive, 1990s-style privatization.

Conclusion

As shown by the coverage in the *Review*, there was a clear progression in the debate over privatization in international public administration. Ken Kernaghan's editorial style was to follow this debate in a clear and useful manner. What began in the late 1980s as a technical discussion – one that regarded privatization as merely a technique –quickly evolved into a political discussion. By the mid-1990s privatization had become such a universal public administration panacea that it almost ceased to be political. It had been adopted by all kinds of governments, from European to African, and by avowedly communist systems as well as avowedly ex-communist ones. That China privatized its health service, according to You, was an immensely important fact. Also noteworthy, privatization had been adopted in francophone Africa even while not welcomed formally in France itself. Yet the high hopes that privatization would change everything for the better have not been realized in Africa or elsewhere.

The countries for which studies have been mentioned here – Germany, the United States, Italy, Ivory Coast, Jamaica, China, France, Canada, Guinea, Niger, Nigeria, Uganda, Senegal, Ghana, Togo, Kazakhstan, New Zealand, Mexico, Malaysia, and Britain – cover all the inhabited continents. Almost no region of the world has been untouched by the privatization wave, and the *Review* under Kernaghan's leadership gave it a fair if not comprehensive accounting. Since the process in some parts of the world has now become a debate about PPPs – a more complex notion than the transfer of activities from one sector to another – it is now time, as Kernaghan has been doing, to examine how the basic ideas work in the context of the twenty-first century. Privatization is an idea whose time has gone in part of the world; but that cannot be said of the entire world. For all the attacks on it by scholars like Farazmand, its potency as an idea has yet to be exhausted.

Ken Kernaghan did not focus solely on privatization during his time as editor of the *Review*. The sixty issues of the *Review* he edited covered many other topics; ethics (his own field), civil service reform and recruitment, poverty, e-governance, sustainability, and so on. But across all fields he showed the same openness and judgment. His coverage was wide ranging and varied, and not only geographically; and it was systematic in giving space to administrative scholars as well as practitioners, reflecting a balance between theory and case studies. An editor does not determine all. He must be in many ways responsive and seek to fill gaps in the literature. Ken Kernaghan did that, and he did it well.

NOTES

1 At the time this was written, the author was Director General of the International Institute of Administrative Sciences, IIAS. He is currently a visiting professor at the University of Portsmouth, England.

2 As *La Revue Internationale des Sciences Administratives*. All quotations in this text are from the English-language *International Review of Administrative Sciences* edition (hereafter *IRAS*).

3 Joseph W. Eaton, 'Bureaucratic, Capitalist and Populist Privatization Strategies,' *IRAS* 55 (1989): 467–92.

4 Peter Curwen, Book review of *Privatization in Western Europe: Pressures, Problems, and Paradoxes,* by Vincent Wright (London: Pinter, 1994), *IRAS* 62 (1996): 418.

5 Klaus König, 'Developments in Privatization in the Federal Republic of Germany: Problems, Status, Outlook,' *IRAS* 54 (1988): 517–51.

6 Hendrik J. de Ru and Roger Wettenhall, 'Progress, Benefits and Costs of Privatization: An Introduction,' *IRAS* 56 (1990): 7–14.

7 Harold Seidman, 'Public Enterprise versus Privatization in the United States,' *IRAS* 56 (1990): 15–28.

8 Peter Curwen, 'Privatization, the Italian State and the State of Italy,' *IRAS* 59 (1993): 463–76.

9 Theophile N'Doli Ahoua, 'The Ivory Coast – Imported Incoherence When the Wisdom of the Market Falters,' *IRAS* 59 (1993): 633–50.

10 Chunmei You, 'Privatization in China: A Case Study of Health-Care Management (Reconciliation between Human Ideals and Economic Limitations),' *IRAS* 60 (1994): 595–607.

11 In recent years, Ken Kernaghan has had an associate editor, Pierre Sadran, from Bordeaux University, who has written that 'Ken applique à sa propre pratique professionnelle les règles de l'éthique administrative moderne dont il est un spécialiste mondialement connu; ajoutez cela à sa grande compétence et à son extrême courtoisie, vous aurez trois raisons du plaisir que l'on éprouve à travailler avec lui.'

12 Asfaws Kumssa, 'The Political Economy of Privatization in Sub-Saharan Africa,' *IRAS* 62 (1996): 75–87.

13 Mouhamadou Rassoulou Deme, 'The Problems of Privatization: The Experience of Sub-Saharan African Countries,' *IRAS* 63 (1997): 79–97.

14 Ibid., 83.

15 Waddah Saab and Mukul Kumar, 'The Influence of Institutional Arrangements on the Progress of Privatization: The Example of Kazakhstan,' *IRAS* 63 (1997): 187–205.

16 Silvia Dorado and Rick Molz, 'Privatization: The Core Theories and Missing Middle,' *IRAS* 64 (1998): 583–609.

17 Ali Farazmand, 'Privatization or Reform? Public Enterprise Management in Transition,' *IRAS* 65 (1999): 551–67.

18 Ibid., 554–5.

19 Ali Farazmand, 'Privatization and Globalization: A Critical Analysis with Implications for Public Management Education and Training,' *IRAS* 68 (202): 355–71.

20 Ibid., 362.

PART II

The Public Service

Part One of this book focused on the institutions and organizations found in the public service. This part focuses on the people who populate those organizations. It is essential to control and motivate public servants to ensure that they are behaving in an ethical and efficient manner and working in the public interest. The three contributions in this part all consider various dimensions of these issues.

In chapter 5, Iain Gow discusses some of the problems inherent in the development and dissemination of a system of ethics and values for public servants. He begins with a general discussion of the current status of ethics in the public service – an issue that in recent years has been at the forefront of much discussion both in and outside government circles. He concludes by asserting that ethics constitutes acting on the right values. This leads into a discussion of the current status of public service values. Gow argues that public service values must be based more on a teleological approach (i.e., whether actions based on values will produce the desired effect) than on a deontological approach (i.e., concerning values that are true no matter what the circumstances). This is because public administration is by its nature primarily concerned with the means for accomplishing goals that are determined elsewhere by politicians.

However, Gow's review of the values espoused by several government organizations suggests that the proliferation of values that public servants are expected to be cognizant of and to act on places those people in a very difficult position. He concludes that the only solution is to focus on the public interest; in doing so, all the other values that are present will be embraced.

In the next section, Gow addresses this difficult issue: politicians and public servants must work together to accomplish common goals even though these two groups may emphasize different values. He concludes that 'the chief values to be defended are the conservation of the liberal democratic state and justice. The role of conservator or steward includes the operation, protection and adaptation of the system within which public servants work.' But he admits that even this general statement poses problems when certain required actions conflict with personal values.

The chapter concludes with a discussion of what Gow calls the ethics infrastructure, which consists of codes of conduct, whistleblowing, and resistance. He concludes the chapter with a plea that the proliferation of values and the possibility of normlessness on the part of the public (i.e., the public may not have strongly developed ideas about what they want done in a particular situation) be countered with an emphasis on constitutional stewardship tempered by justice.

In chapter 6, Evert Lindquist builds on Gow's work by probing what he calls 'the new landscapes for commitment in public service institutions.' He is concerned about a number of factors that have strongly affected the public service in recent years and the impact these factors will have on the ability of public servants to develop and sustain a consistent set of values.

He explores the following three areas: the significant changes in public service institutions; the impact of the changing external environment, in particular 'shifting political approaches to public sector governance'; and the rise of discussions of 'meaning', 'soul,' and 'spirituality' in private and public sector workplaces.

He catalogues many significant changes in the public sector over the past few years, including downsizing, alternative service delivery, and dramatic shifts in policy priorities. He emphasizes, however, that the real problem is the cumulative impact of so many changes occurring so quickly. Rapid change can be a threat or an opportunity, but in either case strong leadership is needed to help the organization survive the turbulence.

The changing external environment has raised questions about the use of exit, voice, and loyalty by public servants. At one point, public servants felt that they had significant voice in that their views were elicited and respected by politicians. With the rising distrust of the public service, individual public servants are more likely to look to the exit option when they are dissatisfied. This has affected the quality of the public service generally.

The next section of the paper discusses the development of commitment or 'spirituality' in the workplace. The latter term is not at all meant to be coincident with religion. Rather, commitment or spirituality refers to a concern for service to community and fellow citizens, or the embracing of a particular program or an organization's goals.

Lindquist recognizes that discussions of spirituality are difficult for Canadians, who are deeply committed to the separation of church and state. But he argues that this discussion is unavoidable, because many spiritual values are already finding their way into the workplace through the attitudes of individual employees. At a systemic level, issues touching on the relationship between religion and the state are becoming more intrusive.

Lindquist argues that we are at a significant juncture: we must begin to examine these new concepts of motivation because we must find new ways to rebuild commitment in the workplace, at the same time remaining cognizant of changing attitudes towards spirituality in the workplace and in society generally.

In chapter 7, Bourgault and Parent consider the growing number of pride and recognition programs in the public service. They begin by discussing the important role that pride and recognition play in motivation, and they argue that it is more important to have well-motivated than well-qualified employees.

'Pride and recognition reinforce professional values and contribute to professionalism by celebrating the implementation of these professional values in public administration.' This constitutes what has been described as a virtuous circle, where pride in performance leads to higher service quality, which leads to greater recognition on the part of the public and greater pride on the part of the worker.

This chapter presents the results of a survey about pride and recognition awards in a variety of governments. The authors report that these awards are increasing in number and that their emphasis is changing. There are still rewards for long service, but these are being accompanied by awards for innovation and good service. There is also a growing emphasis on formal recognition programs, with awards being provided by senior managers.

Bourgault and Parent also identify some obstacles to good recognition programs. An obvious one is that they require a great deal of employee time and some financial resources to administer. A more serious concern is that programs targeted only at certain groups can create jealousies; also, poorly designed programs that reward people who are perceived as undeserving are counterproductive. A more subtle criticism is that these awards often focus on efficiency, but not so much on other public service values such as democracy. The chapter concludes by praising the concept of recognition and awards, albeit with some reservations regarding specific aspects of some programs.

5 Between Ideals and Obedience: A Practical Basis for Public Service Ethics[1]

J.I. GOW

The study of public sector ethics has grown in importance in recent years, under the combined impact of changing political ideas, new management philosophies, fiscal crisis, and growing citizen alienation. In Canada one must be brave to venture into this field, such is the dominance in it of Ken Kernaghan. While in this paper we will encounter some of Kernaghan's many contributions, and those of others such as John Langford, Sharon Sutherland, Ralph Heintzman, and Gilles Paquet, the main purpose of this chapter is to try to synthesize existing writings with a view to ranking values into some sort of coherent order that offers a practical approach to understanding public service ethics.

This look at a possible practical basis for public service ethics advances in three stages. First, the values identified as being core to public administration are considered; this includes discussion about the role of the public interest. The next part deals with the practical implications of public service ethics – including the implicit moral contract that links public servants and elected politicians – as well as their feasibility. The final part deals with the infrastructure of public service ethics and with practical steps that can be taken to foster an ethical public service.

The argument is that there are very few core values involved in public service ethics. Most of the multiple values we see at present are only means to further ends that are the bedrock of ethics. Also, the various categories of values that are currently identified tend to conceal their common nature as sources of ethical obligations. Finally, it is proposed that it is not only useless but also dangerous to encourage public servants to follow the highest moral principles to their logical conclusion, since the final determination of the public interest is not theirs to decide. The role of public servants is to operate, adapt, and protect the democratic state they serve.

The ethical problems that arise in public administration acquire their particular nature from this subordinate quality of administration. In democratic states the administration is there to serve, not to govern. At the same time, the relevant academic disciplines all recognize that it is impossible to control completely the work of public servants. In sociology, Michel Crozier speaks of zones of uncertainty surrounding their work; in economics, principal–agent and transaction cost theories study the problems that result from the difficulties leaders encounter in ascertaining whether their agents are faithfully executing their orders; in political science and law, the existence of discretionary powers has long been seen as a challenge to the rule of law.

Public service ethics, then, concerns relations not only among public servants but above all between public servants and interested 'outside' parties: elected politicians, the media, institutions, and citizens. In what circumstances (if any) can public servants rightfully limit the power of their political and administrative superiors to dictate their conduct? And do public servants have any obligations towards the entire political system that limit their right to reject a request for services from a citizen or a group? The literature suggests that for ordinary public servants the most frequent ethical problem is the one that arises when a superior asks them to do something illegal, wasteful, contrary to good practice, or against the organization's mission.[2] Meanwhile, the ethical preoccupations of elected politicians regarding public servants are more likely to relate to conflicts of interest, declarations of assets, and post-employment activities.[3]

Administrative ethics encompasses a broad range of topics. From down-to-earth questions relating, for example, to conflict-of-interest and post-employment rules, it extends to questions of constitutional significance and, eventually, to the values adhered to by public servants – that is, their administrative culture. In this respect, as in any teaching situation, one must know the people one is dealing with and the situation in which they work. In this paper the goal is to reach, in the words of the Quebec Institute of Applied Ethics, 'a vision of the world based on clear, practicable and shared values.'[4]

So these are the questions I will address: What are the important values in public administration today? Which of those values are fundamental and may serve to evaluate the others? What do we know about the relevant values of public servants and elected politicians? What components are required for a good public service ethics infrastructure? In the conclusion I will return to the problem of rationalism and the limits of any approach to ethics.

The Profusion of Values and the Public Interest

If ethics is acting on right values, what are these values? To begin with, values are, according to Christopher Hodgkinson,[5] 'concepts of the desirable with motivating force.' In his view they are facts of a subjective nature that can never be true or false. In the practical life of the public service, ethics usually means good behaviour. Among the many debates over values, the dominant one opposes the deontological to the teleological approach.[6] The former seeks to identify values that are true no matter what the circumstances. The problem with this approach is that people of good will may differ over fundamental values that find their justification in religion or intuitive experience. The latter asks instead what the chances are that a decision or course of action will produce the desired effects. This seems much more appropriate for analyses of administrative questions, which are essentially concerned with means. In public administration one does not have the luxury of being an absolutist; a value must be adopted with consideration of the effects it will have on different stakeholders and on other values with which it may clash. Langford calls this second approach 'consequentialist';[7] as it is closer to common usage, I will use that term instead of 'teleological.'[8]

The obvious place to look for official versions of public service values is in documents with those words in the title, or with words such as 'public service ethics' or 'mission statement.' However, there are countless such documents. An analysis of the Quebec Public Service and Public Administration Acts by the Quebec Institute of Applied Ethics found many values or standards, which could be boiled down to only four true values: equity, honesty, respect, and trust.[9] Reports of central agencies and parliamentary agents also abound with explicit or implied value statements, as do those of study groups such as Public Service 2000 and the Tait Task Force on Public Service Values and Ethics.[10]

If one wants to know what values are actually practised by public servants, instead of what the official version says they must do, one must look at the public service culture. Some of this information comes from observation, and some from declarations of unions or associations, but most of it comes from interviews or opinion surveys such as those of Zussman and Jabes,[11] Bourgault and Dion[12] (and with Lemay[13]), and Germain Julien.[14] Also, in recent years the federal government has conducted two major surveys of public servants' opinions and attitudes.

This official focus on values has its critics. In particular, Langford is concerned about how the values are chosen that are typically presented in studies of the subject; for example, the Tait Committee noted that its list had come forth 'spontaneously.'[15] Langford suggests that these values merit closer attention. For instance, in documents like PS 2000 and the Tait Report the values presented are more likely managerial values rather than values actually practised. Surveys support this assertion. Langford also points out that many values are not really values; rather, they are competencies (such as professionalism and excellence). Most damning of all is the large number of 'core' values. Langford[16] counts roughly 60 in *A Strong Foundation* and 164 in Ken Kernaghan's survey of ninety-three public organizations. Dwivedi and Gow found thirty values that featured prominently in the reports of the ten working groups of the PS 2000 study.[17] As Kernaghan and colleagues put it, to avoid excessive and therefore ineffective numbers of values, 'public organizations need to dig deeply to the core of their values.'[18]

This profusion of values is one of the reasons why so many are calling for some kind of Code of Ethics or statement of essential public service values. If public servants are to know what is expected of them, that knowledge has to be accessible to them in comprehensible form. Kernaghan has championed this approach for many years though he recognizes that on its own, it will not solve the ethical problems of the public service.[19]

Recent years have seen the widespread adoption of codes of values or ethical behaviour. Four of these are presented in table 5.1 – three Canadian, and one arising from a survey of essential values identified by OECD member countries. The resulting lists are different but comparable. The OECD list is interesting because it ranks the values according to how many countries report them. All values are widely adopted, but impartiality and legality (at 24 and 22 mentions respectively) far outpace equality, responsibility, and justice (11 and 10 mentions).

The longest list in table 5.1 is that of the federal government. Following the lead of the Tait Committee, it distinguishes four kinds of public service values. *Political* values concern the public interest, loyalty, respect for the law, and accountability. *Professional* values include excellence, efficiency, effectiveness, and impartiality. *Ethical* values include upholding the public trust, serving the public interest, and avoiding conflict of interest. Finally, *people* values include respect for human dignity, fairness and civility, openness and respect for diversity, and the merit principle. Some of these, though, are not really values, and furthermore, there is overlap and duplication. At the very least, the third and fourth categories ought to be merged. All values can generate ethical questions, so a separate class for ethical values seems redundant.

Table 5.1. Core values identified in Canada and in OECD countries[20]

Values and Ethics Code for the Public Service of Canada	IPAC Statement of Principles	Quebec Declaration of Values	Public Service Values of OECD Countries
Democratic Values • help ministers, under law, to serve public interest • honest, impartial advice • loyal implementation • support • accountability	*Accountability*	*Public Service Mission*	*Impartiality*
Professional Values • competence, excellence • efficiency, effectiveness • objectivity, impartiality • transparency	*Service to the Public* • courteous • equitable • efficient • effective	*Competence*	*Legality*
Ethical Values • uphold the public trust • serve the public interest • avoid conflict of interest	*Public Service* • respect spirit and letter of the law	*Loyalty* • represent the administration to the population • respect for democratic will	*Integrity*
Personal Values • respect for human dignity • fairness and civility • openness, respect for diversity • merit principle	*Political Neutrality* • knowledge of laws and traditions • loyal service to government	*Impartiality* • neutrality and objectivity • equity • non-partisanship	*Transparency*

Table 5.1. (*Concluded*)

Values and Ethics Code for the Public Service of Canada	IPAC Statement of Principles	Quebec Declaration of Values	Public Service Values of OECD Countries
	Political Rights • fullest possible compatible with neutrality • discretion in public pronouncements	*Integrity* • justice and honesty	*Efficiency*
	Absence of Conflict of Interest	*Respect* • consideration and courtesy • diligence • non-discrimination	*Equality*
	No discrimination nor harassment		*Responsibility*
			Justice

What the categories do usefully, however, is remind us that one may have mixed reasons for doing the right thing. To be polite to the citizen at the front desk or on the telephone is both a matter of common or personal courtesy and a message about how the state deals with citizens.

Searching for Fundamental Values

The profusion of values and the confusion this engenders lead us to try to sort out the basic values on which the others may be based. Can we rank them so that the hard-pressed public servant will have a small number of basic values or standards on which to base his or her reasoning?

Two preliminary remarks are in order. First, there is no prima facie reason for excluding or downgrading any one category of values. Some commentators have chosen to exclude economic values from the list, while others have seen in ethics a way to counter the business values promoted by the public management movement and right-wing politicians.[21]

We cannot leave out economic values even if we want to, for several reasons. First, those who wish to limit public spending do so in the name of personal liberty. We may agree or not, but it is an important value. Second, the fiscal burden caused by expenditures and the public debt affect the health of the entire political system. That burden commits future generations, may expose the system to the intervention of foreign investors, and may affect public opinion about the state. Third, not to waste the taxpayers' money is to respect them and to protect the state's legitimacy. Fourth and finally, forty years of studies, beginning with those on PPBS (planning–programming–budgeting systems), have shown us that the attraction of a value may vary with our awareness of the costs associated with its realization.

The second remark concerns a value that does not appear in the various codes and declarations I have seen: the survival of the political system that the administration exists to serve, as well as its maintenance and adaptation to changing conditions. True, the defence of this value may lead to unwanted side effects (such as the sponsorship scandal) or to excesses (such as in the search for security from terrorism). Even so, it is a primary value that public servants in every country are required to respect. In most systems, public servants swear loyalty to the regime. One of the qualities of democratic regimes is that the courts and some public servants are assigned the task of keeping others within the confines of the constitution, the law, and major public policy traditions.

When we search the literature for fundamental values that might allow us to justify the others, we find several:

- justice (T. Cooper; Morgan and Cass; Stewart and Sprinthall)
- social equity and justice (G. Frederickson)
- the rule of law (Aucoin)
- individual rights (cited by Van Wart 1998)
- regime constitutional values (Rohr)
- loyalty (Tait, Kernaghan)
- stewardship (Aucoin, Dunsire, Heintzman)
- citizenship (C. Stivers)

Others, however, reject the very idea of searching for rational and universal criteria from which we may derive the ethics of public servants. A feminist critique claims that this is a masculinist approach and that a feminist one would be more flexible, for it could be directed towards the solidarity needs of staff and clients.[22] Postmodernists, for their part, say that it is important not to blame and discipline certain individuals and that feedback and accountability should aim at social learning.[23] I will return to these criticisms later in the chapter.

Even this short list reveals that justice may be at odds with the automatic application of the law or with loyalty to the government. Similarly, loyalty to the government may fall into conflict with loyalty to the state. Consideration of these conflicts leads directly to the question of the public interest.

The Public Interest as Focal Point

If any single value is key to ranking all others, it can only be the public interest. But it must be fully recognized that the public interest is an ill-defined concept. It cannot be reduced to a single value; rather, it emerges from competition among values and interests.[24] In 1960, Glendon Schubert found three models of the public interest in American public administration literature: realist, idealist, and broker. For the realist school, the public interest requires the public servant to do what he or she is told to do. The literature discredited this version long ago; even so, Terry L. Cooper writes that many public servants still have to deal with it.[25] For Schubert's idealists, the public interest requires public servants to act according to their conscience and professional knowledge. This version leads straight to conflict with the democratic duty to carry out the will of elected representatives. The third category, that of broker, calls on public servants to deal with all stakeholders in a way that avoids appeal to a higher level, be it political, administrative, or legal. This version is more realistic than the other two but can easily produce corporatist conniving.

In the face of opposing ideas, a traditional solution is to apply procedural criteria: Have the prescribed procedures surrounding consultations, analyses, and deliberation been followed? This is an enhanced criterion of obedience. To address these shortcomings, Manzer has proposed three substantive criteria to accompany the procedural ones: acceptability, authenticity, and justice.[26] It is true that the criterion of acceptability or feasibility is important: many administrative projects have had to be abandoned because they were not politically acceptable. This criterion, then, considers power relations. Authenticity is a more delicate and controversial criterion, yet it arises whenever a group brings its case to the government. Whether it be a grant to a sports team or to a multinational corporation, a raise in welfare payments or a raise in minimum wage, the question will be considered partly according to one's perception of its authenticity. Finally, justice, according to Manzer, is linked to the idea of equity. It is usually determined either as equality or as a form of proportionality (to each according to their contribution, their merits, their efforts, etc.).

Manzer's analysis reminds us that the question of justice may derive from philosophy but also involves political judgment. Morgan and Cass have tried to convert the idea of justice into an administrative model.[27] The administration, in their view, is the place to protect procedural values. Public servants are the guardians of administrative and political history and represent a reservoir of community identity.

The provisional conclusion from these remarks is that the idea of the public interest obliges us to recognize that public servants have other obligations than those of obedience and following the rules to the letter. Public servants must not usurp the place of elected representatives when exercising their duties, yet they also have responsibilities to the political system and to the political community at large. It is this responsibility to the policy system and the community that should be paramount, not some higher level of moral reasoning. Moreover, it is a realistic position that takes into account the complex relations between the administration and ministers and other members of Parliament. Yet a question remains: Is it feasible for both groups?

Feasibility of Values for Public Servants

There is little point in working up codes of values and ethics, or establishing a hierarchy of values, if those who will have to put them into effect do not believe in them or have no interest in them. We therefore have to raise several questions concerning those who share in a sort of contract, some of which is explicit and written but other parts of which are unwritten. This section deals with the values of public servants and elected politicians.

The Values of Public Servants

Most bureaucrats understand their roles. In Aberbach, Putnam, and Rockman's major survey, *Bureaucrats and Politicians in Western Democracies*, the only role in which bureaucrats thought they should have the principal responsibility was policy implementation.[28] When it came to formulating policy, brokering interests, and articulating ideals, they either thought that politicians should have the main responsibility or that responsibility should be shared. Graphs of opinion distribution on a number of ideological issues showed that bureaucrats were more concentrated in the moderate ranges; politicians had flatter curves, indicating more support for positions at either extreme.

Canadian public servants share this image as moderates, even more so than those in some countries where public management reforms have been more radical.[29] In their well-known study of senior federal public servants, Zussman and Jabes found that they were more likely than their private sector counterparts to value intrinsic motivating factors such as public service, interesting work, and recognition of a job well done.[30] The study also found that there was a fault line through the senior public service, with dissatisfaction increasing as one moved downward from the highest levels. Many studies have found that managers and senior public servants want more decision-making power. This is one of the attractions to them of the New Public Management (NPM), and they are willing to be held more accountable in order to acquire it. At the same time, it remains a distinguishing feature of public service that managers and senior public servants take pride in serving the public and the community.[31]

In sum, most higher-level civil servants are committed to their work, have ideals, and want influence. Lower-level civil servants tend to be more affected by the need for security; yet federal higher-level officials tend to favour reducing job security.[32] The former head of the federal civil service, Jocelyne Bourgon, once wrote that there was a 'quiet crisis' in the public service after several years of downsizing and restructuring,[33] while Christian Rouillard found disenchantment rather than a survivor's syndrome among employees of Revenue Canada.[34] The federal employee surveys of 1999 and 2002 found high levels of job satisfaction; almost half the respondents, though, felt that quality had declined as a result of cuts in resources.

If we hope to achieve high levels of employee ethics, employee surveys are important, for they put employee attitudes into perspective and delineate areas of current concern. A shared code of values has more chance of being respected than a code imposed from the top. Moreover, the values of public servants change over time. Eleanor Glor has made a first attempt to apply to the federal public service categories developed for election and opinion studies: civil servants born before 1945 are probably motivated by a sense of duty; the 'baby boomers,' born between 1945 and 1964, are more autonomous and rebellious; and those of 'generation X,' born after 1964, are likely to be more pragmatic and in need of a different type of direction.[35]

Studies by Germain Julien have found that among Quebec's managers and professionals, the collective values of the organization (i.e., its culture) are stronger than personal preferences.[36] In support of this, studies of women managers in the United States do not confirm the notion of a feminist or women's ethics; indeed, they find that women managers exhibit much the same values as their male counterparts.[37] A big problem for a general ethic of the public service is that most employees have a deep attachment to their department or agency – an attachment that may override the common good.

The Values of Elected Officials

As noted above, survival is a primordial but not exclusive value for any political system. However, this value is experienced very differently by public servants and by elected politicians. It is in the interest of public servants that the state survive; their careers depend on it. A government can rarely allow itself to look much beyond the next election. To be sure, it will make decisions affecting the community over the long term, but survival, to it, means being re-elected. There is thus a certain opposition between those whose role is to bring energy, new ideas, and change to the system and those who, in the words of the *Institut québé-*

cois d'éthique appliquée,[38] must defend the intermediary values of prudence, caution, and prevention.

It took a good deal of maturity before politicians collectively came to realize that the merit system served their interests. According to Aucoin, it is now accepted that it is in the public interest to have an impartial administration, recruited and appointed by merit, professional and accountable before elected representatives and the population at large.[39]

But while this principle is accepted in theory, it is not always followed in practice. Earlier, we cited American and British authors who said that officials continue to receive orders that they consider unjust, dangerous, or illegal. A number of public servants testified before the Gomery Commission that they were unhappy with things that were happening in the sponsorship program but lacked the authority to do more than raise questions.

Organization culture plays a role in these problems. Public servants who denounce abuses, waste, or favouritism are often punished or isolated despite the existence of whistleblower protection acts. Here it seems that organization culture at the meso-level overrides democratic and patriotic duties at the macro-level.

Another difficulty arises from the respective roles of the two sides. The world of civil servants is one of action and results; that of politicians is one of conflict, debate, and appearances. Modern-day accountability requirements oblige public servants to enter the world of politics because the information they provide on the results of government programs is necessary for public debates. Also, under the eye of public opinion, governments do not want to admit that the new direction they wish to bring to public policies requires the promotion of certain values at the expense of others. At the present time, we do not see governments admitting that the pursuit of economy, efficiency, and effectiveness may adversely affect equity, justice, and transparency. They want to believe that the list of values public servants must respect can be regularly added to without some of those already adopted being neglected. This is a recipe for confusion or a hypocritical pretence.

This kind of wishful thinking is also present in certain approaches to public management. Only recently have some of our leading administrative authorities admitted that our enthusiasm for innovation, service, competition, and results-based management may have gone too far. After two decades of preaching managerial values and preferring value-for-money audits over financial audits,[40] the auditor general in his October 2000 report proposed that values and ethics in government be promoted, with priority given to clarifying ministers' and officials' responsibilities. The auditor general further recommended 'an extensive dialogue on values and ethics that emphasizes the primacy of principles of respect for the law, the public interest and the public service as a public trust.'[41] Four years later the Clerk of the Privy Council wrote that public administration reforms in the 1990s had been influenced by 'popular management theories [that] emphasized innovation and public service, and devalued rules and control.' Most of the time, he argued, innovations had been successful, 'but we also lost some of our rigour.'[42] The point is that these leaders seemed to be rediscovering the values that are particular to the public service.

The Moral Contract between Politicians and Public Servants

Public servants have interests, but they also have ideals that are influenced by the milieu in which they work. Regarding interests, many observers and practitioners, such as the Tait Committee, have observed that a deep knowledge of the rules of the game in public administration comes with having a career public service. The Tait Report wrote that loyalty to the regime would be less certain without a career system: 'For a public service where employment is more contingent and short-term, public servants would necessarily be encouraged to use their current role to advance themselves and position themselves for future employment.'[43] Savoie summed up the same point by saying that the consultant only has a client whereas the public servant has a minister.[44]

As for ideals, all agree that the public service is not the place for extremists. The government must be confident that it will not be faced with a revolt inspired by an opposing view of the public interest. Kernaghan has noted that the ethics codes of the British and the New Zealand public services clearly state that once their objections are heard, public servants must accept the will of the government or resign, though they still have the right to voice their objections to a government policy or practice.[45] For some observers it is an outstanding feature of the Canadian model of public administration that elected governments have been confident enough about their control of the administration that they do not fear being made prisoners of the public service.[46]

Thus a search for a fundamental value that allows one to derive and rank almost all other values leads to this one: loyalty to the democratic constitutional and political regime. This notion is key to developing a practical basis for public service ethics. For Heintzman and Marson, this criterion becomes 'building democratic citizenship and strengthening the confidence and trust of citizens in the efficiency and values of public institutions.'[47] Such a criterion serves the interests of public servants, politicians, and citizens. To be sure, the possibility exists that the public service will tend to profit from this position by adopting a self-serving and corporatist attitude. However, unlike legally recognized professions, the public service has to live with the dynamics of change brought in regularly through elections and changes of political leadership. Moreover, the public service is quite vulnerable to politicians' criticisms and is also under scrutiny by the media. As a group, public servants – and especially their leaders – have no tribunal from which to defend themselves from attacks launched by various party candidates and the media – attacks that are sometimes unjust and often exaggerated.

An ethical regime based on service to the government within the framework of the constitution, the law, and the customary values of the political system also serves the public by offering them quality services, yes, but within the legal and customary restraints inherited from the past.

As some British observers have remarked, the profession of the public service is government[48] – or, as is more common today, *governance*. Public servants do not govern alone, but they participate in government. Their primary goal is to look after the system, to make it work, to maintain it, and to be attentive to its necessary reform. For this to work, members of the government and of the legislature must respect the moral contract between them and the public service. This contract is described in the Tait Report as the offer by public servants of professionalism, discretion, and non-partisan loyalty in return for a degree of anonymity, a degree of autonomy, and sufficient job security to ensure the existence of a career service.[49] This moral contract is what Donald Savoie is referring to in *Breaking the Bargain*.[50]

This contract has been shaken by several recent trends: more than twenty years of bureaucrat bashing, blame shifting, and flight from ministerial responsibility; new management doctrines that treat government like a business and that downplay the role of citizens; new partnership forms that dilute accountability; and public disenchantment with politicians and bureaucrats.[51] To these, I would add that the federal government seems to want to abandon the idea of a career service in favour of the notion of the learning career, which guarantees public servants the chance to keep learning in order to prepare themselves for future jobs outside government. Such an approach may just fit the danger the Tait Committee foresaw.

Relations between public servants and elected politicians are governed by several laws, such as the Public Service Employment Act and the Financial Administration Act. Other aspects of the relationship, however, depend on conventions such as ministerial responsibility, public service anonymity, and the proper treatment of public servants who testify before parliamentary committees. As Canada has often experienced high rates of turnover among members of Parliament, there seems to be a need for means to transmit to new members a better understanding of the role of the public service.[52] I welcome Savoie's suggestion that a Standing Committee on Public Administration be established, to be served by a new Office of Public Administration.[53] These bodies would elucidate many of the complex questions concerning relations between the House, the political parties, and individual members on the one hand and the civil service on the other. They could be places where other parliamentary agencies, such as the Office of the Auditor General, give account of their own activities – something that they do not at present have to do. Generally, MPs' interest in public service ethics is sporadic, arising either at moments of crisis or when the Public Service Act is revised.

The Fundamental Values of Public Service

It is now possible to summarize the fundamental values to which civil servants, both morally and practically, owe allegiance. As shown in table 5.2, the chief values to be defended are the conservation of the liberal democratic state and justice. The role of conservator or steward includes the operation, protection, and adaptation of the system within which public servants work. Public servants are not alone in these responsibilities. Politicians (crucially) as well as other actors, such as the media, share these obligations.

Except for justice, the other values may be weighed and tested by reference to this stewardship role. They have merit in their own right but are not absolutes. In a democratic state they must be contained by concern for the health of the system. Thus public servants must participate actively in the renewal of the state, in part to protect it from weakness and improper adaptation to changing circumstances. However, ·the

Table 5.2. Hierarchy of values to be respected in the public service

Level 1	Trusteeship/stewardship (operation, maintenance, and adaptation of democratic state)	Justice	
Level 2	Economic and professional values • economy • efficiency • effectiveness	Democratic values • justice • equality • trust • respect	Personal values • equity, fairness • equality • honesty • respect
Level 3	Organizational and professional values		

'new' values of service, innovation, results, and partnerships find their limits in the 'old' values of public service, public interest, accountability, the rule of law, and equity.

For a public servant, even justice must be tempered by what the authorities have legitimately decided. As the Clerk of the Privy Council put it: 'Under the rule of law, the law is supreme over government officials as well as citizens; individual public servants cannot substitute their personal views for the law.'[54] Recognizing that conscientious public servants may wish to bend the rules for a deserving client, I propose that those involved in implementation should follow a moral equivalent of natural justice in administrative law: they should seek social justice for their clients by following their personal and professional conscience as long as they are not explicitly ordered by law, regulation, or directive to do otherwise.

The other values do not follow in logical decision hierarchies. Several values (equality, respect) appear in the democratic *and* personal values columns. Professional values have been subsumed under the economic values of effectiveness and efficiency. This lack of hierarchy seems necessary because there may be personal, professional, and political reasons for doing the right thing.

The argument is that given their role, and given those with whom they must work, public servants must temper their loyalty to certain personal values with loyalty to the system. Obviously, this loyalty may be put to severe test – for example, when a public servant's personal values leave her or him with a sense of 'dirty hands.'[55] In other cases, he or she may wish to 'blow the whistle' on actions that are harmful to the state: a subject to which I return in the next section.

The Means: The Ethics Infrastructure

A comparative federal study by the Treasury Board of Canada in 2002 concluded that an ethics infrastructure generally includes the following elements: a statement of values or principles; norms of conduct; tools of promotion and sensitization to values; control of reprehensible acts; coordination; and management and evaluation of programs of values and ethics. To these, the OECD adds means to ensure accountability of the actors in this area.[56] In other words, ethics is an area that must be taken as seriously as other administrative activities and thus structured from beginning to end.

Values or Discipline?

It seems clear that neither a values-based approach nor a disciplinary one alone will solve all of the problems raised by public service ethics. As Langford has so decisively demonstrated, the hope that a values approach will lead public servants to behave ethically is illusory, as the values they are encouraged to uphold are too numerous, too apt to conflict with one another, and too ill-defined to serve this purpose.[57] The weakness of the 'values approach' (good intentions without clear priorities) is that, as the Tait Committee discussion document put it, public servants feel they have been 'missioned' and 'valued' to death.[58]

On the other hand, repression alone cannot suffice. Studies of the most tightly hierarchical organizations from the command-and-discipline perspective – that is, the armed forces and the police – have found that strict discipline ensures neither ethical conduct nor full accountability.[59] At any rate, we know that the working lives of public servants are full of times when there are no 'normative reference points.'[60]

But what of those numerous other decisions where ethical behaviour is hoped for? For the moment, the answer to the sixty-year-old position of Carl Friedrich or the recent ones of post-rationalists and of Quebec ethicists (Boisvert and Villemeure) is that while it is no doubt illusory to try to cast all values in rules, all decision makers must be able to defend their judgment after the fact. While it is neither possible nor desirable to adopt rules to cover all cases, public servants must always be ready to justify their actions. In cases where important rules have been broken, they will face disciplinary and perhaps criminal proceedings. In other cases they would be called on to explain their behaviour before parliamentary committees, during times of crisis and scandal, or at periodic personnel evaluations.[61] On these occasions, they would need to justify their interpretation of the values both of the current government and of the civil service. As we have seen from various commissions of inquiry – Somalia, Oka, tainted blood, the sponsorship scandal – such after-the-fact mechanisms are costly and time consuming.

One reason to favour a values approach over a disciplinary one – a reason having nothing to do with personal ethics – is the misplaced attention that disciplinary ethics produces. A long-time specialist in police and military affairs, Jean-Paul Brodeur, insists that our reactions to scandals have failed to avoid hunts for the guilty. The capacity to focus on systemic failings that might be remedied is usually lost when the search for the guilty takes priority.[62]

Here, then, is the reason why post-rationalists and the Canadian government emphasize the learning organization. As Savoie points out, we may be past the point where one person or even one department may be blamed in retrospect for a mistake or for reprehensible acts. It would probably be more profitable to place the accent on reform – something that requires a different atmosphere than one of repression and fear.[63]

The Code Solution

Ken Kernaghan promoted the idea of a public service code for a long time before it was accepted in Canada and other OECD countries; even so, he also recognized that having a code is not enough.[64] Other means are surely needed to promote a high level of public service ethics, but a code is a starting point. One benefit to developing a code is that various drafts can be widely discussed and debated, ensuring the broadest possible support for its principal ideas. In the case of the recently fragmented British Civil Service, the Civil Service Code (along with the pension plan) may be one of the few unifying factors.[65]

The codes most relevant to us vary considerably (Table 5.1). Some are laws, as in New Zealand; others are regulations or executive declarations, as in Britain and Canada.[66] Quebec has both a Regulation on Ethics and Discipline in the Public Service and a Declaration of Values of the Quebec Public Administration. Britain and more recently Canada have Codes of Ethics for ministers — a good idea, in terms of the moral contract mentioned earlier. The British Civil Service Code is very short, at fourteen paragraphs and under two pages; the New Zealand Public Service Code of Conduct, at forty-six paragraphs and thirteen pages, is much more detailed. The two British codes and the New Zealand code give a number of specifics relating to relations between civil servants and politicians, including (as mentioned earlier) the reminder that if the civil servant's views have been overridden by ministers, she or he must accept this. The Canadian parliamentary code deals almost entirely with monetary issues such as conflict of interest and post-employment work.[67]

Pecuniary matters are surely of great interest, but the political questions are more interesting. One thing all of these documents reveal is Canadians' reluctance to speak of the state, even in Quebec, which is often seen as more European than the rest of Canada. In this country 'the Crown' is a euphemism for the state; unfortunately, this obscures the true object of loyalty.[68] The one place where we seem to have been willing to embrace the word is in the dangerous area of 'reasons of state.'

Codes are valuable in part because they can be used during training and discussions. New employees and especially those promoted to positions of responsibility are generally required to sign a statement that they have read and accepted the pertinent code. Codes also play a role in evaluations and disciplinary matters. However, a code imposed from on high will not fit the bill if the goal is to produce a declaration of shared values. The widest possible discussion of drafts of the code is needed to ensure its practicability.

Whistleblowing and Resistance

Public servants often find themselves in situations where obedience is at odds with their view of their obligations. What are they to do at these times? A.O. Hirschman offered the classic range of choices in *Exit, Voice and Loyalty*.[69] Certainly, the exit option is mentioned in the British and New Zealand codes: if you cannot accept the position of the government of the day, after your objections have been considered, then you must resign. The price to be paid is much greater, however, for an employee than for a customer: the latter can simply decide to abandon a product or a service; the former places her or his career in jeopardy. And as Hirschman also points out, loyalty to the organization raises the cost of exit. To this range of choices, Lundquist adds obstruction.[70]

There are probably cases where any of us would approve of blowing the whistle: Daniel Ellsberg giving the Pentagon Papers on Vietnam to the *New York Times*; 'Deep Throat' feeding Watergate material to Woodward and Bernstein; the women who blew the whistle on Enron, Worldcom, and the FBI and became *Time*'s Persons of the Year in 2002. However, as a general proposition, providing a safe haven for those who denounce political and administrative practices raises many problems. O. Glenn Stahl worried that encouraging whistleblowers would encourage malcontents and undermine relations of trust between executives and public servants, while giving no recourse to executives who were unfairly accused.[71] He and others, including Peter Drucker (cited by Stahl 1983) and René Villemure,[72] contend that a general climate of denunciation is more in tune with dictatorships than with a free society.

From the point of view defended here, a whistleblowers' protection act that undermined the moral contract between the government and the public service would do harm to the mission of the public service. Even so, as this mission is to protect the constitution and its values, public servants ought not to be coerced into accepting harmful or illegal instructions simply because the government will lose confidence in them if they don't.

Kernaghan and Langford have set the bar high for acceptable whistleblowing.[73] It must deal with serious problems,[74] be supported by unequivocal evidence, come only after internal channels of resistance have been exhausted, and be likely to obtain satisfactory results.

The Public Servants Disclosure Protection Act of 2005 generally conforms to these requirements – which is to be expected, since Kernaghan was chair of the working group whose report led to it.[75] This act provides both recourse and protection for public servants and employees of Crown corporations who in good faith wish to denounce wrongdoing. Two levels of denunciation are envisaged. Clauses in the act relating to internal and confidential disclosure cover a wide variety of misdeeds, including violations of any law or regulation, gross mismanagement, and the misuse of public funds. The person filing the complaint, if not satisfied with his or her organization's response, may take it to the Public Service Integrity Commissioner, who now enjoys the status of an independent agent of Parliament and who has powers of investigation and report. Under the act, going public is justified only when the matter at hand is serious or urgent. The working group recommended that the government submit to Parliament a Charter of Public Service Values, the idea being that this would draw members of

Parliament into a kind of moral contract, since by endorsing those values they would automatically be adopting them. This step hasn't yet been taken; even so, it may.

In early December 2006 the Harper government's Accountability Act (Bill C-2) was adopted. Among other things it has revised the Public Servants Disclosure Protection Act in two ways: first, a new administrative tribunal, the Public Servants Disclosure Protection Tribunal, comprising judges drawn from the Federal Court or provincial Superior Courts, will hear cases concerning reprisals taken against whistleblowers; and second, the law now covers all Canadians, not just the federal public sector, which will allow contractors, for instance, to make complaints.

For the purposes of this chapter, the significance of the Accountability Act lies in what it reveals about the attitudes of the Harper government towards the public service. On 25 April 2006, during debate on second reading, Treasury Board president John Baird stated that 'as Conservatives, we believe in public service, both in the ideal and the institution' and that the goal of the bill was to heighten the public's trust in government. This is reassuring in a government that has often rejected the advice given by senior public servants. A second major innovation proposed by Bill C-2 would have allowed the Integrity Commissioner to make cash awards to those demonstrating noteworthy courage. Faced with pressure from a number of critics (notably the Bloc Québécois and the Public Service Alliance of Canada), this clause was dropped from the law as adopted.

It remains to be seen whether the new act (with or without the amendments of Bill C-2) will make the public service safe for legitimate whistleblowers and whether it will promote or undermine trust between politicians and public servants. As Hirschman has pointed out, voice is much messier than exit.[76] However, voice is all the more necessary if the costs of exit are high, as they are here. The alternative is to create among both parties a culture of loyalty to the moral contract while fostering more open government. Lundquist (1993) notes that there are few problems with leaks in Sweden because of the long tradition there of freedom of information.[77]

Conclusion

Aaron Wildavsky has written about his concern over growing anomie or normlessness in the American public service. It is, he said, a career without orientation.[78] Robert Denhardt has posited that the way to provide 'significance' in public organizations is by developing the values of public service, shared leadership, and pragmatic incrementalism.[79] Public servants are being asked to respect too many values for all of those values to be practicable.

It has been argued in this chapter that the basic values of the public service are 'constitutional stewardship' (Morgan and Kass) or 'regime values' (Rohr), tempered with justice. In their moral contract with politicians, public servants have to uphold the democratic state while bending to the policies of the legitimate government. Whistleblowing policies try to cover these two poles: legality-morality and legitimacy. The other elements of the ethics infrastructure should reflect this. Codes of values and ethics are useful but may lead to confusion and overload unless there are basic values at hand that place the others in perspective.

The contradiction between a rules-based approach and one based on personal and professional ethics is in fact bogus because, while there is no way that rules can effectively cover all situations, even the most high-minded public servant must answer for his or her actions and decisions. A more real divide exists between rationalists and post-rationalists or consequentialists. Public sector reform repeatedly seeks to find the rational 'fix' that will solve today's problems; yet public servants are mostly consequentialists – a position much closer to that of feminist authors than to rational choice thinking.

Public servants have a noble calling: to act with the highest possible ethical standards and benevolence within the constitutional framework and the system values they are there to uphold. That this approach is in their long-tem interest is not a fault, quite the contrary.

NOTES

1 This chapter was presented at the annual conference of the Canadian Political Science Association, University of Western Ontario, London, June 2005. The author thanks for their helpful comments Ken Rasmussen, André Bazinet, J.E. Hodgetts, Sharon Sutherland, David Siegel, Kenneth Kernaghan, and the anonymous evaluators.
2 For the United States: Terry Cooper, 'Big Questions in Administrative Ethics: A Need for Focused, Collaborative Effort,' *Public Administration Review* 64, no. 4 (2004): 395–407; Warren Schmidt and Barry Posner, 'Values and

Expectations of Federal Service Executives,' *Public Administration Review* 46 (1986): 447–54. For Britain: Norman Lewis and Diane Longley, 'Ethics and the Public Service,' *Public Law* (1994): 596–608.

3 The first Codes of Ethics in Canada dealt almost exclusively with these questions, which still occupy a large part of regulations, but not of value statements and codes.

4 Personal communication to author.

5 Christopher Hodgkinson, *Towards a Philosophy of Administration* (Oxford: Blackwell, 1978), 105.

6 Kenneth Kernaghan and John Langford, *The Responsible Public Servant* (Halifax: IRPP, 1990), 23–8; Michel Cloutier and Gilles Paquet, 'L'éthique dans la formation en administration,' *Cahiers de recherche éthique* 12 (1988): 69–90; Margaret Somerville, 'What Does Doing Ethics Mean?' *Literary Review of Canada* (June 1999): 7–10.

7 John W. Langford, 'Acting on Values: An Ethical Dead End for Public Servants,' *Canadian Public Administration* 47, no. 4 (2004): 443.

8 Langford (ibid.) says that most public servants 'are intuitively consequentialist.' An important exception to this remark would be those whistleblowers who plunge ahead without regard for the consequences. As we will see, it is precisely these consequences that raise doubts about widespread encouragement of whistleblowing.

9 Personal communication from René Villemure.

10 John Tait, *A Strong Foundation: Report of the Task Force on Public Service Values and Ethics* (Ottawa: PCO, 1997). This task force was created by the Clerk of the Privy Council in 1995. It was chaired by John Tait, former deputy justice minister, and it produced both a consultation document (1996) and a final report (1997). The latter captured the prevailing opinions on this topic among senior public servants and academics.

11 David Zussman and Jak Jabes, *The Vertical Solitude: Managing in the Public Sector* (Halifax: IRPP, 1989).

12 Jacques Bourgault and Stéphane Dion, 'Canadian Senior Civil Servants and Transitions of Government: The Whitehall Model Seen from Ottawa,' *International Review of Administrative Sciences* 56 (1990): 149–69.

13 Bourgault, Dion, and Jacques Lemay, 'Creating a Corporate Culture: Lessons from the Canadian Federal Government,' *Public Administration Review* 53, no. 1 (1993): 73–80.

14 Germain Julien, 'Les styles de gestion des cadres supérieurs vus par les professionnels de la fonction publique du Québec,' *Canadian Public Administration* 32, no. 3 (1989): 449–61; idem, 'Les valeurs collectives de gestion dans la fonction publique québécoise: la perception des cadres,' *Canadian*

Public Administration 36, no. 3 (1993): 319–48; idem, 'Valeurs collectives et valeurs personnelles de travail dans la fonction publique québécoise,' *Revue québécoise de science politique* 26 (1994): 5–34.

15 Langford, 'Acting on Values.'

16 Ibid., 437.

17 O.P. Dwivedi and James Iain Gow, *From Bureaucracy to Public Management: The Administrative Culture of the Government of Canada* (Peterborough: Broadview, 1999), 142–3.

18 Kenneth Kernaghan, Brian Marson, and Sandford Borins, *The New Public Organization* (Toronto: Institute of Public Administration of Canada, 2000), 59.

19 Kernaghan, 'Public Service Ethics in Canada,' in Kernaghan and Dwivedi, eds., *Ethics in the Public Service* (Brussels: IIAS, 1983), 37–48; idem, 'Rules Are Not Enough: Ethics, Politics, and Public Service in Ontario,' in John W. Langford and Allan Tupper, eds., *Corruption, Character, and Conduct* (Toronto: Oxford University Press, 1993), 174–96; idem, 'Towards a Public Service Code of Conduct – and Beyond,' *Canadian Public Administration* 40, no. 1 (1997): 40–54; idem, 'An Honour to Be Coveted: Pride, Recognition, and Public Service,' *Canadian Public Administration* 44, no. 1 (2001): 67–83; idem, 'Integrating Values into Public Service: The Values Statement as Centerpiece,' *Public Administration Review* 63, no. 6 (2003): 711–19.

20 Treasury Board of Canada, *Values and Ethics Code for the Public Service of Canada* (Ottawa, 2003); IPAC, *Principles Regarding the Conduct of Public Employees* (Toronto, 2004); Conseil du Trésor du Québec, *Déclaration de valeurs de l'administration publique québécoise* (Québec: 2003 [my translation]); OECD, *Building Public Trust: Ethics Measures in OECD Countries* (Paris: 2000).

21 H. George Frederickson, ed., *Ethics and Public Administration* (Armonk: M.E. Sharpe, 1993).

22 Carole Gilligan, *In a Different Voice* (Cambridge, MA: Harvard University Press, 1982); Anneka Marina Scranton, 'Gender Differences and Administrative Ethics,' in Terry Cooper, ed., *Handbook of Administrative Ethics*, 2nd ed. (New York: Marcel Dekker, 2001), 553–81.

23 Michael Harmon, *Responsibility as Paradox: A Critique of Rational Discourse on Government* (Thousand Oaks: Sage, 1995); Kathryn G. Denhardt, *The Ethics of Public Service: Resolving Moral Dilemmas in Public Organizations* (New York: Greenwood, 1988); O.C. McSwite, *Legitimacy in Public Administration* (Thousand Oaks: Sage, 1997); Gilles Paquet, *Governance through Social Learning* (Ottawa: Presses de l'Université d'Ottawa, 1999).

24 Kernaghan and Langford, *The Responsible Public Servant*, 49.

25 Terry Cooper, 'Big Questions in Administrative Ethics: A Need for Focused, Collaborative Effort,' *Public Administration Review* 64, no.4 (2004): 395–407, at 402.

26 Ronald Manzer, 'Policy Rationality and Policy Analysis: The Problem of the Choice of Criteria for Decision Making,' in Dwivedi, *Policy and Administrative Studies* 1, University of Guelph, Department of Political Studies, 1984, 27–40.

27 Douglas F. Morgan and Henry Kass, 'Legitimizing Administrative Discretion through Constitutional Stewardship,' in James S. Bowman, ed., *Ethical Frontiers in Public Management: Seeking New Strategies for Resolving Ethical Dilemmas* (San Francisco: Jossey-Bass, 1991), 286–307.

28 Joel D. Aberbach, Robert D. Putnam, and Bert A. Rockman, *Bureaucrats and Politicians in Western Democracies* (Cambridge, MA: Harvard University Press, 1981).

29 Dwivedi and Gow, *From Bureaucracy to Public Management;* Gow, *A Canadian Model of Public Administration?* (Ottawa: Canadian Centre for Management Development, 2004).

30 Zussman and Jabes, *The Vertical Solitude.*

31 Kernaghan, 'An Honour to Be Coveted,' 70, 75.

32 On this subject they appear to differ considerably from their Quebec counterparts, who are firmly committed to job security for the staff. Jacynthe Demers and James Iain Gow, 'Gestion des ressources humaines et nouveau management public: opinions de gestionnaires fédéraux et québécois,' *Canadian Public Administration* 45, no. 4 (2002): 512–37.

33 Jocelyne Bourgon, *Fifth Annual Report to the Prime Minister on the Public Service of Canada* (Ottawa: PCO, 1988).

34 Christian Rouillard, *Le syndrome du survivant et la fonction publique fédérale du Canada*, PhD diss., Carleton University, 1999.

35 Eleanor Glor, 'Codes of Conduct and Generations of Public Servants,' *International Review of Administrative Sciences* 67, no. 3 (2001): 525–41.

36 See note 14.

37 Debra Stewart, Norman A. Sprinthall, and David M. Shafer, 'Moral Development in Public Administration,' in Cooper, ed., *Handbook of Administrative Ethics*, 2nd ed. (New York: Marcel Dekker, 2001), 457–80; Scranton, 'Gender Differences and Administrative Ethics.'

38 Personal communication from René Villemure, director of the Institut québécois de l'éthique appliquée.

39 Peter Aucoin, 'A Profession of Public Administration? A Commentary on *A Strong Foundation,*' *Canadian Public Administration* 40, no. 1 (1997): 25–39.

40 S.L. Sutherland, 'The Office of the Auditor General of Canada: The Results Trail,' paper presented to the Conference on the Officers of Parliament, University of Saskatchewan, 2001, www.myschool-monecole.gc.ca/Research/publications/html/cmpa/endnotes_e.html; Denis Saint-Martin, 'Managerialist Advocate or "Control Freak"? The Janus-Faced Office of the Auditor General,' *Canadian Public Administration* 47, no. 2 (2004): 121–40.

41 Ch. 12.1.

42 Alex Himmelfarb, *Eleventh Annual Report to the Prime Minister on the Public Service of Canada* (Ottawa: PCO, 2004), 2.

43 Tait, *A Strong Foundation*, 7.

44 Donald J. Savoie, 'Searching for Accountability in a Government without Boundaries,' *Canadian Public Administration* 47, no. 1 (2004): 1–26.

45 Kernaghan, 'Towards a Public Service Code of Conduct.'

46 Aucoin, 'Beyond the "New" in Public Management Reform in Canada: Catching the Next Wave?' in Christopher Dunn, ed., *Handbook of Canadian Public Administration* (Don Mills: Oxford University Press, 2002), 36–52; Gow, *A Canadian Model of Public Administration?*

47 Ralph Heintzman and Brian Marson, 'People, Service, and Trust: Is There a Public Service Values Chain?' *International Review of Administrative Sciences* 71, no. 4 (2005): 553.

48 Brian Chapman, *The Profession of Government* (London: Allen and Unwin, 1959); Richard Clarke, *New Trends in Government* (London: HMSO, 1971).

49 Tait, *A Strong Foundation*.

50 Savoie, *Breaking the Bargain: Public Servants, Ministers, and Parliament* (Toronto: University of Toronto Press, 2003).

51 Ibid., 7–16.

52 Sutherland, 'The Consequences of Electoral Volatility: Inexperienced Ministers, 1949–1990,' in Herman Bakvis, ed., *Representation, Integration, and Political Parties in Canada* (Toronto: Dundurn, 1991); David Docherty, 'Parliamentarians and Government Accountability,' in Martin W. Westmacott and Hugh Mellon, eds., *Public Administration and Policy: Governing in Changing Times* (Scarborough: Prentice Hall, 1999), 38–52.

53 Savoie, *Breaking the Bargain*, 273–5.

54 Himmelfarb, *Tenth Annual Report to the Prime Minister on the Public Service of Canada* (Ottawa: PCO, 2003), 6.

55 Richard Chapman, 'Reasons of State and the Public Interest: A British Variation on the Problem of Dirty Hands,' in Chapman, ed., *Ethics in Public Service* (Ottawa: Carleton University Press, 1993), 93–110; Sutherland, 'The Problem of "Dirty Hands" in Politics,' *Canadian Journal of Political Science* 27, no. 3 (1995): 479–507.

56 OECD, *Building Public Trust: Ethics Measures in OECD Countries* (Paris: 2000).

57 Langford, 'Acting on Values.'

58 Tait, *Discussion Paper on Values and Ethics in the Public Service* (Ottawa: PCO, 1996), 2.

59 Jean-Paul Brodeur, 'Accountability: The Search for a Theoretical Framework,' in Errol P. Mendes, Joaquin Zucherberg, Susan Lecorre, and Anne Gabriel, eds., *Democratic Policing and Accountability: Global Perspectives* (Aldershot: Ashgate, 1999), 125–64; Jacques Bourgault and Gow, 'Le difficile contrôle des activités et comportements de la police: le cas de la Sûreté du Québec,' *Canadian Journal of Political Science* 35, no. 4 (2002): 747–70.

60 Yves Boisvert, 'L'imaginaire éthique des répondants du réseau gouvernemental québécois en matière d'éthique,' *Canadian Public Administration* 47, no. 4 (2004): 475–96.

61 Sutherland, 'The Al-Mashat Affair: Administrative Accountability in Parliamentary Institutions,' *Canadian Public Administration* 34, no. 4 (1991): 573–603; idem, 'The Problem of "Dirty Hands" in Politics.'

62 Brodeur and Louise Viau, 'Police and Accountability in Crisis Situations,' in R.C. Macleod and David Schneiderman, eds., *Police Powers in Canada: The Evolution and Practice of Authority* (Toronto: University of Toronto Press, 1994), 243–308; Brodeur, 'Accountability.'

63 Savoie, 'Searching for Accountability.'

64 Kenneth Kernaghan, 'Rules Are Not Enough: Ethics, Politics, and Public Service in Ontario,' in John W. Langford and Allan Tupper, eds., *Corruption, Character and Conduct* (Toronto: University of Toronto Press, 1993), 174–96.

65 Lewis and Longley, 'Ethics and the Public Service.'

66 The Public Servants Disclosure Protection Act (S.C. 2005, c. 46) calls for a new Charter of Public Service Values as well as a Code of Conduct for the entire federal public sector, both apparently to be regulations, not laws. It is unlikely that they will diverge greatly from the existing code, which has its origins in the Tait Report of 1996. However, the broader coverage of this whistleblower protection act (which includes agencies, corporations, and the RCMP) may bring some differences.

67 C.E.S. Franks, 'The New Code of Ethics for Parliamentarians,' paper presented to the annual meeting of the Western Political Science Association, Albuquerque, NM, April 2005.

68 Kernaghan, 'Public Service Ethics in Canada'; Daniel Mockle, 'La réforme du statut juridique de l'administration fédérale: observations critiques sur les causes du blocage actuel,' *Canadian Public Administration* 29, no. 2 (1986): 282–303.

69 Albert O. Hirschman, *Exit, Voice, and Loyalty: Responses to Decline in Firms, Organizations, and States* (Cambridge, MA: Harvard University Press, 1970).
70 Lennart Lundquist, 'Freedom of Information and the Swedish Bureaucrat,' in Chapman, ed., *Ethics in Public Service*, 75–91.
71 Glenn Stahl, 'Public Service Ethics in the United States,' in Kernaghan and Dwivedi, eds., *Ethics in the Public Service*, 23.
72 Bianca Joubert, 'Dénoncez-vous les uns les autres,' *Relations* (mars 2005): 32–4; Éric Grenier, 'C'est lui! Le philosophe René Villemure et la dénonciation,' *JOBBOOM*, le magazine.joboom.com, 2005.
73 Kernaghan and Langford, *The Responsible Public Servant*, 94–100.
74 Lundquist, 'Freedom of Information and the Swedish Bureaucrat,' 80, limits these to problems that are harmful to citizens.
75 Working Group on the Disclosure of Wrongdoing, chaired by Kernaghan, *Report* (Ottawa: PCO and Treasury Board Secretariat, 2004).
76 Hirschman, *Exit, Voice and Loyalty*, 16.
77 Lundquist, 'Freedom of Information and the Swedish Bureaucrat.' See also Lewis and Longley, 'Ethics and the Public Service,' 608.
78 Aaron Wildavsky, 'Ubiquitous Anomie: Public Service in an Era of Ideological Dissensus,' *Public Administration Review* 48, no. 4 (1988): 753–5.
79 Robert Denhardt, *The Pursuit of Significance* (Belmont: Wadsworth, 1993), 17–18.

6 In Kernaghan's Wake: Navigating the Choppier Seas of Commitment in Public Administration

EVERT LINDQUIST

A few years ago I was invited to address a group of public servants in a functional community who were dealing with the effects of dramatic policy shifts, wholesale restructuring of the B.C. public service, and significant cutbacks in budgets and staff. Bruised and bewildered by these changes, the host asked if I could address the question of 'soul' and 'spirituality' in public administration – a theme surfacing south of the border in conferences and journals in the United States. Simultaneously intrigued and discomforted, I did what most Canadian public administration scholars would likely have done: I sidestepped the specific brief and broadened the topic to consider the sources of commitment and motivation that might sustain public servants in the midst of radical restructuring.

How we think about the values and motivation of employees in public service institutions in Canada and internationally has been strongly shaped by a steady stream of writing and insights from Ken Kernaghan. Early in his career he elegantly set out the precepts underpinning career public service in parliamentary systems: merit, political neutrality, professionalism, career assistance, and so on. He constantly revisited these ideas and principles in light of new developments in the field – as much a 'self-dialogue' as one with practitioners and scholars.[1] Simultaneously, he branched out to address many other topics such as values and ethics, partnerships, whistleblowing, empowerment, service quality, pride and recognition, New Public Management (NPM), and, most recently, information technology. His methodology has been comparative and international in scope, his writing always precise yet accessible to public servants. Beyond his impressive research output, Ken has provided enormous service to our field: editing leading journals and collections, producing several essential books, broadening horizons as a highly valued teacher, and actively contributing to the work of the Institute of Public Administration of Canada (IPAC), the Canada School of Public Service, and the Commonwealth Association of Public Administration and Management.

So where values and motivation are concerned, Ken's forays and well-trodden paths have mapped our world. This paper contends that as we uneasily consider his 'retirement,' we stand at a juncture regarding how we understand public administration, within which many core (and, more than a few would argue, essential) assumptions animating practice have been challenged, sometimes in fundamental ways, to the concern of a great many public servants and observers. First, while there has been considerable writing on the clash between traditional public service values and NPM values,[2] there has been little probing of the cumulative impact of successive waves of restructuring on workplaces, employee morale, and the fabric of our public service institutions. Even recent calls to delineate a 'new bargain' for public service executives and how they relate to ministers and members of Parliament[3] say little about the implications for rank-and-file public servants. Second, our traditional conception of the public administration ethos has long been predicated on separating privately held values or personal beliefs from the expectations of public servants working as professionals.[4] This separation is under challenge, with some observers calling for open discussions of spirituality and faith in both private and public sector workplaces.

This paper probes the new landscapes for commitment in public service institutions. It does not aim to be comprehensive; rather, it provides reconnaissance into three areas. First, it explores the impact and opportunities of sustained and sometimes significant changes to public service institutions over the past twenty years and what this may imply for public service leadership, especially in the context of the demographic rollover now underway. Second, it considers how the external environment, which includes shifting political approaches to public sector governance and the maturing labour market for professional services for the public sector, may be affecting the quality of debate and talent within public service institutions. Third, it reports on several strands of recent writing, largely from the United States, on 'meaning,' 'soul,' and 'spirituality' in private and public sector workplaces, and considers their implications for Canada. The chapter concludes by calling for a more sustained program of research on the sources of motivation and commitment, one that could usefully inform retention, recruitment, and branding strategies for public service institutions.

The Internal Landscape: Acknowledging Sustained Change

Since the early 1990s, duly elected governments have instigated the following kinds of reforms and initiatives to public service institutions:

- Downsizing and across-the-board cuts.
- Off-loading (i.e., withdrawal) from provision of certain services, leaving them to other sectors, communities, levels of government, or individuals to absorb.
- Amalgamation and restructuring of the public services of local governments and the creation of megadepartments at the federal and provincial levels, often involving recombining programs for new policy and operational goals.
- Alternative service delivery initiatives ranging from contracting out core public service functions (payroll, IT functions, etc.) to public–private partnerships with not-for-profit and for-profit entities, all designed to lower human resource costs, increase flexibility for managers, and improve service to clients.
- Deconcentration within governments as part of regionalization strategies, *or* reconcentration in order to secure common standards and economies of scale. Also, experimentation and reliance on information and communication technologies (ICTs) to re-engineer the work of public service institutions, resulting in a new mix of 'service channels.'
- Dramatic shifts in policy priorities as citizens have elected governments with very different political platforms.
- Rebureaucratization and the introduction of new oversight regimes for public servants and departments as part of a political strategy of risk management.

These changes are well known. And they have often been launched in combination, striking at the core of public service institutions. There have also been successive waves of change, sometimes undoing or negating previous reforms.

While many observers associate such widespread change with the early to mid-1990s, it has proceeded apace to this day, with no end in sight. Public servants have navigated incredibly choppy organizational waters and weathered further turbulence from unstable political and governance environments, including fickle electorates. In what follows we explore the negative and positive features of such diverse and sustained change.

The Cumulative Toll of Change

Most literature on public sector reform tends to take a high-level view of its impacts, with the focus on NPM. A considerable amount of attention has been paid to the clashes between traditional values and NPM values[5] as well as among vertical accountability systems.[6] From an organizational perspective, however, what really matters is that constant change has exerted a toll on public bureaucracies. Writing in 1994, Mitchell Lee Marks captured the effects of sustained change:

> Nearly every corporation has gone through a major change or transition in the 1980s and 1990s, be it a merger, acquisition, downsizing, restructuring, reengineering, leadership succession, or culture change. Most, in fact, have experienced several transitions, often overlapping one another. These events have not just changed the structure and style, policies and practices of organizations, they have had a profound impact on the people who spend their working lives in these organizations. And, it has been a mostly negative impact, as employees over the past several years have watched their co-workers get laid off, their career paths and aspirations evaporate, their cynicism increase, and their faith in their leadership diminish. The survivors of these transitions see themselves as working harder for fewer rewards. Some even envy their former co-workers who lost their jobs ... What concerns these employees most is that they see no end in sight to the parade of transitions, and they feel they have no power to avert any subsequent impact.[7]

The effects of such change have been insufficiently recognized, and there has been no lessening in the pace of change *since* the mid-1990s, for a variety of reasons. Let us parse out how similar impacts manifest themselves in public service environments.

Sustained change can lead to insecurity, uncertainty, low morale, and stressful working environments, especially if change initiatives are not well conceived, well led, and properly implemented. In the worst cases this can lead to toxic work environments.[8] However, the costs and turmoil of such transitions are usually not fully accounted for in terms of lost productivity, buy-out and other transition costs, and the loss of top talent. Such costs typically accumulate outside of public view; moreover, governments that initiate such change usually are shielded by public service executives from its impacts on rank-and-file staff and their operations.[9]

Such effects inevitably result even from well-managed transitions, properly resourced and with leaders who communicate effectively and meet symbolic needs. Unfortunately, change is often continuous over many years and often cavalier. In these circumstances one is more likely to encounter insufficient staff in 'finger in the dike' situations – whether as part of the transition or on a longer-term basis – and, as is so often the case, a plethora of 'acting' positions. This leads to burnout, departures, and the adoption of coping strategies; it also results in less 'slack' of the sort that is so essential for good strategic thinking, proper internal dialogue, better horizontal management, and learning across boundaries. Repeated change, well managed or not, all in the name of good or better government, can make these situations even more desperate.

More fundamentally, albeit often in subtle ways, waves of change can lead over time to disengagement from the broader ideals and aspirations that should animate a public service institution. A career, especially when it has begun to level out and when executive-level compensation and psychic benefits are not available, may become less a vocation and more a 'paycheque' or future stream of pension benefits. To the extent that ideals are at play, more public servants may focus on their clients, becoming less interested in advising and serving the public service or duly elected governments. Moreover, whatever the best intentions of governments and public service leaders to provide close political direction and oversight, and whatever their rhetoric to that effect, dramatic and sustained change can create multiple priorities and significantly overdetermined situations in which public servants have to use discretion, consider risks, and strike balances (no longer the domain of street-level bureaucrats!). Public servants shoulder the risk when things go wrong because most ministers are not interested in management and capacity. Yet at the same time, most ministers will not countenance things gone awry, even if the cause is actions taken by their own government or a previous one.

A more worrisome coping strategy is hyper-responsiveness to political or superiors' needs without questioning the implications either for the public or for the public service as an institution.[10] Indeed, ongoing change may result in less incentive to ask hard questions of superiors if there is a good chance that a public servant will be moved to another position as part of that change.

Such environments have led to the departure of many talented public servants, either directly through departure incentives, or indirectly via the pull of better compensation and a different work–life balance in the private sector or more personal fulfilment in the not-for-profit sector. Watching a stream of colleagues departing cannot possibly be good for morale (unless it is the worst performers who are leaving). But the effects do not end there. First, there is the spectacle of watching governments tap into contractors for advice and services at significantly higher rates than before. This willingness of governments and executives to pay considerably more heed and remuneration to outsiders cannot help but lead to cynicism within the public service. Second, staff would be irrational not to view investments in professional development quite differently; common sense suggests that they make choices based as much on the possibility of leaving the public sector as on the prospects of rising within it.

There have been efforts to rebuild trust and engage public servants, to make public service institutions an 'employer of choice' in the face of these morale and renewal challenges. However, as Lindquist[11] argues, many of these initiatives can hardly be construed as serious branding and communications strategies. The latest communication strategies from central agencies and the apexes of departments may not be dealing with how mid-level public servants feel. As Marks observes: 'Spend time with middle managers and other employees who represent the heart and soul and the mind and the muscle of work organizations, however, and you will find that they remain sore and angry over the treatment they and their co-workers experienced over the past several years during turbulent times of transition. They are holding onto their experiences and perceptions of the past, and are neither ready nor willing to heed their leadership's call to charge ahead and capture new business opportunities.'[12]

Zussman and Jabes[13] have observed there can be a significant disjuncture in perceptions about the quality of work between governments and executive cadres on the one hand and senior and middle managers on the other. In an environment of sustained change and soaring rhetoric about 'learning organizations' and high-performing, employer-of-choice workplaces, the risk of gaps between the rhetoric from above and the reality of public service organizations two or three levels down seems even greater. Shallow recognition and renewal initiatives only reinforce scepticism, cynicism, and disillusionment[14] when impossibly high standards are set that the public service cannot meet.

The picture I am painting here is a sobering one. Undoubtedly, cumulative change and its effects have become an abiding dimension of many public service institutions. Neither the public administration literature, nor governments and public service leaders, have fully acknowledged the toll this has taken on public service institutions and their employees. All of this has combined to reduce the possibility that public servants will be willing to make the adjustments and actively exploit opportunities presented by the next wave of reforms, and this will not be overcome by a light 'branding' or recognition strategy. Even dedicated public servants find it difficult to recommend public service careers to their own children. As a consequence of all this, what sort of advice will governments be getting? What sort of talent will public service institutions be attracting? Much later we will discuss the new landscape for loyalty among public servants and its implications for securing input and information on quality.

Continuous Change as Opportunity: An Alternative Perspective

Notwithstanding the stark picture set out above, we all encounter public service executives and managers who thrive in rapidly changing environments, and this goes beyond the leaders who initiated the changes. What qualities can we associate with public servants who thrive in times of change? Here are a few to consider:

- Energy, commitment, and personal resilience.
- A willingness to experiment and consider alternative approaches for developing policy and delivering services.
- Possession of a medium or longer-term vision and an ability to place current turmoil and challenges in perspective.
- The capacity to view change as an opportunity for personal or organizational development.
- An almost evangelical ability to motivate, communicate, delegate, and lead by example.[15]

Such individuals see the chronicling of the negative impacts of sustained change in the previous section as hand wringing, as not reflecting the skills and perspective required to thrive in modern public sector organizations.

Public servants with these qualities view impending change as liberation from old ideas, assumptions, and approaches that have outlived their usefulness or gone unexamined. They are impatient with the status quo; they see no reason not to (at the very least) challenge current practices; and they take an outside-looking-in perspective when doing so. They see change or a succession of changes as opportunities to deal with long-standing problems and issues, move new policy priorities and goals to the top of the agenda, and experiment with different approaches and delivery models for realizing those goals. They are attracted to change initiatives, seeing them as learning opportunities; and they recognize that significant and sustained change creates demands for new perspectives, new types of knowledge and expertise, and often recruitment of talent from different parts of the public service as well as from outside organizations. In short, for these people change involves learning and applying new sets of ideas and skills to meet governance challenges (for better or worse).

To take advantage of this, though, requires adroit leadership. In this connection, we need to distinguish between sustained and ephemeral leadership. The former steers an organization through immediate turmoil, grieving, and the process of moving positively towards 're-commitment' to a new vision, mission, and organization structure in Selznick's[16] sense of an institution acquiring new bearings. The latter involves leaders who alight, instigate change, and leave organizations, not fully engaging in and seeing through the full process of reorientation and transformation and all of its challenges.

From Turmoil to Positive Change: The Need for Superior Leadership

Whichever view one takes of the effects of change – negative or positive – it is clear that highly capable and informed leadership, as opposed to naive and ephemeral leadership, is pivotal for public service institutions. Such leadership must be cultivated not only in the executive suites of departments but also in the senior and middle ranks. An open question, though, is whether there is a sufficient supply of such leadership, especially when so many public service institutions have been through sustained change, have lost some of their most highly talented individuals, and, because of turmoil, have failed to recruit or attract their fair share of the next generation of talented individuals.

Many governments, heeding this issue, have attempted to parachute talent in from other public sector institutions or the private sector, sometimes by means of political appointments. This undoubtedly brings in fresh perspectives; however, mastering the culture and mores of a new and more complex institutional environment involves a steep learning curve. Regardless of the leadership talent attracted, the realities of public sector governance (politics, ministerial ambitions, further restructuring, etc.) steadily intrude on efforts to rebuild ministries and departments and give them the kind of leadership they require over the longer term.

The well-known disjuncture between the rhetoric and undertakings emanating from governments and public service leaders, and the actual experience of rank-and-file public servants, continues to be a serious one. The latter may still be grappling with previous changes and may not yet have experienced either the opportunities and psychic benefits of promised or newly launched reforms or the executive-level benefits for performance. An irony is that new initiatives, though guided by attractive visions and reasonable assessments of the need for change, or by the private sector literature on change, are often not based on fully informed models and understandings of the moral incentives at play in public service institutions – or public sector governance more generally. This may lead to unrealistic change strategies that aggravate the very problems that governments and public service leaders are seeking to remedy through reform initiatives. This is an important point, to which we will return later.

To underscore the crucial issue of superior leadership, we need only consider the stark demographic challenges confronting public service institutions across Canada. Waves of change have deeply affected how these institutions function as well as their cultures. At the same time, downsizing and the use of alternative service delivery (ASD) have meant insufficient hiring of younger staff over several years – staff who would have constituted the feeder groups from which the most talented would have been selected for leadership roles. And every day we are reminded that public sector governance is increasingly more complex and that citizens are more demanding. The demographic rollover now in motion carries the risk of poor policy design, program failure, and political embarrassment if ways are not found to preserve institutional memory. Fresh perspectives and higher energy might go a long way in the new governance environment. Given the challenges and expectations for public service leadership, the search is on for ways to get 'instant smart,'[17] since public service institutions no longer have twenty or more years to groom this talent.

Furthermore, the relatively thin feeder group taking on these challenges will be in demand everywhere, especially outside government at market rates. Attracting and retaining this generation despite the waves of sustained change poses a significant challenge. Finding realistic and smart ways to do so will require an understanding of the new landscape of loyalty in the environments of public service institutions. To this question we now turn.

The Changing External Landscape: Implications for Voice and Loyalty

Another reason for the decline in morale and for the more mercenary perspectives of public servants has to do with episodic and steady departures of colleagues and with the better pay and opportunities offered by the private sector. Yet another factor – a dramatic one over the past twenty years – is the possibility of a professional life *after* public service. Here we consider how this affects debate and discussion about the quality of public service.

Most analysts have explored how to 'improve' organizations; few have considered what happens when quality or performance declines.[18] In this regard, several insights from Hirschman's (1970) *Exit, Voice, and Loyalty* are useful. He identified strategies that customers, members, and their larger organizations applied when handling the challenge of communicating and redressing declines in the quality of services and management.[19] He contrasted and probed two distinct modal strategies from the disciplines of economics ('exit') and political science ('voice'), but his great insight related to how these two strategies worked interactively or in sequence.

Hirschman observed that, though the threat of exit may enhance use of voice inside an organization, that strategy must be credible: the executive or staff member in question must have an option and be willing to leave;[20] and that person, one might add, must be the sort of talent the home organization wants to retain. However, Hirschman suggests that overreliance on the exit option for responding to declines in quality may 'atrophy the development of the art of voice'[21] and lead to the loss of 'quality-conscious' members 'who would be motivated or determined to put up a fight against deterioration.'[22] Pure exit, or departure from an organization without voice, keeps information away from the organization. Hirschman suggests, however, that public servants will be more reluctant to use the exit option if they have had positive experiences exercising voice to deal with declines in quality.

An important feature of Hirschman's analysis is that it assigns an important role to 'loyalty' on the part of members in that it allows an organization to learn of and deal with declines in quality. Loyalty fosters the capture of critical information because 'loyalty holds exit at bay and activates voice'[23] and, more particularly, because it 'neutralizes within certain limits the tendency of quality-conscious customers or members to be the first to exit.'[24] Interestingly, Hirschman notes that when choosing between exit and voice strategies, exit will be chosen not because voice will be ineffective, but rather, because new forms of voices have not been sought out – loyalty helps by buying time and by increasing the chances that creativity will lead to new forms of voice.[25] There are boundaries to this analysis, however: too much loyalty can dampen exit and the exploration of internal options,[26] and, intriguingly, exit can be seen as an act of loyalty when public goods are involved in situations where members are still affected by their delivery after exit; voice within affects use of voice without; quality must matter to the member after exit.[27]

The traditional model of public service worked well so long as public servants knew that their advice was being elicited and considered by ministers and executives. This may be a rosy interpretation of the past, but concerns and alternative perspectives were debated and conveyed within public sector bureaucracies, albeit always qualified by the leadership styles of ministers and executives. However, with more governments in various jurisdictions distrusting the public service (at least early on in mandates), combined with increased public encouragement to 'act' rather than 'reflect,' a dynamic has emerged where governments are more likely to assert policy direction and to view internal challenges and explorations of alternatives from public servants ('voice') as insubordination. Though difficult to prove, it is often said that many ministers and executives find subtle ways to indicate that they do not want certain types of advice. From this there emerges and spreads a perception among public servants that giving 'frank and fearless' advice could be a career-ending move.

In such an environment, more of the best public servants are more likely to leave because their expertise and intellectual capabilities are no longer in demand. In this formulation, loyalty and respect is a two-way street – when governments discount or pre-empt the advice of public servants, the latter are less likely to remain loyal to the institution, regardless of whistleblower protections, and certainly fewer public servants are willing to stay and bear the costs of exercising 'voice.' Those who do stay learn to keep their heads down, likely attaching greater value to employment security. Unless there are clear incentives to encourage open advising, they will tend to focus on their exclusive spheres of authority rather than those of the institution or the government as a whole.[28]

The risks are many. First, such an internal environment will dampen internal debate as well as the vertical transmission of alternatives, not to mention concerns about the risks of various options. This will lead to governments making decisions with less fulsome information and testing, increasing the possibility of bigger and/or avoidable mistakes. Second, this has the potential to influence the nature of recruiting – for new talent and for promotions; if timid, less knowledgeable, or less questioning candidates are chosen because they are less likely to ruffle feathers, the quality of advice will decline further and, of course, the very talented will be less likely to join and stay.

But there is a more fundamental problem here – or, to put it differently, a missed opportunity. All else equal, the prospect of a considerable increase in compensation from private corporations, consulting firms, and associations (sometimes doubling or trebling that of public service executives) reduces the willingness of top public service talent to use their 'exit' as an important and rare opportunity to exercise 'voice.'[29] If a talented and respected public servant wants to keep open the possibilities for employment beyond the public sector, an important consideration is surely to maintain a reputation for loyalty in the sense of *discretion* as opposed to 'speaking truth to power and the public.' These considerations, along with evidence that governments are increasingly averse to frank advice and reluctant to develop full whistleblowing protections for public servants who seek to exercise voice and remain with a public service, combine to increase the potential for 'information impactedness' when it comes to the state and performance of the public service,[30] unless something really goes awry, at which point it is too late for action.

These issues loom large for public service institutions working in constantly changing and precarious environments, where policy development and service delivery take place in networked and complex contexts, the performance expectations are high and tolerance for error is low, and staff complements are lean and aging. The implication is that public service institutions need to recruit and retain the very best talent from the next two generations, fully engaging their advice for governments and their willingness to explore alternatives. Comprehending and improving the quality of these institutions – not only in terms of outputs and their effectiveness on outcomes, but also in terms of their internal environments for dialogue and strategic thinking – is crucial for attracting and retaining governments' fair share of top talent, who otherwise will gravitate to the private sector, no matter how public spirited they are, and work for top dollar on private and public business.

Commitment, Meaning and Spirituality in Public Administration

This paper began with an anecdote about an invitation to discuss the emerging literature on 'soul' in public administration in the context of the B.C. restructuring and the turmoil it generated. The anecdote is notable not only for pointing to the many interpretations of and implications for 'commitment' in periods of great turmoil, but also because the host was aware of a burgeoning American literature on soul and spirituality in public administration, and because of my discomfort in taking up the brief – which I think would have been a typical reaction among most Canadian public servants and public administration scholars. After taking up that speaking opportunity, I scanned the literature and found an intriguing diversity of contributions and perspectives. What follows is an outline of that literature's strands, one with implications for the field of Canadian public administration.

One strand can be traced to Robert Denhardt's *In Pursuit of Significance* (1993), a strong rebuttal of *In Search of Excellence* and *Reinventing Government* and what eventually became known as NPM. Written in a similar style as the NPM progenitors, Denhardt delineated an alternative set of values and motivation that could inform public service and innovation. Later, Robert and Janet Denhardt broadened these ideas into an approach labelled 'the New Public Service' as a contrast to NPM and traditional models of public service. Presented at a *PAR* symposium on leadership, democracy, and public administration, this broader formulation was informed by literature on democratic citizenship, communities and civil society, and organizational humanism and discourse theory.[31] Instead of setting direction and performance objectives, this approach emphasizes serving citizens and communities, fostering engagement with citizens and communities, relying on broader interpretations of accountability, treating people well in public organizations and their larger networks, and promoting stewardship. Others have depicted public service as a 'search for meaning' through the work public servants take on and the citizens, communities, and sectors they serve.[32]

This writing does not explicitly address spirituality and soul in public administration; it does, though, provide a point of departure for practitioners and scholars with such interests. Lynch, Omdal, and Cruise's[33] quirky contribution argues that the secularization of public administration since its origins (along with logical positivism) has severed the links between the spiritual wisdom that could be derived from several religious traditions, and that opening up this line of inquiry makes sense to the extent that values and ethics are considered important and worth probing. In their view, broader lines of human inquiry should be brought to the discussion of many issues in public administration. A seminal work argued that renewal in the public sector requires benevolence and civility, essential elements of the 'spirit' of public administration.[34] In 2001 the Denhardts initiated an online column with the American Society for Public Administration (ASPA) on 'the soul of public administration'; here they tapped into their earlier work and emphasized meaning and serving the common good, rather than spiritual perspectives, but they also asked questions such as these: 'What values lie at the core of public service?' 'What is the essential character and meaning of what we do?' 'What is the moving force that compels our actions?' 'What gives us strength and inspiration when the trials and turmoil of our work gets [sic] us down?'[35] More recently, Donald Menzel has surveyed the literature and different institutional loci such as codes of ethics, professional associations, associations for teaching public administration, and journals, regarding where the 'soul' of public administration resides in the discipline and profession.[36] Menzel has also reported on a study that surveyed members of ASPA about the extent and influence of spirituality in their lives and whether it should be discussed in a professional context.[37]

A second strand of literature keys on spirituality in the workplace, with a focus on the experience of private sector organizations. The much-cited work of Mitroff and Denton[38] explored, among other things, the difference between spirituality and religion, the meaning of both for respondents, their relevance for workplaces, and how to foster conversation about spirituality in workplaces. The authors encountered many definitions of spirituality and suggested that, among other things, it is informal, non-denominational, inclusive, timeless, and fundamental;

that it emphasizes calm and interconnectedness; and that it is a source of faith and power. They developed a typology of organizations based on degree of engagement with spirituality and religion. In their view, workplaces that foster spirituality and that allow workers to engage their 'complete selves' at work can 'deploy more of their full creativity, emotions, and intelligence; in short, organizations viewed as more spiritual get more from their participants, and vice versa.'[39] Their respondents were interested in, but neutral or tentative about, discussing spirituality in the workplace; generally, though, they would not countenance discussions of religion. Mitroff and Denton concluded: 'We have gone too far in separating the key elements. We need to integrate spirituality into management. No organization can survive for long without spirituality and soul. We must examine ways of managing spirituality without separating it from the other elements of management.'[40]

Writing in *Public Administration Review*, Garcia-Zamor[41] offers a dispassionate review of the burgeoning literature on spirituality in private sector workplaces,[42] describing how it emerged in the 1990s and speculating that it was a reaction to corporate excesses of the 1980s and later rounds of restructuring. Garcia-Zamor provides a wide-ranging review of various aspects of workplace spirituality, exploring different ways that corporations have provided support, echoing the notion that acknowledging or supporting spirituality is fundamentally different from promoting religion, and affirming findings that organizations which foster spirituality seem to perform at higher levels. He acknowledges the rise in Christian-based writing,[43] but he also points to other writing inspired by many other spiritual and religious traditions. He explores how spirituality has been addressed through ethics discussions and professional development. Indeed, anyone who has reviewed literature or participated in courses on leadership development and change management will have found that the matter of exploring self, and the need for personal transformation and to serve ultimate individual, organizational, and societal goals, are never far from the surface of discussions. However, Garcia-Zamor never suggests that public sector organizations should embrace spirituality.

A third strand of literature explores motivational factors and processes in public sector organizations. Seminal work in this area includes that of Perry and Porter,[44] who set out a framework for considering how public service work and motivation differed from the private sector context[45] and how the characteristics of individuals, specific jobs, the work environment, and external environments may vary, as well as motivational techniques. Perry and Wise[46] reviewed the literature and developed a typology of public service motives, distinguishing between *rational* ones (participation in policy process, personal identification with programs, advocacy for special interest), *norm-based* ones (serving the public interest, duty and loyalty to government, social equity), and *affective* ones (conviction about programs, patriotism of benevolence), as well as several propositions to stimulate empirical research. These authors draw on the work of Frederickson and Hart[47] to posit that the 'patriotism of benevolence' embraces 'love of regime values and love of others.' But this is as close as they get in their article to broaching the topics of spirituality and religion. Perry reported empirical results of a study of MPA students indicating that 'public policy making, commitment to public interest, compassion, and self-sacrifice were confirmed as dimensions of public service motivation.'[48]

Perry identifies and tests the antecedents to public service motivation and concludes that parental socialization, religious socialization, professional identification, political ideology, and demographic characteristics are relevant.[49] He provides an interesting discussion of how different types of religious commitment (mainstream versus fundamentalism) may explain some anomalous findings (religious socialization was negatively correlated); he also reports on a study which found that different indicators of public service motivation correlate with willingness to blow the whistle. Crewson reports that there are differences in the reward motivations of employees between the public sector and private sectors, that the public sector has more service-oriented personnel, and that 'service-motivated federal employees will be more productive than economic-oriented employees.'[50] He suggests that providing recognition and clarifying the organization's objectives may be more effective than relying on monetary incentives, though these need to be carefully balanced. Brewer, Seldon, and Facer used Q-sorting methodology to interpret the results of surveys of public servants and arrived at four somewhat overlapping categories of motivation: *samaritans* (who are deeply concerned about the disadvantaged and for whom helping provides personal gratification); *communitarians* (who are motivated to serve the community, as opposed to the underprivileged, and who seek meaningful work); *patriots* (who serve larger causes, duty, and idealism); and *humanitarians* (who care most about social justice and inclusion).[51] These findings all suggest that economic incentives and engagement in policy advocacy are not important motives, but that the desire to perform public service is. It is interesting that the authors did not explore the potential spiritual and religious dimensions underpinning the motivations.

This review only skims the surface of the literature; each article contains numerous references to contributions from other authors. But even this selective review reveals a fairly wide-ranging discourse on questions of meaning and spirituality in public service, especially in the context of continuous change. Panels have been devoted to probing these issues at the meetings of the ASPA and the PAR Forum; research has appeared in leading journals such as *Public Administration Review* and *Journal of Public Administration Research and Theory*; and ASPA has established an online forum for this purpose. The Association for Public Policy Analysis and Management's recent research conferences have held several panels on faith-based initiatives. Even more interesting is the literature emerging on how to introduce the topic of spirituality into management education. In addition to stand-alone articles in journals such as *Journal of Management Inquiry* and books, there have been special issues in *Journal of Organizational Change and Management* (eleven articles in two issues of the 1999 volume) and in *Journal of Management Education* (eight articles in a 2000 special issue). The National Association of Schools of Public Affairs and Administration's *Journal of Public Affairs Education* recently published an article exploring how to incorporate discussions of spirituality into the curricula of MPA programs and the rationale for doing so; this was a dispassionate piece that was sensitive to the provocative subject at hand.[52]

The mention, let alone the prospect, of engaging in research and dialogue on motivation and spirituality in our public service institutions will be disconcerting for Canadians. We have a strong tradition of separation of church and state, and spiritual and religious beliefs are not to interfere in the workplace. But can we avoid probing these issues? There are several reasons to think not. First, we already know that many public servants who have experienced great turmoil have tapped into personal reservoirs of different kinds to sustain themselves, and we should know more about the extent to which different motivations are at play. Governments' compensation, retention, and branding strategies may overlook or underemphasize important sources of motivation, which is particularly interesting when so many leadership and change management specialists and courses seem to recognize these dimensions of engagement. Second, as Leland and Denhardt[53] suggest, good leaders need to develop good understandings of work colleagues, which may involve learning more about personal beliefs and motivations as well as understanding the drivers of one's own engagement with public service institutions. There are important lines to be drawn here, but it seems that a debate may be warranted on this subject. Third, the high-profile faith-based initiatives of the Bush administration have highlighted the fact that many governments rely on non-secular organizations to deliver public services, and there is growing interest in whether this leads to superior outcomes.[54] Canada relies on faith-based organizations to deliver services as well, and in an ASD world they may do so more in the future. We need frameworks for understanding and drawing lessons from our jurisdiction as well as others. Fourth, the new security regime has placed religious values squarely on the table: many Muslim citizens and immigrants may not see Canadian governments as 'secular' or 'neutral,' as we would like to pretend they are; in Australia, for example, the prime minister has asserted that 'Australian values' take precedence over the religious and spiritual values of certain immigrant groups.

I am not suggesting that spirituality should be promoted in the workplaces of Canadian public service institutions or be integrated into the curricula of public administration programs. Having said that, interesting lines of inquiry have emerged south of the border, and at the very least they deserve attention in the Canadian context, if only to explore the differences in administrative cultures and to develop more complete frameworks for ascertaining the motivations of public servants in rapidly evolving work environments, and what strategies might lead to retaining and recruiting the best possible people and creating the most productive work environments.

Conclusion: Researching and Rebuilding Commitment

This paper has argued that we stand at an interesting juncture with respect to the nature and our understanding of commitment in public service institutions. So much that we have taken for granted about the motivations of public servants, the environment in which they work, and how we conceive of and study commitment and motivation is changing radically. For practitioners and observers alike, this is simultaneously discomforting and exciting. This paper has explored three themes:

- Governments and observers have insufficiently recognized the extent to which continuous change and turmoil in public service institutions have exacted a toll on public servants in terms of their levels of commitment and trust. While change produces opportunities, and some individuals thrive in these environments, there is cause for worry about whether a sufficient amount of sustained leadership to navigate these internal waters will be available, particularly as our public sector institutions experience the demographic rollover in earnest.

- External factors – demands for advice from governments and the governments' own demands for outside professional services such as policy analysis and service delivery – may be dampening public servants' willingness to exercise voice within public service institutions and on exit. This may have profound consequences for securing timely information on declines in the quality of work environments. Such information is essential for remedies and strategies for retaining and attracting the best talent.

- Recent writing has explored the sources of motivation and commitment for public servants. This literature has emerged as a reaction to the often profound restructuring in many public sector workplaces, which has left staff to fend for themselves, and to traditional and NPM value systems, which may not resonate with many public servants. The issue of 'soul' or 'spirituality' in private and public sector workplaces, and whether either should be broached in management curricula, has been considered in American conferences and journals. The new security environment, the promise of sustained change in public sector workplaces, and partial reliance on faith-based ASD service providers suggest this will be a lively area of debate.

This paper has not aimed to provide a general survey of developments affecting public service institutions, which could easily be extended to include issues such as electoral and democratic reforms and the impact of information technology, to name only two. Rather, the focus here has been on exploring how the landscape has changed with respect to the nature of commitment in public service institutions.

The challenge of rebuilding and sustaining commitment in public service institutions will be squarely on the agenda for the foreseeable future. Moreover, this is a critical time, with demographic rollover starting in earnest and the prospect of continuing, often episodic, change in varying degrees across public service institutions. It may be difficult to rebuild trust in fast-paced operating environments; it may be easier to foster commitment and loyalty as well as interest in public service careers, so long as there is good appreciation of the different motivations driving public servants and potential recruits. This will require a better understanding of the sources of commitment. Here I suggest seven modalities:

1 Service to customers (providing service quality moments).
2 Service to citizens/communities (helping professions and communities).
3 Meaningfulness (fulfilling values, philosophy, spirituality).
4 Stewardship (cultivating organizations, resources, sectors).
5 Professional excellence (application of expertise, discipline, knowledge).
6 Instrumental/goal achievement (changing society, sectors, government).
7 Ideas and problem-solving (learning, working with top people).

There is not the space in this paper to consider whether this list is more robust than the categories produced to date by the American literature; this would require empirical research similar to that done by Perry[55] and by Brewer and his colleagues.[56] But it seems likely that public servants and recruitment prospects are motivated to varying degrees by these categories. Moreover, the distribution of the sources of commitment may vary according to different roles: front-line workers, program managers, executives, ministers, and so on. Different levels and kinds of work may have different distributions of motivations, and this has important implications for the design and use of incentive regimes and for retention, recruitment, and branding strategies. All of this raises the question whether rhetorical and branding strategies cater only to what top executives believe to be the motivations of certain groups.

Where do we go from here, and can we navigate these choppier waters of commitment without the sure hand of Ken Kernaghan? The foregoing suggests that we need an equally productive and committed set of scholars to conceptualize and follow through with a long-term research agenda in the Canadian context. Ken has left us with an impressive corpus of work that will continue to serve as a beacon as others take up this agenda, and he provides an important personal model of the engaged scholar. To pursue this agenda fully will require a new generation of scholars who, like Ken, are not only committed to research but also willing to regularly test their ideas and interact with public servants, and who take strong interest in the need for public servants to reflect and sort through these challenging issues. This role becomes even more important as the cycles of change shorten and the time available to public servants becomes even more precious.

NOTES

1 A recent IPAC volume, *Government Restructuring and Career Public Service in Canada* (2000), can be seen as a dialogue with Ken using his formulation as a point of departure.
2 Kenneth Kernaghan, Brian Marson, and Sandford Borins, *The New Public Organization* (Toronto: IPAC, 2000); O.P. Dwivedi and James Iain Gow, *From Bureaucracy to Public Management: The Administrative Culture of the Government of Canada* (Toronto: IPAC, 1999).
3 Donald Savoie, *Breaking the Bargain: Public Servants, Ministers, and Parliament* (Toronto: University of Toronto Press, 2003).
4 Kernaghan and John W. Langford, *The Responsible Public Servant* (Toronto: IPAC, 1990).
5 Dwivedi and Gow, *From Bureaucracy to Public Management*; Kernaghan, Marson, and Borins, *The New Public Organization*; Task Force on Values and Ethics, *A Strong Foundation: Report of the Task Force on Values and Ethics* (Ottawa: Canadian Centre for Management Development, 1996).
6 Savoie, *Breaking the Bargain*.
7 Mitchell Lee Marks, *From Turmoil to Triumph: New Life after Mergers, Acquisitions, and Downsizing* (Toronto: Maxwell Macmillan, 1994), viii.
8 Peter Frost, *Toxic Emotions at Work: How Compassionate Managers Handle Pain and Conflict* (Toronto: McGraw-Hill Ryerson, 2003). Aside from my own research perspectives on public service institutions, our school has encountered this when arranging co-op placements: sometimes a potential co-op client has chosen not to hire fully capable students where there is a good match for work assignments because the work environment is so toxic, either during or in anticipation of a change, that it would not be a good introduction to a public service career.
9 Evert Lindquist, 'The Bewildering Pace of Public Sector Reform in Canada,' in Jan-Erik Lane, ed., *Public Sector Reform: Rationale, Trends, and Problems* (London: Sage, 1997), 47–63.
10 In the parlance of Chester Barnard, *The Functions of the Executive*, and Herbert Simon, *Administrative Behavior*, repeated change may expand the zones of acceptance or indifference of public servants. It is interesting to consider

which of our models of public service have implicit in them notions of how broad these zones should be. The very notion of 'speaking truth to power' and providing professional advice suggests an expectation, first, of working outside the zones in giving advice and reacting to initial proposals, and, second, of working inside these zones to implement duly considered decisions.

11 Lindquist, *A Critical Moment: Capturing and Conveying the Evolution of the Canadian Public Service* (Ottawa: Canada School of Public Service, 2006).

12 Marks, *From Turmoil to Triumph*, vii.

13 David Zussman and Jak Jabes, *The Vertical Solitude: Managing in the Public Sector* (Halifax: IRPP, 1989).

14 Isabelle Fortier, 'From Skepticism to Cynicism: Paradoxes of Administrative Reform,' *Choices* 9, no. 6 (2003): 3–19; Christian Rouillard, 'From Cynicism to Organizational Disillusion: New Public Management as Confusion Factor,' *Choices* 9, no. 6 (2003): 20–36.

15 Robert Quinn, *Building the Bridge as You Walk on It: A Guide for Leading Change* (San Franciso: Jossey-Bass, 2004).

16 Philip Selznick, *Leadership in Administration: A Sociological Interpretation* (New York: Harper and Row, 1957).

17 This phrase was coined by Ted Semmens, a well-known Victoria-based consultant.

18 In the public administration literature, we typically approach these sorts of questions through the lenses of whistleblowing and codes of values and ethics (Kernaghan, 'Whistleblowing in Canadian Governments,' *Optimum* 22, no. 1 [1991/92]: 34–43; John W. Langford, 'Acting on Values: An Ethical Dead End for Public Servants,' *Canadian Public Administration* 47, no. 4 [2004]: 429–50; Langford and Allan Tupper, 'How Ottawa Does Business: Ethics as Government Program,' in G. Bruce Doern, ed., *How Ottawa Spends, 2006-07* [Montreal and Kingston: McGill-Queen's University Press, 2006], 116–37) as well as through varying approaches to and processes for exercising accountability (Peter Aucoin and Mark D. Jarvis, *Modernizing Government Accountability: A Framework for Reform* [Ottawa: Canada School of Public Service, 2005]; Canada, Commission of Inquiry into the Sponsorship Program and Advertising Activities, *Restoring Accountability: Recommendations* [Ottawa: Public Works and Government Services, 2006]).

19 Albert O. Hirschman, *Exit, Voice, and Loyalty: Responses to Decline in Firms, Organizations, and States* (Cambridge, MA: Harvard University Press, 1970).

20 Ibid., 82. Despite its seminal nature, *Exit, Voice, and Loyalty* was overlooked because it was published when government was expanding rapidly. Its relevance looms larger now because of the stresses that public organizations have experienced in the past few years. Perhaps it is not surprising that

Hirschman's insights emerged because of his experience dealing with development issues at the time.

21 Ibid., 43.

22 Ibid., 41. Such individuals can be identified as 'rare talent' who are critical when it comes to managing any sort of public service at high levels (Evert Lindquist and James Desveaux, *Recruitment and Policy Capacity in Government* [Ottawa: Public Policy Forum, 1998]).

23 Hirschman, *Exit, Voice, and Loyalty*, 78.

24 Ibid., 79.

25 Ibid., 80.

26 Ibid., 92.

27 Ibid., 104–5.

28 This should not be interpreted as suggesting that public servants would condone such activity; I am saying, rather, that if it lies outside their sphere of authority, they have much less incentive to deal with the matter.

29 There are some examples of important public servants who have pursued this exit followed by voice route, such as Arthur Kroeger, David Good, Ian Clark, and Harry Swain. However, this limited number is very much the exception rather than the rule.

30 Harold Wilensky, *Organizational Intelligence: Knowledge and Policy in Government and Industry* (New York: Basic, 1967).

31 Robert Denhardt and Janet Denhardt, 'The New Public Service: Serving Rather Than Steering,' *Public Administration Review* 60, no. 6 (2000): 549–59. See also Robert Bellah, Richard Madsen, William Sullivan, Ann Swidler, and Steven Tipton, *Habits of the Heart: Individualism and Commitment in American Life* (Berkeley: University of California Press, 1985); and Robert Putnam, *Making Democracy Work: Civic Traditions in Modern Italy* (Princeton: Princeton University Press, 1993).

32 Alex Pattakos, 'The Search for Meaning in Government Service,' *Public Administration Review* 64, no. 1 (2004): 106–12.

33 Thomas Lynch, Richard Omdal, and Peter Cruise, 'Secularization of Public Administration,' *Journal of Public Administration Research and Theory* 7, no. 3 (1997): 473–87.

34 H. George Frederickson, *The Spirit of Public Administration* (San Francisco: Jossey-Bass, 1997).

35 Robert Denhardt and Janet Denhardt, 'The Soul of Public Administration,' ASPA Online Columns, 20 July 2001, www.aspanet.org.

36 Donald Menzel, 'Public Administration as a Profession: Where Do Body and Soul Reside?' *Public Integrity* 5 (2003): 239–50.

37 Willa Marie Bruce, 'Public Administrator Attitudes about Spirituality,' *American Review of Public Administration* 30, no. 4 (2000): 414–35.

38 Ian Mitroff and Elizabeth Denton, 'A Study of Spirituality in the Work-place,' *Sloan Management Review* (1999): 83–92; idem, *A Spiritual Audit of Corporate America: A Hard Look at Spirituality, Religion, and Values in the Workplace* (San Francisco: Jossey-Bass, 1999).

39 Ibid., 83.

40 Ibid., 91.

41 Jean-Claude Garcia-Zamor, 'Workplace Spirituality and Organizational Performance,' *Public Administration Review* 63, no. 3 (2003): 355–63.

42 For a recent example, see John Dalla Costa, *Magnificence at Work: Living Faith in Business* (Ottawa: Novalis, 2005).

43 Garcia-Zamor, 'Workplace Spirituality and Organizational Performance.'

44 James Perry and Lyman Porter, 'Factors Affecting the Context for Motiva-tion in Public Organizations,' *Academy of Management Review* 7, no. 1 (1982): 89–98.

45 Terence Mitchell, 'Motivation: New Directions for Theory, Research, and Practice,' *Academy of Management Review* 7, no. 1 (1982): 80–8.

46 James Perry and Lois Recascino Wise, 'The Motivational Bases of Public Service,' *Public Administration Review* 50, no. 3 (1990): 367–73.

47 Frederickson and David Hart, 'The Public Service and the Patriotism of Benevolence,' *Public Administration Review* 45 (1985): 547–53.

48 James Perry, 'Measuring Public Service Motivation: An Assessment of Con-struct Reliability and Validity,' *Journal of Public Administration Research and Theory* 6, no. 1 (1996): 20.

49 James Perry, 'Antecedents of Public Service Motivation,' *Journal of Public Administration Research and Theory* 7, no. 2 (1997): 181–97.

50 Philip Crewson, 'Public Service Motivation: Building Empirical Evidence of Incidence and Effect,' *Journal of Public Administration Research and Theory* 7, no. 4 (1997): 515.

51 Gene Brewer, Sally Coleman Seldon, and Rex Facer, 'Individual Concep-tions of Public Service Motivation,' *Public Administration Review* 60, no. 3 (2000): 254–64. Since this chapter was submitted, several interesting articles pertaining to motivation in a public service context have emerged: Wouter Vandenabeele, 'Toward a Public Administration Theory of Public Service Motivation: An Institutional Approach,' *Public Management Review* 9, no. 4 (2007): 545–56; Barry Bozeman and Alex Murdoch, 'Public Managers' Reli-giosity: Impacts on Work Attitudes and Perceptions of Co-workers,' *Inter-national Public Management Journal* 10, no. 3 (2007): 287–306; and David H. Coursey and Sanjay K. Pandey, 'Public Service Motivation Measurement: Testing an Abridged Version of Perry's Proposed Scale,' *Administration and Society* 39 no. 5 (2007): 547–68.

52 Pamela Leland and Kathryn Denhardt, 'Incorporating Spirituality in the MPA Curriculum: Framing the Discussion,' *Journal of Public Affairs Education* 11, no. 2 (2005): 121–31.
53 Ibid., 31.
54 Fredrica Kramer, Kenneth Finegold, Carol De Vita, and Laura Wherry, 'Federal Policy on the Ground: Faith-Based Organizations Delivering Local Services,' discussion paper in the Urban Institute's Assessing the New Federalism series, presented to the annual research conference of the Association for Public Policy Analysis and Management, Washington, D.C., 3–5 November 2005; Steven Rathgeb Smith, 'Comparative Case Studies of Faith-Based and Secular Service Agencies: An Overview of Synthesis of Key Findings,' paper presented at as above.
55 Perry, 'Measuring Public Service Motivation,' 5–22; idem, 'Antecedents of Public Service Motivation.'
56 Brewer, Seldon, and Facer, 'Individual Conceptions of Public Service Motivation.'

7 Inspiring Exemplary Practices in Canada: Ken Kernaghan's Contribution to Professionalism, Pride, and Recognition

JACQUES BOURGAULT AND ESTHER PARENT

This chapter explores Ken Kernaghan's contribution to the development and protection of professional values in the public service. Throughout his career he has been concerned with the behavioural norms of professional public servants. This led him to work on, among other subjects, professionalism, ethics, and pride and recognition as well as threats to these values, which arise from such things as growing politicization and – as Heclo would put it – a government of strangers.[1] This chapter deals with professionalism among public servants and the concepts of pride and recognition that have become part of this sense of professionalism.

In addressing the subjects of professionalism and pride and recognition in Ken's work, one is immediately overwhelmed with the task: he has contributed at least thirty-three pieces in these fields, which have become the core of the literature as well as benchmarks for policies, programs, and judicial decisions. The first section of this chapter examines his extensive scholarship to demonstrate how the topics of professionalism and pride and recognition are intimately linked. The second shows how programs of pride and recognition are alive and well in Canada in 2005, reflecting the tremendous influence that Ken has had in this important area.

Professionalism

Public servants provide professional advice and assistance to the politicians who have been mandated to conduct a country's affairs. Public servants' contributions are based on two principles: first, politicians are not necessarily specialists in their fields of responsibility; and second, politicians do not have the time to conduct all the work needed to prepare policies and decisions as well as to fully monitor their implementation. The important issue is the relationship between the contributions of public servants and politicians' responsibility for final decisions.

This raises a number of questions: What is the appropriate contribution of public servants? What are their rules of engagement? What are the standards for their performance? How should they behave when confronted with political pressures, partisan or not? The answers to all these questions are related to the concept of professionalism. This is especially the case in the Canadian public service, where the civil service model in place corresponds neither to a career model such as those in continental Europe, nor to a spoils system in the American sense. It is seen, rather, as a professional model, meaning that while guarantees of career employment are not absolute, public servants have a reasonable expectation in terms of progressing in the organization so long as they perform their tasks according to a set of standards.

What are these standards? They can be found in the other dimension of a professional public service, which is characterized by the non-partisan status of public servants and the application of the merit principle in decisions concerning them, thus allowing the 'hired help' to be of the highest possible quality.

Kernaghan referred to Holtan Odegard's description of administrative responsibility to highlight the development of 'professionlike attitudes in the civil service.'[2] Besides 'professional commitment to fact, expertise, rationality, skill and learning,' the elements included 'dedication to the public interest, refusal to take a stand on issues of partisan politics [and] identifying relevant publics';[3] these elements correspond to commitment, neutrality, and partnership.

In his more recent writings, Kernaghan has added to these intrinsic (or profession-like) elements an extrinsic one: serving the government and the public. In 2001 he classified components of professionalism in terms of reliability, loyalty, and courtesy: 'The public service is seen to be reliable because it meets its commitments to the public and respects the rule of law, and it is seen to be loyal because it respects the democratic authority of political leaders and the hierarchical order of management in government departments. The fact that our public servants, compared to those in other countries, are notably courteous in their dealings with the public is based on public servants' belief that effective public service is a right of all taxpayers, not a privilege.'[4]

This description incorporates both democratic and professional values that lead to fairness and quality of service. Democratic values such as duty and loyalty stem from responsible cabinet government. Professional values such as excellence and effectiveness stem from duty and service performance.[5] However, self-proclaimed personal or professional interpretations of 'service to the public' can never become more important than the orientations of government. Public interest or duty to the public, which gives wide and often unchecked power to those who attempt to speak in the public interest, often ends up being self-interested.

Kernaghan has addressed the issue of professionalism throughout his career, yet he never becomes hostage to a strict definition of professionalism. Having introduced the term 'profession-like,' he applies the criteria of the traditional professions to define the status of professional public administrators. These criteria include 'a high degree of knowledge and/or skill based on education and/or training, membership in a professional organization with a high set of standards for admission, dedication to public service above personal interest, and a code of ethics.'[6] However, he concludes that 'it is clear that public administration is gradually moving closer to satisfying some of the criteria noted above but can only be considered a profession if a much looser definition of the term is accepted.'

In 1990, Kernaghan and Langford addressed other difficulties in defining professionalism within the public service, noting that 'there is obviously room for considerable debate about the exact definition of the duty of service to the public ... [However] some variation on this theme is held out by most governments and professional groups involved in government as an essential obligation of all public servants.'[7]

In 1997, Kernaghan addressed certain elements that are intrinsically related to professionalism, such as values and ethics: 'The term "ethics" is frequently used interchangeably with the word "values" and both values and ethics are closely linked to the concept of professionalism ... Writings on these subjects in general either provide or imply a variety of meanings for these terms.' However, 'what is clear is that these several concepts are closely linked by their common focus, in whole or in part, on right and wrong, or good and bad, behaviour.'[8] Professionalism in public administration is, therefore, seen in relation to ethics. Individuals are accountable for their actions, and there should be standards for this accountability. Furthermore, Kernaghan explains that the word 'unprofessional' is often used in conjunction with words such as 'unethical' and 'corrupt.'[9] Clearly, the concept of professionalism can only exist when ethics and values are in place and are respected. Ethics and values are thus prerequisites to professionalism. This may explain the evolution in Kernaghan's approach to the elements of professionalism mentioned earlier, which refer to reliability, loyalty, and courtesy.

According to Kernaghan, another reason to promote professionalism is that it can help counter the public's negative view of the public service. Certain activities seem to increase or decrease the trust that Canadians have in government and the public service. First of all, the public service's role in wealth creation should be recognized: 'Key actors in Canadian society are beginning to recognize – and to publicize – the vital role of the public service in sustaining our democratic institutions and in fostering economic prosperity and social well-being. There is a growing realization that a highly competent, professional and non-partisan public service, at all levels of government, is central to meeting the formidable challenges facing Canada in the new century.'[10]

Second, the performance of public servants must be observed and celebrated. To overcome long-held perceptions of low performance, public servants must improve their performance and the public must understand their contributions.[11] The logical extension to this is that a charter, or norms of service, is required in order to improve service delivery to the public. Because the public views the performance of public servants at first hand, members of the public will be the first witnesses of this improvement in performance. Furthermore, service delivery is a professional value, an extension of a professional's duty to clients. As Kernaghan says, 'Canadians are more likely to have more trust, confidence and pride in a non-partisan, professional public service than in a politicized one.'[12] As well, professionalism places priority on the client rather than on the government hierarchy.

Professionalism also reduces the possibility of a politicized public service. This in turn increases the legitimacy of the government and the state. In the modern context, the image the government needs to maintain will profit from professionalism. This reality is pushing the government towards a professional public service that has an ethic based on skills, competence, and service.[13] Government is becoming a values-based institution.

Kernaghan has been quick to note that the various pride and recognition programs that have been developed across Canada have the potential to contribute to this growing professionalism by institutionalizing values relating to excellence with the goal of improving service to clients and thereby changing the public's negative view of the public service. As Kernaghan has recognized, pride and recognition encourage excellent practices in government as well as the institutionalization of particular values. The next section of this chapter discusses how pride and recognition programs have evolved in Canada in recent years and how they have helped increase professionalism in the public service.

Professionalism, Pride, and Recognition

According to Kernaghan, *pride* refers 'to a proper sense of regard or respect, either for oneself or other entities,'[14] whereas *recognition* 'includes overt expressions of approval and appreciation as well as feelings of regard and respect.'[15] One of his most significant contributions to the study of pride and recognition in the public service is a project he launched in 2001 while he was editor of *International Review of Administrative Sciences*. This project involved convening an international round table, which he chaired, and following up with a special issue of *IRAS*.[16]

His approach to merit and motivation in 1982 was a precursor to his approach to pride and recognition, in that the objectives of merit and motivation at that time were comparable to those for pride and recognition today. As he wrote, 'the effective management of [human] resources is essential to achieving organization and government objectives. The challenge is to design a personnel management system that ensures a high level of merit and motivation in the public service.'[17] Much later, empirical evidence was developed indicating that utility to society was one of the key motivations for public servants.[18]

In the same paper Kernaghan suggested that government should change its emphasis and hire well-motivated rather than merely well-qualified employees.[19] One of the arguments in this chapter is that motivated employees help foster administrative values. Here the elements involved are similar to those relating to pride and recognition: to successfully realize government objectives, employees must be motivated, and the quality of work life affects their performance. This is an echo of the virtuous circle (recognition, pride, performance) that Kernaghan discusses later on.[20] In two papers[21] Kernaghan analyses the background to low public service morale, which in his view is caused principally by the negative reputation the public service has among the media, the public, and some politicians. He sees this as a serious problem because public servants are key players in the government's efforts to meet new challenges.[22] He then argues that recognition and pride are part of the solution. One of his contributions is therefore to explain how recognition practices constitute a solution to problems in the operation of the public service.

Another of his contributions is an attempt to pinpoint how the public service's negative image can be changed, since this is necessary for employees to feel valued. He made this contribution in the IPAC round table study *Rediscovering Public Service*, the purpose of which was to 'determine how to improve Canadians' recognition of the crucial role that a high-quality professional public service plays in facilitating democracy and sustaining the country's social and economic development.'[23] Ideas on pride were the dominant theme of the round table discussions, which helped generate perspectives and consensus relating to pride-oriented action in government. His study has often been mentioned as a catalyst for establishing recognition practices in several jurisdictions.

How Pride and Recognition Contribute to Professionalism

Pride and recognition reinforce professional values and contribute to professionalism by celebrating the implementation of those values in public administration. For example, the goal of excellence values is to establish a culture of quality service that reflects professionalism. The advantages of service excellence were noted by Kernaghan and Langford in 1990: 'Clients that are treated efficiently, effectively, fairly, and courteously are happier clients. They complain less, thereby increasing the efficiency and morale of the organization and reducing need for "catch-up" efforts to bring them on side or redress their procedural grievances.'[24] This was not written in the particular context of pride and recognition, but it can be seen that the virtuous circle of pride and recognition is a logical extension of the benefits of values associated with excellence. In *The Responsible Public Servant*, the values Kernaghan would later categorize as 'professional' (client reaction, notion of duty to the public, service excellence) are the same values as are recognized in pride and recognition programs today.[25]

Pride sets the level of quality for services and personal involvement. In 'An Honour to Be Coveted: Pride, Recognition, and Public Service,'[26] Kernaghan points out that solid data concerning the relationship between pride and increased performance in the public service have yet to be gathered. He therefore marks the way by examining the links among components of the 'virtuous circle': pride, performance, and recognition. First he examines three concepts that help determine the quality of work performed: organizational commitment, job satisfaction, and motivation. Organizational commitment is 'the desire to work hard for the organization, and a desire to stay in the organization.'[27] Since government wants this kind of commitment from its employees, the logical approach is 'to strengthen the major elements of organizational commitment so as to move public servants towards the highly committed pole of the continuum and, thereby, to foster higher performance.'[28] He does not discuss, however, what constitutes the 'major elements of organizational commitment.' Job satisfaction is related to the amount of job challenge, a sense of accomplishment, the possibility for independent thought and action, respect from superiors, and satisfaction in the department.[29] Motivation follows when these elements are satisfied. Kernaghan also maintains that what motivates private sector employees is very different from what motivates public sector employees. A focus on these factors may therefore lead to increased job performance.

He then explains how improved performance leads to increased public recognition. He points out a first contradiction: the public service has a negative image even though citizens admit that they have a high level of satisfaction with specific government services. Public recognition is therefore the most difficult part of the cycle, as it has to involve creating a new, positive image for the public service to counter an unjustified negative one.[30] Finally, he states that one of the major causes of low employee morale is that employees do not feel valued.[31] This could be corrected by increasing recognition through a more positive image, as well as through intrinsic and extrinsic recognition and awards.

To help the public service meet the challenges of this century, Kernaghan has proposed three initiatives: first, to foster a learning organization; second, to use information and communications technology to promote citizen-centred service, thereby enhancing service delivery and improving its image; and third, to move the public service from a rules-based institution towards a values-based one in ways that balance core public service values such as law, integrity, and neutrality with new service values.[32] Throughout this essay, Kernaghan explains how increased pride leads to increased performance and how that pride can contribute to a high level of quality among workers. His theory converges with that of Bourgault and Gusella, which appeared in the same year.[33]

In a 2001 essay,[34] Kernaghan stated that recognition is advantageous for the public service since many public servants say they chose the milieu from a sense of duty and commitment to the community. This is not to say that money is not an incentive; recognition and praise for contributions are necessary, but they need to be supplemented by adequate and tangible rewards.[35]

Recognition can be a tool for easing everyone's tasks. Kernaghan suggests that the role of the public service is much broader than implementation: the public service also supports democratic, economic, and social development. To perform its role, the public service must cooperate with other social institutions and therefore requires their trust. To obtain their trust, the public service must prove its competence, its aptitude for performance, and its motivation, and recognition can help achieve this. Recognition improves organizational performance. Kernaghan lists the links between pride and performance that are related in some way to professionalism: (1) recruitment and retention by attracting and motivating a highly skilled workforce; (2) reward and recognition via the idea that public servants respond more to non-monetary recognition; (3) empowerment, which allows public servants to be more innovative; (4) innovation, which comes with continuous learning; (5) accountability, which increases the public's pride in public service by making it more effective; and (6) citizen engagement, which leads to greater openness and trust in government.[36]

Pride and recognition programs contribute to learning from exemplary practices; they also identify specific people who serve as models of quality. Such programs may celebrate the success that individuals or teams have had in delivering services or implementing innovations. Recognition can involve a learning event for the organization and may improve efficiency across the whole organization. The strategic importance of pride and recognition programs prompts us to examine the extent of Kernaghan's influence in this domain. Next we survey pride and recognition programs across Canada.

What Is the Status of Pride and Recognition in Canada Today?

Are pride and recognition programs disappearing, having been a 'flavour of the month' in the late 1990s? Are they being institutionalized and thus bureaucratized, as Kernaghan has feared? In February 2005 the authors attempted to determine the direction that provincial and federal governments were taking in terms of recognition practices. Since most of the new programs appeared between 1995 and 2000,[37] and the point of this study was to pinpoint fresh evolutions, the interval of time that was chosen for examination was 2000 to 2005. We chose the respondents after a Web search for responsible agencies; phone calls were then made to find the responsible officials and validate their titles and addresses. Then we sent a letter to each, explaining our research and guaranteeing confidentiality. Finally, interviews were conducted by telephone. The respondents were asked to describe what their government had done during this period. Our resources did not permit us to search all federal and provincial departments; however, we interviewed at least one person in every province, having chosen four types of federal departments. We found that the value of pride and recognition programs was well recognized.[38]

Our first observation is that most provincial governments and federal ministries have recognition programs. In many cases, programs had been entirely revamped during the interval we examined or were being redesigned. Over the past five years, programs of pride and recognition have turned towards recognizing values reflecting excellence. This is most notable at the provincial level: the federal ministries interviewed generally had taken this direction shortly before 2000.

Origins of Programs and Strategies of Pride and Recognition

The objectives of recognition programs have changed over the years. The traditional type of recognition – that is, rewards for long service – was in place well before 2000 in all fourteen institutions studied and still is today. However, most respondents were quick to add that this form of recognition does not work in terms of today's expectations for recognition programs. New awards that recognize excellent work are the priority for almost all governments today.

Half the respondents stated that their institution had such awards ceremonies in place before 2000; some have since added new awards to already existing programs. Most of the earlier awards took the form of banquets. We call these events 'formal' because they meet these four criteria: (1) they are part of an official program; (2) they are made part of an awards process that includes nominations and selections; (3) there are established rules that must be followed; and (4) they include some form of celebration ranging from a group meeting to an official dinner. Informal recognition, which is characterized by immediacy, is also gaining in importance. Examples range from verbally recognizing employees, to providing access to electronic greeting cards with messages of recognition that can be sent to peers, subordinates, or managers, to online gift catalogues from which managers may choose gifts to recognize employees' excellent work. Most of the respondents considered this an efficient and effective form of recognition and said that more of it needed to be done. In half the cases studied, informal recognition existed at the departmental level before 2000. Three departments had informal recognition guidelines elaborated at the corporate level for the entire government. Three others took this route after 2000.

Types of Recognition Programs

Programs of recognition take different forms, and most governments have more than one program in place. The vast majority of departments had formulated their own recognition practices, with the strongest trend being towards formal awards ceremonies. One ministry preferred to present these awards at the regional rather than the corporate level. Informal recognition programs, including immediate recognition actions, were in place in six organizations at the time of the study. Two federal ministries had elaborate informal recognition programs that included framed certificates as well as an online gift catalogue from which managers across the country could choose gifts. The purpose of the online catalogue was to have a variety of gifts that responded to cultures across the country and that could be ordered and received in a timely fashion.

Other interviewees said that informal recognition was not used as much as it could be; individual managers basically took on the task, and perhaps the risk, of deciding when and how to recognize employees informally. Recognition has been integrated into the management plan of one government. Another said that its approach to recognition was integrated with its policy for health at work. Four governments indicated that they had elaborated a recognition template at the corporate level that was distributed to departments, which then used the template according to their needs. These templates included guidelines for formal and informal recognition. When guidelines are drawn up at the corporate level and distributed to departments, this allows for common values to be highlighted across the government. Two governments were using National Public Service Week as a platform for many recognition activities. Two governments had awards to recognize the community work and civic spirit of employees.

Evolution of Pride and Recognition Programs

The most important change in recognition programs over the period under review was the addition of programs providing more opportunities to recognize excellence. More than half the jurisdictions surveyed have created formal recognition programs or new awards for existing programs. This illustrates the greater importance being assigned to recognition of excellent work. Six institutions stated that the programs they had in place in 2000 were still in place. Some of these had been modified over time. Four respondents mentioned the creation of a new template, designed at the corporate level, containing the values the government wanted to instil but flexible enough to be adapted to the various departments.

Abandonment of Programs or Strategies concerning Pride and Recognition

Most governments have added recognition programs over the past five years – so recently that there has been little opportunity to evaluate them. This is probably why respondents stated that none of the programs in place in 2000 had been abandoned – perhaps modified or added to, but not abandoned.

There were some exceptions to this trend. In one jurisdiction, two awards programs were abandoned after a change of government and replaced by more prestigious programs. One ministry temporarily abandoned a suggestion program in order to redesign it. A more efficient version was to be reintroduced the following year. Another ministry noted that its entire program would be abandoned in the summer of 2005 and replaced with a completely new one that was more in line with that of Canada's Public Service Commission.

Modifications to Programs and Strategies

Only six governments stated that they had not modified their programs. Modifications to existing programs in governments and ministries affected the programs, the awards, the nomination processes, the selection of candidates, and management of the programs.

One government has tied in its recognition program to its corporate business program, in this way integrating recognition with performance and results. Another government now takes a humanist approach to recognition instead of tying it to excellence. The new values the program addresses will target human dignity in a healthy work environment. This is the only exception in what seems to be a national tendency towards excellence.

Two federal ministries have adjusted their informal recognition practices. One now uses an online gift catalogue; the other has introduced standardized certificates for informal recognition.

Many jurisdictions have made changes to their awards ceremonies. Two changed the dates of awards ceremonies in order to increase media coverage and have more time to prepare for them. One ministry noted that awards were no longer presented at yearly awards ceremonies; instead they were presented locally for the sake of timely recognition. This reflected its employees' wishes, in that they felt more comfortable receiving awards locally.

One respondent said that to improve the success of the program, a selection committee had been established to choose award recipients – an improvement over past practice, in which only one public servant was responsible for this. Sometimes changes were implemented as a result of resource cutbacks. In one government a suggestion program lost its full-time administrator, whose job included helping employees fill out nominations. The nomination process had been revised so that employees could complete the entire procedure on their own. Two organizations noted that the nomination procedure for awards was constantly being simplified. The goal in this was to encourage more people to nominate employees.

Various other changes have been made in awards systems. Again, these reflect new values of excellence in government. For example, one government has added an award for people outside the public service who have worked in teams with the public service. Other new awards recognize excellent management of personnel and partnerships. One government has changed the name of its awards, adding the term 'deputy minister' to associate that person with the awards.

Implementation

Almost all interviewees stated that multimedia communication strategies are necessary to encourage recognition practices. These media include the Internet, intranets, internal articles and memos, and bulletin boards. Also, managers are reminded during congresses and through managerial guides as well as the *Bravo* guide (at the federal level).

The participation of senior managers is essential, since in most cases recognition is conducted through them. For this reason, meetings are held with management teams; also, recognition is treated as a component of human resources strategies and as a priority. When senior managers participate in recognition, they encourage others to do the same.

Departmental coordinators are one means of improving communication and assisting managers. Two interviewees mentioned that this was a way of ensuring that the message was getting across.

Two respondents emphasized the importance of evaluation procedures for ensuring that recognition practices were followed. For example, interviews and surveys can be conducted during which employees are asked if they feel that recognition is a current practice in their department, if they feel recognized, and so on. This is one way to ascertain whether managers are applying recognition in their sector. One interviewee stated that recognition was part of the performance component in managers' evaluations.

Many respondents emphasized the importance of integrating recognition into human resource policy as a part of government management plans and human resources strategies. One person said that working in concert with the central agency responsible for it (in this case, the PSC) ensured that the message of recognition got across more effectively. One government noted that its managers were required to implement recognition programs.

Two respondents made a very basic point: managers are overwhelmed with other tasks and are not prepared to either enact the programs with maximum efficiency or to optimize those programs' benefits. If you want managers to recognize their employees, you must give them the tools to do so and make those tools as simple as possible to use. In other words, when recognition tools are effective, accessible, and inexpensive, managers are encouraged to provide more recognition.

Good Practices

When thinking about the 'good practices' of an organization regarding recognition, one tends to think about high-visibility events. From the perspective of the government, formal awards are a best practice because the government highlights its values through them. But from the perspective of employees, formal and informal awards at the ministerial level are the most effective since these respond to their local culture.

Half the respondents said without hesitation that the best practice is actually a diversity of practices. Formal recognition generates a maximum of pride for a limited number of employees, whereas informal recognition reaches a larger number of employees several times a year. The latter also recognizes diverse examples of 'excellence.'

Four respondents said that formal awards are the best practice because of the amount of pride involved and the visibility given to excellent practices. Two stated that for several reasons, informal recognition is the most effective form for governments *and* employees. First, it is a low-cost practice that allows a maximum number of employees to be recognized; second, it answers to the new generation of employees, who are much more sensitive to immediate recognition of their work; and third, informal recognition can be adapted to different cultures and work environments.

Only one of the respondents felt that the traditional long-service recognition was a best practice. Note that this person's government did not have in place a structure for recognizing excellence. Another respondent noted, however, that long-service recognition was still a best practice for the older generation of employees, since it responded to their traditional values of stability and loyalty.

One interviewee mentioned that his government's best practice at the time was an unofficial 'community of thought,' a discussion forum for managers from different departments that was born spontaneously and that was not at all part of government policy. This practice, though, did not target employees; rather, it was a forum for managers – one that has produced important results.

Expectations for Pride and Recognition Programs

Respondents stated their expectations for recognition practices, but in no order of priority. The expectations were diverse and related mainly to having a *proud* workforce and a *prepared* workforce.

FOR EMPLOYEES: POSITIVE ATTITUDE, CULTURE OF EXCELLENCE, AND SENSE OF PRIDE

The idea that received the most attention from respondents was that of encouraging a positive attitude. Five stated that recognition practices are a means to foster a positive work environment with positive energy, positive employee behaviour, and employee engagement. One government mentioned positive competition. Three respondents said, in more general terms, that one goal was 'happy employees.'

The 'virtuous circle' was mentioned by four governments. Through recognition practices, they hoped to increase employee pride and employee productivity and thereby improve services. The various components of the virtuous circle were also mentioned individually by respondents.

Other goals focused on employees included honouring employees' contributions (two mentions) and recognizing the talents of each employee (one mention). Unlike the goals noted earlier, these were not stated in the context of pride, performance, positivism, and so forth. Rather, they were mentioned in terms of individual employees.

FOR THE WORKING ENVIRONMENT: A POSITIVE, CONVIVIAL, AND
STIMULATING ENVIRONMENT

The major goal here was to create an attractive work environment in order to retain personnel. The literature distinguishes among morale, motivation, pride, and positivism; that said, most interviewees used these terms in a manner that reflected the desire to foster a stimulating work environment in which employees could be happy and proud of their work. This was in line with Kernaghan's point that the public service attracts workers who have a sense of duty to the public and who for that reason are more sensitive to recognition practices than to monetary awards.[39]

FOR THE ORGANIZATION: CORPORATE PRIDE, TRANSMITTING COMMON
SHARED VALUES, AND RETAINING PERSONNEL

Representatives of two governments noted that their organizations' objectives for recognition practices included organizational pride. Such practices were a means of highlighting and adjusting organizational values in an ongoing manner, and formal events provided a forum for doing so. One respondent noted that recognition practices were a way to improve links between the centre and the regions by transmitting common values. Another noted that his government did *not* use recognition practices as a way to increase performance. Its approach was a humanist one that targeted employees as individuals with the goal of improving employee, workplace, and organizational health. It was hoped that this would lead to an organizational culture of recognition. Nearly half the respondents mentioned that recognition practices aimed at attracting and retaining personnel. One respondent said that the goal was to make the public service an 'employer of choice.'

Obstacles Faced in Relation to These Programs

All respondents expressed a belief in recognition programs, but they were also quick to add that there had been problems and obstacles in implementing these programs. There was general agreement that while recognition practices are a positive thing, commitment to them must be demonstrated by allocating sufficient resources. Almost all respondents noted either that recognition programs were too expensive, that budget cuts were making the programs suffer, or that they were underfunded.

A second major obstacle flowed directly from the first: human resources for such programs were lacking. One respondent pointed to frozen budgets and changes in personnel. Half the respondents mentioned difficulties arising from cuts in personnel, deficient human resources, and managers who were too busy to pay sufficient attention to these programs.

Four respondents mentioned the role of top leaders and managers. Managers, directors, CEOs, and deputy ministers have a key role to play in recognition programs, which can be a problem when they do not show appropriate support, when they do not believe in the programs, when they do not attend awards ceremonies, and when they are uncomfortable with the process of recognizing employees.[40] For recognition practices to work, leaders must set the example and managers must support the programs. When senior people do not participate, it becomes an obstacle to the success of the program.

Some respondents described the designing of recognition programs as a delicate task that, if not done well, could end up targeting only part of the workforce instead of all employees, in this way marginalizing some individuals. Another risk was that the program would not reflect the cultural differences across the government. Five respondents mentioned that creating uniformity across the government was an extremely difficult task. Also, programs could backfire if expenses exceeded norms; the media would be quick to exploit such abuses.

Two governments noted that various 'deficits' needed to be addressed before constructive recognition could take place. These deficits included cognitive ones – for example, finding creative ways to recognize employees and comprehending the role of recognition in an organization. Other deficits were more ideological – four interviewees noted that unions were a significant obstacle to recognition practices because of the contradictory discourses that resulted. It is hard for employees to believe that their employer appreciates them and wants to recognize their contributions when a strike or a difficult collective bargaining process is taking place. Two respondents pointed out that unions were not fond of recognition practices, for such programs attempted to instil values that conflicted with union demands relating to salaries, working conditions, and so forth. Other attitudinal problems included employee cynicism.

Many respondents noted that a poorly designed recognition program can become a major embarrassment. One observed that it was easy to fall into the trap of thinking that recognition is easy, since it is for positive purposes, when actually it is a very delicate task. Three respondents pointed out that there was always a risk that the programs would lack meaning for employees and thus not motivate them. One noted that ensuring immediate recognition was extremely difficult.

Two respondents said that negative public attitudes towards recognition programs for public servants were an obstacle; it is more difficult to justify the costs of such programs when the public views them as a waste, as rewarding the undeserving, or as a logrolling exercise among public servants. Pride and recognition programs try to reverse this trend by showcasing for citizens the value of public administration and the quality of civil servants.[41]

Culture and Communication

For a program to succeed, it must first of all be credible. This means that the nomination criteria and procedures must be fair, clear, and transparent. The program must also demonstrate consistency in what it recognizes and how it recognizes it. One goal of recognition practices is to instil a culture of recognition within the organization; however, one government spokesperson noted that to succeed, the organization must already have in place a culture of excellence and recognition. Another mentioned that to succeed, there must already be a 'community of thought' regarding recognition that enables ideas to be shared among departments. A community of thought and of dialogue helps preserve the integrity of the program as well as its direction. Another element that helps the program gain credibility is a communication plan that talks about recognition publicly as much as possible.

Involvement of People

The vast majority of respondents mentioned that the support of leaders at all levels was essential for a well-functioning recognition program. Leaders could show support by providing the necessary funds and human resources, by giving their time, and by setting an example. One respondent mentioned that managers could not be expected to apply recognition practices immediately; they needed to be trained to apply effective recognition and had to be sensitized to the practice. Two government spokespeople noted that those organizing the program had an important role to play in establishing recognition practices.

PROGRAM CONTENT

The program also has to be meaningful and flexible, meaning that it has to be adaptable to all areas and levels of government and also flexible in terms of human resource management strategies. One respondent noted that having an array of diverse programs in place increases their chances of success since a maximum number of people come into contact with recognition. Two respondents referred to the need for proper tools to encourage managers to practise recognition in their departments.

Two respondents mentioned that since recognition programs were paid for with public monies, funds had to be managed transparently and efficiently if such programs were to be sustainable. This is, of course, important for all public programs, but especially for recognition programs, whose managers have to justify the topping up of employee compensation. Two governments advised that these programs had to be evaluated from time to time so that improvements could be made to them.

During the interviews it was often noted that in the present day there is a national tendency towards embracing the concept of excellence as a means to strengthen organizations and restructure their values. Two jurisdictions stand out as exceptions to this trend. The first is Quebec. In most other jurisdictions, recognition practices are part and parcel of a 'virtuous circle' in which performance and quality of services are gradually increased. Quebec's objectives for recognition practices are very different. Perhaps owing to cultural differences that affect how merit and recognition are given and received, Quebec's approach to recognition programs does not primarily target increased performance, but rather increased human dignity through employee, workplace, and organizational health and well-being.

The second exception is Prince Edward Island, where the researcher encountered a 'culture of familiarity' in public sector recognition practices. At present, some of that province's awards programs do attempt to realign values (e.g., there is a Diversity Award designed to support an innovative and inclusive workforce) and to encourage employee innovation (e.g., through suggestion programs). This is similar to approaches in other jurisdictions. However, the forms that many recognition practices take in that province reflect a workforce that already has a solid community base. One example given by the respondent is the great interest that civil servants take in the employee profile page of a government newsletter.

Furthermore, recognition practices in that province, and the events surrounding them as described by the respondent, are not based on grandeur and size. Rather, they constitute simpler events that focus on socializing among all members of all levels of government. The activities during National Public Service Week are of this flavour; they include ministers and deputies serving dinner to employees as well as friendly sports challenges. As the respondent pointed out, the goal is for representatives of all levels of government to have fun together. Here, familiarity and socializing become a mode for recognition.

Conclusion

This paper has tried to demonstrate general links between, on the one hand, professionalism, and on the other hand, pride and recognition. Pride matters to anyone who has chosen public service as a vocation and who has demonstrated excellent work; so does recognition. All employees ask themselves: Do I do my work well? Do those around me think I perform my tasks well? What are the best ways to perform my tasks? All employees are proud of a job well done. It is well recognized that civil servants are 'vocational' and want to believe in the social utility of their work. Pride and recognition allow them to feel that their career choice was not useless; in this way their professional life becomes more meaningful.

Recognition has also retained our attention: as we have seen, it does exist, but only for some aspects of professionalism, such as comradeship, excellence in tasks, and service delivery. Other dimensions of professionalism are difficult to observe and thus to celebrate. For example, it is not easy to tell who in the organization is the most loyal, who has the most respect for democracy, who is the most competent, and who is the most honest in a given year.

This chapter has differentiated between two distinct but related types of professionalism: individual and collective. It is possible to celebrate individual professionalism in certain dimensions; that said, organizations also tend to encourage the development of collective professional values. This is done through all-encompassing tools such as selection mechanisms, codes of conduct or ethics, and corporate programs for pride and recognition.

This chapter has observed the evolution of professional values and of professionalism over the past forty years. Findings show that professionalism has moved from a rather static and reactive perspective towards a consideration of traditional profession-like standards in public service. Also, greater emphasis is being placed on values such as respect for democracy and excellence in service to the public, as well as on continuous learning spread across the organization. This chapter has also shown, albeit indirectly, the pioneering role that Professor Kenneth Kernaghan has played in setting the pace for this journey.

Recognition practices have evolved from long-service awards given at national banquets towards awards presented in an appropriate format for excellence in service delivery as well as informal recognition initiatives given in a timely manner with the involvement of senior managers.[42] Informal recognition initiatives tend to express broader organizational values and to be structured along those lines.

Recognition practices for the most part celebrate excellence (in service delivery, partnerships, and so forth); thus they do not seem to target democratic values. This would support Kernaghan's view that the public service is moving away from a rules-based regime towards a values-based one.[43] Of course, it is easier to observe excellence in service delivery than in 'democratic values,' in the same way that it is easier to observe attitudes towards users or clients than attitudes towards a keyboard, photocopier, or purchasing form!

The values emphasized in pride and recognition practices inject professional values into government. The goal is for these values to become part of the organizational culture. This may then lead to a more professional public service as these professional values become intrinsic to the organization. Efforts are made to disseminate professional values to the overall public service. While striving to achieve this goal, one must still keep in mind Kernaghan and Langford's warning that the institutionalization of values may lead to their bureaucratization. In practice, heed must be taken of the bureaucratization of values when a culture of recognition is being created and when a values-based institution is being developed. Flexibility for organizational adaptation makes a difference.

This chapter has allowed us to observe some of Ken Kernaghan's contributions to the present high professional standards of our bureaucracy. Throughout his long career, in articles, chapters, and books, he has initiated and animated discussion and contributed as an expert. He has also been an educator and a participant in continuous learning, and he has encouraged organizations to promote professionalism, foster pride and recognition, and adopt codes of conduct. He is, for me, as an academic and a citizen, a role model. I hope I have not betrayed his thought, and I fear I have reduced its reach. And I trust that this modest article has given adequate credit to him for his immense contribution.

NOTES

1　Hugh Heclo, A Government of Strangers: Executive Politics in Washington (Washington, D.C.: Brookings Institution, 1977).
2　Kenneth Kernaghan, 'Responsible Public Bureaucracy: A Rationale and a Framework for Analysis,' *Canadian Public Administration* 16 (1973): 578.
3　Ibid.
4　Kenneth Kernaghan, working paper, 'Rediscovering Public Service: Recognizing the Value of an Essential Institution,' IPAC, 2000, 8–9.
5　Kenneth Kernaghan, introduction to symposium on 'Values, Ethics, and Professionalism in the Public Service,' *International Review of Administrative Sciences* 63 (1997): 292.
6　Kenneth Kernaghan, *Canadian Public Administration: Discipline and Profession* (Toronto: Butterworths, 1983), 7.
7　Kernaghan and John Langford, *The Responsible Public Servant* (Halifax: IPAC, 1990), 115.
8　Kenneth Kernaghan, Introduction to 'Values, Ethics, and Professionalism,' 292.
9　Ibid.
10　Kernaghan, 'Rediscovering Public Service, 2.
11　Kenneth Kernaghan, Editorial Statement, *International Review of Administrative Sciences* 67, no. 1 (2001): 11–15.
12　Kernaghan, 'Rediscovering Public Service,' 18.
13　See whistle-blowing acts, competency development approach, codes of conduct, etc.
14　Kenneth Kernaghan, editorial statement, 'Pride and Recognition in the Public Service,' *IRAS* 67, no. 1 (2001): 69.
15　Ibid.
16　Ibid., 11–15.
17　Kenneth Kernaghan, 'Merit and Motivation: Public Personnel Management in Canada,' *Canadian Public Administration* 25 (1982): 711.

18 Gregory B. Lewis and Susan A. Frank, 'Who Wants to Work for the Government,' *Public Administration Review* 62, no. 4 (2002): 399–400.

19 Kernaghan, 'Merit and Motivation,' 698.

20 Jacques Bourgault and Mary Gusella, 'Performance, Pride, and Recognition in the Canadian Federal Service,' *IRAS* 67, no. 1 (2001): 43.

21 Kernaghan, Editorial Statement; 'Rediscovering Public Service.'

22 Kernaghan, 'Pride and Recognition in the Public Service,' 68.

23 Kernaghan, 'Rediscovering Public Service,' 2.

24 Kernaghan and Langford, *The Responsible Public Servant*, 119.

25 Ibid.

26 Kenneth Kernaghan, 'An Honour to Be Coveted: Pride, Recognition, and Public Service,' *Canadian Public Administration* 44 (2001): 67–83.

27 Kernaghan, 'Pride and Recognition in the Public Service,' 73.

28 Ibid., 74.

29 Ibid., 75.

30 Ibid., 77.

31 Ibid., 77.

32 Ibid., 80.

33 Bourgault and Gusella, 'Performance, Pride and Recognition,' 38.

34 Kernaghan, 'Pride and Recognition in the Public Service,' 68.

35 Ibid., 79.

36 Kernaghan, 'Rediscovering Public Service,' 13.

37 In fact a first wave of programs existed in federal government in the early 1980s. Many were put aside after 1988, after cutbacks and a lost sense of purpose for the programs.

38 Bourgault and Gusella, 'Performance, Pride and Recognition,' 40.

39 Kernaghan, 'Pride and Recognition in the Public Service.'

40 Roy Saunderson, 'Survey Findings of the Effectiveness of Employee Recognition in the Public Sector,' *Public Personnel Management* 33, no. 3 (2004): 267.

41 Bourgault and Gusella, 'Performance, Pride and Recognition,' 46.

42 Saunderson, 'Survey Findings,' 271.

43 Kernaghan, 'An Honour to Be Coveted,' 80.

PART III

Service Delivery

Service provision has always been one of the key roles played by government. In fact, this is the face of government that most citizens see every day. For a variety of reasons, there has been an increasing emphasis on better service provision over the past few years. However, better service provision has come to be defined not just as delivering a better widget, but also as being in touch with citizens to ensure that the services provided are of the kind and quality desired by them. Governments have adopted new philosophies and begun to use new technologies to ensure that they are in touch with citizens.

In chapter 8, the first in this part, Sandford Borins and David Brown discuss how governments have been using computer technology to consult with citizens. The authors' use of a channel choice framework is a reminder that governments have been consulting with citizens for some time in a variety of different ways, including public meetings, formal hearings, and written submissions. In this vein, the use of computer technology amounts to a conscious choice to employ a new method of consultation.

The chapter then presents information about four e-consultations conducted by the federal government and four by Ontario. Here, the authors identify five common themes:

- The creation of organizational capacity for consultation. This has been difficult because it has required both the use of a new technology and the development of more interdepartmental and interdisciplinary interaction.
- Relationships between websites and portals used for consultation.
- Coordination and timing of consultation initiatives during a government's mandate.

- Consultation and channel choice.
- The potential to move beyond consultation to more intensive citizen engagement.

Borins and Brown conclude that 'experience with e-consultation in both the federal and Ontario governments has been positive enough to launch and sustain electronic channels as a permanent feature of the policy development landscape.' They go on to provide some very useful detailed findings relating to the implementation of the initiatives.

In chapter 9, Jennifer Berardi discusses another recent innovation in service delivery – partnerships. Specifically, she examines the partnership between the Ontario Lottery and Gaming Corporation (OLGC) and the Falls Management Company (FMC), which operates two casinos in Niagara Falls, Ontario. She notes that the Ontario government has been reluctant to call this a partnership, but she argues that it meets a number of the criteria that are traditionally employed to distinguish partnerships.

This particular partnership has been dogged with controversy from the very beginning, when the acceptance of FMC's proposal was accompanied by allegations of conflict of interest. This has been followed by an ongoing controversy relating to the fact that FMC has not built an 'off-site attractor' such as an amphitheatre to spread the tourism benefits beyond the casino itself.

Berardi laments that the confidentiality of the agreement between OLGC and FMC makes it difficult to determine whether all the components of a partnership have actually been met. She does conclude that by the available evidence, most but not all characteristics of a partnership are present.

She ends her chapter with a list of seven lessons learned about establishing future partnerships. She cautions that a 'difficulty of utilizing alternative methods of service delivery such as the FMC-OLGC operating agreement, is that it requires a shift in thinking on behalf of the public. In this case, accountability, openness, and transparency are diminished as the cost of doing business with the private sector. This was the tradeoff. As shown in this case study, the consequence of this secrecy is general confusion about who is really in charge and whether the OLGC is really upholding the public interest.' The general impression is that this partnership has provided significant benefits in the form of increased tourism and the jobs that go along with that, but that there has also been some level of local dissatisfaction with the partnership.

Chapter 10 documents the development of the Citizen Centred Service Initiative as told by one of the primary architects of the system – Brian Marson. Citizen Centred Service is an action research approach to determining the wants and expectations of Canadians with regard to service delivery, which leads to improvements in systems of service delivery.

Marson explains how Canada has become a leader in service quality by using extensive surveys to develop a 'citizens-eye view' or an 'outside-in' approach to service delivery. The Citizen Centred Service Network created the Common Measurement Tool – a bank of questions that can be used by any service organization to compare citizens' perceptions of service delivery. The network also identified the drivers of citizen satisfaction, which turned out to be these: timeliness; knowledge and competence; courtesy and the 'extra mile'; fairness; and outcome. The practical application of this approach is visible in the fact that when managers learned that timeliness was both the most important driver and the one most in need of improvement, they applied this finding to improve citizen satisfaction with services.

The improvements have come in the form of blue pages in the telephone book, single-window approaches that co-locate many services from several governments and provide advice about the locations of others, and a single-window Web portal for all government services.

More significantly, the Citizen Centred Service Network has brought together service professionals from many governments as well as academics interested in the field to study the issue in more depth and to determine what the next major improvements in the quality of service delivery will be.

In his conclusion, Marson argues that Canada has become an international leader in the field of measuring the quality of service delivery and instituting improvements in the quality of services as a result of undertaking the forms of systematic review inherent in this initiative.

8 E-consultation: Technology at the Interface between Civil Society and Government

SANDFORD BORINS AND DAVID BROWN[1]

This contribution deals with Ken Kernaghan's most recent interest: the ever-expanding role of information technology (IT) in public administration. This interest has emerged from his work on service delivery and organizational restructuring, discussed in his co-authored book *The New Public Organization*.[2] As the importance of IT's role as a facilitator of change has become evident, Kernaghan has begun looking more closely at the management of IT within the public sector. Two of his most recent papers[3] deal specifically with IT, the first integrating it into public administration theory and practice, and the second examining its role in the development of integrated service delivery. Both papers display the hallmarks of his research: interest in new developments, and the ability to relate that which is new to pre-existing intellectual and organizational structures. Guided by a careful reading of the evidence, Kernaghan steers a middle course between the utopianism of the techno-enthusiasts and the cynicism of the techno-critics.

Our research shares a similar understanding as we look at IT as a new medium for interaction between society and government. Interactions occur in three main areas: the political system, service delivery, and policy making. The third is the focus of this chapter, in particular the impact of IT on public consultation, a vital link between policy making and the other two areas. This research employs a channel choice framework; thus online consultation is seen as an alternative to other forms, for example, written communications or attendance at public meetings or hearings chaired by legislators or regulators.[4] We deal mainly with citizen consultation, which involves government receiving information about citizens' views, and less with citizen engagement, in which government enters into deliberative dialogue and shared decision making with citizens.[5] This is because most of what we have observed was consultation rather than engagement, and also because we see the former as a prelude to the latter. This chapter begins with eight short case studies of recent consultations – four in Ontario and four at the federal level. The cases were chosen to display the diversity of consultations at each level of government: for the federal government, consultations on policy development and on regulation; and for the Ontario government, consultations initiated by Cabinet Office and consultations initiated by line ministries. We then discuss five common themes that emerge from the cases: the creation of organizational capacity for consultation; relationships between websites and portals used for consultation; the coordination and timing of consultation initiatives during a government's mandate; consultation and channel choice; and the potential to move beyond consultation towards more intensive citizen engagement.

E-Consultation in the Federal Government

While this has never been central to its policy process, the federal government has historically made use of various public consultation tools, most notably Royal Commissions and White and Green Papers, to solicit input on major public policy issues and public opinion research for both policy and political purposes. Consultations became more common in the early 1990s – for example, the Mulroney government's Green Plan of 1990 included an extensive public consultation exercise.[6] In the early Chretien years, then-Finance Minister Paul Martin made extensive use of public consultation in developing budget measures to reduce the deficit, and the Department of Finance was an early adopter of the Internet to publish and obtain feedback on budget documents. In 1996 a requirement to consult stakeholders and Canadians in general became part of a major reform of the government's regulatory process. A fundamental element of all consultation activities has been the requirement, based on the Official Languages Act, that they be equally accessible in all channels in both English and French.

The emergence of the Internet in the early 1990s and the launch of the Government of Canada website[7] in 1995 were paralleled by experiments with online citizen engagement methodologies, including a project initiated by Public Works and Government Services Canada (PWGSC) in 1996 for the G7 Government On-Line and Democracy initiative. By 2000 the Privy Council Office Communications Secretariat had taken an interest in online consultation and begun to partner with the PWGSC to sponsor the development of online methodologies as well as an e-consultation community of practice within the federal government to put them to use. An important step was the establishment within the PWGSC of the On-Line Consultation Technical Centre of Expertise, headed by Elisabeth Richard, a pioneer in government use of the Internet.[8]

The idea of establishing an online consultation portal was first considered in 2000 in discussions led by Debbie Cook at the Privy Council Office. In 2001 she spent six months on exchange in the British Cabinet Office studying the Blair government's approach to online consultation, which was by then a prominent feature of its official website. Subsequently, Heritage Canada took the lead in launching a pilot public consultation portal, in 2003, and then in developing a business case for a permanent portal.[9] The deputy minister of Heritage, Alex Himelfarb, became Cabinet Secretary in 2002 and was an important supporter of the initiative in both positions. In December 2004 the Treasury Board Government Communications Policy was revised to include a section on consultation and citizen engagement. This mandated a permanent Consulting With Canadians portal,[10] which went live on the Canada Site in April 2005. The policy required that all public consultations be publicized on Consulting With Canadians and set out procedures to be followed when the consultations were online, including ensuring that public feedback was adequately processed. At the same time it was decided to give the Consulting With Canadians portal a low profile, with access through the 'What's New' button on the Canada Site homepage rather than on the homepage itself.[11]

While most of the impetus for these developments came from the public service, this effort was backed at needed points by the Cabinet Secretary and by Prime Minister Martin, who declared his support for online consultation at a Crossing Boundaries Conference in April 2003.[12] The various policy changes also required endorsement by two cabinet committees: Treasury Board, which provides funding and sets the policy framework for federal government communications and consultation; and Operations, which oversees the government's communications activities. Operations has in the past often been chaired by the deputy prime minister; in the absence of such a portfolio in the Harper government, it is chaired by Jim Prentice, the minister of Industry.

Consultations are generally considered to be related to three areas of public policy development: major national policy issues, regulations, and service delivery.[13] The first two in particular engage ministers, while the third is largely the domain of officials. The most fully prescribed area is the development of regulations. *Canada Gazette*, the official government newspaper published by the PWGSC, has online and paper editions, both legally authoritative. The government's 2007 Cabinet Directive on Streamlining Regulation, administered by the Treasury Board Secretariat, requires that all draft regulations be prepublished in Part I of the *Gazette* for 'timely and thorough consultation with the interested parties,' using the channel of the public's choice. The final texts must be published in Part II, showing the results of the Part I consultations.[14]

Four cases illustrate the federal government's experience with e-consultations. Without necessarily being fully representative, two of these illustrate uses of e-consultation in the policy development context: the 2003 foreign policy review, in which the sponsoring minister was actively involved; and the spam task force, which worked at the level of officials and stakeholders. The COX-2 inhibitors and Spike TV are two quite different examples of e-consultation in the regulatory context.

1 *Dialogue on Foreign Policy*

On 22 January 2003, Foreign Affairs and International Trade Minister Bill Graham announced a Dialogue on Canadian Foreign Policy, based on a public discussion paper and an extensive program of public consultations, which continued until 1 May 2003. The process ended with a 'Report to Canadians' from Graham dated 27 June 2003. The consultations were informed by the philosophy that 'foreign policy must be informed by public advice fully representative of our country's diverse population and regions.' They involved an intensive range of activities, including fifteen town hall meetings across Canada, nineteen expert round tables, a national Youth Forum, meetings with the provinces, and parallel activities by the House of Commons Standing Committee on Foreign Affairs and International Trade.

Technology-based methodologies were integral to the process. Consultation documents were available online, and some 28,000 copies of the discussion paper were downloaded. More than 3,400 responses to the paper's five themes were submitted online in English and another 378 in French. (A subject for further inquiry is how to explain the disproportionately small number of submissions in French.) A bilingual, moderated online discussion forum was available for each of the five themes, with almost 2,000 participants; the town halls were webcast, and the documents from the expert round tables were posted to the consultation site along with video interviews with participants and weekly summaries of the round tables and the online discussion forums. All of this was supported by an extensive consultation website on the DFAIT site containing numerous information resources.[15]

Graham was actively involved in the process; for example, he participated personally in all fifteen town halls, and five of his cabinet colleagues participated in various ways. This undoubtedly stimulated public interest in the process and raised expectations about the outcome. The use of the website was seen by DFAIT as one of the innovative aspects of the consultation, and there was a conscious effort to expand the traditional array of consultative tools, including considerable care to establish proper rules of conduct for participation in the online discussion forum.[16] This added dimension clearly broadened the reach of the consultation by providing an accessible and accurate source of information about the process and a record of what was being said. It is unlikely that such extensive consultations could have been carried out in a three-month period without the website and online tools. Multichannel approaches to individual events such as town halls (in-person events complemented by advance online notice, simultaneous webcasting, and online posting of the results) made them more widely accessible and probably also gave them greater depth.

In the end, however, the consultation was an 'artistic success' but a political failure. Coming at the end of the Chretien government and for practical purposes feeding into a policy-making vacuum, Graham's Response to Canadians was essentially a personal statement in which he could only assert that the results of the consultation would inform his discussions with cabinet colleagues.[17] In any event, he was moved to the Defence portfolio when Paul Martin came into office in December 2003, and the new prime minister chose to launch a completely new process for reviewing foreign policy, which resulted in an international policy statement written by officials without any further public consultation.

2   Spam Task Force Online Forum

Spam, or unsolicited commercial email, is an artefact of the online environment. In May 2004, Lucienne Robillard, the minister of Industry, created a Special Task Force on spam to oversee implementation of a comprehensive action plan to reduce the volume of unsolicited commercial email. The task force brought together experts and stakeholders representing Internet service providers, businesses that use email for legitimate commercial activity, and consumers. The action plan was itself the product of earlier consultative activity, and the ten members of the task force were asked to consult through implementation working groups in each of the action plan's five areas.

The task force met nine times over six months, issuing its report in May 2005. Each working group hosted an online forum in which the public was invited to comment on a discussion paper and other task force documents with the promise that comments would be taken into account by the task force. This yielded 171 postings on the online bulletin board (which was not, however, carried on the Consulting With Canadians portal). In addition to this were a webcast stakeholder round table and a private online forum for the members of the task force and working groups.[18]

The exercise was sponsored by the branch in Industry Canada that had supported the Information Highway Advisory Council in the mid-1990s and later efforts to consult the IT-related business community. The online element was considered to be one part of the larger task force effort. The public forum was judged to have introduced a broader range of views and to have been more conversational in nature. The stakeholder discussions were more expert but less lively. The private forum turned out to be an effective method of disseminating information and documents to task force participants, but not as strong as more traditional means such as email and listservs for group discussion among them. While both the internal and the public online forums involved some initial cost to construct, they required limited resources to run. In the final judgment, the online element was considered worthwhile and worth using again in appropriate circumstances.[19]

3 *Selective COX-2 Inhibitors NSAIDs Expert Panel and Public Discussion*

Health Canada's Health Products and Food Branch is responsible for regulating pharmaceutical products. It does its own product testing and monitoring; it also convenes advisory panels of experts to review available information and provide advice on related issues, including product safety and effectiveness. An effort is made to tap into academic, scientific, patient, and other stakeholder concerns. Typically, the department provides the panel with a statement of the advice it is looking for and a series of questions to shape the panel's discussion. Health Canada considers the panel's advice but is not bound by it. The consultations are organized by the Office of Consumer and Public Involvement, a unit within the Health Protection Branch.

In 1999, Health Canada approved the marketing of COX-2 inhibitor non-steroidal anti-inflammatory drugs (NSAIDs) – a family of arthritis medication designed to reduce gastrointestinal side effects such as ulcers. Celebrex, Bextra, and Vioxx were widely distributed. In 2004, Vioxx and Bextra were withdrawn by their manufacturers because of concerns about increased incidence of heart attacks and strokes among users, including reported deaths. In the spring of 2005 the Health Protection and Food Branch established an expert panel to advise on the risks and benefits of the COX-2 inhibitor NSAIDs, including additional research that might be required. This advice would inform specific regulatory decisions, which are subject to prepublishing in *Canada Gazette*.

The Expert Advisory Panel met in Ottawa on 9 and 10 June 2005, and its report was made public on 5 July 2005. It recommended that Celebrex and Vioxx be permitted to stay on the market and that additional measures be taken to ensure that the risks in using the drugs were addressed. In the lead-up to the panel meetings, a public forum was opened on the Health Canada site from 18 May to 9 June 2005, to permit input from members of the public, including patients who had been both positively and adversely affected by COX-2 inhibitors, and from interested organizations. Some sixty responses were provided in paper and electronic form to the Office of Consumer and Public Involvement, which posted them on the website within five business days of receipt. The first day of the panel meeting was open to the public and included a presentation by the Office of Consumer and Public Involvement of the results of the public forum, as well as presentations from Health Canada and pharmaceutical manufacturers, all of which were also posted on the website. The second day of the panel meeting involved a closed discussion among panel members of the various communications they had received.[20]

The consultation was posted on the Consulting With Canadians portal and reflects a methodology designed by the Health Protection and Food Branch to keep regulatory decision-making at arm's length from politicians, while recognizing its considerable public sensitivity. An important part of the process was, therefore, to ensure that the affiliations and interests of all official contributors to the Expert Advisory

Panel were declared and that participants in the public forum were encouraged to declare their interests voluntarily.

4 *Distribution of Spike TV – Call for Comments*

In March 2004 the Canadian Radio-television and Telecommunications Commission (CRTC) issued a call for comments on a request from the Canadian Association of Broadcasters (CAB) that Spike TV be removed from the list of non-Canadian programming services that could be carried by Canadian cable and satellite distribution companies. The consultation, which was posted on the Consulting With Canadians site, was open to all interested parties, including the general public. It was conducted entirely online, and the posted submissions formed the basis of the commission's decision – to reject the CAB application and approve Spike TV for distribution in Canada – issued in January 2005.

The issue arose when the Nashville Network (TNN), based in the United States, was taken over by Viacom in August of 2003 and re-branded as Spike TV, a 'men's lifestyle' programming service. The CAB, representing Canadian-based television networks including pay and specialty channels, argued that the programming changes were so extensive that Spike TV was no longer covered by the previous approval for TNN and that it posed a competitive threat to Canadian broadcasters and distributors.

The CRTC consultation lasted two months and generated 219 submissions, 184 opposed to the CAB submission. Submissions – from individuals, corporate stakeholders, national associations, and several MPs – were sent by mail, email, or fax. All were posted on the CRTC website in downloadable form and were also available in paper form for consultation in CRTC offices across the country. The CRTC made it clear that its decision was based solely on this material, combined with its own internal staff work.[21]

This case illustrates the use that a regulatory agency can make of the online medium in addressing a relatively straightforward and non-technical issue with a wide range of public and stakeholder perspectives. The input and discussion was entirely in writing, as an alternative to public hearings, but the focal point of that exchange was the postings on the CRTC website. The chosen medium does not seem to have been controversial, perhaps helped by the fact that the participants in the consultation could be expected to be reasonably technologically oriented. (The Spike TV target audience – males between eighteen and forty-nine – is also among the highest users of the Internet.) It seems likely that this will become a standard part of the public consultations toolkit for the CRTC and perhaps other regulatory agencies.

E-consultation in Ontario

The Harris government, elected in 1995, believed that by winning power on the basis of a detailed election manifesto – the Common Sense Revolution – it had ipso facto consulted the voters, and that its obligation was to enact the provisions of that manifesto. Premier Harris had little enthusiasm for extensive public consultation about particular pieces of legislation and saw elaborate consultation exercises as simply giving the government's political enemies a platform. His successor, Ernie Eves, who took power in March 2002, was more pragmatic, as evidenced for example by his departing from the Common Sense Revolution's commitment to privatize Ontario Hydro. The Eves government took the first steps in e-consultation. Some low-key e-consultations were initiated by individual ministries, such as Municipal Affairs and Housing's province-wide consultation on 'smart growth' and Transportation's consultation on aggressive driving. The most significant central e-consultation dealt with the 2003 Throne Speech, which was placed on the government's homepage on a consultation site. There were 9,100 visitors to the website, and 2,700 of them completed an online questionnaire.[22]

The government's IT organization, based in the Management Board Secretariat, was responding to the politicians' emerging interest in e-consultation. Corporate chief strategist Joan McCalla, a senior IT official, hired Melissa Thomson to do background work on e-consultation. Thomson had entered the Ontario Public Service (OPS) through its internship program, which is geared towards attracting talented recent graduates. Thomson established a staff-level working group that met monthly to compare departmental experience in and plans for consultation. But without strong political support, public servants were reluctant to do much more. That political support came when the McGuinty government took office. One of the six themes in the Liberal election campaign had been 'strengthening democracy,' and included in this were commitments to mandatory public hearings for major legislation and the use of citizens' juries.[23]

Below we offer four case studies showing the diversity of consultations launched during the McGuinty government's first year. The first three were central initiatives; the last involved six consultations initiated by the Ministry of Municipal Affairs and Housing.

1 *Ideas Campaign*

The Liberals' campaign document included a commitment to a valued public service, and it was to this commitment that the McGuinty government first turned. In a letter emailed to all public servants the day he took office, McGuinty wrote that 'our team is excited about working with you to implement real, positive change. Ontario is fortunate to have a public service that is second to none.'[24] He asked the OPS for ideas about ways to improve the quality, delivery, and efficiency of public services.

The Ideas Campaign was launched on 18 December 2003, less than two months after McGuinty took office. It involved a call centre, group brainstorming, and an Intranet site available to all public servants on a common desktop platform. By the time the campaign concluded on 31 January 2004, Ontario's 62,000 public servants had made a total of 11,500 suggestions, 92 per cent of which were submitted through the Intranet site. This was a far greater response than expected. The popularity of online submission indicates that Ontario public servants are comfortable with this technology and also that the software employed was user friendly.

In a sense, the Ideas Campaign was *too* successful. So many ideas were received that committees of middle managers required considerable time and effort to categorize and evaluate them. Ideas that made it through the initial assessment were sent to the relevant ministry – though it often took time to determine which ministry that was – and some have since been implemented. In many cases, public servants were suggesting things that the OPS was already doing. And given the ultimate decentralization of the exercise, the government has not attempted to produce a global list of the top ten or twenty ideas emanating from the campaign.[25]

2 *2004 Budget Consultation*

The Eves government had forecast a budget roughly in balance in the 2003–04 fiscal year, and all three parties used this forecast in developing their platforms for the 2003 election. The Liberals promised many new initiatives that would be funded by expected revenue growth and by the cancellation of some proposed Conservative tax cuts. During the campaign, however, independent analysts began to forecast a deficit approaching $5 billion. During the transition period, McGuinty asked a former provincial auditor to analyse the forecasts, and he confirmed the pessimistic view of the analysts. As a consequence, the key issue that faced the Liberals on taking office was how to deal with the large and unexpected deficit as well as its implications for their election platform.

The McGuinty government could have made the spending cuts and tax increases necessary to balance the budget unilaterally, and blamed the Eves government. Instead it launched a public consultation process regarding priorities for budget cuts and speed of eliminating the deficit. In effect, it was attempting to renegotiate its mandate with the electorate. The public consultation was conducted by a full panoply of traditional approaches – travelling legislative committee meetings, meetings between representatives of the Finance Ministry and interest groups, and town hall meetings chaired by MPPs – as well as new ones, such as citizens' juries and an online questionnaire. Citizens' juries and meetings heard from 2,500 individuals and 540 interest groups and organizations. The online consultation was established at a new site[26] located just below the premier's site on the Government of Ontario homepage. It used the slogan 'Delivering Change' and a graphic of diverse faces — both reminiscent of the Liberals' campaign website. The consultation site was visited by 14,000 people. It contained a comprehensive policy paper laying out deficit projections and policy alternatives, such as new taxes and user fees, spending cuts, and asset sales. This was followed by a questionnaire that asked for preferences among these alternatives and priorities for government spending. A measure of interactivity was provided, in the sense that respondents could see the distribution of responses to date, including their own. The questionnaire was completed by 1,500 people, only 10 per cent of visitors to the site, which suggests that it was too long and complicated.

The budget focused on health care and elementary and secondary education as the two key priorities, set out a three-year schedule for eliminating the deficit, introduced a progressive tax earmarked for health care spending, and increased a variety of user fees; but it did not attempt to raise revenue through asset sales. All of these directions were broadly consistent with the results of the public consultation.

The health tax (termed the employer health levy) became a source of controversy because, during the election campaign, McGuinty had made a high-profile commitment not to raise taxes. His critics, in particular the media and taxpayer groups, argued that McGuinty had been well aware of the province's deteriorating fiscal situation during the campaign and that, cynically, he had promised new programs he knew he would not be able to deliver without raising taxes. The McGuinty government had not anticipated these attacks and did not respond effectively.

The view in the Premier's Office, Cabinet Office, and Finance was that the 2004 budget had established clear fiscal directions for the government's mandate, so the objective of the 2005 budget was to implement those directions. The people had been consulted in 2004 and they had spoken, so the government would look indecisive if it launched another full-scale consultation.[27] Thus, the e-consultation on Town Hall Ontario for the 2005 budget was simply a paragraph outlining the government's approach to tackling the deficit and asking three questions: What other measures should be taken to constrain spending and modernize government? Where should there be cuts to fund any spending increases? And how should the federal government, which by the province's estimate receives $23 billion more in taxes from Ontario than Ontario receives in return, help solve the problem? The questionnaire was not at all interactive; individuals completing it did not see other responses or even a summary of them.

3 Ontario Conserves

The Ontario Conserves initiative was driven by the Premier's Office, which wanted to promote a culture of conservation and sustainability. The broad theme of conservation was subdivided into four subthemes – air, earth, water, and energy – and fifteen ministries contributed to the consultation document. This consultation differed from the others in that its objectives were education and raising awareness rather than soliciting public reaction. It provided substantial information about why and how to conserve – for example, a conservation guide in eleven languages. It also featured a moderated ideas exchange that allowed visitors to the site to read others' suggestions and submit their own. Since the consultation began in July 2004, 113 ideas have been posted on the exchange, but it is not clear how many had come from individual citizens, as opposed to the bureaucracy. The consultation, still ongoing at time of writing, appears both on Town Hall Ontario and on a URL of its own.[28] This consultation could change to the more common approach of asking for public reaction if the government decides to propose legislation.

4 *Ministry of Municipal Affairs and Housing Consultations*

The Ministry of Municipal Affairs and Housing (MMAH) was the most active of all ministries in consultation, launching consultations on the following six topics: rent reform, protection of the green belt surrounding Toronto (in two phases), planning reform, rural planning, and a review of the Municipal Act. In addition to public meetings and facilitated stakeholder consultations, all had an online component that included consultation documents and online surveys. Only the three most significant consultations – green belt protection, rent reform, and planning reform – were linked to the Town Hall Ontario website. The expertise for this work was found internally in the Technology and Business Solutions Branch and Communications Branch. The latter developed and managed the web pages and questionnaires for the different branches of MMAH that had overall responsibility for each consultation. Content management software already in use by the ministry was employed. The incremental cost of adding an e-consultation component to each consultation was approximately $22,000, consisting mainly of software modification, server testing, and staff time.[29]

The balance between online and paper questionnaires varied from consultation to consultation, depending largely on how the two alternatives were promoted to target groups. In the second phase of the green belt protection consultation, 90 per cent of approximately two thousand surveys were submitted online, while in the rent reform consultation, the ratio was fifty–fifty. In the case of rent reform, concern about the digital divide prompted an emphasis on, and widespread distribution of, postage-paid paper questionnaires. One instance of an entirely online component was the display of detailed maps of the green belt on the MMAH website. It was considered too expensive to publish and distribute paper maps. Landowners in the green belt area were intensely interested in how green belt protection policies would affect them, and as a consequence the map pages had 62,000 visits.[30]

Seeing the Big Picture

The objective of this section is to develop a 'big picture' of consultation in the federal and Ontario governments based on the smaller pictures of the eight cases. Electronic consultation is relatively new to the federal and Ontario governments, and its development has largely paralleled the general evolution of their use of technology in dealings with the public. That is, it has moved from a marginal to an increasingly central role in combination with other, more traditional channels. With the development of the Internet, there has been a systematic effort in the federal government at the working and middle management levels, encouraged by the central agencies and a few key senior managers, to explore and entrench e-consultation tools and activities. It was not adopted as a government-wide priority by the Chretien government; since then, however, e-consultation has gradually been taken on board by individual ministers, in particular as part of the regulatory process, where it offers clear advantages for arm's-length decision making. Under the Martin government, e-consultation gradually became more structured and was cautiously linked to efforts to address the democratic deficit.

In Ontario there was interest in e-consultation at the level of individual ministries. At the political level, the Harris government lacked interest in consultation of any kind; the Eves government showed greater receptiveness. The McGuinty government took office with a strong commitment to consultation, which led to central initiatives and a much more receptive climate for ministerial initiatives.

The themes presented below are the components of a bigger picture of practices that both governments have been developing to manage e-consultation.

1 *Organizational Capacity*

The federal government's organizational capacity to use e-consultation has matured over the past ten years. From the outset, a priority for the PCO Communications Secretariat and the PWGSC – the public service leaders in this area – was to understand the nature and implications of the technology and its potential applications. At early stages this primarily involved facilitating the emergence of a 'community of practice' among interested departments and bringing in outside expertise. With the establishment of the Centre of Expertise on On-Line Consultation Technologies at PWGSC, a permanent source of technologically oriented but policy-sensitive advice became available. The Treasury Board Secretariat Chief Information Officer Branch and Government Communications Policy Office (initially combined, more recently not) have supported these developments without actively promoting them.

The 2004 changes to the Government Communications Policy provided the backbone for the current federal approach. Specifically, that policy recognized the Consulting With Canadians portal as the permanent government consultation site; also, PCO approval would be required from now on for all consultation initiatives, which were to be posted on Consulting With Canadians. The policy now also requires departments engaging in online consultation to develop a capacity to deal with the input that is provided electronically. These policy changes were approved by two cabinet committees; combined with the ongoing role of the Operations Committee and Prime Minister Martin's known interest, this provided a basic level of collective ministerial support for the adoption of e-consultation by individual ministers.

The biggest challenge has been to embed e-consultation in the ongoing processes of government. E-consultation is by its nature multidisciplinary in that it links together program managers, policy makers, the public communications community, and the information management community – not a natural alliance. Part of the continuing evolution has been that there is no standard model for locating the lead responsibility for e-consultation within departments, and in different parts of the government it can be found in any number of areas. Similarly, e-consultation requires new combinations of public service skills that are still relatively scarce. A key element of the 2004 changes in communication policy was the creation of a more formal role for Directors General of Communications, whose responsibilities now include media relations, publishing, advertising, and polling on behalf of ministers. This group had been cautious about e-consultation owing to concerns about managing public expectations and the potentially large volumes of input. The policy changes have ensured that any e-consultations will be managed, but they have not by themselves brought the methodology into the policy and decision-making mainstream.[31]

Regulations constitute a distinct subset of federal e-consultations. The starting point is policy requirements for public consultation in the early stages of the regulatory process. Each of the seven key regulatory departments (Agriculture, Environment, Finance, Health, Industry, Justice, and Transport) has a regulatory coordinator, and each is a heavy user of the Consulting With Canadians portal. The PCO Orders in Council Division supports the Cabinet Operations Committee, which processes Orders in Council and considers draft primary legislation and the government's legislative strategy, among other functions. The Treasury Board Secretariat Regulatory Affairs Division takes an overview of the regulatory process and has a close working relationship with *Canada Gazette* (the government's newspaper of record) and with the legislative drafting office in the Justice Department.

E-consultation has also been indirectly supported by Government On-Line (GOL), Ottawa's initiative for delivering government services electronically. When established in 1999, GOL excluded initiatives relating to the policy process, including e-consultation. While that has remained the formal position, there is no doubt that the general success of GOL has strengthened the institutional environment and technology infrastructure for e-consultation and fostered a considerably higher level of awareness and support for electronic tools among government program and information managers.

The situation in Ontario has been somewhat different. Without comparable maturity of ministerial capacity for consultation, with fewer central agency resources devoted to supporting ministerial initiatives, and with several central consultation initiatives as an immediate priority, the McGuinty government moved quickly to create capacity in the Consultation Projects Office (CPO). That office was led by Lee Allison Howe, an associate deputy minister with a background in communications, and Joyce Barretto, a senior manager with a similar background, and was staffed by a handful of younger public servants who were or had recently been in the OPS's internship program. One of these secondments was Melissa Thomson, who had been working on consultation strategy in the Office of the Chief Corporate Strategist. She was given primary responsibility for negotiating an agreement to lease and then adapt consultation software from a private sector provider. Another secondment was Allison Killins, a member of MMAH's e-consultation team.[32]

The CPO worked hard to get the Ideas Campaign and budget consultation underway within eight weeks and to run them simultaneously. One of the consequences of the Ideas Campaign's success is that the office was bogged down for several months after the campaign deadline of 31 January 2004 analysing and evaluating submissions. When it came up for air in late spring, the CPO also was given responsibility for Ontario Conserves because of that initiative's interministerial nature.

While the CPO was handling three centrally launched initiatives, other ministries were showing that they, too, had the capacity to manage consultations, including those with an online component. As a result, Cabinet Office decided to wind down the CPO, and it closed in April 2005. All of its staff were reassigned to Cabinet Office, CPO's original home, or to other ministries. Cabinet Office moved away from active engagement in consultation; the CIO's office moved back into the area. In fall 2004 the latter established a small e-Citizen Engagement Support Office with a mandate to support consultation and citizen engagement initiatives in other ministries – for example, by developing guidelines for e-citizen engagement, undertaking pilot projects such as public access terminals in libraries in several rural communities, and chairing a committee where ministries could share consultation experiences.[33]

2 *Websites and Portals*

The Consulting With Canadians portal developed in the context of the federal government's primary site – now the Canada Site – which has evolved considerably since it was first launched in 1995. From the outset, important considerations in developing the Canada Site and related sites were to ensure that the federal presence on the World Wide Web was clearly identifiable as belonging to the Government of Canada, that the site was readily accessible, and that it conformed with official-language requirements. While every government agency and major program has established its own website within common guidelines, the focal point since 2000 for federal dealings with the public has been three gateways and approximately thirty clusters located on the Canada Site. These are structured around defined segments of the Canadian and international population.

Even though public consultation fell outside the formal scope of GOL, the citizen-centred philosophy and well-developed infrastructure of the Canada Site made it an obvious place to start when it came to taking a similar portal-based approach. The two-step approach – a pilot project sponsored by a department, with central agency encouragement, followed by the embedding of the e-consultation site in the Canada Site – was also consistent with the GOL approach. The major debate focused on what profile to give to Consulting With Canadians. When it was relaunched on the Canada Site, access was provided through the What's New button on the Canada Site homepage rather than through a listing on the homepage itself. Departments were given six months from the relaunch in April 2005 to list all of their consultation activities on Consulting With Canadians. Central agency officials thought it might be two or three years before the level of activity was sufficient to warrant placing the Consulting With Canadians link on the homepage itself. Even then, Consulting With Canadians is not a consultation site as such; rather, it is a listing of consultations. Actual online consultations are found on the departmental sites concerned.[34]

In the early days of Consulting With Canadians, most of the listed consultations related to regulatory activity. Besides linking to the departmental sites, Consulting With Canadians linked to two other sites that bear on regulations:

- *Canada Gazette*, which is the authoritative source of proposed and existing regulations.
- House of Commons sites related to the legislative process.[35]

It is rather curious that the Regulations cluster (www.regulation. gc.ca), which is linked to the Canada Business Service Centre on the Canada Business Gateway, was at first not linked to this network even though its purpose was to help the private sector navigate the regulatory maze. Following the enactment of a new Cabinet Directive on Streamlining Regulation in April 2007, the site is now the locus for the government's regulatory policy. The companion Treasury Board Secretariat Regulatory Affairs website provides links to a wide range of federal and other governmental websites concerned with regulations.

After assuming office in February 2006, the Harper government retained the policy framework for government communications, consultation, and regulations that had been developed by its predecessors, though it made some adjustments to the central agency and to the common service machinery linked to that framework. The most important change was that the regulatory affairs policy centre was transferred from PCO to the Treasury Board Secretariat; however, the Cabinet Operations Committee retained its decision-making role for communications matters. In our review of the listings on the Consulting With Canadians portal in November 2006, we found that after the Harper government had been in office for ten months, the site was still being used for regulatory and policy consultations, just as it had been during the Martin government.

In Ontario the most significant development was the spectacular rise and fall of the Town Hall Ontario portal.[36] That portal was started shortly after the 2004 budget consultation was launched, and it was assigned a prominent button on the right sidebar of the Government of Ontario homepage, just under the button for Premier McGuinty's site. Soon afterwards a number of consultations were posted on Town Hall Ontario. As we discuss below, so many consultations were happening that Cabinet Office started deciding which ones would be posted on Town Hall Ontario and which would be left on ministerial homepages. By the time the intense consultation that characterized the first year of the McGuinty government came to an end, Town Hall Ontario's role had greatly diminished and it had been removed from the Government of Ontario homepage. At the time of writing, it hosts only one active consultation, Ontario Conserves. However, it also serves as an archive of completed consultations.[37]

The rise of Town Hall Ontario coincided with the McGuinty government's intensely consultative first year. A portal provided two advantages in that context. When members of the public searched online for a particular consultation of interest, they were likely to find it through the portal, which facilitated searching and also exposed them to other consultations that might be of interest. The portal also established a place where public servants conducting a consultation could see other ongoing consultations; in this way it supported a developing community of practice.[38]

When the McGuinty government reduced the pace of consultation, less new business appeared on Town Hall Ontario. Individual ministries had mixed opinions of Town Hall Ontario. They were happy to have a link to it, but they also preferred to publicize the consultation pages they had built on their own sites. For example, MMAH[39] wanted to create a web presence directly related to its issue – green belt protection – rather than an indirect link to a general-purpose portal.[40] When the green belt consultation was a top priority for the government, it had its own link on the Government of Ontario homepage. Similarly, the Premier's Office now prefers to create a separate website for each new initiative and to display it as a button on the Government of Ontario homepage. For example, in mid-July 2005, besides buttons for the premier's page and the premier's kids zone, which are ongoing, there were buttons for major policy initiatives (the 2005 budget, Results Ontario) as well as buttons for various flavours of the month: Fair Share – Strong Ontario (Ontario's case for greater federal funding), tsunami relief, consultations about the New City of Toronto Act, and the Shared Air Summit held on 20 June 2005. These buttons have changed over time, but the point to recognize is that the Premier's Office is using the government's homepage for its major consultation initiatives instead of a consultation portal.

Ontario's recent experience does raise questions about the future of consultation portals. A consultation portal is intrinsically different from a service portal. In the latter, individuals approach the government for service and are encouraged to do so through a portal structure that will ultimately lead them to the right door. With consultations, the government is approaching individuals and groups and encouraging them to comment. But citizens are less likely to be interested in consultation in general than in consultation about issues of concern to them. Citizens are therefore unlikely to go to a consultation portal to see if there is something there they want to comment on; rather, they need to be informed that there is a consultation happening on an issue of concern to them. And from the point of view of the ministry or ministries doing the consultation, the best way is to frame the consultation in terms of that particular issue. This being so, the most a consultation portal can do is provide a back door for individuals who saw an ad for a specific consultation, but who forgot the URL, to find their desired consultation. Portals may be more useful for institutional users and for individuals who participate regularly in specific areas of public policy, such as regulations.

3 Consultation, Coordination, and a Government's Mandate

In the early years in particular, the impetus for developing an e-consultation capacity in the federal government came primarily from interested officials in central agencies and in departments that had a history of public consultation. It was not driven by either top management or politicians, and for some time it had a 'below the radar' quality. This hesitation had several elements, including concerns among politicians that direct online contact between public servants and the public would risk creating competition with the roles of MPs and ministers, as well as concerns among the communications community that e-consultations would create unmanageable expectations and resource pressures. These concerns were gradually assuaged by the gradualist approach adopted by the PCO and the PWGSC, by an accumulation of experience with the e-consultation medium, and by the movement of electronic channels into the mainstream of government interactions with the public. Because the central agencies were involved from the outset, albeit not always enthusiastically as institutions (though some individuals played leading roles), it was a natural step for e-consultation to be embedded in central agency policy and coordination machinery. Less clear is whether a single model will develop in departments – leaving aside the regulatory process – given the number of different disciplines involved. The fact that the PCO, in support of the Cabinet Operations Committee, signs off on new consultation initiatives whether or not they have an online component ensures that departmental ministers are also involved.[41]

A new element was introduced with the announcement in the 2005 budget that the Canada Site would be made part of Service Canada. It was not clear what kind of role this would assign to Service Canada, given that its mandate essentially coincides with that of the Canadians Gateway whereas the Canada Site provides services on behalf of the government as a whole.

To date, the impact of the electoral mandate cycle at the federal level is also unclear. The Martin government, which came to office at the end of a mandate cycle, did not launch major public consultation exercises though it did strengthen the policy and institutional framework for consultation, in particular online. However, the final year of the Chretien government saw at least two ministerially led public consultation exercises, on foreign policy and on a national identity card. Both, however, turned out to reflect the personal agendas of ministers who expected to leave their portfolios; thus they did not lead to changes in government policy. The election of minority governments in 2004 and 2006 rendered the issue of planning for a mandate cycle irrelevant, since neither government expected to complete a full cycle.

The McGuinty government's first term was completely different, since it was elected with a strong majority and had the luxury of planning for a full cycle. In its first year in office it started numerous consultations. Besides the ones discussed earlier, there were consultations about waste diversion (Ministry of the Environment), sustainable development of the Great Lakes Water Basin and provincial parks (both Ministry of Natural Resources), postsecondary education (Ministry of Colleges and Universities), and mandatory retirement (Ministry of Labour). The Liberals came to power with ambitious plans and a deficit that was higher than anticipated when the plans were made; consultation, then, was a means to realign plans and fiscal realities. Some of the McGuinty government's plans were vague, and perhaps consultation helped bring precision to them. Finally, the McGuinty government believed that democracy demands consultation and that the Harris government's disinclination to consult had been undemocratic.

Launching so many consultations at the same time threatened to lead to consultation overload; to avoid this, Cabinet Office played the role of 'air traffic controller,' coordinating consultations in order to set priorities and ensure that ministries were aware of one another's efforts. Cabinet Office allocated space on the Town Hall Ontario website, restricting it to the most high-profile consultations. A second aspect of this coordination was interministerial. Most consultations were conducted by a single ministry, which had lead responsibilities. In some cases, though, such as green belt protection, the lead ministry consulted with other ministries that would be affected by any initiatives.[42] The most extensive coordination involved Ontario Conserves. Launching a consultation on such a broad theme necessarily brought to the table multiple ministries (fifteen of them, eventually), each with a different piece of the theme, and got them all involved in developing a common document to publish in hardcopy and post online.[43]

The pace of consultation eventually slowed; ministries completed their consultations and began drafting laws or regulations and implementing them. The government moved from the policy development phase that characterizes the first year of a first mandate to a program development phase and ultimately a program delivery phase.[44] In the run-up to the election scheduled for 10 October 2007, the McGuinty government hoped to focus the voters' attention on the results it had achieved. Additional consultations would have distracted voters from that.[45]

4 Consultation and Channel Choice

The federal government's 2004 consultation and public engagement policy makes it clear that consultations should as a rule be conducted through a range of channels. Unlike transactional services to the public, there was little serious suggestion that consultations should only be conducted electronically. Discussions of e-consultation methodology had highlighted the importance of recognizing that participants in online consultations are not necessarily fully representative of the population, though they can represent defined – and often geographically dispersed – communities of interest. Electronic consultations were generally seen as supplementing other channels. It was judged that a clear business case could not be made that electronic tools and channels on their own significantly expand the reach of public consultations or realize major cost savings.[46]

The foreign policy review did, however, demonstrate that electronic tools can be woven effectively into more traditional methodologies such as public meetings and written input to provide a process that is richer overall. Indeed, electronic channels may sometimes be the central element of public consultation. The spam task force found that electronic tools of various kinds facilitated the work of the task force and its working groups. The COX-2 advisory panel used its Public

Forum to organize public input to its meetings, ensuring a broader range of submissions than would have been possible in a single day. Both it and the CRTC's Spike TV consultation used the website as a vehicle for disseminating a definitive compendium of submissions, including those originally submitted in written form, and the CRTC used its online process as an alternative to public hearings. The spam task force judged that its online input was at times less expert than in-person discussions. In any event, all four consultations accepted public online input as a legitimate contribution to the process, and the online vehicles were key to making available the documents of record that formed the basis for the consultation.

In Ontario, given the deficit, considerations of channel choice are more strongly affected by cost factors. In this analysis, the two main alternatives are face-to-face consultation (the spoken word) and written consultation. Two types of face-to-face consultation are facilitated workshops – for example, citizens' juries – and public meetings. Facilitated workshops involve fewer people but greater depth of engagement, while public meetings can accommodate a larger number of people, but often with little engagement. Both are relatively expensive in terms of design work done by staff or consultants, travel and accommodation for speakers or facilitators, and facility and equipment rentals.[47]

Regarding written consultation, four alternatives are written submissions, paper surveys, online surveys, and telephone polling (the latter defined as written because its final product is in written form). Written submissions provide substantial engagement for the writer; their impact, however, clearly depends on who reads them. Based on its considerable experience with surveys, MMAH estimates that online surveys are substantially cheaper than telephone polling or paper surveys.[48] Telephone polling is labour intensive, and in recent years its costs have been driven up by the high percentage of people who refuse to answer. The advantage of telephone polling is that, despite the high percentage of refusals, it attempts to be representative of the population. Online surveys are less expensive than telephone polls because they eliminate the individuals who do the surveying; they are also less expensive than paper surveys because they eliminate manual data entry. This was a distinct advantage for MMAH, which lacked resources for its consultations.[49] The concern with online surveys is representativeness; to the extent that widespread diffusion of the technology will erase the digital divide, this problem will eventually diminish.

MMAH also observed that when paper *and* online surveys are used, the balance between the two may depend on how aggressively each is marketed. For example, a ministry could choose mass distribution of paper questionnaires to the group it wants to consult, or alternatively, it could display a URL prominently in media advertising about the consultation. One of the other advantages of online consultation is that it is less expensive for government and more convenient for an increasingly large proportion of the population provided that consultation documents are posted online. An example of this was MMAH's online posting of more than one hundred detailed maps of the green belt; publishing hardcopies of those maps would have been much more expensive and would also have taken much longer.

One distinction between the spoken word and written consultation is that written consultation leaves a paper trail that is subject to freedom-of-information requests, whereas the spoken word, unless official notes are taken, is not. This distinction may explain a greater willingness on the part of politicians to engage in face-to-face consultations. In addition, at least some politicians believe that the art of representation involves assessing the views of citizens in face-to-face meetings and that this art cannot be replaced by the written word, whatever form it takes.[50]

5 *Beyond Consultation to Citizen Engagement*

The 2004 consultation section of the federal government's Communications Policy recognizes citizen engagement as a component of public consultation, but without providing a very precise definition. Government departments have experimented with citizen engagement, working with organizations such as the Canadian Policy Research Network and the Public Policy Forum to pilot methodologies such as deliberative polling. Also, it was suggested in interviews that consultation – and in particular e-consultation – was a way to provide a role for citizens between elections. More generally, e-consultations were seen as a potential means of addressing the democratic deficit that is a growing concern to many politicians, in particular with respect to new and younger voters who have been raised in a networked environment. The continuing emergence of new technologies such as text messaging and wireless ensures that the issue will always have an open-ended dimension.[51]

The McGuinty government's experience to date has been primarily with e-consultation, in which individuals submit their views to government. Rare instances have approached genuine interactivity: in the Ideas Campaign, participants were able to see one another's views with minimal moderation; in the 2004 budget consultation, participants could see the numerical totals for the questionnaire; and in Ontario Conserves, there was a moderated exchange of ideas. In contrast, the face-to-face approach has been fully interactive – for example, in the use of facilitated workshops for some consultations, a stakeholder task force for the green belt protection consultation, and the citizens' juries for consultations on electoral reform and campaign financing. Are we to conclude that the electronic channel is best for written questionnaires but that face-to-face is the best way to provide interactivity? Is there a place for greater online interactivity in the Ontario government's consultations? There appears to be interest at two levels. Individual ministries have young, computer-savvy web developers who will want to push this envelope.[52] There is also interest at the political level in exploring online discussion forums.[53]

In the final analysis, the move towards more systematic, online citizen engagement in the policy process will depend on the willingness and ability of politicians to include citizens in a domain that has traditionally been assigned to the institutions of representative democracy. But it will also depend on citizens themselves – on their willingness to have public institutions evolve in this manner, to participate in these new institutions, and to accept the results.

Conclusion

The case studies illustrate that e-consultation can provide an effective input into policy development, including providing a more visible, accessible, and effective policy deliberation process and reducing its costs. At their best, e-consultations constitute online conversations, preparing and supplementing face-to-face deliberations but not replacing them.[54] The nature of the policy issues may also be a factor. The federal government's spam task force addressed an issue arising from the 'new economy' that lent itself to the use of new economic tools. Similarly, the Spike TV consultation drew the attention of two groups – media institutions and males between eighteen and forty-nine – that are known to be more oriented to the Internet than the mainstream of the population. In contrast, the provincial government's e-consultations have been on broader issues (the budget, urban development, conservation) directed at the entire population. Experience with e-consultation in the federal and Ontario governments has been positive enough that electronic channels have been launched and are being maintained as a permanent feature of the policy development landscape. Both governments have been working out issues of how to manage e-consultation. As technology evolves to provide greater opportunities for citizen engagement on the electronic channel, we expect them to continue working on these management questions.

We end with these specific findings:

- The federal government slowly developed an e-consultation portal and is allowing experience to determine the role it will play. The McGuinty government quickly developed and just as quickly abandoned its portal, instead providing access to individual consultations through the government's or individual ministries' homepages. This suggests that the value of a consultation portal depends on a government's overall approach to public consultation and policy deliberation.

- It is now well within the ability of communications branches of individual ministries to develop and manage e-consultation. The role of central agencies is now to enforce policy and priorities, provide endorsement and technical expertise, and serve as a focal point for developing a community of practice. They also provide a vital link to the government's political agenda and its operating style.

- In a majority government with a normal five-year mandate, the primary time for consultation is early in the mandate. Nevertheless, specific issues may arise throughout the mandate necessitating consultation, and end-of-mandate consultation can help departing ministers develop their political legacies or raise their profile before the coming election. The life of a minority government is too short and uncertain for such timing considerations to be relevant. The regulatory process, in contrast, exists independently of the electoral mandate cycle and drives consultation at any time.

- Electronic consultation has begun at a minimal level of engagement, with governments making documents available online and asking for responses that are not posted. However, the federal and Ontario governments have been moving towards greater engagement – for example, by posting responses online, creating moderated discussion forums, posting video online, and webcasting in-person town hall discussions. It seems there is an appetite in both governments for greater experimentation as part of the progressive integration of online tools into the broader process of public policy consultation and decision making.

- Both governments have been much more aggressive in online services than in online policy consultation. It will bear watching whether this is simply a case of policy making lagging behind service delivery – but eventually catching up – or whether an inherent tension is developing within the triangle formed by the political system, service delivery, and policy making that will have long-term implications for how government and society interact.

NOTES

1 The authors acknowledge the financial support of the Social Sciences and Humanities Research Council of Canada's Initiative on the New Economy, the research assistance of Eliza Jiang Chen and Patrick Kirby, and the copy editing of Beth Herst.
2 Kenneth Kernaghan, Brian Marson, and Sandford Borins, *The New Public Organization* (Toronto: University of Toronto Press, 2000).
3 Kenneth Kernaghan and Justin Gunraj, 'Integrating Information Technology into Public Administration: Conceptual and Practical Considerations.' *Canadian Public Administration* 47, no. 4 (2004): 525–46; Kenneth Kernaghan, 'Moving towards the Virtual State: Integrating Services and Service Channels into Citizen-Centred Delivery,' *IRAS* 71 no. 1 (2005): 119–31.
4 Sandford Borins, Kenneth Kernaghan, David Brown, Nick Bontis, Perri 6, and Fred Thompson, *Digital State at the Leading Edge* (Toronto: University of Toronto Press, 2007).
5 Democratic Renewal Secretariat, 'Citizen Engagement: Definition and Scope,' PowerPoint presentation to Deputy Minister's Committee on Transformation, February 2005.
6 Robert J.P. Gale, 'Canada's Green Plan,' in *Nationale Umweltpläne in ausgewählten Industrieländern* (Berlin: Springer-Verlag, 1997), 97–120.
7 www.canada.gc.ca.
8 Interview with Elisabeth Richard, director of E-Government Technology Partnerships, Public Works and Government Services Canada, 18 April 2005; interview with Debbie Cook, director of Public Engagement, Canada Corps, Canadian International Development Agency, 26 April 2005.
9 Interview with Stephanie Ashton, director of Service Improvement and GOL, Canadian Heritage, 15 April 2005.
10 www.consultingcanadians.gc.ca.

11 Interview with Luc Gauthier, analyst, Strategic Communications Planning, Privy Council Office, 27 April 2005.

12 Transcript of remarks by Paul Martin, 'Finding our Digital Voice: Governing in the Information Age,' to the Crossing Boundaries National Conference, 8 May 2003. www.crossingboundaries.ca/files/paul_martin_david_zussman_tr anscript.pdf.

13 Interview with Elisabeth Richard, 18 April 2005.

14 Interview with Carol Kennedy, director of *Canada Gazette*, Public Works and Government Services Canada, 19 April 2005.

15 William Graham, *Dialogue on Foreign Policy: Report to Canadians* (Ottawa: Department of Foreign Affairs and International Trade, 2003). www.foreign-policy-dialogue.ca/en/final_report/index.html.

16 Ibid., www.foreign-policy-dialogue.ca/en/welcome/index.html.

17 Ibid., www.foreign-policy-dialogue.ca/en/final_report/index.html.

18 Industry Canada, Task Force on Spam, 'Stopping Spam: Creating a Stronger, Safer Internet' (2005), e-com.ic.gc.ca/epic/Internet/inecic-ceac.nsf/en/h_gv00317e.html.

19 Interview with David Charter, policy analyst, Industry Canada Task Force on Spam, 20 April 2005.

20 Health Canada, 'Selective COX-2 Inhibitor NSAIDs – Expert Advisory Panel Meeting and Public Forum (2005), www.hc-sc.gc.ca/ahc-asc/public-consult/consultations/col/cox2-cos2/index_e.html.

21 Broadcasting Public Notice CRTC 2005-9, 'Distribution of Spike TV by Broadcasting Distribution Undertakings' (2005), www.crtc.gc.ca/archive/ENG/Notices/2005/pb2005-9.htm

22 Interview with Steven Green, manager of Creative Services and New Media, Ontario Cabinet Office, 16 June 2005.

23 Ontario Liberal Party, 'Government That Works for You: The Ontario Liberal Plan for a More Democratic Ontario' (2003), ontarioliberal.com.

24 Dalton McGuinty, Memo to All Ontario Public Servants, 23 October 2003.

25 Interview with Joyce Barretto, executive director of Consultation Projects Office, Ontario Cabinet Office, 8 April 2005.

26 www.townhallontario.gov.on.ca.

27 Interview with Karen Rosen, director of Citizen Engagement, Office of the Premier of Ontario, 31 May 2005.

28 www.ontarioconserves.gov.on.ca.

29 Interview with Louise Simos, manager of Corporate and Electronic Communications, Ontario Ministry of Municipal Affairs and Housing, 15 April 2005.

30 Ibid.

31 Gauthier interview.
32 Simos interview.
33 e-Citizen Engagement Support Office, 'Electronic Citizen Engagement by the Ontario Public Service,' PowerPoint presentation to Deputy Ministers' Committee on Transformation, 16 February 2005. Also, interview with Glen Padassery, manager of e-Citizen Engagement Support Office, and Barbara Swartzentruber, manager of I & IT Strategy, Policy, and Planning, Office of the Corporate CIO, 14 April 2005.
34 Gauthier interview.
35 Kennedy interview.
36 www.townhallontario.gov.on.ca.
37 Green interview.
38 Rosen interview.
39 www.greenbelt.ontario.ca.
40 Simos interview.
41 Interview with Dave Thompson, director of Canada On-Line Services, Public Works and Government Services Canada, 25 April 2005.
42 Interview with Michael Bunce, member of Greenbelt Task Force, 13 April 2005.
43 Barretto interview.
44 Interview with David Guscott, associate secretary to Cabinet for Communications, Ontario Cabinet Office, 20 April 2005.
45 Rosen interview.
46 Cook interview.
47 Ministry of Municipal Affairs and Housing, *Greenbelt Consultation: Increasing Citizen Engagement*, PowerPoint presentation, October 2004; also, Simos interview.
48 Simos interview.
49 Ibid.
50 Perri 6, *E-governance: Styles of Political Judgment in the Information Age Polity* (Houndsmills: Palgrave Macmillan, 2004).
51 Cook interview.
52 Simos interview.
53 Green interview.
54 Cook interview.

9 The Niagara Casinos Partnership: Game of Chance?

JENNIFER BERARDI[1]

There are very few fields in public administration that have not been enlightened by the intellectual inquiry and contributions of Kenneth Kernaghan. His distinguished career is founded on a true love of the discipline and the utmost respect for the men and women who comprise our public service. One of the central themes of Kernaghan's work has been how the public service has evolved to meet (and even surpass) the demands of its citizenry. Kernaghan is especially interested in how government reform and renewal efforts affect the traditional relationship between public servants and politicians. In essence, how does one implement public service reforms and innovations while keeping the public service accountable?

Always on the leading edge of government innovations, Kernaghan has written several pivotal articles that have served as the foundation for further academic study. One of these is 'Partnerships and Public Administration: Conceptual and Practical Considerations.'[2]

In 1993, when that article appeared, academics and practitioners alike were abuzz with the promise or prospective downfall of the New Public Management (NPM). Many governments around the world, be they from the political right (e.g., Conservative governments in Canada and the United States) or from the political left (e.g., Labour governments in Australia and New Zealand), embraced NPM as an approach to public service reform and renewal. There was widespread debate about what exactly NPM entailed, as solid definitions of the strategy were just beginning to appear. It was understood, though, that it called for a change from the traditional ways that governments did business. A new 'managerialism' was emerging that encouraged reforms in public sector management based on management practices in the private sector. The rising management culture emphasized the need to utilize scarce resources efficiently and effectively and to embrace change and innovation; it also stressed the importance of management – not just policy making.[3] In this climate, partnership developed into an important component of the NPM agenda to revitalize the public sector.[4] In 1997 Marcel Masse, in his speech 'Governing for the Future,' noted that 'the future of governance is partnerships and shared responsibility.'[5]

Almost a decade later, partnerships continue to thrive as an alternative service delivery mechanism. For example, in the case of public–private partnerships, Partnerships British Columbia notes that eleven large-scale public–private partnerships are currently operating in B.C. in addition to between twenty and thirty small-scale public–private partnerships at the municipal and regional levels.[6] The B.C. government has invested around $3.6 billion in various public–private partnership arrangements throughout the province.[7] Partnerships continue to be popular in Canada. According to a 2004 Environics Research Group study, six in ten Canadians agreed that governments should invest in public–private partnerships in the provision of infrastructure and the delivery of public services.[8]

Partnerships are no longer considered a new phenomenon in the public sector; even so, the practice still requires study, as they are being utilized in many different ways. Partnerships come in many shapes and sizes, which makes some arrangements difficult to label. One example is the operating arrangements that currently exist between the Ontario Lottery and Gaming Corporation (OLGC)[9] and the three private sector companies that run the commercial casinos in Rama, Windsor, and Niagara Falls, Ontario. Under these arrangements, private sector companies are operating and managing commercial casinos under the aegis of the Ontario government.

In recognition of Professor Kernaghan's long-standing ties to the Niagara Region, this chapter profiles the public–private partnering arrangement involving the OLGC and the Falls Management Company (FMC), which operates both Casino Niagara and the Niagara Fallsview Casino and Resort. Thus it will be the first academic review of the Niagara casino operations. The public–private partnership agreement – referred to as an 'operating agreement' – is bound by a confidentiality agreement that is protected under the Privacy Act. The Ontario government has invested more than $1 billion in the government-owned Niagara Falls casinos, yet there is very little public information or knowledge about this arrangement, nor does the government want to share this information with Ontarians. In fact, the government does not openly refer to the operating agreement as a 'partnership in the traditional sense,' though neither does it view the arrangement as an example of contracting out.[10] This chapter shows that despite the government's reluctance to use the term partnership, the operating agreement between the OLGC and the FMC is in fact a public–private partnership. This reluctance to use the term stems more from political reservations and possible legal ramifications than it does logistical ones.

This chapter investigates the Niagara casino operations and assesses the various issues that have arisen. The first section defines partnerships by highlighting Kernaghan's partnership typology. The second section is a case study of the Niagara Falls casinos. The concluding section reviews the lessons to be learned and offers general comments on the future of partnerships in Canada.

It will be argued that although public–private partnerships are a viable form of service delivery, concessions relating to accountability, openness, and transparency have sometimes been made. Specifically, the Niagara Falls casino operating arrangement defies a long-standing expectation of government operations in that the arrangement is shrouded in secrecy, uncertainty, and political posturing. The question is, is this political arrangement a bad deal for Ontarians or is it an inescapable requirement in the 'high stakes' environment of today's casino operations?

What Are Partnerships?

Kernaghan notes that strictly defined, a partnership 'is a formal agreement to share power with others in the pursuit of joint goals and/or mutual benefits.'[11] But then he adds that this definition is too restrictive to apply to all partnerships, since many interactions described as partnerships involve minimal power sharing.[12] He therefore suggests that a 'broad working definition' of partnership may be more appropriate, one that defines partnerships as a 'relationship involving the sharing of power, work, support and/or information with others for the achievement of joint goals and/or mutual benefits.'[13]

Complementary to Kernaghan's definition, governments have provided similar definitions based on the concept of power sharing. For example, at the federal level the Policy on Alternative Service Delivery guidelines define partnerships as follows: 'Arrangements between a government organization and one or more parties in which they agree to co-operate on the delivery of a program or service that fulfils the objective of the Government of Canada, where there is: delineation of authority and responsibility among partners; joint investment of resources (such as time, funding, expertise); allocation of risk among partners; and mutual or complementary benefits.'[14]

The Ontario government has a similar working definition for partnerships, describing public–private partnerships as arrangements in which 'government provides services with another party where each contributes resources and shares the risks and rewards.'[15]

Some of the common components found in the preceding definitions of partnership seem to suggest that power sharing, mutual benefits, and joint risk taking are all characteristics of a 'true' or a 'real' partnership – that is, the collaborative partnership. According to Kernaghan, a collaborative partnership goes beyond consultation and can be viewed as collaboration in that such arrangements 'involve the pooling of resources such as money, information and labour to meet shared or compatible objectives. Each partner gives up some autonomy.' Ideally, in this type of partnership 'decisions are made by building consensus.' He describes this as the true form of partnership, in that partners are 'mutually dependent' and 'bring roughly equal resources to the decision-making table.'[16]

In practice, however, there are many different forms of partnership that do not meet these criteria. In fact, the diversity of partnerships found throughout Canada's public services is overwhelming. Partnerships are customized to suit the specific goals and objectives of the participants involved; hence, each partnership is distinctive. As Evert Lindquist notes, this diversity can present several challenges for those study partnerships. To begin, any innovations or claims of service improvements resulting from a partnership are difficult to compare and contrast as 'what works when managing one partnership may not be appropriate for another.'[17] Furthermore, the diversity of partnerships makes it even more difficult to articulate what the basic or recognizable features of partnerships are. As noted, 'partnerships are not like some innovative government structures, such as ministries of state or special operating agencies, which have generally understood generic forms or functions so that even when operationalized in particular contexts, there is agreement on essential qualities.'[18]

Nevertheless, the diversity of partnerships in the public sector does not necessarily cripple the study of partnerships; lessons can still be drawn from all types of partnership experience. In fact, the diversity of partnerships should in some ways be celebrated, for it is evidence that public sector managers have the flexibility to design partnerships to meet their own goals and needs.

Given the breadth of partnerships found across Canada, Kernaghan includes a number of partnership models in his typology based on 'the nature and extent of power (i.e. control or influence) exercised by the partners.'[19] This classification was a pivotal contribution to public administration as it was one of the earliest means for classifying the various forms of partnership.

Besides collaborative partnerships, Kernaghan's typology includes operational partnerships, contributory partnerships, and consultative partnerships. According to him, operational partnerships 'are characterized by a sharing of work rather than decision-making power. The emphasis is on working together at the operational level to achieve the same, or compatible, goals.' Some operational partnerships may have 'a strong element of collaboration in that the partners share resources.' In this form of partnership, 'power, in the sense of control, is retained by one partner, almost invariably the public organization involved, especially if it is providing the bulk of resources.' These partnerships may not empower those involved, but they can lead to better coordinated and more responsive operations.[20]

Kernaghan defines contributory partnerships as 'those in which an organization, whether public or private, agrees to provide sponsorship or support, usually in the form of funding, for an activity in which it will have little or no operational involvement.' This form of partnership is generally not considered a 'true' partnership because it does not 'require active involvement in the decision-making process of all players' as 'a financial contribution alone is not considered sufficient to make the contributor a real partner.' In practice, though, the 'success of the partnership depends primarily on the performance of the partners receiving support.' The sponsoring organization's partners are not without influence.[21]

The final form of partnership that Kernaghan profiled was consultative partnerships: 'those in which a public organization solicits advice from individuals, groups and organizations outside government.' This form of partnership 'usually takes the form of advisory committees or councils whose main task is to advise government in relation to a particular policy field or policy issue.' The partner's influence is contingent on a number of factors such as the credibility of the partner, whether or not the partnership is formalized, and even whether the recommendations are going to be made public. Unlike a one-time consultation exercise, these partnerships provide ongoing consultation and may gradually evolve towards collaborative arrangements and increased power sharing.[22]

Though this typology provides a useful framework for studying all different types of partnerships (e.g., public–private partnerships, public–public partnerships, public–not-for-profit partnerships), it is recognized that these compartments are not watertight. As Kernaghan notes, 'some partnerships evolve from one category to another and some have elements of more than one category (e.g. a collaborative arrangement involving a few partners complemented by a consultative arrangement involving several others).'[23] The typology, however, has unquestionably served as a valuable tool for guiding our understanding of government partnerships. In practice it may not be simple to slot each partnership into a single classification; even so, this approach does provide a general understanding of the criteria that may be present in a variety of partnership agreements.[24]

Kernaghan's typology applies to all forms of government partnership. Other models of partnership specific to public–private partnerships (P3s) have also been developed. For example, the Canadian Council for Public–Private Partnerships suggests an approach for describing partnership arrangements in Canada in which a key consideration is the level of risk sharing. Thus:

> *Operation and Maintenance Contract (O & M)*: A private operator, under contract, operates a publicly-owned asset for a specified term. Ownership of the asset remains with the public entity.
> *Design-Build-Finance-Operate (DBFO)*: The private sector designs, finances and constructs a new facility under a long-term lease, and operates the facility during the term of the lease. The private partner transfers the new facility to the public sector at the end of the lease term.
> *Build-Own-Operate (BOO)*: The private sector finances, builds, owns and operates a facility or service in perpetuity. The public constraints are stated in the original agreement and through on-going regulatory authority.
> *Build-Own-Operate-Transfer (BOOT)*: A private entity receives a franchise to finance, design, build and operate a facility (and to charge user fees) for a specified period, after which ownership is transferred back to the public sector.
> *Buy-Build-Operate (BBO)*: Transfer of a public asset to a private or a

quasi-public entity usually under contract that the assets are to be upgraded and operated for a specified period of time. Public control is exercised through the contract at the time of transfer.

Operation License: A private operator receives a license or rights to operate a public service, usually for a specified term. This is often used in IT projects.

Finance Only: A private entity, usually a financial services company, funds a project directly or uses various mechanisms such as a long-term lease or bond issue.[25]

This model is a useful complement to Kernaghan's typology in that it seeks to categorize the very specific roles of each partner. Unfortunately, for the purposes of trying to define the FMC–OLGC operating agreement, it does not provide enough detail to determine the key characteristics of partnership such as the extent of mutual dependency and shared decision making. Even so, after this chapter has assessed the nature of the FMC–OLCG agreement, it will be interesting to determine whether the agreement is similar to any of these basic forms of P3 arrangements.

Casino Case Study

Two casinos are operating in Niagara Falls: Casino Niagara, which opened in 1996 as an 'interim' casino (though in April 2003 the government decided not to close it); and the Niagara Fallsview Casino and Resort, which opened its doors in 2004. Some consider the Niagara Falls casino properties to be the 'sparkling jewel in Niagara's crown';[26] however, their image has been tarnished by controversy surrounding the public–private agreement that was struck between the OLGC and the Falls Management Company (FMC), which won the bid to 'finance, design, build and operate' the Fallsview Casino.[27]

Background

The approval to open a casino in Niagara Falls was granted by Bob Rae's NDP government on 29 November 1995, but it was not until the Harris Conservative government took power that the project began to flourish.[28] From the beginning it was understood that a temporary interim casino would be operated until a permanent operator was selected.

In April 1996 the site for the interim casino was announced. Later that summer the Navegante Group was chosen as the temporary private sector developer and operator. The Navegante Group is a Las Vegas–based consulting firm that specializes in casino implementation and international marketing.[29] A temporary agreement was struck between the Navegante Group and the Ontario Casino Corp (OCC; OLGC's predecessor) under which Navegante would act as an agent of the OCC, which owned and managed all provincial casinos.[30] Navegante would be responsible for the property's development and day-to-day operations. For instance, the company would be involved in completing construction of the casino, furnishing and equipping it, recruiting and training staff, marketing the casino, and developing its operating procedures. Domenic Alfieri, the past president of the OCC, stated that 'the selection of The Navegante Group ensures we have some of the most talented industry professionals involved in developing this world-class facility.'[31] The Navegante–OCC partnership flourished, and Casino Niagara opened its doors on 9 December 1996. It was estimated that 30,000 people visited the attraction in the first twenty-four hours.[32] In its first year Casino Niagara attracted close to ten million visitors and generated more than $500 million in gross revenue, making it the most profitable casino in Ontario.[33]

On 12 September 1996 the OCC issued a request for proposal (RFP) for the permanent casino in Niagara Falls – the Niagara Falls Casino/ Gateway Project. Niagara Falls City Council lobbied the OLGC for the RFP to include not only a 'world class Casino Complex' but also 'one or more prestigious, first-class, year-round Tourist Attractors.'[34] At the time, Niagara Falls was suffering an economic downturn. Several important industries had left the area, and even the tourism industry was declining. The jobs, economic development, and various economic spin-offs associated with a new casino were welcomed, but local politicians were leery of creating a 'black hole,' as had happened in Atlantic City.[35] In particular, they were concerned that tourists would only be drawn to the casino for the day and that they wouldn't spend more than a few hours or visit any other attractions beyond the casino complex. An offsite attractor, especially a year-round one, was a strategy not only to lure tourists to the city but also to entice them to stay longer, visit the multitude of attractions that Niagara has to offer, and come to the city in the off season. The OLGC agreed, and an off-site attractor became a requirement in the RFP.

The tourism development required under the RFP was not prescriptive; the government did not want 'to inhibit the imagination of developers by spelling out precisely what might be incorporated into the tourism development portion of the RFP.'[36] The government felt that it was 'issuing the private sector a challenge': 'The objective is to challenge the development industry to use its imagination, creativity and expertise to create a year-round attraction in Niagara. We envision a tourist attractor or attractors that will be unique in the world of family entertainment.'[37]

Four companies submitted bids: Fallsview, Seven Wonders of Niagara, Trump International Casinos, and Falls Management Company (FMC).[38] The latter was a consortium of five firms: Hyatt Development Corporation, Shiplake Gaming Corporation, Highland Gaming, Olympic V Associates, and Falls Entertainment Corporation.[39] On 18 February 1998, Al Palladini, the minister of Economic Development, Trade, and Tourism, announced that the FMC had been chosen. Negotiations ensued, and on 14 September 1998 the OCC announced that an agreement had been reached. The time between the official announcement that the FMC had won the bid (February) and the press release announcing that a successful operating agreement had been reached (September) was tumultuous to say the least. There were several allegations of unethical conduct and influence peddling, and opposition MPPs called for an inquiry into the selection process. Kevin Donovan, a *Toronto Star* investigative reporter, covered the developments in what he eventually called the 'saga of the Niagara Casino … a mystery thriller involving lawyers, political operatives, wealthy land barons and high-stakes gamblers.'[40]

The conflict-of-interest accusations related mainly to the tendering process. From the outset there was speculation about how the FMC won the bid. There were allegations that it had ranked third in the tendering process and that its bid had prevailed only because it had made political contributions to the Conservatives. Dalton McGuinty, now premier but at the time leader of the opposition, declared that 'the best proposal didn't win. The second best proposal didn't win. It turns out that the winner was a company with significant ties to your party.'[41] In fact, the FMC did rank third, but it ranked third in its ability to deliver a 'world class attractor.' The corporation ranked first in its ability to operate the 'world class casino complex.' Owing to the agreement's confidentiality terms, details like this were never made public, allowing opposition members to question the integrity of the partnership. For instance, NDP MPP Peter Kormos argued in the legislature that the tendering process had amounted to blatant influence peddling: 'It looks like influence peddling and it stinks like corporate influence peddling.'[42] Liberal MPP Dwight Duncan asked the government, 'If you are so confident about your process, will you release the process that the tourism review group has done, so we can see ... why [the government] is not dealing with the company rated best?'[43]

It was also reported that an international gaming consultant for Coopers Lybrand (now PricewaterhouseCoopers) who was involved in running the Niagara selection process was concurrently employed by a member of the FMC's business team (Falls Entertainment Corporation) as a consultant on casino bids 'outside of Ontario.' After several of these allegations were brought forward, and the Fallsview Company launched a lawsuit,[44] the provincial government finally agreed to an inquiry and selected the OCC's law firm to conduct an investigation.[45] That investigation revealed that the consultant did have a dual role and that he had not disclosed this in writing to the OCC when he had been asked to 'tell of any current or prior business relationships with members of the four bidders.' Yet, unbelievably, the inquiry found no conflict of interest here. Instead it concluded that the 'Niagara Falls bidding process was detailed, complex, open and fair' and that the selection process had been 'beyond reproach.'[46]

At the local level as well, the choice of the FMC was criticized, as it was the only bid that did not have any local connections. For instance, the Fallsview bid was headed by Niagara Falls businessmen, and so was the Seven Wonders of Niagara bid. And the Trump International bid was a partnership between Donald Trump and yet another local resident. Niagara Falls City Council, which had no authority or involvement in the bidding process, demanded to know why a business without any ties to the community had been chosen. At this writing, the local MPP still does not know exactly who sits on the FMC board. As a result of all this, the public perception was that the partnership was inherently flawed. There is an element of 'sour grapes' with every bidding process. Here, the rumours surrounding the FMC were left to fester, and the public came to believe that the process had not been as fair and open as it should have been. Despite the controversy, on 1 November 1998, the FMC assumed responsibility for the operation of Casino Niagara.

On the political front, in April 2000, as part of its Common Sense Revolution, the Harris government merged the OCC with the Ontario Lottery Corporation to form the OLGC. This streamlined Crown agency continued to work in partnership with FMC. In April 2003 the Eves Conservative government announced that Casino Niagara would remain open and that the FMC would be responsible for both casinos in Niagara: Casino Niagara and the planned Fallsview Casino and Resort.[47]

On 8 June 2004 the opening gala for Fallsview Casino and Resort was held. Political dignitaries, businesspeople, and citizens alike were awed by the spectacular billion-dollar entertainment complex overlooking Horseshoe Falls.[48] It was a moment of praise and congratulations for what had been accomplished.

Within a year, however, the mood had darkened. Revenues were down, but the real issue that began to emerge related to the FMC's promise to provide 'world class attractors.' Various stakeholders such as City Council and the local MPP tried to pressure the FMC and the OLGC to ensure that those attractions were built. Frustrated citizens even formed the grassroots interest group 'Fair Share' as a means to pressure the 'FMC to build the attractors they proposed when they bid on the Casino project.'[49] In many respects the city was torn. On the one hand, the casinos had generated jobs, revenue, and development opportunities for the people of Niagara Falls; on the other hand, citizens and government officials alike were perplexed as to why the FMC was not making good on its RFP promises to build a world-class attraction.

Making the situation even worse, the actual operating agreement reached between the FMC and the OLGC was confidential. Since the details of the arrangement and the allocation of responsibilities could not be disclosed, Niagara Falls City Council, local interest groups, and citizens in general became increasingly confused as to who owed what to whom. The honeymoon was over. The FMC–OLGC 'operating agreement' was now in the public spotlight, and it was becoming increasingly clear that serious questions of accountability, integrity, and transparency needed to be addressed.

Two core issues began to dominate the political discourse: (1) the confidentiality of the operating agreement, and (2) the lack of an attractor.

Issues and Analysis

1 The FMC-OLCG Operating Agreement

WHY IS IT CONFIDENTIAL?
In the Niagara Falls Casino/Gateway RFP, very little was disclosed about the future structural arrangement with the province. Statements such as 'there will be a high degree of private-sector involvement' and

'the successful Proponent will ... act as the agent of the Ontario Casino Corporation' provided very little insight into the agreement.[50] After the FMC was selected, its role was usually confined to statements relating to its function to 'finance, design, construct and operate the development.'[51] The exact level of power sharing, collaboration, and joint risk taking exercised by the partners was still unknown.

In fact, no locally elected politician or city official – not the mayor, the councillors, the city clerk, the MPP, or the MP – could state definitively what type of agreement had been reached.[52] The question, 'Is the FMC–OLGC agreement a public–private partnership or is it just a situation of basic contracting out?' was a mystery to officials and citizens alike. No one was aware of exactly who was paying for what, who controlled what, or how much power each party held in the agreement. Niagara Falls Liberal MPP Kim Craitor even made a freedom-of-information request in an attempt to unveil the details of the agreement, but met with no success. He says that even as a member of the current Liberal government, he is not privy to the casino arrangement.[53]

The confidentiality of the agreement has some justification. According to the OLGC, the arrangement needs to be kept confidential for 'proprietary' reasons.[54] Specifically, it is argued that, given the increasing competitiveness of the gaming marketplace (e.g., in New York state the Seneca Niagara Casino opened in 2002, and the Seneca Allegany Casino, just south of Buffalo, opened in 2005), the confidentiality clause ensures that the OLGC will keep its 'competitive edge.' Also, the OLGC does not want prospective vendors and companies studying the winning bid to gain an advantage when it comes time for renewal in the years to come.[55]

IS IT A PARTNERSHIP?

Unfortunately, owing to the confidentiality of the agreement, a full investigation of it is not possible. The information collected to describe and analyse the agreement is based largely on interviews with the FMC and the OLGC, supplemented by City of Niagara Falls records, various press releases, newspaper articles, corporate websites, and the original RFP Casino/Niagara Gateway proposal. The FMC–OLGC operating agreement would probably be difficult to classify even if its contents were made public; however, enough information has been revealed to confidently provide an overview and general assessment of the agreement.

To determine whether the operating agreement is indeed a partnership, criteria were selected based on Kernaghan's partnership typology. These criteria serve as the 'common elements' found in partnerships, certainly not the 'only elements.' Though these criteria help distinguish among the different types of partnership arrangements, once again, these are generalized forms. The criteria used to differentiate the types of partnerships are (1) mutual dependency, (2) shared decision making, (3) shared work, (4) shared financial resources, (5) shared risk taking, and (6) shared rewards. It is according to these criteria that the FMC–OLGC operating agreement will be assessed.

Table 9.1 serves three functions. First, it provides some clarity to Kernaghan's typology by allowing us to easily compare and contrast the various criteria that may be found in the different types of public–private partnerships.[56] Second, as the criteria outline the generalized characteristics found in various forms of partnership, they may be compared to the characteristics found in the FMC–OLGC operating agreement to determine whether it is or is not a partnership agreement.[57] Third, as public–private partnerships are so often confused with contracting out or even basic consultation (many of those interviewed were unclear on the distinctions), these organizational forms are included in the analysis in order to demonstrate how they differ from a typical partnership arrangement.

It is important to understand that while partnerships may exhibit different levels of power sharing, risk taking, and investment in resources, what truly defines a partnership and differentiates it from other government arrangements such as contracting out is the 'spirit' of partnership, or the teamwork, coordination, and mutual dependency that the partners exhibit. Partnership differs from contracting out in that there is mutual trust or at least the presence of some form of mutual consultation that is genuine and respected by the partners. There is a sharing of power, either through direct (i.e., control) or indirect (i.e., influence) intervention.

Furthermore, partnership and consultation are similar in that both concepts involve sharing and exchanging information, but with the latter there is not the same sense of mutual dependency that comes from sharing risks, resources, and/or decision making. As Kernaghan, Marson, and Borins note, 'certainly the process of partnering necessarily involves some measure of consultation. However, consultation can take place in isolation from partnership, and so-called "real" partnerships go beyond consultation to collaboration and include shared power, risks and benefits.'[58]

As shown in table 9.1, the FMC–OLGC operating agreement shares at least four, and possibly five, of the six characteristics found in a collaborative or a 'real' partnership arrangement. Specifically, the agreement allows for mutual dependency, shared decision making, shared work, shared financial resources, shared rewards, and (arguably) shared risk taking. Ironically, owing to the strong level of mutual decision making between the partners, it can be argued that the FMC–OLGC operating agreement is more similar to a collaborative partnership than to the contributory or consultative models (i.e., in the operational model, decision making is not shared and in the consultative model decision making is shared but the government is typically the dominant player). Clearly, the FMC–OLGC operating agreement is a partnership in disguise.

Determining Characteristics

MUTUAL DEPENDENCY

Both the FMC and the OLGC attest to a significant sense of mutual dependency between the two parties. In fact, both characterize the feeling of mutual dependency as 'strong.'[59] From a legal standpoint the FMC has a strong sense of dependency on the OLGC because it cannot operate a casino in Ontario legally without the partnership agreement. Specifically, in 1985 the federal government gave the provinces the exclusive authority to operate and/or license particular forms of gambling under Section 207 of the Criminal Code. Games of chance, including casinos, are legal only if they are under the authority of a provincial government.[60] Thus without the OLGC there would be no casino. From a business standpoint, the OLGC depends heavily on the FMC because the OLGC has no experience in the gaming industry. As it did with the Navegante Group beforehand, the government has chosen to partner with the FMC because of its vast casino experience and expertise.

Whatever the sources of mutual dependency, however, the parties do feel more than a contractual obligation to each other. Both partners feel that the FMC and the OLGC work as a team towards a common goal, but they also recognize that they play different roles. The OLGC's mandate is to 'deliver gaming entertainment to maximize economic benefits for the people of Ontario in an efficient and socially responsible manner.'[61] Essentially, both parties want to generate revenue, but the OLGC also wants to ensure that the public interest is upheld. This has led to

Table 9.1 A comparison of the characteristics of partnerships and related organizational structures.

	Consultation	Consultative partnership	Operational partnership	Operating agreement	Collaborative partnership	Contributory partnership	Contracting out
Mutual dependency	X (based on non-commital information exchange)	√	√	√	√	√	X (based on market transaction relationship)
Shared decision making	X (gov't has no obligation to utilize information)	√ (gov't dominant)	X (gov't controlled)	√ (strong, but gov't has final say)	√ (equal sharing)	X (usually business controlled)	X (gov't controlled)
Shared work	X (business has no authority to be involved)	X (gov't controlled)	√ (business dominant)	√ (business dominant)	√ (equal sharing)	X (usually business controlled)	√ (business dominant)
Shared financial Resources	X (business has no authority to be involved)	X (gov't controlled)	√ (gov't dominant)	√ (gov't dominant)	√ (equal sharing)	√ (usually gov't dominant)	X (paid by gov't for services rendered)
Shared risk taking	X (business not involved)	X (gov't controlled)	X (gov't assumes risk)	? (FMC & OLGC disagreed on response	√ (equal sharing)	√ (usually business dominant)	X
Shared rewards	X (but possible indirectly, if business gets desired outcome)	√	√	√	√	√	X (possible if incentives built into contract)

difficulties in their relationship over the years, but the spirit of working together and respecting what each side brings to the table is still there.[62]

SHARED DECISION MAKING

The FMC and the OLGC agree that there is a 'high level of consultation' in the decision-making process. The arrangement between the two parties dictates that the FMC is responsible for the day-to-day operations of the properties, hence the description in the RFP that 'there will be a high degree of private-sector involvement.' This is not, however, a situation of unilateral decision making. The FMC is required to get approval from the OLGC for important business matters such as setting a budget plan and launching a marketing campaign. The OLGC 'works in conjunction with the FMC on the bigger issues' as its role is 'beyond a regulatory function.'[63] For instance, FMC executives are in frequent contact with OLGC personnel. The FMC's CEO explains that there is daily interaction between the FMC and the OLGC and that the two CEOs usually meet every two weeks to discuss strategies and current issues.

SHARED WORK

As mentioned, the FMC is responsible for the day-to-day operations of the casino properties. The OLGC plays an active role in setting policy, and it shares in decision making, but it does not involve itself at the operational level. The OLGC, however, is responsible for 'all construction of the two facilities including any upgrades.'[64]

SHARED FINANCIAL RESOURCES

The Niagara Fallsview Casino and Resort is a government-owned facility. Details on how the partnership is financially structured are closely guarded; this is probably the most 'secretive' element of the operating agreement.

As a condition of the RFP, the FMC was required to 'finance, design, and construct' the property; later it was reimbursed for the money it spent, in addition to an undisclosed development fee.[65] In terms of the revenue generated by the casinos, the OLGC automatically receives a 20 per cent 'win tax' from the gross revenue as well as all of the profits left over once the operating expenses (including interest on the debt) and an undisclosed operating fee have been paid to the FMC. The government uses this revenue to finance other public services. The OLGC used to report to the Ministry of Consumer and Commercial Relations but has recently been moved to the Ministry of Public Infrastructure and Renewal.[66] This was a strategic decision by the government, which can now include casino revenues in the public infrastructure budget. Critics such as NDP MPP Peter Kormos contend that this was merely a 'political manoeuvre' so that the government could 'pad its public investment budget.'[67]

SHARED RISK TAKING

This is the only characteristic about which the FMC and the OLGC do not agree. The OLGC does not view the relationship as including the sharing of risks; rather, it sees the government as the dominant financial player. Though the details cannot be disclosed, the operating agreement does include provisions to provide 'protection for both sides' to ensure that both parties are fulfilling the conditions of the agreement.[68] The government has leverage to ensure the FMC's compliance; for example, it can financially penalize the FMC or not approve certain plans on an annual basis. But the agreement also includes stipulations that protect the FMC, though owing to confidentiality concerns, no examples were given.[69] On the other side, the FMC sees itself as sharing risks in that it must 'operate under certain parameters' and is required to show a substantial profit.[70] The FMC's CEO believes that the FMC and the OLGC are both 'frustrated by the results of the new casino' but that they share a common goal in trying to increase its revenues.[71] He states that both parties are currently under pressure, though he admits that 'the OLGC is probably under more pressure than the FMC.'[72]

The differing perspectives on the level of shared risk taking perhaps can be understood better when one separates the risks associated with the development agreement from the risks associated with the operating agreement. In the development agreement that was outlined in the RFP, the OLGC was to collaborate with the FMC to design, construct, and finance the facility within a defined budget, thereby ensuring that a detailed scope definition was met (e.g., specific square footage, details of all amenities). The FMC did share resources throughout this process. It contracted with PCL Contractors as the construction manager through a GMP (gross maximum price) contract. The FMC entered a GMP contract with PCL; however, it continued to share considerable risk with the OLGC in that it was responsible for all overruns and for meeting the scope definition report. For instance, if there were construction delays or cost overages, the FMC would be held financially responsible. Clearly, the FMC did share risk in building the Fallsview facility. Regarding the actual operating agreement, however, it can be argued that the OLGC is correct to state that there is minimal risk taking. Even though the FMC is required to perform and meet the expectations of the business plan as agreed on by the OLGC, it is still paid an operating fee from the government regardless of the actual profits collected. Even if the OLGC does financially penalize the FMC for a lack of profits, it is questionable whether a reduction in the incentive fee could be considered a risk. The FMC is at risk only of losing a percentage of its operating fee. From the CEO's perspective it is easy to understand why he may consider it a risk to lose profits; his salary is paid by the FMC, not the OLGC. The CEO is responsible to his board of directors, which, given that his is a private sector organization, is looking for profit maximization. Arguably it is worth asking whether this represents true risk taking.

SHARED REWARDS

Both parties agree that they share in the rewards. As mentioned earlier, each partner receives an undisclosed portion of the gross gaming revenue generated by the casinos. The government can utilize those resources to bankroll other public services; the FMC is granted a sizable operator's fee.

As expected, the FMC–OLGC operating agreement does not exactly emulate one of the general types of partnerships as defined by Kernaghan; this, however, does not mean it is not a partnership. As noted earlier, partnerships are difficult to classify as there is no 'one size fits all' model. What *can* be said is that the operating agreement seems to share many of the characteristics of partnership, including the all-important factor of mutual dependency as well as shared decision making, financial resources, rewards, and (perhaps) risks. It also can be argued that the OLGC–FMC operating agreement is a variation of the design–build–finance–operate P3 arrangement as outlined by the Canadian Council for Public–Private Partnerships, in that the FMC has been responsible for all four with regard to the Niagara casinos, and will be so for an undisclosed length of time. So the agreement may well warrant the term partnership, even if the government chooses not to use it.

This question needs to be addressed: Why does the government not publicly refer to the operating agreement as a public–private partnership when it meets the general criteria of a partnership? The situation is usually reversed: organizations are more likely to claim that they are working in partnership when actually they are not. Overuse of the terms 'partner' and 'partnership' has undermined the potency of this practice, as both are used so often in a rhetorical sense; but in this case the government has chosen deliberately to avoid the term.

Then again, given how politically volatile the issue of gambling is, one can easily hypothesize that government may not want to be seen as a true 'partner' in the gaming industry. In a government-commissioned study of gaming in Ontario, it was revealed that approximately '4.8% of Ontario adults have moderate to extreme gambling problems ... 36% of the Ontario gaming revenue is generated by people with gambling addictions ... [and] problem gamblers account for up to 60 per cent of the revenue generated from slots.' The government has tried to combat problem gambling through various programs and hotlines. For example, on 23 March 2005 the OLGC established the Responsible Gaming Code of Conduct to ensure the 'corporation's pledge to reduce the risk of problem gambling in Ontario.'[73] However, it is still a fact that it was the government that allowed legalized gambling to occur in the first place. The current government 'is not going to build any more commercial casinos,' but it certainly has no plans to close any of the existing commercial casinos either.[74] As Premier McGuinty stated: 'There's no doubt about it, we have come to rely on gambling revenues ... Perhaps in a better world we wouldn't but the fact of the matter is, it's here, it's here to stay.'[75] Economic Development Minister Joe Cordiano states that 'it wouldn't be "prudent" for Ontario to get out of the gambling business ... We need that revenue ... It is a significant contributor to the province's revenue base.'[76] Despite the recent concerns in Niagara, no one is calling for the casinos to be closed. In fact, the City of Niagara Falls is worried that the FMC may choose to close Casino Niagara since it is not as profitable.[77]

Another hypothesis as to why the government has chosen not to call the operating agreement a partnership may have to do with legal concerns involving the province's gaming authority. As stated earlier, the Criminal Code stipulates that only the provincial government has the right to operate, license, and regulate legal forms of gambling. The government is very careful to use terminology such as the FMC acts as an 'agent of the government' and 'FMC has been contracted by the OLGC.'[78] The OLGC admits that while the agreement is not a 'collaborative partnership,' neither is it a contracting-out relationship. Table 9.1 confirms this, yet analysis reveals that the operating agreement does meet enough criteria that it can be considered a form of partnership. This leads to the hypothesis that since the term 'partner' implies a relationship of equal standing and collaboration, it cannot be utilized in this situation as only the provincial government has the legal right to operate a gambling facility. Given that collaborative partnerships are considered the 'real' partnerships, perhaps for legal reasons the government does not want to imply a relationship that legally cannot exist.

2   *The Lack of an Attractor*

Not long after the FMC–OLGC negotiations were completed, the FMC released some of the details of its winning bid, including its plans for the on-site 72,000-square-foot meeting space and convention facility and the off-site attraction of a 12,000-seat indoor/outdoor amphitheatre.[79] At this writing the on-site convention space has been built, but it is only 28,000 square feet. FMC has offered to give the City of Niagara Falls $15 million as 'seed money' towards building a convention centre; City Council has declined to accept it.[80] The amphitheatre, or an equivalent 'year-round world class attraction,' has yet to be built.

Dealing with the Local Community

For those parties outside the FMC and the OLGC, very little has ever been known about the attractions. According to the local press, 'promised tourism commitments may or may not have been fulfilled already, depending on who you talk to.'[81] City Council asked the FMC's CEO to appear before council to sort out the attraction issue; he did not do so. The FMC argues that the attraction would have been built by now, except that back in 2001 the city could not decide what it wanted.[82] The FMC contends that it owes $15 million in attractions; other parties, including Fair Share, contend that the amount is closer to $100 million.[83] Given the lack of communication between the FMC and the local community, the confusion is inevitable.

The proposed 12,000-seat indoor/outdoor amphitheatre is at the centre of the debate. FMC now argues that Niagara does not have the market to sustain it since it 'would need long term sponsors and contracts to sustain the inevitable losses … and Niagara does not have the population base during the summer to pay for it.'[84] The OLGC agrees with this conclusion.[85] Confused citizens such as the members of Fair Share argue that even if an amphitheatre is not built, the FMC is still responsible for building a year-round world-class attraction in accordance with the RFP. Fair Share's $100 million request arises from the belief that the indoor/outdoor amphitheatre attraction would have cost at least that much.[86]

What has resulted is a flurry of rumours and unsubstantiated opinions as to who owes what to whom. Even more worrisome is that the OLGC admits that 'what was announced in the winning bid is not the same as what was hammered out in the final contract talks with the FMC.'[87] Concerned citizens and politicians are trying to get some public accountability, but that has proven difficult when dealing with an agreement that is confidential and possibly not based on the original RFP conditions.

Dealing with the OLGC

The FMC is feeling the pressure from the local community; moreover, this issue has led to tensions with the OLGC. Even though the OLGC has 'no direct involvement in the financing, development and operation of the Tourist Attractors,' it is responsible for 'ensuring that they occur.'[88] In March 2005 a 'stiffly worded letter' was sent by the OLGC to the FMC.[89] In that letter (which was leaked to the press), the OLGC criticized the FMC for not making enough money for the province; for not providing a 'full entertainment experience' that includes restaurants, shows, and retail stores; and for not building the off-site tourist attraction.[90] Under the operating agreement the OLGC is allowed to penalize the FMC for non-compliance, but no details have been released, nor is it known whether the current events warrant such sanctions.

Most noteworthy in this situation is the recent leadership change in the FMC, which is said to be 'influenced' by the OLGC. Actually, the OLGC has characterized its current relationship with the FMC as 'challenging in points, but optimistically positive with the new leadership in place.'[91] Unlike the former CEO, the newly appointed CEO, Clare Copeland, has experience with the Ontario public service. According to the OLGC, 'having someone with both private as well as public sector experience is very important.'[92] Copeland, who has served on many public sector boards such as Toronto Hydro, agreed that his public sector experience is valuable; he understands that 'the public sector doesn't move as quickly and there are a lot of bosses and agendas that have to be met.'[93] Conceivably, to blend two worlds – the public and private sectors – the change in leadership was essential. All of this reveals that the mandate of the partnership is perhaps better shared with someone who has experience serving the public interest. Even though the issue of the attractor has created some tension within the partnership, the OLGC has chosen to support the FMC. Other stakeholders are still trying to figure out who, if anyone, is accountable for the lack of the attractor.

Lessons Learned

In the end, whether it is called a partnership or an operating agreement, several lessons can be drawn from this experience.

1 *A confidential agreement can undermine public service values and put the credibility of the partnership at risk.* Public perception that this was a flawed agreement from the outset was only reinforced when the FMC failed to provide a world-class attraction. Once the public began to demand answers, it became apparent that the confidentiality of the agreement took precedence over public accountability, transparency, and openness. As a result, the credibility of the partnership was brought into question, as was the appropriate role of government in the partnership.

2 *Culture gaps[94] can occur between public and private sector partners because business works with a different set of rules and expectations.* For example, the FMC has been criticized for not appearing before City Council to discuss the issue of attractors. In fairness to the FMC, it has no direct or formal obligation to this group. The FMC's obligations are to its shareholders and the OLGC, not Niagara Falls City Council. The city received $2.5 million from the FMC to alleviate costs associated with hosting the casino (e.g., road maintenance); however, it has no authority to make demands. From a business perspective this is clear; from a government perspective it is not. Government is used to working in a fishbowl and to being accountable to multiple groups, even if just for appearance's sake. The private sector partner was perhaps not always willing to take into account the political dimension of the partnership.

3 *The private sector partner will be expected to uphold public accountability standards.* The public expected the FMC to account for why the promise of an attractor had not been fulfilled. Regardless that it is a privately owned company, the public expected answers because public money went into the casino project.

4 *The partners need to maintain communication with their stakeholders.* Communications between the OLGC–FMC partners and the local

politicians and residents of Niagara have been relatively poor. The
FMC is not required to be open and transparent with the city as a
condition of the agreement; even so, some information exchange
would have helped dispel the rumours, misinformation, and general
confusion surrounding the attractor issue. The OLGC recognizes
that this is an ongoing problem, but believes this will be addressed
with the FMC's new CEO, who unlike his predecessor has experience working with the public sector.[95]

5 *The traditional model of governance does not always apply in public–private partnerships.* In this case the minister of Public Infrastructure and
Renewal is twice removed from the OLGC–FMC agreement: not
only is it a public–private partnership with its own set of confidential rules and conditions, but it is also headed by the OLGC, a Crown
enterprise that works at arm's length from the ministry. Thus ministerial responsibility can be only loosely applied. Citizens have pick-
eted the minister to remedy the attractor situation but have met little
success. The direct lines of accountability and responsibility that are
typically enjoyed in traditional public sector operations are not
always applicable in a partnership arrangement, especially when
that arrangement is confidential.

6 *Partnerships with a profit-based mandate may weaken the government's
ability to uphold the public interest.* For example, aside from the profits,
the OLGC is required to uphold the public interest by ensuring
responsible gaming. This may prove to be a quandary for the OLGC,
as statistics reveal that approximately 36 per cent of Ontario casino
revenue is generated by gambling addicts. Banning ATM machines
on casino floors is one example of a precaution the OLGC could take
to promote responsible gaming, but it would not be a wise business
decision.

7 *Partners must respect one another by honouring the roles and conditions
on which they agreed.* The attraction issue has become a political
embarrassment for the OLGC, especially now that its differences
with the FMC have been aired publicly.

Conclusion

As Rob Nicholson, the Niagara Falls MP, stated, 'Niagara Falls isn't
Vegas.'[96] Canadians have had a long history of government intervention; we feel comfortable having governments oversee various markets,
especially in areas such as alcohol (e.g, the Liquor Control Board of

Ontario) and gaming (e.g., the OLGC). Usually government involvement fosters transparency, clear lines of accountability, and a definitive understanding of the state's roles and responsibilities. This surely has not been the case with the FMC–OLGC operating agreement.

It is certainly expected that industry confidences and details might be withheld from public disclosure, but the fact that the very nature of the agreement has been withheld is highly unusual. The OLGC does not publicly state that the operating agreement is a partnership, though it does recognize that its relationship with the FMC goes beyond just contracting out. Neither have specifics about what an operating agreement entails been open for public scrutiny. According to Kernaghan's typology, the FMC–OLGC operating agreement can be considered a partnership agreement. As relationships and agreements between government and business continue to evolve, his typology and general characteristics of partnership such as mutual dependency, shared decision making, shared work, shared financial resources, shared risk-taking, and shared rewards will serve as an increasingly important foundation for assessing various forms of arrangements.

The accountability issue of this partnership would most likely never have been brought into question had the FMC provided the promised attractions. The general public and local politicians have found it difficult to accept that unlike most government operations, the FMC–OLGC operating agreement does not provide for clear lines of accountability and transparency. This agreement has been shrouded in secrecy owing to the nature of the competitive casino industry. The OLGC has upheld the secrecy of the agreement despite public backlash and acknowledgment that the FMC has not lived up to the RFP agreement. This has been confusing for many stakeholders as they are accustomed to governments adhering to the principles of responsible government, not actively participating in blurring the lines of accountability.

The difficulty of utilizing alternative methods of service delivery such as the FMC–OLGC operating agreement is that it requires the public to adjust its mindset. Here, accountability, openness, and transparency have been diminished as the cost of doing business with the private sector. This has been the tradeoff. As this case study has shown, the consequence of this secrecy is general confusion as to who is (a) in charge and (b) upholding the public interest. Mixed as it is with misinformation, rumours, and old-fashioned political posturing, the current situation with the FMC-OLGC has become a fascinating case study to learn from and possibly, to advance our understanding of the complexities that each partnership (or operating agreement) may encounter.

NOTES

1 The author would like to thank the editors, Andy Sancton and Jackie and Carm Dix, and the anonymous reviewers for their helpful comments and suggestions on an earlier draft.
2 See Kenneth Kernaghan, 'Partnership and Public Administration: Conceptual and Practical Considerations,' *Canadian Public Administration* 36, no. 1 (1993): 57–76.
3 Donald Savoie, *Thatcher, Reagan, and Mulroney: In Search of a New Bureaucracy* (Toronto: University of Toronto Press, 1994), 172–3.
4 See Michael Barzalay, *Breaking Through Bureaucracy: A New Vision for Managing in Government* (Berkeley: University of California Press, 1992); Anna Yeatman, 'The Reform of Public Management: An Overview,' *Australian Journal of Public Administration* 53, no. 3 (1994): 287–95; Peter Aucoin, *The New Public Management: Canada in Comparative Perspective* (Montreal: IRPP, 1995); Mohamed Charih and Arthur Daniels, eds., *New Public Management and Public Administration in Canada* (Toronto: IPAC, 1997); and David Osborne and Ted Gaebler, *Reinventing Government: How the Entrepreneurial Spirit Is Transforming the Public Sector* (New York: Penguin, 1993).
5 Marcel Masse, Treasury Board President, 'Governing for the Future' (speech), Quebec City, 15 July 1997.
6 For further elaboration, see Partnerships British Columbia at www. partnershipsbc.ca.
7 Interview with Mina Laudan, director of Communications, Partnerships British Columbia, 8 August 2005.
8 Canadian Council for Public–Private Partnerships, *The People Speak on P3: A National Survey on Attitudes to Public–Private Partnerships* (22 November 2004), 3.
9 Shortly after this article was written, the OLGC became known as OLG (Ontario Lottery and Gaming). Note that though OLG is now the 'preferred name,' OLGC is still the official corporate name. See www.olgc.ca.
10 Interview with Joe Vecsi, director of Public Affairs, OLGC, 13 August 2005.
11 See Kernaghan, 'Partnership and Public Administration.'
12 Ibid., 61.
13 Ibid.
14 Canada, Treasury Board Secretariat, Alternative Service Delivery Division, Service and Innovation Sector, *Policy on Alternative Service Delivery* (Ottawa, 2002), 9 (emphasis added).
15 Ontario, Management Board Secretariat, *Alternative Service Delivery Framework*, (Toronto: Queen's Printer, 1997), 22.
16 Kernaghan, 'Partnership and Public Administration,' 62.

17 Evert Lindquist, 'Taking a Step Back: Partnership in Perspective,' *Optimum* 24, no. 3 (1993): 24.

18 Ibid.

19 This partnership typology developed by Kernaghan is a synthesis of several different partnership typologies, including the classifications made by the Ontario Ministry of Natural Resources in its submission to the IPAC Award for Innovative Management, 15 January 1992, and Susan Phillips, 'How Ottawa Blends: Shifting Government Relathionships with Interest Groups,' in Francis Abele, ed., *How Ottawa Spends: The Politics of Fragmentation* (Ottawa: Carlton University Press, 1991), 183–228. This typology of partnership continues to serve as the leading conceptual framework for classifying different partnership arrangements. See Kernaghan, 'Partnership and Public Administration,' 61–5.

20 Kernaghan, 'Partnership and Public Administration,' 63–4.

21 Ibid., 64.

22 Ibid., 64–5.

23 Ibid.

24 For more information, see Treasury Board, *Managing Collaborative Arrangements*, at www.tbs-sct.gc.ca/fcer-cfre/documents/mca-gec/mca-gec01_e. asp#a1.

25 Canadian Council for Public–Private Partnerships, www.pppcouncil.ca/ aboutPPP_definition.asp.

26 FMC, 'Niagara Fallsview Casino Resort: A View to the Future,' discoverniagara.com/casino/about/media/body.php, 8 June 2004.

27 Ministry of Economic Development, Trade, and Tourism, news release, 'Falls Management Company Chosen as Preferred Proponent for the Niagara Falls Casino/Gateway Project,' 18 February 1998.

28 Casino Niagara, 'Milestones,' www.discoverniagara.com/casino/about/ media/body.php, 8 June 2004.

29 Members of the Navegante team had held 'key positions' in launching casinos such as the MGM Grand Hotel and Bally's Grand (Las Vegas), the Diamond Beach Hotel Casino (Darwin, Australia), Caesar's Atlantic City, and Casino de Montreal. See 'Corporate Profile,' www.navegantegroup.com.

30 Note that as part of the agreement, the Navegante Group was not allowed to submit a bid for the permanent casino.

31 Ontario Casino Corporation, news release: 'Temporary Operator Selected for Casino Niagara,' 25 July 1996.

32 Falls Management Company, 'Chronology,' www.fallsmanagement.com/ About_FMC/chronology.html.

33 Falls Management Company, press release, 'Navegante Welcomes Falls

Management Company,' www.discoverniagara.com/casino/about/media/body.php, 14 September 1998.

34 Interview with Kim Craitor, MPP for Niagara Falls, 22 August 2005. (Note: Craitor served on the Niagara Falls City Council during this time.) Description used in the Ontario Casino Corporation, 'Request for Proposals: Niagara Falls Casino/Gateway Project,' 12 September 1996, 7.

35 Kim Craitor interview.

36 Ontario Ministry of Economic Development, Trade, and Tourism, 'Background: Niagara Falls Development – the Casino/Gateway Project,' n.d., 9.

37 Ibid, 9.

38 Falls Management Company, 'Milestones,' www.discoverniagara.com/casino/about/media/body.php.

39 'Niagara Falls Casino/Gateway Project, Falls Management Company' (information collected by the City of Niagara Falls, n.d.), 1.

40 Kevin Donovan, 'Intrigue Flows over Casino Bid: Documents Turn Up in Suit over Niagara Deal,' *Toronto Star*, 3 March 2002, A1.

41 Donovan, 'Liberals Call for Inquiry into Casino Contract,' *Toronto Star*, 28 May 1998, A1.

42 Donovan, 'Minister Defends Casino Award Process,' *Toronto Star*, 29 May 1998, A1.

43 Ibid.

44 The Fallsview Company sued the OCC over this issue and received an undisclosed settlement. Kim Craitor interview.

45 Donovan, 'Lawyer in Casino Probe Had Dual Role,' *Toronto Star*, 12 June 1998, A1.

46 Donovan, 'Niagara Casino Cleared of Conflict Taint,' *Toronto Star*, 21 August 1998, A1.

47 Falls Management Company, 'Chronology,' www.fallsmanagement.com/About_FMC/chronology.html.

48 Ibid.

49 www.fairshareniagara.ca.

50 Ontario Casino Corporation, 'Request for Proposals: Niagara Falls Casino/Gateway Project,' 12 September 1996, 15.

51 Ontario Ministry of Economic Development, Trade, and Tourism, press release: 'Falls Management Company Chosen as Preferred Proponent for the Niagara Falls Casino/Gateway Project,' 18 February 1998. Also see www.olgc.ca and www.fallsmanagement.com.

52 This conclusion was drawn based on the interviews with the respective parties (August 2005).

53 Kim Craitor interview.

54 Teresa Roncon, OLGC spokesperson, quoted in Paul Forsyth, 'Who Owes What and to Whom?' *Niagara This Week,* 12 August 2005, 10.

55 Interview with Joe Vecsi, director of Public Affairs, OLGC, 13 August 2005.

56 Kernaghan's typology does apply to partnerships involving a diversity of partners such as public–not-for-profit partnerships and public–public partnerships. For the purposes of this paper, the criteria and types were profiled using a public–private partnership model.

57 Information pertaining to the characteristics of the operating agreement was obtained through interviews with Clare Copeland, the CEO of FMC, and Joe Vecsi, the OLGC director of Public Affairs.

58 Kenneth Kernaghan, D. Brian Marson, and Sandford Borins, *The New Public Organization* (Toronto: IPAC, 2000), 179.

59 Interview with Clare Copeland, CEO of FMC, 24 August 2005; interview with Joe Vecsi, 23 August 2005.

60 See Colin Campbell, Timothy Hartnagel, and Garry Smith, 'The Legalization of Gambling in Canada,' report prepared for the Law Commission of Canada, responsiblegambling.org/articles/legalization_of_gambling_in _canada_july2005.pdf.

61 OLGC, 'Corporate,' corporate.olgc.ca/corp_about.jsp.

62 Vecsi interview.

63 Ibid.

64 Email correspondence with Vecsi, 26 August 2005.

65 Craitor interview.

66 Ontario Realty Corporation (ORC) and the Liquor Control Board of Ontario (LCBO) were also moved under the Ministry of Public Infrastructure and Renewal.

67 Interview with Peter Kormos, MPP for Welland–Thorold, 19 August 2005.

68 Vecsi interview.

69 Ibid.

70 Copeland interview.

71 Ibid.

72 Ibid.

73 OLGC, 'Corporate Responsibility,' www.corporate.olgc.ca/ corp_responsible.jsp.

74 Craitor interview.

75 April Lindgren, 'Gambling Addicts Fuel Ontario's Gaming Revenue: Province Doesn't Plan to Scale Back Gaming That Took in $2.28 Billion Last Year,' *Kingston Whig-Standard,* 3 November 2004, A1.

76 Ibid.

77 Interview with Dean Iorfida, Niagara Falls City Clerk, 9 August 2005.

78 OLGC, 'Niagara Fallsview Casino Resort Fact Sheet.'
79 Casino Niagara and Hyatt Niagara Falls, 'Niagara Falls Casino/Gateway Project Highlights,' n.d. 1–3.
80 Copeland interview.
81 Forsyth, 'Who Owes What to Whom?'
82 Copeland inteview.
83 Interview with Patricia Mangoff, member of Fair Share, 8 August 2005. (Note: Fair Share's platform is outlined in a pamphlet, 'Where's My Fair Share?' which was sent to local residents. See www.fairshareniagara.ca for more information.)
84 Copeland interview.
85 Vecsi interview.
86 Interview with Margaret Done, Fair Share spokesperson, 18 August 2005.
87 Editorial, 'End the Secrecy,' *Niagara This Week*, 17 August 2005, 6.
88 Ontario Casino Corporation, 'Request for Proposals: Niagara Falls Casino/Gateway Project,' 20.
89 Donovan, 'Gaming Officials Demand Casino Shape Up,' *Toronto Star*, 14 March 2005, A1.
90 Vecsi interview.
91 Ibid.
92 Ibid.
93 Copeland interview.
94 The argument that there can be a 'culture gap' between the public and private sectors was originally outlined in Alti Rodal, 'Managing Partnerships,' *Optimum* 24, no. 3 (1993): 50.
95 Vecsi interview.
96 Interview with Rob Nicholson, MP for Niagara Falls, 22 August 2005.

10 Citizen-Centred Service in Canada: From Research to Results

BRIAN MARSON

Current Status of the Field of Public Sector Service Delivery

During the past ten years, public sector service delivery has been the subject of significant research by scholars and by governments regarding citizens' service needs, and also regarding best practices in service delivery, especially within the Canadian public sector. Thus public sector service delivery has begun to emerge as an important part of public sector management science, including performance metrics and measurement. This chapter examines contemporary concepts and approaches to citizen-centred service delivery and looks at emerging trends and issues. In addition, Kenneth Kernaghan's contributions to the field of public sector service delivery are reviewed. Kernaghan has played an important role in the citizen-centred service research agenda, especially in the fields of service partnerships, e-service, and integrated service delivery. In this regard he has been an active partner with practitioners at all three levels of government in identifying and communicating citizens' service needs as well as emerging best practices in citizen-centred service delivery.

Kenneth Kernaghan's contributions include research and publications in the following areas: integrated service delivery and 'single window' service; e-service; and intergovernmental service partnerships, including governance arrangements for intergovernmental service delivery.

Perhaps his greatest contribution has been to the emerging field of integrated and intergovernmental service delivery. He has documented the innovative world of one-stop service delivery in the public sector; he has also developed a conceptual model of the ideal future state of citizen-centred integrated service delivery towards which the public sector can strive and has identified the political and bureaucratic barriers that must be overcome to get there. Through his work he has helped public managers in Canada and elsewhere create innovative and citizen-centred improvements in public sector service delivery. He is also a good example of a scholar who has partnered with practitioners to undertake 'action research' aimed at practical service improvement.

Canada: A World Leader in Citizen-Centred Service

Since 1997 the Canadian public sector has become an acknowledged world leader in developing a citizen-centred strategy for improving government services to citizens. In 2005, for example, Accenture ranked Canada number one in the world among twenty-two countries both in e-government and in citizen-centred service more broadly.[1] Other governments, such as Britain and New Zealand, acknowledge Canada's leadership role in service improvement and have adopted elements of the 'Canadian model.'

The Canadian strategy to improve government service to citizens and businesses has its roots in the Citizen Centred Service Network, an action research initiative created by the Canada School of Public Service (then the Canadian Centre for Management Development) in 1997, which involved more than 220 public sector executives and academics from across Canada. The impetus for this work was the desire by public servants and their governments to improve public sector service delivery, as documented in successive IPAC surveys of deputy ministers over the past decade and driven by technological changes and public pressure for improved service delivery (www.ipac.ca/Survey_DMs_and_CAOs). The application of action research and performance measurement techniques to service improvement across the Canadian public sector has been the driver of steadily improving results.

The Citizen Centred Service Network's initial award-winning research in 1998 on citizens' needs and expectations evolved into the ongoing Citizens First research series, funded by governments across Canada. It also led to the founding of the Institute for Citizen Centred Service.[2] Through ongoing research into citizen's expectations, into measurement systems, and into best practices, public sector service delivery in Canada is rapidly moving from an 'art' to a research-driven management discipline.

Defining Citizen-Centred Service in the Public Sector Context

As noted above, improving service delivery for citizens has been a management priority of Canadian deputy ministers for a decade, driven by public pressure for better service and by technological innovations such as the Internet. According to the surveys of deputy ministers conducted by IPAC,[3] service delivery is one of four clusters of management challenges facing Canadian public organizations (the others are human resource issues, performance measurement and accountability, and aligning government operations with fiscal realities). The term citizen-centred service has been in wide use across the Canadian public sector since 1998, when the intergovernmental Citizen Centred Service Network[4] published a series of research reports[5] on citizens' needs and expectations, including the award-winning *Citizens First* national survey.[6] The previous year, the Clerk of the Privy Council had stated in her annual report to the prime minister:

> We have learned that focusing on citizens' needs often leads, over time, to
> - integrated service delivery among departments and agencies, to better serve citizens;
> - integrated service delivery among governments, as they share the responsibility of serving citizens;
> - strategic alliances and partnerships with private-sector, volunteer and non-profit organizations (everyone can contribute to the collective interest); and
> - the exploitation of the potential of information technology as a means for government to reach out and for Canadians to access government on their terms.[7]

Over the intervening decade, increasing attention has been paid to citizen-centred service delivery across the Canadian public sector and in other countries. This has included the development by almost all governments of the Internet as a new service channel for citizens. In addition, in recent years most of the provinces have created 'single window' service agencies; examples include Service New Brunswick, Access PEI, Service Quebec, Service Ontario, Service Manitoba, Service Alberta, and Service British Columbia. Likewise, Australia has created Centrelink in 1997, and the British government has espoused both e-government and 'joined-up government.' In 1999, Canada's federal government initiated Government On-Line and piloted Service Canada; and in 2005 it expanded Service Canada so that it became a separate delivery agency. In 2000 the federal Treasury Board issued its management manifesto *Results for Canadians*, which stated: 'This document sets out a framework for management in the Government of Canada and an agenda for change in the way that departments and agencies manage and deliver their programs and services. This framework and agenda recognize that a "citizen focus" must therefore be built into all government activities and services.'[8]

How should citizen-centred service be defined? According to a federal Deputy Ministers' Task Force on Service Delivery Models,

> Citizen-Centred Service incorporates citizens' concerns at every stage of the service design and delivery process; that is, citizens' needs become the organizing principle around which the public interest is determined and service delivery is planned:
> - Citizens are treated as active participants in the design and delivery of services;
> - Service is planned using a holistic approach, clustering service needs around a targeted client group;
> - Governments, not the citizen, are responsible for integrating service;
> - The government concentrates on setting the goals and ensuring the outcomes;
> - Service partnerships between government departments, levels of government, and other providers are fundamental to this approach;
> - Obstacles – jurisdictional, organizational or legal – to a partnership approach are removed; and
> - Service design and delivery systems are continuously measured, questioned and improved.[9]

Citizens First,[10] which interviewed 2,900 Canadians, constituted the first comprehensive 'outside-in' citizens' view of government service delivery. The result was the following model, which outlines the way that citizens actually experience public sector service delivery. This model shows that citizens start with a need, not a service. Then they must find and access the service(s) that meet their needs. Once at the point of service, their service delivery experience determines their satisfaction levels as well as their priorities for service improvement. This model is discussed in more detail later in the chapter.

Note, however, that in the public sector the needs of clients must be

Figure 10.1. The *Citizens First* service model

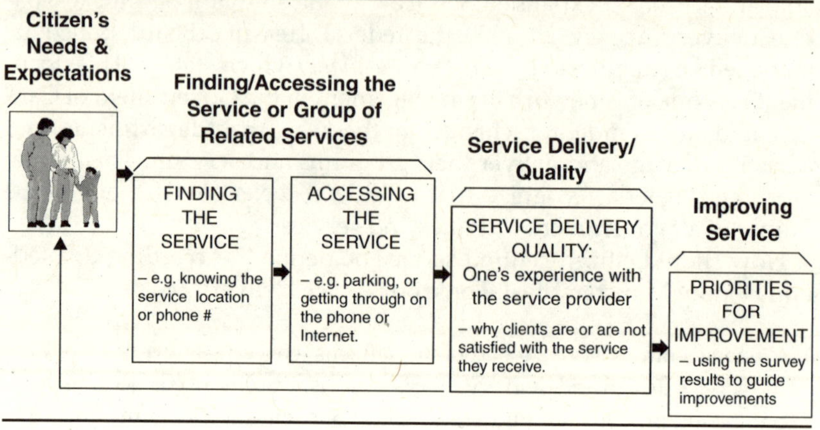

balanced with the public interest, as pointed out earlier in the quote from the Deputy Ministers' Task Force. This is especially true in the regulatory and enforcement activities of government, where protecting the public interest is the predominant objective. This notion of balancing client service needs with the broader public interest in public sector service delivery was captured in the Deputy Ministers' Task Force on Values and Ethics: 'The true role of public servants is not only to serve the "customers" but also to balance the interest and preserve the rights of "citizens."'[11]

In *The New Public Organization*,[12] the authors outline a similar framework for thinking about public sector service delivery. They suggest that as one moves from service activity towards regulatory activity, the emphasis shifts from serving clients to protecting the public interest. Thus in travelling along that continuum, the nature of service delivery changes from service to control. For example, if a government service involves selling a map, the focus is on serving the client's needs; however, a prison service must restrain and control prisoners in order to protect the public interest. Kernaghan and his colleagues use a special nomenclature to capture this complex reality of service in the public sector:

From: Customer-Interest Dominant

↑

❏ **Customer** (e.g., someone renting a campsite)

❑ **Client** (e.g., an elderly recipient of ongoing community health services)
❑ **Claimant** (e.g., someone who must qualify for the service – Workers Compensation or Employment Insurance)
❑ **Complier** (e.g., a tax filer; paying a parking ticket)
❑ **Captive** (e.g., a person arrested by police, a convict, or a prisoner of war)

↓

To: Public-Interest Dominant

Within this framework, they note that the customers, clients, claimants, compliers, and captives are simultaneously citizens (or organizations) with legal rights and obligations, and that this fact may affect their expectations with respect to their interactions with government agencies. This is akin to the difference between being a 'customer' of a private sector bank and being a 'member' of a credit union. Expectations of the service experience may be very different for someone who is a 'member' of an organization, just as they are for citizens who are 'members' of the body politic, when they interact with government agencies. Moreover, as pointed out in *A Strong Foundation*, the role of citizens is much broader than the role of customers, and the interests of both must be balanced in public sector service delivery. For example, in current times, that could involve balancing the desires of customers for improved service with the desires of citizens and taxpayers for lower-cost service delivery and lower taxes.

Research Findings on Citizens' Service Needs and Expectations

Since 1997, Canada has been considered a world leader in the implementation of citizen-centred approaches to service, both within and across jurisdictions. According to Accenture's survey of twenty-two countries, 'Canada's focus on self-examination and its relentless pursuit of user feedback have allowed it to continue to build what is clearly one of the world-leading customer-focused government online programs.'[13]
Likewise, the UK Cabinet Office has identified Canada's citizen-driven action research as a major driver of Canada's public sector service improvement:

Canada, the world's seventh largest economy, has a thriving public sector and can teach us much about responding to our customers. I visited the

country last year with one of my colleagues from the Office of Public Services Reform in the Cabinet Office. I was surprised at the extent to which
public servants embraced the needs of those who used their services – and
how much they seem to have been personally empowered by the experience ... The Canadian authorities put a lot of effort into finding out about
those who use public services, what they like about them and where they
would welcome changes. Surveys are conducted every two years to measure trends in customer satisfaction. And these are published independently by a small but powerful body, known as the Institute for Citizen
Centred Service.[14]

As noted by the UK Cabinet Office, federal, provincial, territorial,
and municipal governments across Canada collaborate to identify citizens' (and businesses') service needs, satisfaction, and priorities for service improvement. Based on the biennial *Citizens First* survey, which is
sponsored by more than twenty governments and agencies, an overall
picture of citizens' views on public sector service appears (figure 10.2).

This 'citizens-eye view' helps governments to understand how to
improve access and service delivery from the citizens' perspective, as
well as how to focus on those improvements that will make the most
difference for citizens. There are three areas where improvement is
required: finding and accessing the services required; clustering the
services that citizens and businesses need around client groups and life
events; and improving the quality of the actual service provided, especially the timeliness of service. Similar 'outside-in' perspectives from
the business community are gathered through *Taking Care of Business*,[15]
the biennial national survey conducted by the Institute for Citizen Centred Service.

Improving Access and Clustering Services

According to the *Citizens First* and *Taking Care of Business* national surveys, Canadians and Canadian businesses have problems knowing
what services are available and where to find them. This problem is
compounded by the fact that services can be provided by three or four
levels of government in Canada, in addition to the not-for-profit sector
(often on behalf of governments). How can governments help citizens
to easily ascertain where to go to obtain relevant services? Two concepts are being used to make it easier for citizens to find government
services: 'no wrong door' and 'single window' information services.

Figure 10.2. How citizens experience public service

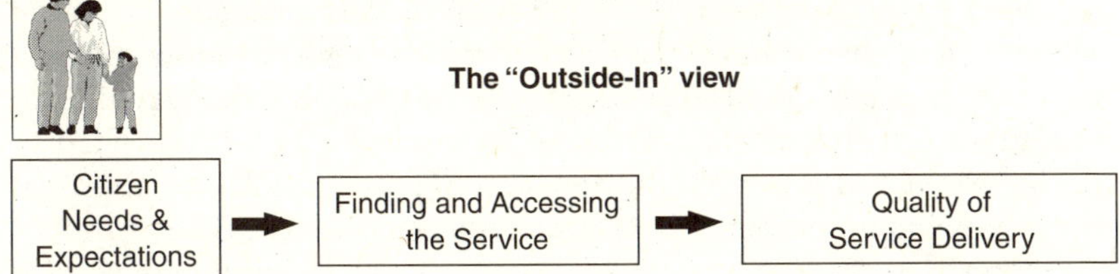

• Citizens (97%) expect service from the public sector to be as good or better than the private sector.

• 16% of the time citizens need a group of related services – e.g. dealing with a life event – and often across multiple levels of government.

When trying to find a service, 33% of citizens did not know where to go before they started.

• More than 67% had at least one problem when accessing the service:

  • Busy phone lines
  • Bounced around
  • Trouble with phone trees

• Telephone is the most common channel and also the one with the most access problems.

• In half of all service experiences, citizens use more than one service channel.

• Five factors drive satisfaction with service: timeliness, competence, extra mile, fairness, and outcome. Internet drivers include navigation, completeness, and visual appeal.

• Addressing these drivers can make the difference between service quality scores of 87 (out of 100) and 22.

• Citizen priorities for service improvement include:

• Access: one-stop service
• Telephone and e-service
• Timeliness

'No wrong door,' a concept pioneered by the State of Delaware's State Service Centres, is based on the idea that citizens should be able to go to any government point of service and get help in finding the services they need. This concept has been further developed in Prince Edward Island through GovInfo, an online system that contains information on accessing services at all three levels of government. So at least in theory, a citizen in Charlottetown can enter a provincial social services office and inquire where to apply for a passport – the social services staff can call up that information from the GovInfo Internet site[16] and provide it to the citizen. Or the citizen can access it directly via the Internet from home.

More commonly, the Canadian public sector has implemented single-window information services for each service 'channel' – that is, telephone, in-person, and Internet. For the telephone channel, governments have collaborated to create integrated 'blue pages' in the telephone directory, along with keyword indexes to make it easier to find government services. Consistent with citizen-centred principles, the new blue pages have been designed with help from focus groups of citizens. Most governments have also installed single-window call centres such as 1-800-OCANADA (federal) and Inquiry BC (provincial) through which citizens can dial a single number and be connected to the department or service(s) they are looking for. The CRTC's approval of the telephone number 311 for municipal service access by citizens[17] is another step towards providing easier access to government service for citizens.

Likewise, on the Internet channel, governments have installed single window 'portals' such as the Canada site[18] and the Ontario Government site,[19] which allow citizens to self-navigate to the services they need. For the in-person channel, many governments have created information counters for citizens looking for help in accessing the government services they need. Examples are the federal Service Canada counters, Ontario's information counters, Service New Brunswick offices, Access PEI outlets, and BC's Service British Columbia offices. It is interesting that all of these information services receive requests for services provided by other levels of government. For example, the Ontario information counter on Bay Street in Toronto and the Toronto City Hall information counter both receive many inquiries about federal services such as Social Insurance Number and passport applications, and pensions and employment insurance. Consistent with the 'no wrong door' philosophy, clients coming to these Ontario and Toronto counters are given information about how to reach the federal points of service and may even be provided with the federal forms.

The second part of the access issue is that citizens often need a bundle of services provided by several departments and more than one government. The former Clerk of the Privy Council, Jocelyne Bourgon, argued that it was wrong to make citizens 'manage the white space' between programs that should be coordinated. In an attempt to make service more responsive to citizens' needs, therefore, many governments are providing 'single window' service, or what the British government calls 'joined-up government.' These single-window services fall into three main categories: 'information kiosks' (e.g., 1-800-OCANADA); 'department stores' (e.g., Service New Brunswick), and 'boutiques' (e.g., the Canada Business Service Centres). The latter two types focus on providing seamless, one-stop service for citizens and businesses. For example, Service New Brunswick is a Crown corporation that provides a wide range of services to citizens and businesses via telephone and the Internet as well as at its retail outlets in convenient shopping locations.[20] Service New Brunswick:

- provides over two hundred services to the public through a network of office locations, online services, and Service New Brunswick TeleServices (call centres);
- provides one-stop delivery of federal, provincial, and municipal government services;
- operates New Brunswick's Real Property Registry;
- operates New Brunswick's Personal Property Registry;
- operates New Brunswick's Corporate Affairs Registry;
- assesses all land, buildings, and improvements for property taxation purposes and operates the province's Property Assessment and Taxation System; and
- maintains New Brunswick's land information infrastructure.

Service New Brunswick has analogues in most provinces (e.g., Service Ontario, Access PEI, Service Quebec, Service Alberta, and Service BC) as well as the Government of Canada (Service Canada). Some of these one-stop 'department stores' are set up as megadelivery departments (e.g., the Ontario and Nova Scotia models), and some are set up as separate Crown agencies that deliver services on behalf of a wide range of departments (e.g., Service New Brunswick).

In addition to these public sector 'department stores,' the Canadian public sector has established an increasing number of 'service boutiques' to serve particular life events (e.g., unemployment) or particular client groups (e.g., new businesses). Some of these boutiques are storefront (e.g., Canada Business Service Centres[21]), and some are Internet-based (e.g., the intergovernmental Seniors Portal).[22] Others are both Internet and telephone based, such as Toronto 211,[23] a multijurisdictional partnership that provides one-stop access to health and social services in the Greater Toronto Area. Because of the ease of creating integrated service delivery via Internet 'clusters,' the public sector has seen a proliferation of 'virtual service boutiques,' though for the time being most of them are limited to providing information and simple self-service transactions such as downloading and completing forms online.

Improving Access and One-Stop Delivery

Despite the many initiatives to improve access, Canadians still indicate through the *Citizens First* surveys that finding out where to go to get the service, then actually getting to the point of service, is still a major problem.[24] Businesses appear to have fewer access problems, partly because experienced intermediaries (e.g., accountants and lawyers) are available to them, and partly because service requirements often repeat over time.[25] Improving access for Canadians will require service improvements in many areas: well-marketed one-stop government 1-800 numbers; one-stop government portals; walk-in information counters; improved, citizen-centred blue pages in the telephone book; and the development of an intergovernmental electronic blue pages on the Internet. Overall, this will mean creating a pan–public sector 'no wrong door' approach.

The second problem for citizens in access is actually getting to or into the point of service once it is known. The main barriers to be overcome here are on the telephone channel: limited hours of service, busy phone lines, and complex interactive voice response systems. Improved service on the telephone channel, combined with a 'no wrong door' philosophy across the public sector, will be required to overcome the remaining barriers to citizen-centred service access.

The third element of the access issue is clustering related services so that citizens can conveniently access the multiple services they need in one place. This is a difficult challenge since it often requires governments to collaborate to provide seamless service. In his report to Treasury Board, *Integrated Service Delivery – Beyond the Barriers*,[26] Kernaghan argued that interjurisdictional, integrated service delivery will have to overcome many challenges to succeed in the coming years. The competitive banking industry had to create collaborative joint ventures like Interac and Visa to provide commonly owned service 'utilities' to serve clients seamlessly. Kernaghan argues that in much the same way, interjurisdictional service utilities may be required in the decades ahead to provide truly seamless service to Canadians. Such 'horizontal' intergovernmental service platforms will have to overcome the 'vertical' nature of political accountability of the Canadian political system, as well as challenge technological, turf, and governance issues.

Government Online: Developing the Internet Channel for Service Delivery

In the 1999 Speech from the Throne, the Government of Canada announced that 'the Government will become a model user of information technology and the Internet. By 2004, our goal is to be known around the world as the government most connected to its citizens,

Figure 10.3. Why did you visit this site?

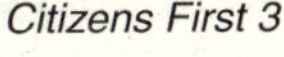

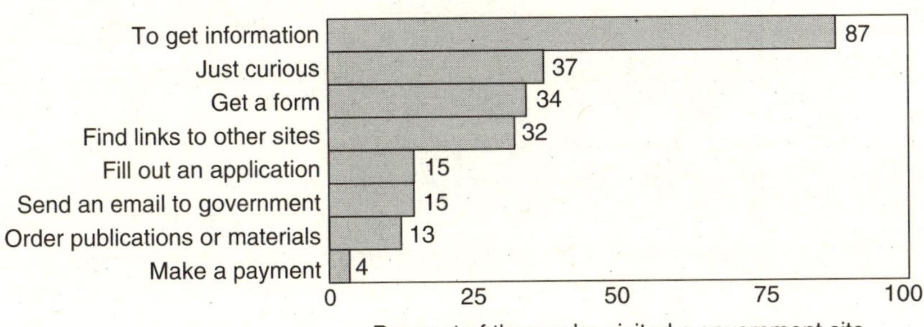

with Canadians able to access all government information and services on-line at the time and place of their choosing.'[27] Subsequently, the federal government announced the Government On-Line (GOL) initiative, which would seek to place the 130 most heavily used government services online for Canadians by 2005. Since that time the Internet channel has become one of the most popular channels for Canadians because of its 24/7 availability and because of the time it can save in conducting business with government.

The Government of Canada established an Internet Panel of ten thousand Canadian Internet users to guide the government in the design of the Internet channel. As a result, Canada has been ranked number one in the world by Accenture for several years for its effective delivery of government services via the Internet.[28]

According to *Citizens First-3* data, in 2003, 70 per cent of Canadian Internet users visited Government of Canada websites, and 66 per cent visited provincial websites. Both figures were significant increases over 2000. By 2003 the Internet was being used mainly for information gathering rather than transactions, as shown in the following chart from *Citizens First-3* (figure 10.3).

However, more and more citizens are also conducting transactions online, such as e-filing their income tax forms. For example, in the 2003 tax year, 43 per cent of Canadians filed their tax returns electronically.[29] Moreover, citizen satisfaction with the Internet channel is higher than for other channels, as documented in the following chart (figure 10.4).

The development of the Internet channel has had a strong impact on the ability of Canadians to find and access the services they need, as

Figure 10.4. Service quality ratings for high-channel services

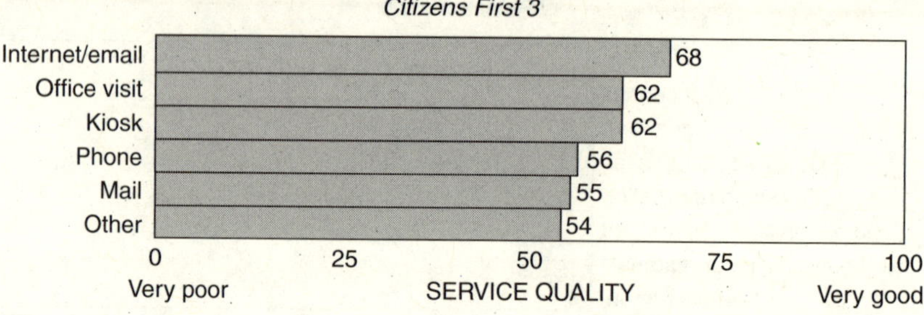

well as to save time and effort visiting government offices or dealing with complex and cumbersome Interactive Voice Response systems on the telephone channel. Recently we have begun to see the merging of the Internet and telephone channels, as Canadians visit departmental websites and then ask departmental call centre personnel questions about information on the departmental website. This 'multichannel' service phenomenon is resulting in call centres evolving into multi-channel client contact centres across the public sector.

Improving Citizen Satisfaction with Service Delivery: Research Findings

Turning from the access issues outlined in the *Citizens First* model described earlier, to the quality of the actual service experience itself, what has the Canadian research uncovered? And how are the research findings being used in the public sector to improve citizen/client satisfaction?

Before the *Citizens First* national survey was launched in 1998 by the Canadian Centre for Management Development (now the Canada School of Public Service), much public opinion research had been done in Canada, but little operational research had been completed that would help public sector managers actually improve service to their clients.[30] For example, before the *Citizens First* research it was not known (a) how satisfied citizens were with a wide range of public services, (b) what factors 'drove' client satisfaction in the public sector (i.e., what factors contributed to high or low satisfaction scores), (c) what citizens' priorities were for service improvement by program, by service channel, or by service element (e.g., courtesy), and (d) what service standards Canadians thought were reasonable (e.g., waiting times). What was discovered through the award-winning *Citizens First* research was groundbreaking and laid the foundation for a focused strategy for service improvement. The results were surprising in some respects.

Perhaps the greatest surprise was that citizens rated their satisfaction with public services in a statistical tie with private sector services. Moreover, a number of public sector services such as libraries and fire services outperformed all private sector services measured in the study.[31] Among the remarkable findings was that Canadians rated their satisfaction with service from Revenue Canada higher than the service they received from Canadian banks. Previously it was thought that public sector service was poorly regarded by citizens. These findings were all the more remarkable because over 90 per cent of Canadians surveyed indicated that their expectations were that the public sector should offer the same or better service than the private sector.

But perhaps the most important finding in the *Citizens First* research was that five 'drivers' of service satisfaction accounted for about 70 per cent of the outcomes in public sector service transactions. In order of importance across a wide range of services, these drivers were

- timeliness,
- knowledge and competence,
- courtesy and extra mile,
- fairness, and
- outcome.

Moreover, the research demonstrated that timeliness was not only the most important 'driver' but also the element of service most in need of improvement across the Canadian public sector. Interestingly, the top four drivers are within the control of managers; sometimes outcome ('I got what I needed') is not, particularly in services that are adjudicated or that have a regulatory component. *Citizens First* provided managers with even more specific guidance because the survey asked Canadians about expectations for service standards. Most of these centred on the timeliness driver; the research demonstrated that most Canadians expect to be served in a maximum of ten minutes at the counter, expect the telephone to be answered in four telephone rings, expect an email or telephone message to be answered the next day, and expect a letter to be answered in two weeks. This information has ushered in a new era in service improvement activity in the Canadian public sector, since managers can now focus their improvement strategies on the key client satisfaction drivers (which are now known by individual channels and by major types of services) and on meeting citizens' expectations for service standards.

Improving Client Satisfaction with Service Delivery – a Results-Based Approach

Research undertaken by the federal Treasury Board in 1999 of more than 200 best practice cases in the federal public service resulted in the development of an empirically based methodology as well as a *How-to Guide*[32] for improving client satisfaction with public sector services. In addition, in 2000 the Treasury Board created a service improvement policy for government services, setting a goal of a 10 per cent improvement in client satisfaction to be achieved by 2005.[33] The recommended approach to improving client satisfaction involved a four-phased, continuous improvement approach comprising nine steps.

Using the service improvement model noted in figure 10.5, many federal departments have significantly improved their service in the eyes of Canadians.[34] For example, Veterans Affairs Canada has focused its efforts on significantly improving satisfaction for its Armed Service clients:

Satisfaction Rating (%)

Client Type	2001	2003
War Veterans	89	90
Canadian Forces Veterans & Clients	72	80
Survivors	84	86
Overall Rating	85	87

Between 2001 and 2003 the satisfaction of Armed Forces clients increased from 72 per cent satisfied to 80 per cent satisfied. In the Quebec Region the increase was from 80 to 87 per cent, in the Atlantic Region from 83 to 89 per cent. Total client satisfaction rates across the department improved from 85 per cent satisfied to 87 per cent satisfied, which shows that even high ratings can be improved over a two-year period. These improvements were achieved by focusing on the drivers of client satisfaction and on those geographic regions that most needed improvement – Atlantic Canada and Quebec. Here is VAC's analysis of

Figure 10.5. Overview of the SIPI Methodology

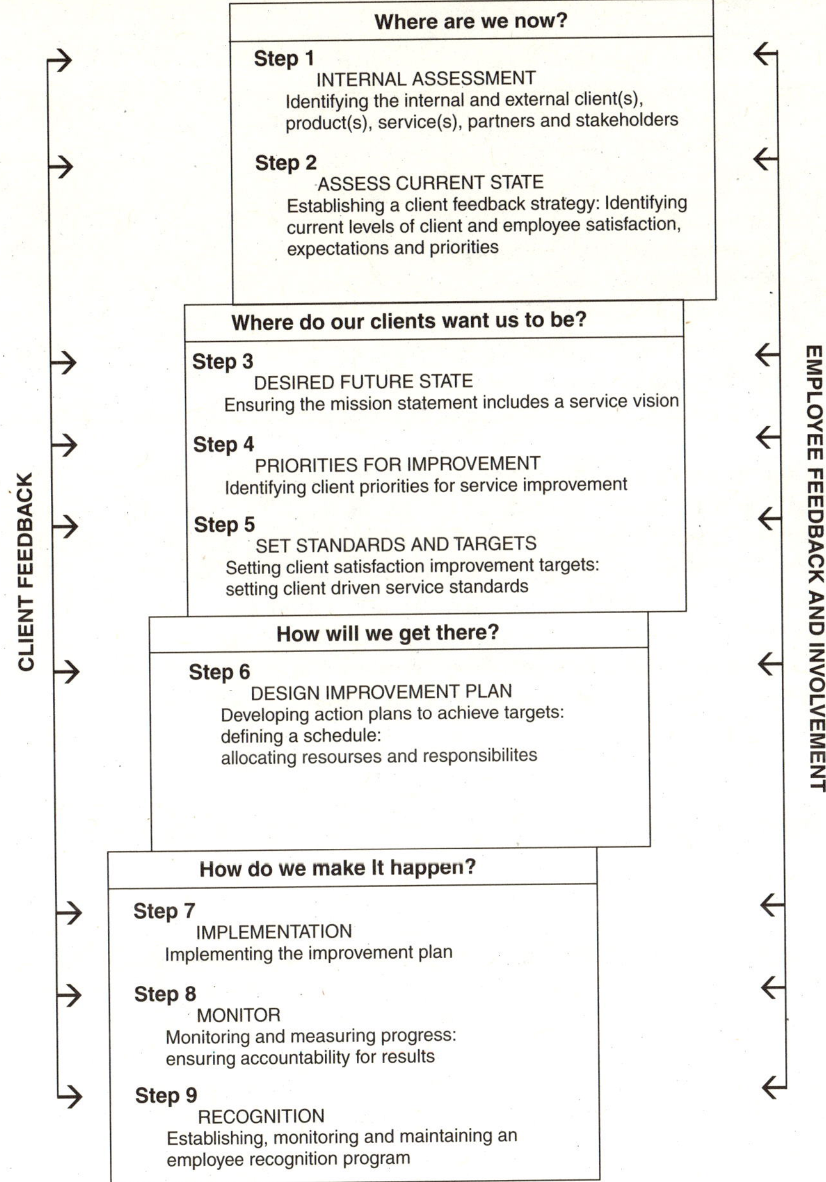

the service elements ('drivers') that most needed improvement in 2001 and 2003:

	2001	2003
❏ Waiting time	X	X
❏ Ease of finding information	X	
❏ Information for applications	X	X
❏ Staff knowledge	X	
❏ Questions answered	X	X
❏ Staff sensitivity to Armed Forces issues	X	X
❏ Waiting time for an appointment	X	X

Between 2001 and 2003, VAC concentrated on three areas of service: improving access, timeliness, and staff knowledge. While progress has been made, there are still opportunities for improvement (2003 column), and this provides VAC managers with precise knowledge of where to focus their improvement efforts in the next round.

Public organizations as disparate as the RCMP and the Ontario Ministry of Labour have used a similar approach to service improvement. Between 2003 and 2006 the RCMP dramatically improved its performance on the main drivers of service satisfaction, based on results from its annual CMT-based surveys of clients and stakeholders (www.rcmp-grc.gc.ca/surveys/index_e.htm). Similarly, the Ontario Ministry of Labour learned from its CMT surveys that the service driver most needing improvement was staff knowledge; it then focused its efforts on this specific area of service, knowing that doing so would make the most difference for clients. Using this scientific approach to service improvement, many public organizations are achieving higher levels of client satisfaction. For example, between 1998 and 2005 Canada Post improved from a 5.7 to a 7.0 mean satisfaction score; the Canada Revenue Agency improved from 5.5 to 6.2; and the Employment Insurance program improved from 4.5 to 5.7.[35] These scores are impressive in that they show steady upward trends in client satisfaction over several years of measurement.

In Canada the public sector as a whole has seen a significant improvement in terms of 'service reputation' (overall rating of an organization's service) and in terms of a recent service experience. Canada seems to be the only country so far that has been able to document these positive trends. For example, according to the 2005 survey results[36] the federal government's overall service reputation score improved from

Figure 10.6. American Customer Satisfaction Index

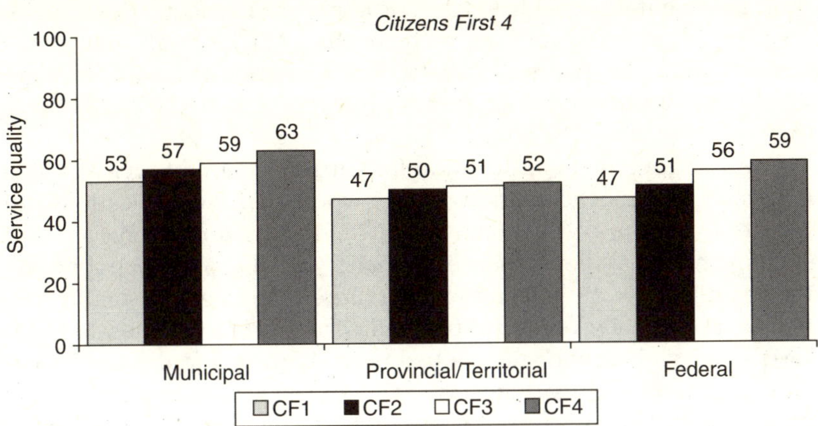

4.7 to 5.9 out of 10 between 1998 and 2005 (service reputation scores are always significantly lower than recent service experience scores). Provincial and municipal governments have seen similar improvements in citizens' evaluations of public sector service. Likewise, for recent service experience a basket of eighteen commonly used federal services scored an average of 6.7 out of 10 in 2005, compared to 6.0 in 1998. Over the same period, private sector service scores remained relatively stable or improved only marginally, according to the University of Michigan's American Customer Satisfaction Index (figure 10.6) and *Citizens First-4* data.

Measurement and benchmarking – the Common Measurements Tool

Another key feature of the citizen-centred service strategy in the Canadian public sector has been the commitment to measurement and benchmarking. Performance is measured at two levels: macro (*Citizens First* and *Taking Care of Business* national surveys), which measures the overall performance of the public sector and of individual governments, as we saw earlier; and micro (program level). In the latter regard, in 1998 the Citizen Centred Service Network developed the Common Measurement Tool (CMT),[37] a bank of questions with standard measurement scales that program managers across the public sector can use to measure client satisfaction. Before CMT, few public organizations measured client satisfaction and the ones that did tended to choose a different vendor and a different measurement system each time, making it impossible to track progress or to benchmark with others. The dozen or so core questions in the CMT are built around the research-derived drivers of satisfaction. However, organizations can also choose from about one hundred more focused CMT questions; they can even add customized questions.

The intergovernmental Institute for Citizen Centred Service in Toronto maintains a benchmarking centre where public organizations can register to use the CMT, submit their CMT results, and receive a report showing how their performance compares with that of other public sector organizations. By the end of 2006 more than one thousand public managers and their organizations had registered to use the CMT, 245 CMT client satisfaction surveys had been submitted to the CMT database, and 176 benchmarking reports had been issued to participating public organizations. To date, the highest client satisfaction performance in the public sector is found in single-window service agencies such as Service New Brunswick and Service British Columbia, which sometimes show mean CMT client satisfaction scores greater than 9 out of 10 – results almost unknown in the private sector.

Ensuring accountability for performance in devolved service delivery models is an important challenge for public management. The 2002 IPAC Deputy Ministers' issues survey noted that 'challenges include the development and implementation of guidelines that ensure that agencies adhere to the principle that accountability obligations and clients' needs are the responsibility of service delivery partners along with governments' (www.ipac.ca/Survey_DMs_and_CAOs). The intergovernmental CMT and the Institute for Citizen Centred Service's CMT benchmarking service can help governments ensure service accountability for those services they have devolved to NGOs, to private companies, or to other levels of government by requiring delivery partners to use the CMT to report service performance results.

Benchmarking using the CMT is an important new development in Canadian service delivery, for it allows organizations to benchmark their results against those of similar public sector organizations and to learn from those organizations which are best-in-class in service delivery.

The Human Dimension of Service Delivery

There are several human resource management features of citizen-centred service. The most interesting of these relates to the possible relationship between employee commitment and client satisfaction. Over the past decade the literature on private sector management has posited that human resource outcomes, service outcomes, and bottom-line outcomes are all linked. The most influential work – *The Value Profit Chain: Treat Employees Like Customers and Customers Like Employees* – was by James Heskett and his colleagues at the Harvard Business School.[38] More recently, Northwestern University has published an important study demonstrating that employee commitment in the service sector influences both client satisfaction and corporate profits.[39] Building on these studies, the idea of a public sector service value chain has been proposed.[40] The authors hypothesize that the public sector chain has the following structure:

Staff commitment ⇔
Client satisfaction ⇒
Public trust and confidence

Citizens First-3 and *Citizens First-4* and other studies[41] have already demonstrated that client satisfaction is a driver of citizen confidence in the public sector. This is a striking finding, for it links two very important areas of public sector theory and performance.

Intergovernmental research is now being conducted to determine whether staff commitment is a driver of client satisfaction in public organizations. Other research by the federal Public Service Human Resources Management Agency, the Treasury Board Secretariat, and several provincial governments is aimed at identifying the drivers of staff satisfaction and commitment. New intergovernmental work on the human resource dimension of public sector service delivery is aimed at identifying competencies, developing training courses, and creating a community of practice for public sector service managers. In addition, efforts are being made to identify the drivers of public trust and confidence in the public service. New research indicates that among the drivers are service quality, service benefit, fairness, and perceptions of how well public organizations are led and managed.[42]

Communities of Practice: Institutionalizing Citizen-Centred Service Delivery

Communities of practice have been an important feature of the citizen-centred approach to service delivery in Canada since 1997. As noted earlier, the Citizen Centred Service Network assembled service officials and academics from across Canada to design an action research approach that would, over time, significantly improve service to the public. Initially there were 40 members; by the spring of 1998 there were more than 220, including academics and federal, provincial, and municipal executives. After the network completed its work, a smaller intergovernmental Public Sector Service Delivery Council (PSSDC) was established to carry on the work and to move from research to coordinated action. The federal, provincial, and territorial CIOs had already established the Public Sector CIO Council (PSCIOC); now, members of the two councils collaborated with the annual Lac Carling Conference to create a citizen-centred approach to service improvement across the entire Canadian public sector. In 2001 the two councils founded the Institute for Citizen Centred Service[43] as an intergovernmental platform with three business lines: research; the CMT; and learning and best practices.

Compared to other countries, Canada is fairly unique in developing these strong intergovernmental communities of practice. The research on citizens' service needs, satisfaction, and priorities is performed collaboratively; the result is a commonly understood service improvement agenda based on citizens' input. We might term this the demand side of the service equation. There is also extensive collaboration on the supply side, ranging from best practice exchanges to collaborative projects for developing common standards, systems, and delivery platforms. In the United States, France, Britain, Australia, and other Western countries, these collaborative pan–public sector approaches to research, measurement, best practices and systems do not seem to exist to the same degree, which makes Canada somewhat unique in the horizontality and inclusiveness of its citizen-centred service work. Marson and Heintzman[44] have argued that the creation of these communities of practice, which have gradually evolved into more permanent institutional arrangements, are a key feature of Canada's success in service improvement and of its perceived leadership position in public sector service delivery.

Next-Generation Service Delivery

According to Accenture,[45] Canada has almost finished building its public sector e-channel. The future will see a stronger focus on integrating the service channels (as we have seen above) and on citizen-centred service delivery. The most recent IPAC survey of deputy ministers sug-

Figure 10.7. The service management agenda

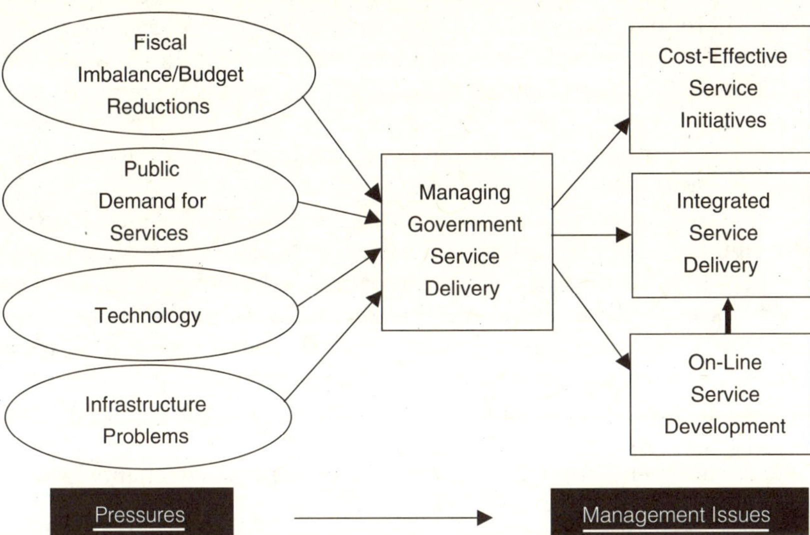

gests that the next generation of public sector service delivery in Canada will focus on improving (a) the cost-effectiveness of service delivery and (b) citizen satisfaction.[46] It will almost certainly be characterized by whole-of-government service strategies, such as Service Canada and common government-wide internal services organizations, and by whole-of-public-sector initiatives, such as the Secure Channel (infrastructure) and Business Canada (integrated intergovernmental service delivery).

At a time of tightened fiscal environments, governments across Canada are looking for ways to improve the efficiency of internal and external service delivery. The above graphic (figure 10.7) illustrates the dynamics of the forward service management agenda within the Canadian public sector.

One of the new approaches to service improvement in the public sector is often referred to as 'service transformation.' This alludes to the efforts many governments are making to rethink and re-engineer service delivery methods; the goal is to drive costs down while improving service from the clients' perspective. The concept includes the idea of process mapping as well as whole-of-government and whole-of-public-sector approaches to service improvement.

Going forward, we can expect a strong focus on multichannel integration and on encouraging clients to migrate to lower-cost channels. This will require that service channels (mail, in-person, telephone, and Internet) be integrated, because more than half the time clients are using more than one channel to complete a service experience.[47] This is especially noticeable with the e-channel and the telephone channel: many clients look up information on government websites before calling the appropriate departmental call centre.

For example, a taxpayer may go to the Canada Revenue Agency website, then call the agency with specific follow-up questions. This happens so often that the CRA has integrated its telephone and Internet channels through an electronic link that allows a taxpayer to move seamlessly from the website to a specific call operator who has expertise in the particular issue that the client is researching. Among the implications of this phenomenon for public organizations is that the databases supporting call centres and Internet sites must be integrated, and the independent organizations supporting the two channels need to be coordinated or merged.

The second emerging element of channel management is that governments now want to reduce the costs of service delivery for taxpayers by encouraging the clients of public services (a) to use lower-cost channels such as the Internet channel and the telephone channel, and (b) to use self-service options on those channels wherever possible. This trend will inevitably generate tensions between the interests of taxpayers for lower-cost service delivery and the interests of clients for improved service and channel choice. To encourage Canadians to use self-service channels such as Interactive Voice Response (IVR) systems, where appropriate to the service, management of the telephone channel will have to improve significantly, since Canadians are not very satisfied with service on that channel and are especially unhappy with the way IVR services are designed and managed. The *Citizens First* studies indicate that Canadians are willing to use automated systems as long as they have a choice of channels, the systems are user friendly, and they are able to reach a real person if necessary.

Another trend when it comes to significantly reducing the costs of service delivery involves a concept referred to as service transformation, popularized by the federal government in recent years. The idea behind service transformation is to create major breakthroughs in service delivery by focusing on cost reductions and integrated service delivery. Generally, these breakthroughs involve whole-of-government and intergovernmental service delivery innovations. Following are some examples: creating government-wide common service organizations for internal services (Ontario, Canada, British Columbia); creating service utilities to support service delivery among several governments (Atlantic Canada OnLine; the federal government's Secure Channel initiative); creating a single lead service department or agency within a government (Service Ontario; Service BC; Service Canada; Service New Brunswick); and integrating service delivery among several governments to reduce costs and to provide more integrated service (the Canada–Ontario Service Agreement; the intergovernmental Seniors Portal; the intergovernmental Canada Business Service Centres).

As Kenneth Kernaghan has pointed out,[48] the emerging world of intergovernmental service collaboration is posing new challenges for Canadian public administration and will require innovative new partnerships and governance arrangements. Some of the issues he has identified include these: the need to meet 'vertical' political accountabilities in a world of integrated intergovernmental service; the need for governments to retain individual visibility in partnership arrangements; the need for new intergovernmental governance arrangements such as service delivery utilities; and the need for public managers to find effective ways to mesh various financial, human resource, and technical systems within partnered-service initiatives.

A final emerging issue in citizen-centred service is the service value chain concept, discussed earlier in the chapter. Significant research and action is being conducted in the Canadian public sector to determine whether the linkages between, and drivers of, people performance, service performance, and public trust and confidence in the public sector can be documented.

Conclusion

Over the past decade Canada has played an international leadership role in developing methods and tools for measuring citizens' expectations, their level of satisfaction with services, and the drivers of that satisfaction. The implementation of this research and measurement activity by public managers across Canada has resulted in strong and quantifiable improvements in service quality as measured from the citizens' perspective. What improvements have Canadians seen in public sector service delivery over the past ten years? First, it is a lot easier to find public sector services though the intergovernmental blue pages in the telephone book, through one-stop telephone numbers like 1-800-OCANADA, through government websites, and through government information counters. Second, services are delivered in a much more integrated way compared to ten years ago. With the creation of Service Canada, Service Ontario, Service Quebec, and other single-window agencies at the municipal, provincial, and federal levels, citizens and organizations are finding it easier to do business with government. In addition, taxation services, postal services, pension services, RCMP services, and other services, are providing better delivery now that management is focusing on improved timeliness, improved staff knowledge and competence, improved fairness, improved courtesy, and improved outcomes (the five drivers of service satisfaction). As a result of these improvements, Accenture in 2005 ranked the Canadian public sector as number one in the world in citizen-centred service delivery.

In this remarkable achievement, Ken Kernaghan has served as an important academic research partner with senior government managers, helping them identify citizens' emerging service needs as well as strategies and best practices for responding to those needs. His work has also helped shed light on the next phase of citizen-centred service in Canada, as the public sector begins working towards integrated service delivery across departments and governments, and towards government services that are high in quality and easy to access, anywhere, any time, and by whatever channels citizens choose.

NOTES

1 Accenture, 'Leadership in Customer Service: New Expectations, New Experiences' (2005), www.accenture.com/xdoc/ca/locations/canada/insights/studies/ leadership_cust.pdf.
2 www.iccs-isac.org.
3 Brian Marson and Peter Ross, 'Targeting Managers,' *Public Sector Management* 16, no. 1 (2005): 4–119; idem, 'The 2002 IPAC Deputy Ministers' Issues Survey – the Results,' *Public Sector Management* 14, no. 1 (2005): 6–8.
4 www.myschool-monecole.gc.ca/Research/themes/servicequality_e.html.
5 Stephen Bent, Brian Marson, and Kenneth Kernaghan, *Innovations and Good Practices in Single-Window Service* (Ottawa: CCMD, 1999); Marie Blythe Marie and Brian Marson, *Good Practices in Citizen-Centred Service* (Ottawa: CCMD, 1999); Geoff Dinsdale and Brian Marson, *Citizen/Client Surveys: Dis-*

pelling Myths and Redrawing Maps (Ottawa: CCMD, 1999); Faye Schmidt
and Teresa Strickland, *Client Satisfaction Surveying: A Common Measurements
Tool (CMT)* (Ottawa: CCMD, 1999).

6 Erin Research, *Citizens First* (Ottawa: CCMD, 1998).

7 Canada, Privy Council Office, *Sixth Annual Report to the Prime Minister on
the Public Service of Canada* (Ottawa, 1997), www.bcp.gc.ca/default.asp?
Language=E&Page=InformationResourc es&Sub=Publications&doc=
6rept98/6rept98intro_e.htm.

8 Canada, Treasury Board, *Results for Canadians* (Ottawa, 2000).

9 Task Force on Service Delivery Models, *Discussion Paper on Service Delivery
Models* (Ottawa: CCMD, 1996), 21, www.ccmd-ccg.gc.ca/Research/
publications/pdfs/srdel1.pdf.

10 Erin Research, *Citizens First*.

11 In Dinsdale and Marson, *Citizen/Client Surveys*, 32.

12 Kernaghan, Marson, and Sandford Borins, *The New Public Organization*
(Toronto: IPAC, 2001).

13 Accenture, 'e-Government Leadership – High Performance, Maximum
Value' (2004), 11, www.accenture.ca/content/en/insights/
Egov%20Research%20final.pdf.

14 Mary Tetlow, 'The Canadian Experience,' *Public* (2004), www.cipfa.org.uk/
publicfinance/search_details.cfm?News_id=18 526&keysearch=canada.

15 Phase-5, *Taking Care of Business* (Toronto: IPAC, 2004).

16 www.gov.pe.ca/govinfo/index.php3.

17 www.crtc.gc.ca/archive/ENG/Decisions/2004/dt2004-71.htm.

18 www.gc.ca.

19 www.gov.on.ca.

20 www.snb.ca.

21 www.canadabusiness.gc.ca.

22 www.seniors.c.ca.

23 www.211toronto.ca/splash.jsp.

24 Phase-5, *Citizens First-4* (Toronto: IPAC, 2005), 19.

25 Phase-5, *Taking Care of Business*, 17.

26 Kernaghan, *Integrated Service Delivery: Beyond the Barriers*, report prepared
for the Treasury Board Secretariat (Ottawa, 2003).

27 Canada, PCO, Speech from the Throne to Open the Second Session of the
Thirty-Sixth Parliament of Canada, (Ottawa, 1999).

28 Accenture, 'Leadership in Customer Service.'

29 www.camagazine.com/index.cfm/ci_id/24142/la_id/1.htm.

30 Dinsdale and Marson, *Citizen/Client Surveys*.

31 Erin Research, *Citizens First*.

32 Canada, Treasury Board, *A How-to Guide for the Service Improvement Initia-tive* (Ottawa, 2000), www.tbs-sct.gc.ca/si-as/howto-comment/howto-commentpr_e.asp?format=print.

33 Canada, Treasury Board, *A Policy Framework for Service Improvement in the Government of Canada* (Ottawa, 2000), www.tbs-sct.gc.ca/pubs_pol/sipubs/si_as/pfsi_e.asp; Ralph Heintzman, 'Toward Citizen-Centred Ser-vice: The Government of Canada's Service Improvement Strategy,' *Cana-dian Government Executive* 4 (2001): 26–30.

34 Phase-5, *Citizens First-4*, 9.

35 Ibid.

36 Ibid.

37 Schmidt and Strickland, *Client Satisfaction Surveying*.

38 James L. Heskett, W. Earl Sasser Jr, and Leonard A. Schlesinger, *The Value Profit Chain* (New York: Free Press, 2003).

39 www.performanceforum.org/PFM/research_employee.asp#27.

40 Heintzman and Marson, 'People, Service, and Trust: Is There a Public Sec-tor Service Value Chain?' *International Review of Administrative Sciences* 71, no. 4 (2005): 549–75.

41 Canada Information Office, 'Listening to Canadians' (Fall 2000), dsp-psd.communication.gc.ca/Collection/PF4-7-2000E.pdf.

42 Phase-5, *Citizens First-4*, 78.

43 www.iccs-isac.org.

44 Marson and Heintzman, 'Citizen-Centred Service Improvement in Canada: From Smart Practices to Smart Results,' paper presented to the Interna-tional Political Science Association – SOG Smart Practices in Government Conference, University of British Columbia, June 2004.

45 Accenture, 'Leadership in Customer Service.'

46 Marson and Ross, 'The 2002 IPAC Deputy Ministers' Issues Survey,' 6–8.

47 Erin Research, *Citizens First 3*, 32.

48 Kernaghan, *Integrated Service Delivery*.

PART IV

Spreading the Word

Public administration does not have all the attributes of a profession; it does, however, share some of its characteristics and is moving towards becoming more professionalized. A general attribute of a profession is that its current members play a role in moulding future members. This part of the book looks at how current members of the developing profession of public administration spread the word about the field in order to attract and develop future professionals.

In chapter 11, Patrice Dutil and Michael McConkey describe the history of Canada's pinnacle association of those interested in public administration, the Institute of Public Administration of Canada. IPAC began as a member-based association of senior public servants in 1947 and thrived in that role for almost forty years. By the mid-1980s, though, storm clouds loomed over IPAC, as they did over similar organizations in other countries. IPAC's British counterpart ceased to operate, while its counterpart in the United States emerged relatively unscathed.

Dutil and McConkey document how IPAC's forward-looking board of directors converted the institute from a member-based association to a non-government organization, thereby assuring its future. The fiscal problem emerged in the mid-1980s in the form of a flattening in the number of individual members as governments reduced employment, and a decline in grants from governments as they reduced expenditures. IPAC realized that it would have to follow the same course as the government organizations it studied. Its 'solution was found in an emphasis on markets and partnerships, looking to new sources of revenue with exercises in commercialization and entrepreneurship.' Initially, the board considered partnerships with similar organizations and the development of training programs. Ultimately, however, it survived by developing international programs in conjunction with the Canadian International Development Agency (CIDA). This was an obvious avenue, and one that allowed IPAC to draw on its members' expertise in governance and management and to share that expertise with developing countries. IPAC earned significant overheads by administering these contracts. As Dutil and McConkey describe, this led to changes in the institute's governance model; more important, it introduced an element of financial security that guaranteed the continued existence of IPAC as the main professional organization of public administrators.

Chapters 12 and 13 focus on how the existing members of a profession renew their profession by disseminating knowledge and values to new members. In chapter 12, Barbara Wake Carroll reflects on her experience as editor of the pinnacle journal of the profession, *Canadian Public Administration*. A good professional needs a sound theoretical grounding that reflects the practical world in which practitioners operate. Carroll laments that the theoretical and practical sides of public administration sometimes seem to be going their separate ways. She contends that academics enjoy publishing abstract theoretical works that have little use in practice, while practitioners need practical advice. This has resulted in a lack of connectedness between theory and practice; it has also created a situation where neither the need for good theory nor the need for practical advice is satisfied.

Carroll is quite forthright that there is a serious split between the interests of academics and those of practitioners, and she is not sanguine about the possibility of closing that gap. She notes that very few journals succeed in appealing to both groups. She concludes that it is imperative that journals like *Canadian Public Administration* keep trying to close the gap, and she provides some suggestions about how they might do so.

In chapter 13, which concludes this book, Carolyn Johns reflects on her experience as editor of the Case Program in Canadian Public Administration. The Case Program, administered by IPAC, has developed more than one hundred cases over the past thirty years that have been widely used in both academic and professional-development venues.

Johns describes the case method and then provides an overview of how cases are used in teaching. She admits that the case method has both strengths and weaknesses; not surprisingly, she concludes that overall, cases have significant value. She then discusses how the use of cases has increased in Canada as more public administration programs have been introduced. The high practical content of cases seems to be something of an answer to Carroll's concerns about relevance in chapter 12.

11 The Road to NGO: The Transformation of the Institute of Public Administration of Canada, 1985–95

PATRICE DUTIL AND MICHAEL McCONKEY[1]

A deep recession was ravaging Canada in the spring of 1991 when the Ontario government told the Institute of Public Administration of Canada (IPAC) that it would have to vacate the small Queen Anne house it had occupied for almost twenty years. Built in 1882, the charming house featured stained glass in the front windows, upstairs and down, a marble fireplace in the 'library,' porcelain bathroom fixtures, and a marble shower stall. The only mulberry tree on Bay Street in Toronto stood on its lawn. Staff had invested their own time and money in making the house attractive and had made the best possible use of old, government-issue furniture. The walls, though, were mostly painted public-works green. The house, dwarfed by the enormous complex of Government of Ontario buildings across the street, proudly announced itself with a big bilingual sign. It was a cosy place for a small association to occupy. It promised close attention to detail and, quite literally, an over-the-counter experience for walk-ins from the street. There were consequences to being so accessible, naturally. Staff often answered calls only to inform strangers that the birth-control clinic was next door, and many pedestrians thought the IPAC office would be a good place to vent frustrations about the provincial government, the federal government, and just plain government.

But by 1991 the four creaky floors of that arthritic Victorian stuffed with books, journals, files, and archives could no longer meet IPAC's needs. This was hardly surprising. The 1970s and 1980s had been turbulent decades for membership organizations in North America and Europe, and the ones with regional chapters were especially rocked by these changes. The newer organizations had narrow mandates and clear political objectives and seemed more aggressive in terms of promoting themselves.

The field of public administration associations was affected by this same phenomenon. Some similar organizations, like the American Society for Public Administration, would survive while changing very little. Others, like Britain's Royal Institute of Public Administration, would perish. IPAC followed a different course and in the process was almost completely reinvented. In the spring of 1991 it moved its offices uptown to Eglinton Avenue, to a typical Toronto mid-rise building. It was an anonymous place, but that hardly mattered anymore: the days of over-the-counter service had ended. The nature of associations was changing rapidly, and IPAC was caught in that current. It had to make room for computers, servers, modern equipment, and new staff who could promptly service public servants and scholars from all parts of Canada and around the world.

IPAC was transformed in the years between 1985 and 1995. Many people had been arguing for years that it had to change in order to survive, and in that regard 1985 was an important year for a number of reasons. First, that was the year it was generally recognized that IPAC's pattern of deficits and debts was structural. It was also the year that an aggressive new marketing strategy, with an emphasis on products and customers, was introduced and discussed extensively by the board of directors.[2] Up until then, IPAC had catered to a select group of senior public servants and scholars through an extensive network of volunteers. Its mission had been to develop a literature for the discipline of public administration, and in this it had met its objectives. For example, it had organized annual meetings and a few smaller yearly events across the country. The organization had been funded by a combination of membership dues, base grants from governments, and sales of its products. It had a small staff that included an executive director, an assistant executive director, and a handful of assistants.

By 1995, IPAC had slightly increased its membership rolls; it had also staked its future on a number of new areas. It had set out to lead a profession, albeit in an informal way. It had offered a Statement of Principles on the Conduct of Public Employees, and it had published Ken Kernaghan and John Langford's path-breaking *The Responsible Public Servant*.[3] It had founded a suite of awards to recognize managerial accomplishments in the public sector and in scholarship, adopted a mission statement to reflect the priorities of the public service, initiated an issues review by polling deputy ministers across Canada, and transformed its governance from a board of forty-six members to one with twenty-seven. Last but not least, it had started to sell its services.

No longer was IPAC merely a learned organization, an association or a think tank with charity status.[4] In the language of the late twentieth century, it was now a 'non-governmental organization': an NGO delivering services to government, driven from headquarters, accountable to an effective board, and dramatically less dependent on government base grants and membership for its funding. Operating now much like a trade association, it would launch efforts to recognize and promote public sector innovation and to showcase Canadian managerial talent around the world. Though IPAC never lost sight of members' needs, its board and management realized that it could not rely on individuals to support a growing, vibrant organization. Nor could it count on government grants to stabilize its budgets. IPAC would have to become entrepreneurial.

These changes were brought about by a remarkably innovative generation of board members, and a prominent member of that board was Kenneth Kernaghan. Boasting a reputation as an exceptional researcher and writer in the field of public administration, the Brock University professor assumed the presidency of IPAC in 1987–8. It is hardly surprising that he was a dynamic part of IPAC's governance at a time when tough decisions had to be made. He had already made an enormous contribution to IPAC as Chair of the Research Committee, founder and first director of the Case Program, editor of the IPAC journal, and co-author of IPAC's *The Responsible Public Servant*. He was an integral part of a team that would transform the institute.

IPAC's transformation amounts to a case study of the very difficult lives of Canadian membership organizations in an era of interest group politics, changes in government policy, and civil society transformations. IPAC was now behaving like an NGO and selling services to governments to ensure its survival. It had been confronted with changes in civil society and government policy, and it had responded to those changes with creativity and resolve.

IPAC to 1985

IPAC was founded in 1947 by a handful of dedicated senior public servants who were eager to build relations with their counterparts in the various levels of government across Canada. It was created as a *confrérie* – that is, an informal gathering place where senior, educated public servants and academics could exchange ideas, share insights, and perhaps 'unify the country and make it great.'[5]

IPAC had assigned itself a strong educational mission. Its leaders referred to it as an 'institute,' not an 'association.' Education was central to its mandate as a learned society. Because public management was still very much in its infancy in Canada (and 'public administration' as a discipline would have to wait for Carleton University to adopt that term in its curriculum), the education it provided would have to be mutual, as in 'between friends.' It was in this spirit that the first IPAC meeting took place in Quebec City in 1949.

IPAC's early years have already been documented.[6] It slowly gathered strength as its board of directors became more confident and as regional groups were created in the early 1950s. In 1958 it launched *Canadian Public Administration*, its flagship periodical. Governor General Georges Vanier lent the prestige of his name and office to the institute's recognition of individual merit. In the early 1960s it organized the Clifford Clark Lectures in honour of the distinguished mandarin. A few years later, books began appearing under IPAC's imprimatur.

But what truly transformed IPAC was the securing of government funding in the early 1960s. Once it was assured that membership donations would be supplemented by government grants, IPAC was able to hire an executive director. Support staff were also hired, and in 1968 Joseph Galimberti was named corporate secretary and research director to bring logic and organization to what was becoming a burgeoning field of intellectual activity.

IPAC enjoyed relative tranquillity between the mid-1960s and the mid-1980s. Most years brought new members. In 1970 it had 1,500; by 1985 there were roughly 2,800 (see figure 11.1). Even so, the board worried that these numbers weren't healthy enough, and it devoted considerable effort to developing strategies for increasing the membership. Throughout the 1960s and 1970s, base funding from governments boded well for IPAC's future. In 1971, 71 per cent of IPAC's revenues were provided by government grants. The recession of the early 1980s hit IPAC hard, however. Governments began to flat-line their contributions to the point that within a few years, their financial aid constituted only 49 per cent of revenues. IPAC was entering a decade of deficits and mounting debt.

The institute was facing difficulties on all fronts. And it was not alone in this: like many associations in North America, it was having to come to terms with the limits of its appeal and of its financial health. As of 1985, IPAC was mainly what it always had been – a professional service organization, albeit one that exercised none of the regulatory or disciplinary powers and responsibilities that are characteristic of professional organizations. The institute had an educational mission, and from time to time it resembled a think tank, though it never played the advocate for any cause except the betterment of public service. IPAC's role was difficult to define and difficult to sell in terms of membership.

Membership in Question: A Continental Perspective

IPAC's evolution from a membership-intensive organization to an NGO seems consistent with global trends, both American and international. The institute was faced with a stagnant membership base and reduced government funding; moreover, it was now competing with membership-based organizations such as the Association for Professional Executives in the Government of Canada (APEX). And other government-sponsored institutions were competing with IPAC for attention. The Institute for Research on Public Policy, richly endowed by the federal government in the early 1970s, was taking its place as an innovative policy-oriented organization. Twenty years later the federal government established the Canadian Centre for Management Development to bring clearer focus to research and education in public administration. All of these newcomers were forcing IPAC to turn to market-based entrepreneurial innovation as a means to generate operating revenues.

The minutes of various IPAC committees, covering the years of funding roll-backs between 1985 and 1998, show an organization caught up in precisely the kinds of dilemmas described in the theoretical and historical literature. At first there was much tinkering with old approaches despite their increasingly evident inadequacy. There was also some experimenting with new ways to apply old thinking. Eventually, though, a new strategic orientation became more convincing to the board: one that emphasized entrepreneurship and commercialization. This new thinking enabled IPAC to survive and eventually thrive on the shifting terrain of the latter 1980s and 1990s.

In the late 1980s, governments around the English-speaking world were shrinking. During this search for a 'new order,' they gradually withdrew their financial support for all not-for-profits. To IPAC's pain, this meant cutbacks in public service staffing and in departmental discretionary funding. Both developments had a severe impact on the institute's membership rolls, besides contributing to a fiscal crisis at the institute.

Though neither unique nor specific to the not-for-profit sector, the 1990s social capital debate provides a useful lens through which to view the developments experienced by IPAC. In a series of seminal works, Robert Putnam of Harvard University argued that society had suffered a marked decline in popular participation in voluntary membership-based associations. He contended that this was having a dramatic impact on the culture and politics of American society, in that it was leading to a decline in civil participation, an increase in citizen alienation, and the atrophy of civil society and democratic governance.[7]

Putnam's critics took issue with his findings on a number of fronts.[8] Some questioned his focus and process, while others argued that his very conception of the problem was misplaced. In the view of these latter critics, he was examining outdated venues for public participation. They countered that civil society was not in fact declining; it was just that its vital energy was being directed differently.

A noteworthy contribution to this debate was made by Theda Skocpol, also of Harvard University. Taking her cue from her colleague, she argued that civic America had made a transition from membership-based activities towards professionally managed institutions and advocacy groups in which individual Americans functioned mainly as cheque writers and sporadic (non-member) volunteers.[9] Acknowledging the arguments of some of Putman's critics, she contended that the roots of this transition from hands-on, structured, membership-based organization activity were to be found in the rise of the more amorphous social movements of the 1960s: the Civil Rights Movement, the Antiwar Movement, women's liberation, and so on. These civil society agents were less structured and more fluid. Ongoing individual commitment to them was less tangible; however, these movements wielded far higher levels of individual involvement, albeit in a more *episodic* manner.[10] This phenomenon paralleled the blossoming of rights advocacy and was fuelled by many of these new civil society agents.[11]

Skocpol argued that the displacement of committed, member-intensive organizations by more fluid, amorphous networks of social movements had left unattended some important activities – notably education and nationwide, grassroots-sensitive political, social, and cultural action. As a result, democracy in America has been diminished, for professionally managed organizations, with staffs skilled in communications, policy analysis, and fundraising, had emerged to fill the void and take over activities that had once been conducted by membership-based organizations.[12]

This is all theory, and Skocpol herself tells us that it has yet to be thoroughly tested with case studies. One would expect, however, that the historical trend towards increased reliance on entrepreneurial fundraising would have caused not-for-profit agencies to rely more and more on professional managers.

There may be few grounds to presume a causal relationship between the professionalization of civil society and the shift towards a more entrepreneurial and managerial orientation in the not-for-profit sector. It may be helpful, however, to think of the events described by Skocpol as a prevailing current that shaped the not-for-profit sector in Canada, and in IPAC in particular, between 1985 and 1995.

Regrettably, attempts to compare IPAC's experience with that of other Canadian associations are frustrated by the absence of a literature. Scholars have not launched any sustained discussion of this topic, and except for Statistics Canada's 2003 study (which was a snapshot profile), there have been no surveys, historical or otherwise, of not-for-profit governance and revenue practices in Canada.[13] There *are* a number of studies of not-for-profits, but these tend to fall into one of two camps: they examine either the social impacts of not-for-profits or the impacts of government policy on them. Moreover, they are almost all industry specific (either the arts or housing), besides often being regionally focused. However, international findings *are* available, and these paint a vivid picture of a not-for-profit sector in great upheaval: the same context that was experienced by IPAC.

The Changing Relationship between State and NGO

There seems to be no dispute that a sea change occurred during the 1980s in the operations of not-for-profits. The Johns Hopkins Comparative Non-Profit Sector Project, a major international comparative study, documented this transformation quite comprehensively.[14] Its research revealed that there is a compelling connection between the capacity of the not-for-profit sector and the extent of public funding. This is not to say, as some have argued, that the size of a country's welfare state is directly related to the size of its not-for-profit sector.[15] However, the study confirms that the countries with the largest not-for-profit sectors are the ones that have the most public funding.[16]

The growth pattern of NGOs is evident in the American context. A review of the number of applications for not-for-profit status, as approved by the Internal Revenue Service, reveals steady growth over four decades. There are two glaring exceptions to this expansion. The first, which seems to confirm the international findings of the Johns Hopkins study, is the near doubling in the number of registered not-for-profits in a single year: 1964–5. This dramatic jump is attributed to the impact of President Johnson's Great Society initiative, a major mobilization of U.S. government resources that used the not-for-profit sector as its primary delivery vehicle.[17]

The second striking anomaly was the 1980s. The first half of that decade saw steady growth in the not-for-profit sector, in keeping with the trend over earlier decades. The second half, however, saw the only period of sustained decline – a decline that was not reversed until 1992. This trend was mimicked internationally as many Western governments began to embrace the view that government welfare services were in competition with the not-for-profit sector. This prevented either sector from operating at optimum efficiency and constituted a counter-productive incursion by the state into the domain of civil society. In keeping, then, with the theme of reducing the role of government, the not-for-profit sector was promoted as both administratively efficient and politically correct.[18]

But that support did not come with money, and in the absence of private giving's capacity to fill the void created by the pull-back of public funding, the not-for-profit sector was compelled to turn more and more to revenue-generating activities as demands and needs for its services increased.

As a consequence, the financial profile of not-for-profits has been permanently reconfigured.[19] The Johns Hopkins study of twenty-two countries found that not-for-profits' revenues generated by fees and other charges (49 per cent) almost equalled combined revenues from public funding (40 per cent) and private giving (11 per cent).[20]

In Canada there has been a cumulative reduction in government funding of not-for-profits since the 1980s; the real blows, however, came in the 1990s. In 1995 the Chretien government initiated a four-year series of funding cuts ranging from 10 to 25 per cent.[21] At the same time, tax incentives for donations to registered charities were increased.[22]

Shifts in government priorities placed intense pressure on not-for-profits to locate non-donor sources of revenue. At the same time, not-for-profit organizations had to respond to charges that they were unaccountable, unrepresentative, and overly bureaucratic.

One obvious approach to palliating losses and demonstrating competency was to impose user fees and commercial initiatives. There is evidence, though, that not-for-profits had to reach far beyond that practice.[23] One study found that some types of not-for-profits, including recreational organizations, private foundations, and arts and cultural charities, were relying on earned revenues for anywhere between 40 and 58 per cent of their funding.[24] Another study documented the forms and consequences of not-for-profit entrepreneurship among several Ontario organizations. Indeed, this trend was so pronounced that the authors considered it conceptually invalid to presume any clear-cut distinction between not-for-profit charitable and for-profit commercial activities.[25] The two categories had merged so thoroughly that even the most mission-directed activities had some revenue-generating dimension. At the same time the authors found that without exception, every commercial activity had some mission-related underpinning.[26]

NGOs are now tapping into other sectors in ways that often place them in direct conflict with commercial enterprises. For example, food banks have built food-processing plants and churches have operated travel agencies. These sorts of initiatives have triggered significant blowback, with commercial enterprises questioning the propriety of organizations directly competing with them in the marketplace while receiving the various tax benefits of not-for-profits.[27]

The moral legitimacy of not-for-profits was also tested when they began collaborating rather than competing with commercial firms. For instance, not-for-profits' practice of "selling" their moral authority by endorsing commercial products has come under fire.[28] A Canadian example was Pollution Probe's endorsement of various products in Loblaw's President's Choice line. In the United States the March of Dimes generated similar controversy.[29]

IPAC Responds to the Crisis

The reality of declining government grants to not-for-profits was the key transforming agent in the later 1980s and the 1990s (see figure 11.1). This development was evident in the IPAC board's deliberations. In April 1987 the institute's treasurer, Ed Power, warned in a sixty-page report to the Executive Committee that IPAC's deficits were growing steadily.[30] Eight months later he observed that the organization was generating a structural deficit of $15,000 to $20,000 per year.[31]

The board responded to this finding in traditional ways – by economizing on operations, attempting to recover a solid foundation of grants, and, most consistently, devising new ways to increase membership levels and fees. The economizing took many forms; the option most debated was restructuring the board (which had forty-six members) in ways that would reduce the associated travel costs.[32] On one occasion the discussion around this matter generated a number of dire suggestions, including one that would have subjected executive members to a financial means test. Other related suggestions:

- Members should have to prove to IPAC's national treasurer that they had asked their employer to pay for executive committee travel.
- National conference revenues should support this travel.
- Only people who can afford the costs should be selected for the executive.
- The size of the Executive Committee should be reduced.
- Regional groups 'could' make a partial contribution to the travel expenses of their representatives on the executive committee.[33]

These proposals came to nothing but, meanwhile, a host of other scrimping suggestions were being considered. Among them were measures to shrink the journal by thirty-two pages; to reduce the in-house newsletter *Bulletin* from six to five issues; to discontinue the bibliography; and to cut back on the number of publications and events.[34] All of this amounted to micromanagement and did not address underlying problems.

The board of directors also stubbornly pursued efforts to salvage the government grants. Certainly it was appreciated that government approaches to grant giving had changed considerably and perhaps irreversibly;[35] even so, the hope died hard that IPAC could return to relying on such grants. The board still hoped to recover lost ground with provincial and federal governments[36] and often expressed its intention to begin seeking municipal grants.[37] The latter notion was sustained throughout the period, despite occasional acknowledgment that municipalities seemed uninterested in playing such a saviour role and might well be unable to do so.[38] As late as 1992, when there were already signs that international consultancy programs were lifting IPAC out of its fiscal woes, many board members were expressing grave concerns over the erosion of government grants.

The board could not bring itself to discard the idea that membership could be the key to financial solvency.[39] Year after year, Finance Committee reports to the Executive Committee indicated that the rosy prognostications for fiscal well-being rooted in revitalized membership rolls had not come to pass.[40] And each time, it seems, this gloomy news was greeted as unexpected and unfortunate. (Naturally, the board often debated increasing membership fees to compensate for the stagnant membership rolls.[41]) Whether it was owing to IPAC's failure to serve its potential markets well, to government staffing cutbacks during those years, or to the general decline in membership-based organizations, IPAC's capacity to solve its financial woes by growing its membership had clearly reached a ceiling.

The ongoing disappointments of the membership drives led to revisionist thinking – that is, to the search for new solutions using old premises. Most of the solutions sought were internal in nature – that is, within the organization or within its conventional and traditional portfolio of options. An exception to this was the drive for corporate memberships – this, at least, meant looking outside the organization and its usual collaborators. This was also a first step towards more outward-looking and dynamic partnership practices. In any event, the corporate membership drive proved to be no more successful than the endlessly disappointing individual membership campaigns.[42]

Typical of the revisionist approach were ideas proposed for building up the new IPAC Endowment Fund, such as canvassing existing members, soliciting contributions from the wealthier regional groups, and creating a list of '1000 friends of IPAC' to whom an appeal could be made.[43] But new ways of thinking gradually emerged from IPAC's financial dilemma of the late 1980s and 1990s, ways that were characterized by an increasingly outward-looking perspective. Just as in the governments that IPAC was studying in its research and publications, the solution was found in an emphasis on markets and partnerships, on seeking new revenue sources through commercialization and entrepreneurship.

This panoply of new ideas did not spring full-fledged into existence. Rather, the IPAC board groped slowly towards these potential solutions. As early as 1985 the benefits of partnerships were being discussed in response to the IRPP's decision to extend its interests into the field of 'governability.'[44] In 1989 a lengthy motion was passed by the Executive Committee, 'Recommendations Re: Building Alliances and Partnerships.'[45] This constituted an assertive and ambitious strategy for moving IPAC into the new, 'horizontal' era of partnership. The recommendations included the following:

- Closer relations should be forged with other organizations of an A and B type.[46]
- The national executive should create a short list of organizations to be approached. For example:

- ○ The Association of Professional Executives of Canada
  - ○ The Canada Centre for Management Development
  - ○ The Conference Board of Canada
  - ○ *L'École nationale d'administration publique*
  - ○ The Federation of Canadian Municipalities
  - ○ The Canadian Association of Municipal Administrators
- A point person should be designated for each discussion with an organization.
- Point persons should develop a plan with relevant parties.
- Regional groups should be asked to consider such a policy.
- An ad hoc committee should be retained to coordinate the project.

Also during this period, the board members began to recognize that IPAC had an important contribution to make to international development. In the same Executive Committee meeting where the IRPP partnership was raised, the potential for IPAC to contribute to the developing world was discussed.[47]

Clearly, while this outward-looking entrepreneurship was emblematic of the not-for-profit sector of the 1980s, IPAC's board members had an immediately relevant role model in the very governments the institute was studying. Governments were by now embracing the New Public Management (NPM) agenda, which emphasized integrating proven business practices into the exercise of government; similarly, IPAC was now looking to learn from commercial practices. For the IPAC seminar 'Best Management Practices in Complex Operational Departments,' business executives were recruited for the first time to participate in discussions of public sector management issues.[48]

In a similar vein, in 1986 the Executive Committee put itself through fiscal contortions in scraping together the money to help Bill Stanbury prepare a half dozen business–government relations cases for the Case Studies program. These efforts were perceived as having great potential for helping IPAC raise its profile in the business community.[49]

An illustration of this more commercial approach was the resort to marketing and advertising strategies as revenue generators. A new marketing strategy was extensively discussed in 1985, with an emphasis on products and publics, as well as objectives and strategies.[50] Advertising was welcomed in both the *Bulletin* and *Canadian Public Administration*.[51] A new magazine was identified as a solution to many problems: *Public Sector Management/Management secteur public* was conceived from the start as a self-financing membership tool, with a potential for twelve full-page advertisements at a cost of $2,000 to $2,500 each. The sales packages for these ads would include a right of first refusal for exhibits at the annual conference, placement on the publications mailing list, and an invitation to attend the presentation luncheon for the new Innovative Management Award (IMA), founded in 1990.[52]

The IMA was part of a series of new awards introduced by the institute around this time. To recognize distinguished contributions to *Canadian Public Administration*, the board had already sanctioned the J.E. Hodgetts and Roland Parenteau Awards. The IPAC IMA was different from these in a number of ways. First, the board of directors, in partnership with the IMA funders, adopted a new theme every year to showcase a different aspect of public sector management. Second, the finalists appeared before a jury of their peers drawn from all parts of the country, all levels of government, and academia. This approach generated a considerable amount of publicity for innovative public management, created incentives for further innovation, and boosted IPAC's profile. And all of this was achieved through a process that generated revenues instead of consuming them. The IMAs were first presented by President Brian Marson and Executive Director Joseph Galimberti but soon found sponsors in PricewaterhouseCoopers and IBM.

IPAC's commercial projects did not all flourish. Joseph Galimberti returned from a trip to Washington in 1986 enthusiastic about IPAC adopting the training program model employed by the American Society for Public Administration.[53] This idea was not transformed into action – it would be twenty years before IPAC started a similar program. Still, there was a strong trend towards commercialization and entrepreneurship during this period.

As IPAC extended its reach, the greatest successes came from an unexpected direction: international work. IPAC began operating internationally after the Canadian government joined the International Institute of Administrative Sciences (IIAS) in 1980 and invited IPAC to serve as that organization's non-governmental Canadian member. In 1982, IPAC established an International Committee to explore options in international involvement. Discussions continued in the latter half of the 1980s. There was a growing sense that the Canadian public service tradition had valuable lessons to offer the developing world.

International consultancy preoccupied IPAC's committees during the late 1980s – a vivid reminder that new ways of thinking were struggling to emerge. First raised during an Executive Committee meeting in 1985, this theme was again discussed at length in 1987. At the time, the expressed view was that 'there was a lot of expertise in IPAC that would be valuable in Third World countries and that IPAC should be a linking body working through CIDA in this regard.'[54] The topic was debated thoroughly in the Management Committee in 1990, where it was declared that IPAC was not achieving its international potential. A new thrust in this direction was planned for the coming year.[55]

There was another important development around this time: IPAC's executive director, Joseph Galimberti, was invited to present a paper at a conference in the Seychelles. During the planning stages of IPAC's own international conference, he presented an examination of NPM in the Canadian context. This paper was well received and confirmed that Canada's experience in public administration could be relevant to many developing countries. The following year saw a formal proposal to study the prospect of doing international work in collaboration with CIDA.[56]

All of these developments came to fruition in the early 1990s, with IPAC hosting an international conference on the theme 'Public Administration Without Borders.' In the spring of 1992 the international consultancy program was formally adopted.[57]

IPAC's first two international projects were in the Philippines and Indonesia. In the Philippines, working closely with the Canadian Centre for Management Development (CCMD), IPAC contributed to needs analysis projects in order to develop training programs. The Indonesian project focused on decentralization. Drawing from the Canadian experience, IPAC matched the needs of Indonesian public servants with the expertise of specialists in Manitoba, Quebec, and Nova Scotia. IPAC was now doing on the international stage what it had been doing in Canada for almost fifty years: creating networks of knowledge to share expertise, insights, and experience.

The move into partnerships generally, and international consulting in particular, reversed the endless spiral of structural deficits that had confronted IPAC in the 1980s. By the time the Liberal budgets of 1995 to 1998 devastated Canadian non-profits, IPAC had ended its reliance on government grants and membership drives.

Indeed, in the summer of 1992 the Finance Committee was able to announce that, as a result of the international programs, IPAC had suddenly – after years of scrimping and penny-pinching – reduced its deficit by $20,000 in one fell swoop. (By the end of that year the treasurer would be able to report approximately $80,000 in overheads and salaries provided by the international program.[58]) Furthermore, it was predicted that with the benefit of this lucrative consulting, within just six years IPAC would be able to eliminate its accumulated deficit.[59] By the spring of 1995 there was talk of founding a second organization, IPAC International, to shelter IPAC's charitable status from the revenues generated by the international consulting work.[60]

IPAC's now well-established ability to work productively with partners eventually opened up new opportunities. In 1995 it would join a private Quebec City consultancy, Groupe TS et Associés, to collaborate in a consortium for a local government support project, again in the Philippines.[61] This initiative would be further proof that IPAC had reinvented itself by embracing the 'new thinking'; it would also be an example of the institute's new orientation towards partnerships, entrepreneurship, and commercialization through international consultancy.

But the old ways of thinking did not disappear overnight. The treasurer ended his 1992 report on a cautionary note: 'We shouldn't rely on international programs to resolve our financial concerns.' And at the next Executive Committee meeting, much concern was expressed over the prospect of eroding government grants. Some board members suggested that the recent revenue windfalls might be best spent on membership recruitment.[62]

Transformation of Governance

In the beginning, IPAC's seven full-time employees were governed by a forty-six-member board of directors. Twenty were chosen by regional groups; twenty were elected by the membership at large; the other six were 'invited' by the board executive to 'compensate' underrepresented stakeholders. The board structure was popular because it allowed individuals who enjoyed name recognition but who were not directly involved in regional groups to play a role on the national board. This feature of board representation proved highly beneficial to scholars. However, the task of gathering such a large group three times a year was cumbersome and expensive. Moreover, the board's ability to set directions was increasingly called into question.

The first attempts at reform were made in 1991. It was recommended that the number of board members be cut in half and that more seats be opened for non-elected members, who would be chosen by the Executive Committee based on merit and on the institute's corporate needs. It was also recommended that board members be held responsible for the expenses of attending the meetings. The proposal was not widely supported, and a revised version was tabled during the Executive Committee meeting of May 1994. This revised proposal called for a dramatic reduction in the representation of regional groups on the board. What became known as the 'Minto model' proposed only a single member from each province and territory, as selected by the regional groups of that jurisdiction.

The recommendations were hotly contested. Regional groups contended that the new arrangement would diminish their clout. It was argued that IPAC would suffer from not having substantive input from across the country that direct representation of regional groups facilitated. It was also argued that IPAC would be less democratic if the reforms were adopted. Finally, it was argued that the economic savings from these changes would be a mere $6,000 a year.[63]

The response to these criticisms was the 'Winnipeg model.' Under this one, IPAC's board would have twenty-seven members. Each of the seventeen regional groups would send one delegate; five additional members would be 'co-opted' by the IPAC executive committee based on their ability to represent a wide base of stakeholders; the other five members would be ex officio: the editor of *Canadian Public Administration*, the president of the Canadian Association of Programs in Public Administration, the chair of the IPAC Research Committee, the chair of the IPAC Endowment Fund, and the past president of IPAC. This model was adopted at the 1994 annual conference in Charlottetown.[64]

This model addressed the concerns of the regional groups but also represented a sharp departure in governance. No longer would there be direct elections to the national board of IPAC, and no longer would deserving members who were not involved in regional groups be eligible to sit on the board. The reaction among scholars was especially strong; more than two hundred chose not to renew membership. It is clear that in changing its governance model, IPAC had crossed another threshold in its journey towards becoming an NGO. Board members would now be appointed by local and regional activists, or they would be 'co-opted' as a means to compensate key stakeholders. 'Membership' would take on another meaning in the minds of many; instead of being 'contributors' to governance, they would be 'consumers' of IPAC goods and services.

Conclusion

IPAC provides a revealing example of how an association that depended heavily on servicing a particular clientele, in terms of both its mandate and its revenues, was forced to respond to new realities. In a context where public servants were offered a variety of memberships based on their specific occupations and governments, fewer chose an institute whose principal mandate was broad-based research and informal learning. Faced with a decline in membership and a shift in government financing from operational to project funding, the board of directors adopted a range of new measures. In so doing, IPAC moved from an organization driven mostly by membership concerns to one driven mostly by the managerial concerns identified by the board of directors and by the staff at the national office. Accountability shifted as well: no longer did IPAC focus exclusively on membership and the board of directors; now it also encompassed funders and clients.

As IPAC moved from the old Victorian on Bay Street to a modern office building, the transformation was almost total. It is interesting that today's IPAC is clearly recognizable with regard to the strategic plan developed in 1988–9. In the late 1980s most of IPAC's revenue was drawn from memberships and from stable base funding by the federal and provincial governments. After 1992 those two revenue streams shrank as a proportion of IPAC's funding. (Thirteen years later, only 7 per cent of IPAC's revenue would be drawn from these sources.) Instead, IPAC received government funding on a service basis. Working with a smaller but ever more dedicated membership, IPAC adopted a dynamic program of international involvement, magazine publication, surveys of deputy ministers, an entrepreneurial approach to research, and awards to both practitioners and scholars.

IPAC today is unique in the world in that it combines membership with service delivery to governments in the field of public administration. Though it incurred the wrath of many scholars in the mid-1990s, it did not abandon its mission to work with them and to provide a bridge between practitioners and academics. In 1997 it celebrated its fiftieth anniversary with flourish and a new sense of purpose. The popularity and influence of its quarterly academic journal would continue to grow, and its publications of the work of scholars would continue to build on strengths. At the same time, IPAC grew more attentive to the needs of the public service, both in Canada and around the world. That it has survived is a testament to Ken Kernaghan and to his generation of board members.

The IPAC experience also brings to light a highly effective relationship between the board of directors and the institute's staff, which was led by Joe Galimberti (1941–2006) after 1976. Inevitably, the institute

Figure 11.1. IPAC, 1986–1995

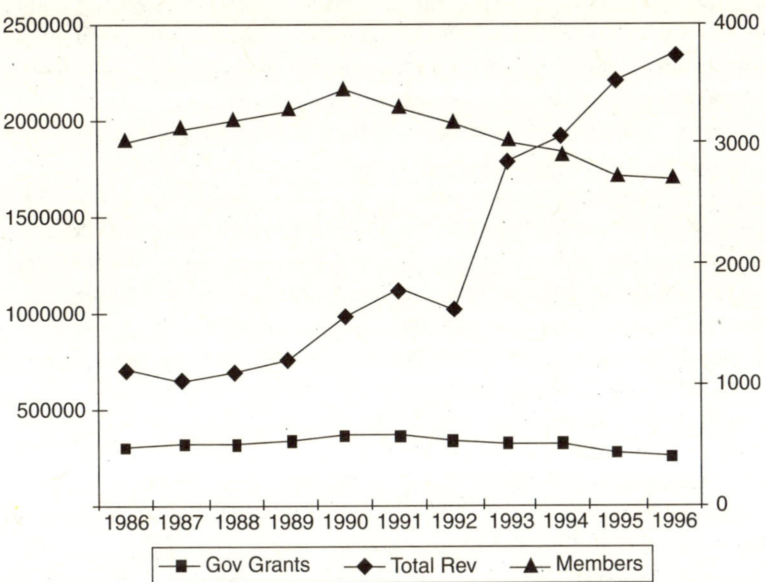

suffered some changes in staff through these tumultuous years, but it was able to count on doggedly determined personnel who were eager to see IPAC survive the turbulence. Joe Galimberti's role in IPAC's transformation was pivotal, but he would never allow himself to take credit for it. His leadership in helping IPAC dramatically adjust its business model and its governance was immeasurable, and his guidance was deeply appreciated by his dear friend Ken Kernaghan.

NOTES

1 The views expressed in this essay, written by two former employees of IPAC, are not to be interpreted as representing an official history of IPAC or in any way expressing the views of the Board of Directors of IPAC. The authors assume full responsibility for the contents of this paper.
2 IPAC, Executive Committee, 11 March 1985, 9–10.
3 See Kenneth Kernaghan, 'The Statement of Principles of the Institute of Public Administration of Canada: The Rationale for Its Development and Content,' *Canadian Public Administration* 30, no. 3 (1987): 331–51.

4 The Canadian Income Tax Act describes a non-profit (i.e., not-for-profit) organization, in paragraph 149(1)(l), as a club, society, or association that is organized and operated solely for social welfare, civic improvement, pleasure, or recreation, or for any other purpose except profit. Also, to be considered a NPO, no part of the income of such an organization can be payable to or available for the personal benefit of any proprietor, member, or shareholder, unless the proprietor, member, or shareholder is a club, society, or association whose primary purpose and function is to promote amateur athletics in Canada. See www.cra-arc.gc.ca/E/pub/tg/t4117/t4117-e.html#P65_1095. According to the U.S. government's Internal Revenue Service, non-profits include nine types of organizations: business leagues; charitable organizations, including religious, scientific, and literary organizations; employee associations; fraternal societies; labour and agricultural organizations, including trade organizations, chambers of commerce, and real estate boards; political organizations; social clubs; and social welfare and veterans' organizations.

5 Frank McKinnon, reflecting on Chester Walters's ambition for IPAC in V. Seymour Wilson, *Value for Many: The Institute of Public Administration of Canada, 1947–1997* (Toronto: IPAC, 1997), 4.

6 See Wilson, *Value for Many*, 1–9. See also Laura Freeman and Joseph Galimberti, 'The Institute of Public Administration of Canada,' in Jacques Bourgault, Maurice Demers, and Cynthia Williams, eds., *Public Administration and Public Management: Experiences in Canada* (Montreal: Publications du Québec, 1997), 375–80.

7 See Robert Putnam, *Making Democracy Work* (New York: Putnam, 1993); idem, *Bowling Alone: The Collapse and Revival of American Community* (New York: Touchstone, 2000); idem, *Democracies in Flux: The Evolution of Social Capital in Contemporary Society* (New York: Oxford University Press, 2002); and idem, *Better Together: Restoring the American Community* (with Lewis Feldstein and Don Cohen) (New York: Simon and Schuster, 2003).

8 See Margaret Levi, 'Social and Unsocial Capital: A Review Essay of Robert Putnam's *Making Democracy Work*,' *Politics and Society* 23 (1996): 45–55; and Stephen Baron, John Field, and Tom Schuller, eds., *Social Capital: Critical Perspectives* (New York: Oxford University Press, 2000).

9 Theda Skocpol, *Diminished Democracy: From Membership to Management in American Civic Life* (Norman: University of Oklahoma Press, 2003), 127–8.

10 Ibid., 135–8.

11 Ibid., 140–2.

12 This might be considered the local cause (see, for example, p. 140). Her

argument provides a more general explanation for the rise of the new advocacy groups that sketches out a complex web of influences: cultural, ideological, socio-economic, and technological (p. 178).

13 Statistics Canada, 'Analytical Report: Cornerstone of Community' (2003), www.statcan.ca/english/freepub/61-533-XIE/2004001/report.htm.

14 This is a study of twenty-two countries. Lester Salamon, *Global Civil Society: Dimensions of the Non-Profit Sector* (Baltimore: Johns Hopkins Center for Civil Society, 1999).

15 Ibid., 14–15.

16 Ibid., 26.

17 Michael O'Neill, *Non-Profit Nation: A New Look at the Third America* (San Francisco: Jossey-Bass, 2002), 17–18.

18 Dennis R. Young, 'Third Party Government,' in Ott, *The Nature of the Non-Profit Sector*, 367; Salamon, 'The Current Crisis,' in Ott, *The Nature of the Non-Profit Sector*; Jeffery M. Berry, *A Voice for Non-Profits* (Washington: Brookings Institution Press, 2003).

19 Karen A. Froelick, 'Diversification of Revenue Strategies: Evolving Resource Dependence in Non-Profit Organizations,' in Ott, *Understanding Non-Profit Organizations: Governance, Leadership, and Management* (Boulder: Westview, 2001). There are also a number of relevant essays in Burton A. Weisbrod, ed., *To Profit or Not to Profit: The Commercial Transformation of the Non-Profit Sector* (New York: Cambridge University Press, 1998).

20 Salamon, *Global Civil Society*, 24–5.

21 See Chris Miller, 'Canadian Non-Profits in Crisis: The Need for Reform,' *Social Policy and Administration* 32, no. 4 (1998): 406.

22 Michael Hall and Keith G. Banting, Introduction, in Banting, ed., *The Non-Profit Sector in Canada: Roles and Relationships* (Montreal and Kingston: McGill-Queens University Press, 2000), 2.

23 Dennis R. Young, 'Non-profit Entrepreneurship,' in *Understanding Non-profit Organizations*. (Note that these international figures may be skewed somewhat by the fact that they reflect some countries with very high levels of government funding of not-for-profits. If those countries were factored out, the contrast would be even more dramatic. Also, it is important to be alert to an additional element with skewing potential – one that will be illustrated when all of this is brought back to the Canadian context: the lion's share of public funding to not-for-profits is bestowed on a small group of resource-demanding institutions, especially hospitals and higher education organizations.)

24 Hall and Banting, *The Non-Profit Sector in Canada*, 13.

25 Raymond Dart and Brenda Zimmerman, 'After Government Cuts: Insights

from Two Ontario "Enterprising non-profits,"' in Banting, *The Non-profit Sector in Canada*.

26 Ibid., 145.

27 Many of the essays in Weisbrod, *To Profit or Not to Profit,* address these issues. See particularly Richard Steinberg and Weisbrod, 'Pricing and Rationing by Non-Profit Organizations with Distributional Objectives.' For an approach considerably more critical, see James T. Bennett and Thomas J. DiLorenzo, *Unfair Competition: The Profits of Non-Profits* (Lanham: Hamilton Press, 1989).

28 Alan R. Andreasen, 'Profits for Non-Profits: Find a Corporate Partner,' in Ott, *Understanding Non-profit Organizations*.

29 Weisbrod, 'The Future of the Non-Profit sector,' in Ott, *The Nature of the Non-Profit Sector*, 400–1. See also Michael H. Hall and Paul B. Reed, 'Shifting the Burden: How Much Can Government Download to the Non-Profit Sector?' *Canadian Public Administration* 41, no. 1 (1998): 1–20.

30 IPAC, Executive Committee, 27 April 1987, 19.

31 Ibid., 7 December 1987, 11.

32 Ibid., 27 August 1985, 3–4; 7 December 1987, 10–14.

33 Ibid., 8 December 1986, 7.

34 Ibid., 7 December 1987, 10–14; 27 November 1989, 3–4; 26 August 1990, 5–6; 9 December 1991.

35 IPAC, Management Committee, November 1990, last page.

36 IPAC, Executive Committee, 27 August 1985, 11; Report of the National Treasurer [Ed Power], 1985–6, 2. With hindsight, one senses the misplaced, even obsolescent, enthusiasm and hope at the announcement that the Province of Quebec had returned to a formal financing of IPAC; IPAC, Executive Committee, 1 and 2 May 1988, 11.

37 Ibid., 9 December 1985, 11; 26 August 1986, 6–7; 27 April 1987, 10–13; December 1991, item 13.

38 Ibid., 8 December 1986, 16. As late as 1992, when there were signs that the program in international consultancy was bailing IPAC out of its fiscal woes, many board members expressed deep concerns over the erosion of government grants. See Ibid., 7 December 1992, 6.

39 Ibid., 27 August 1985, 11; 11 March 1985, 9–12; Report of the National Treasurer, 1985–6, 2; IPAC, Executive Committee, 26 August 1990, 7

40 Ibid., 7 December 1987, 11; 24 August 1991, item 8.

41 Ibid., 26 August 1986, 6–7; Ibid., 1 and 2 May 1988; 30 April 1990, item 10.

42 Ibid., 9 December 1985, 11; 26 August 1986, 6–7; Report of the National Treasurer, 1985–6, 2; IPAC, Executive Committee, 8 December 1986, 8–10; 1 and 2 May 1988; 27 August 1989, 6.

43 Ibid., 9 December 1985, 13; 2 September 1987, 3; 1 and 2 May 1988.
44 Ibid., 9 December 1985, 8. See also IPAC, Research Committee, 7 April 1986, 8.
45 IPAC, Executive Committee, 27 November 1989, 5–7.
46 These types were developed in the 'Report from the Ad Hoc Committee on Certain Interdependent Strategic Projects' (CISP). Type A relationships referred to formal alliances with written general agreements that were largely strategic in focus. Type B relationships were more contingent but also reflected a compatibility of strategic interests. Written agreements would prescribe specific common activities; see CISP, 2–3.
47 Ibid., 18.
48 Executives from the Canadian Consulting Group and Exxon Chemical were involved. Report of the National Treasurer, 1985–6, 1–2.
49 IPAC, Executive Committee, 8 December 1986, 7.
50 Ibid., 11 March 1985, 9–10.
51 Ibid., 31 January 1987, 2.
52 Ibid., 27 August 1989.
53 IPAC, Research Committee, 7 April 1986; see also undated document from 1986, 'Executive Director's Trip to Washington: A Report,' 3–6.
54 IPAC, Executive Committee, 27 April 1987, 15.
55 IPAC, Management Committee, November 1990, 5.
56 Ibid., 15 November 1991.
57 IPAC, Executive Committee, 4 May 1992, item 14.d.
58 Ibid., 7 December 1992, 5–6.
59 Ibid., 30 August 1992, 4–5.
60 IPAC, International Public Administration Committee.
61 Ibid., 7 May 1995.
62 IPAC, Executive Committee, 7 December 1992, 7.
63 For a detailed summary of the debates arising from the Minto Model, see ibid., 1 May 1994, 2–7.
64 For discussion of these events, see Wilson, *Value for Many*, 101–2.

12 Is There a Gulf between Theory and Practice in Public Administration Journals? Can It Be Overcome?

BARBARA WAKE CARROLL

A thing may look specious in theory, and yet be ruinous in practice; a thing may look evil in theory, and yet in practice be excellent.'

Edmund Burke

This chapter is about the role of academic journals – in particular, their role in bridging the gap, or what some people have called the gulf, between theory and practice in public administration. So the short answers to the questions asked in the title of this paper are yes, and probably not. Academic journals are intended by some to be the means by which knowledge is disseminated to students, practitioners, and the broader academic community. They provide new knowledge that has been considered relevant and important, and they stimulate discussion and debate. This is not a universal viewpoint. Some view academic journals as links between academics and practitioners; others maintain that the role of journals is to disseminate academic ideas which will find their way into the policy discourse through other routes.

Most journals that focus on public policy and administration (see below) are used mainly by graduate students or senior undergraduates as the 'language of discourse' (i.e., the terminology is often sufficiently esoteric as to be incomprehensible to any but the initiated). Many such journals are intended to help practitioners, but most seem to rely on some form of 'ideas lite' to filter the ideas. Increasingly, the articles are written *by* PhDs *for* PhDs. As one of the correspondents for this research pointed out, journals are on average read by only five people, and it is not clear whether that includes the editor of the journal and the reviewers. I recently read an article published in a journal on public policy in

2005 in which I found that I could not understand the first line of the abstract. The question is, if I can't understand the first sentence of the abstract, is this my failing or the author's (or perhaps the editor's)? I might point out that I have never had to resort to my 10,000-page Oxford English Dictionary to read an article written by Ken Kernaghan.

My PhD supervisor was fond of saying that 'if the theory does not work, it is not a very good theory.' I contrast this with a colleague who, when it was pointed out that his favourite theory could not be empirically verified, and that furthermore the empirical evidence indicated that the theory was wrong, responded that this was irrelevant, it was still a great theory. Much of the literature on organizational theory is based on what two authors have called 'myths and wishful thinking.'[1] This point, which is covered in an article on 'surreal management' in *Canadian Public Administration*,[2] was first discussed by Chester Barnard[3] when he referred to management theory as asking 'water to flow uphill.' The relationship, or lack thereof, between theory and practice is one of the major preoccupations in public administration – there are wonderful theories; it is just that they do not work. Sometimes it is because they are incorrectly applied, but more often it is because they do not meet the test of practice.

This chapter has been a challenge to write because the topic has received little attention.[4] Yet it strikes a chord with many people. When asked to comment on the subject, most of the people I contacted went on at considerable length and then apologized for the length of their response. Whether theory and practice are mutually exclusive is a difficult question. I recently heard an interview with Larry Diamond, an eminent scholar on transitions to democracy who had been asked to be a leading adviser in the rebuilding of institutions and the transition to democracy in Iraq. During the interview he lamented that the transition team was unwilling to put into practice the theoretical lessons that had been learned in thirty years of research in this area. He attributed much of the current chaos in Iraq to this error. But there was little consensus on the reason for the problem. Some attributed it to the reluctance of practitioners to read, but most attributed it to the failure of academics to write with clarity.

In this chapter I begin by discussing how the distinction between theory and practice developed. As time goes by, it is viewed as less and less important that academics be relevant, yet some journals, such as *Optimum* and *Harvard Business Review*, do place the relevance of theory to practice front and centre in their editorial policy. It ought to be important that practitioners and academics be mutually engaged in the field; but increasingly, as one person commented, 'even though they [practitioners] are professional public administrators, many of them don't see themselves as part of the profession of public administration.' I move on to discuss how this disjunction has been reflected in various journals and how editors have responded. After a brief digression to consider the future role of electronic journals, I conclude with a discussion of what the future holds for those journals which do try to meet the needs of both theory and practice. I should point out here that my emphasis is less on who writes the articles than on who reads them, or should read them, or is intended to read them.

How We Got from There to Here – How 'Unreadable' Became 'Profound'

In the early days of academic journals little distinction was made between academic and practitioner articles – articles by both had both a theoretical and a practical component. Many of the 'classic' theoretical articles in public administration and management were in fact written by practitioners. The most notable of these might be the articles gathered in *Papers on the Science of Administration*[5] and Woodrow Wilson's essay 'The Study of Administration.'[6] This was a time when one article could cover a wide range of topics that had not been discussed in the literature. There was what we would probably call today 'theoretical capacity,' and we ought to bemoan today's lack of it. The theoretical field is now so fragmented that rarely does one article convey the full richness of any one theme.

This could be a function of the increased complexity of public administration; more likely, though, it reflects the pressure on academics to publish, and to publish in what one former editor referred to as 'high impact' journals – those which have high ratings in the Social Science Citation Index. One of the hallmarks of these journals is that, though they are often very sophisticated empirically, they are written in the kind of social science jargon that is not easily accessible to non-academics, or even to academics not specializing in the particular narrow field. As one person put it, 'the degree of difficulty in understanding an article was highly correlated with academic readers' impressions of its profoundness and originality.'[7] Journal rankings are in turn used to rank the 'quality' and prestige of academic departments.[8] Also, academics are facing increased pressure to publish often, so they are tempted not to waste two good ideas on one article when those same two ideas could serve as the basis for two articles. As a consequence, many articles end up being padded with arch and self-serving literature reviews. As I endlessly tell my students, the purpose of the literature review is to place the article in context, not to impress the reader with how well read you are or how much access you have to obscure papers, or to cite yourself and your friends. I mentioned earlier the article on policy making the abstract of which I could not understand. This is hardly going to appeal to a practitioner! The 2004 Presidential Address of the Academy of Management pointed out that 90 per cent of that organization's services and activities were aimed at 25 per cent of its members.[9] This is an organization with three separate journals: one for practitioners, one for theory, and one for empirical research.

As one result, a disconnect has developed between the world of the theoretical academic and the world of the practitioner. This is especially evident in field of the public policy, but we also see it in public administration/public management. Academics strive to succeed in their careers; practitioners strive to solve practical problems. The goals of these two groups have diverged. No longer do they engage in a debate over the normative *and* empirical aspects of public administration. Academics are less involved in problem solving. Except in business schools, 'consulting' or 'practical problem solving' is viewed as vaguely suspect,[10] as something that real academics don't do. Some of the editors who responded to me pointed out that it is no longer very clear what academics in public policy and administration do, in that they spend what some consider an inordinate amount of time writing theoretical work that has no practical application. And there is an even more insidious component to this: coining a neologism means that you don't have to do much of a historical literature review. I believe this is now referred to as 'diaconic' or 'path dependency' theory. If you are putting old wine into new bottles, you don't have to spend a lot of time on the old bottles that have gone to the recycling bin.

The second part of 'how we got there' relates to the nature of research and the concept of theory. The issue here is that what is often meant by theory in public administration has little to do with the true meaning of theory – that is, it does not help us understand relationships in the world, presumably in order to explain, predict, or alter them. Much of the debate over the lack of theory in public administration studies has been carried out in the pages of *Public Administration Review.* It started with an article by Howard E. McCurdy and Robert E.

Cleary, 'Why Can't We Resolve the Research Issues in Public Administration,' published in 1984.[11] They argued that there was insufficient 'theory building' in public administration because too little of public administration followed the 'standard science'[12] model of social sciences, which attempted to emulate the natural sciences model. In a rebuttal to the McCurdy and Cleary paper, White argued that there are different kinds of research and different kinds of theory, including 'theory development with regards to administrators' interests in positive, interpretive and critical research.'[13] White here was attempting to bridge the theory/practice dichotomy, which he felt McCurdy and Cleary had set up as a straw argument. Even so, the argument has not gone away.

Houston and Delevan came back with a further analysis of public administration research. Their findings 'support the argument that public administration research is engaged in little theory testing.'[14] They attributed this problem to reporting 'only univariate and bivariate statistics ... [thus] causal arguments drawn from these projects are weak, as plausible rival arguments often cannot be dismissed.'[15] They admitted that their emphasis on large-scale quantitative studies might be biasing their findings but argued that there was no evidence that alternative research strategies were being used rigorously. The second reason they gave for the problem was that 'the historical character of the field with its focus on practice may well contribute to the lack of theoretical research.' They concluded that the fundamental problem was that the field 'lacks a broad theoretical framework or paradigm.'[16] In 1992, Bailey responded that since case studies were central to the work of physics, chemistry, and other 'hard' sciences, this was one area of complaint that could not be supported. She then attacked the bias against qualitative research. She argued that it is possible to embrace a 'practitioner orientation' that incorporates a rigorous methodology and contributes to theory building in the field. She considered the workplace to be the laboratory of public administration research, and she deplored the tendency to view those who work with practitioners as 'second class.'[17]

In 2000, Chester A. Newland entered the debate, arguing for greater 'connectedness' and more appreciation of the need to reflect historical trends – a perspective reflected in Vince Wilson's perspective on public administration in Canada.[18] A subsequently published analysis of research in public administration journals[19] compared the professional needs of practitioners with the research reported and found a 'somewhat mismatch.' Two other practitioners found a disconnect between research and practice, attributing it to the emphasis on data-supported versus logic-driven knowledge and to the pressure for academic tenure versus the need for organizational effectiveness, among other factors.[20] A series of articles in *Public Administration Review*[21] in 2005 on the relationship between academic and practical research suggested that the two could be brought together through different forms of research that were less concerned with grand (be it meta, meso, or micro) theory and that instead emphasized a more practicable form of theoretical knowledge. These articles also championed the relevance and rigour of narrative research – something that Kernaghan had done more than twenty years earlier.[22]

A similar debate took place in Canada. In the 25th Anniversary edition of *Canadian Public Administration*, one of the articles by Kernaghan[23] reported on a panel that was critically analysing the theory and practice of public administration. He mentioned that one panellist referred to public administration as atheoretical because 'most approaches are middle-range theory which are tied to a particular problem, but which are not used to tie together a wide variety of concerns within the public sector.'[24] That this debate did not continue may reflect the pragmatism of the editors, but it may also be a function of the tendency to be less critical of public sector management in Canada, as well as the size of the academic community in Canada. Several former editors and associate editors commented that publishing a negative book review in *Canadian Public Administration* was simply not acceptable, though damning with faint praise seemed quite acceptable.

What Is an Academic Journal (or Its Editor) Gonna Do?

All of the editors surveyed commented that it was a challenge to balance the demands of practitioners with those of academics in one journal. As one former editor expressed it:

> Editing a journal for a professional association is significantly different from editing a journal for one or more academic disciplines. The majority of practitioners are looking for something of 'value' which they can use to make sense of their 'reality' and perhaps to change that 'reality.' The academics who write in journals are mainly interested in writing for their academic colleagues, gaining favourable recognition and advancing their academic careers.'

Or as another expressed it:

> I can fully appreciate the difficult situation editors face in their endeavour to make the contents 'interesting and appealing' to both academics and practitioners who are interested in different things. One group is keen to become familiar with new developments and thinking, and is driven by the pressure to publish in top academic journals, while the other seeks information and guidance on how to perform their tasks in the public service ... Practitioners enjoy reading brief practice-oriented articles and have neither the time to read lengthy academic articles, nor the academic background to absorb theoretical discussions, which often have no relevance for their jobs.

Much of the literature stressed that one of the problems with public administration journals is that they tend to be overly descriptive and uncritical. A large part of this problem has been attributed to the 'thin skins' of practitioners. Consulting contracts may dry up (this is a bigger problem in the United States than in Canada, where academics are rarely used as consultants). Access may become limited – a particular problem in Canada, where the public administration community is smaller. Several Canadian academics have reported writing papers critical of government and later being taken off government distribution lists.

Various journals have met in different ways the needs of practitioners and academics (see table 12.1). Some have always been academic journals. Either they are stand-alone journals or they represent a membership that is largely academic. *Canadian Public Policy* and *Canadian Journal of Political Science* are solely academic journals. Other journals have moved from serving both communities to serving only one; these are noted in the table by an arrow. *Governance* started out trying to meet both needs but has since evolved into a primarily academic journal. *Public Administration* has evolved into an academic journal since ceasing to be the official publication of the Royal Society for Public Administration. The field of 'practice' has generally been left to softer journals such as *Policy Options*.[25] Some journals, however, do not have such an easy option.

Public Administration Review (*PAR*) is effectively two journals in one. It has published special sections for practitioners such as 'Professional Practices of Public Administration' in the 1990s and, more recently, 'The Reflective Professional.' *International Review of Administrative Sciences* (*IRAS*) probably has the highest practitioner component, with contributions made through symposia. Also, it has faced more pressure to be a

Table 12.1 Primary audience of selected **public administration journals**

Practitioners	Both	Academics
	→	*Governance*
		Canadian Journal of Political Science
	→	*Public Administration*
Academy of Management Executive		*Academy of Management Review/Journal*
	Canadian Public Administration	
Optimum		
Harvard Business Review		
		Canadian Public Policy
	Public Administration Review	
	International Review of Administrative Sciences	
	Public Administration and Development	
	Indian Journal of Public Administration	
	Asian Journal of Public Administration	

practitioners' journal. It is, after all, the official journal of the International Institute of Administrative Sciences, which means that most of its members and sponsors work in public administration; it is also the official journal of the Commonwealth Association of Public Administration and Management, whose members are almost all practitioners. (Besides these two, it is the official journal of the International Association of Schools and Institutes of Administration and the European Group for Public Administration.) *PAR* and *IRAS* have access to a large number of academic practitioners who may not only write for but more importantly read academic journals.

Similarly, some Asian journals, such as *Public Administration and*

Policy (Hong Kong), *Indian Journal of Public Administration,* and *Asian Journal of Public Administration* (the journal of the Eastern Regional Organization for Public Administration [EROPA]), have had practitioner input and have catered to practitioners. In large part this is because they are funded by governments (and in some cases donors). The same is true of *Public Administration and Development,* the journal of the Commonwealth Secretariat.

Canadian Public Administration has tried to keep the two sides integrated. Ron Burns and Al Johnson, both distinguished senior public managers and academics, made various attempts to meld theory with practice;[26] unfortunately, they had limited success. All editors have tried to involve more practitioners. Paul Thomas introduced a series of point/counterpoint debates that were intended to engage practitioners. Ken Kernaghan and Vince Wilson both maintained a 'Notes' section. They were also quite proactive in commissioning articles.

Other editors have tried to achieve integration during the editorial process – for example, by asking academic authors to provide material on the practical significance of their articles (which many authors have strongly resisted), and by working with practitioners to inject a theoretical component into articles. As one former editor expressed it: 'My approach was to ask authors to explain why their work was important, and I received the response that either this was not their obligation or that an insistence on relevance was inappropriate.' Another tactic has been co-authorship, but this has not succeeded very well. Finally, ongoing efforts have been made to get practitioners to review books and write review articles. This has been made easier recently by the tendency for some professional associations to require accreditation; this means that practitioners have to do some form of 'professional skills upgrading,' and working with academic journals is viewed as one way.

But efforts to get practitioners to work on scholarly articles are probably doomed. Regarding practitioners, one individual noted that 'even those who see themselves as part of the profession operate at work as clinicians, basing their decisions and actions on their actual experience (or the experience of their mentors or superiors). They do not engage in evidence based decision-making; they do not need to read any research.'

The same view is encountered in the opinion of Carol Weiss, albeit in the context of policy making rather than public administration: 'For most people, social science reports seem to have little effect on policy makers in and of themselves ... Policy makers are busy people, and reading is low on their list of activities.'[27]

But blaming the victim may not be the answer. If academics are not producing and disseminating research that is read by, or of use to, practitioners, what *are* they doing? One individual suggested that most public administration research is 'vacuous.' This may be true (though I would like to think it does not apply to my own research). More probably, the issue is not so much who *does* the research but who *reads* it. *Harvard Business Review* may be the most successful of the journals when it comes to making cutting-edge research accessible to managers. It publishes rather short articles, but by some of the best-known academics in the field. Its editorial guidelines focus on five questions: (1) What is the central message, and what is new and important about it? (2) What are the article's real-world implications, and how could its findings be implemented? (3) What is the audience, and why should that audience read the article? (4) What research supports the article? And finally, (5) what are the author's credentials, and why should people listen to the author?[28] To be more succinct, the articles must be credible and relevant and must avoid neologisms and obscure references.

Regarding public administration journals, one solution might be to assess each article both for its theoretical/conceptual contribution and for its practical contribution. (Many of Ken Kernaghan's articles are subtitled 'Conceptual and Practical Considerations.') It also helps if the writing is as clear and simple as possible. We need to abandon the idea that the incomprehensible is profound. Especially with empirical, quantitative research, too many authors tend not to bother to explain their findings in clear English or French; instead, they focus on charts packed with obscure statistics; and, in those dreaded words of Blalock, the 'fail to reject their null hypothesis.'[29]

All of the academic/practitioner journals used to rely heavily on papers given at annual conferences, where academics and practitioners had opportunities to interact and to blend theory with practice (or try to). Past editors of these journals tend to agree that PowerPoint presentations – and to a lesser degree theme conferences – have dried up this source in that oftentimes, formal conference papers are no longer required. Which brings us to the issue of technology.

A Digression on the Subject of Electronic Journals

Electronic journals take two forms: existing journals that are also available online, and journals that are *only* available online. Regarding the first kind, the advantage is that you don't have to leave your office to find an article. You can download and print it, albeit often at considerable time and expense. But this affects how research is done. When you search for articles with a search engine, you end up accessing only those articles that are about the topic of interest. This is easy and fast; the downside is that there is no cross-fertilization of ideas. Some excellent research has emanated from a chance reading of an article while browsing through a journal. In other words, online journals tend to narrow research even further, making it of interest and relevance to only a few specialists.

Yet there are success stories. *Optimum* has for thirty-five years been the Canadian government's management journal, but with editorial independence. It was one of the first journals to also publish online. 'Optimumline' now reaches more than 10,000 subscribers – an impressive feat for a Canadian management publication. All the while it has been able to hold the middle ground, publishing articles by consultants, academics, and practitioners that are thoughtful and that contain useful ideas and solutions. It may be that online materials are more accessible to practitioners, who do not have time to visit libraries and who rely heavily on what they can quickly access from their desks.

Nowadays, too many researchers are accessing *only* online publications. If it is not available digitally, then it does not exist. As a consequence, we are losing our collective memory of ideas, which means we are finding it increasingly difficult to recognize supposedly new ideas as old ones with new names. Online journals and other materials do offer some advantages. For example, content analysis is much easier to perform. Also, the Internet allows you to search more journals than you or your library might subscribe to. Finally, online materials are infinitely cheaper, and this makes them attractive to libraries. To save money and space, more and more libraries are getting only the electronic version of journals. Journals that are not available online are nowadays at a disadvantage in terms of being cited.

I make a distinction here between journals that are also available online and those 'e-journals' which are *only* available online. E-journals are even more of a problem (I am limiting myself here to formal online journals, as opposed to papers available on websites, etc.). The major concern is quality. Many online journals simply are not edited well. One individual, who sits on the editorial board of two electronic journals, pointed out that she would not submit her own work to online journals because they tended to lack both rigour and editing. This point was disputed by the former editor of an online journal, who suggested that there is just as much lack of rigour and bad editing in print journals. Nevertheless, the ease of starting an online journal – doing so costs almost nothing – tends to encourage less than stellar scholarship. There are so many academic journals already that publish questionable research. Online journals simply compound the problem. There are already too many academics who write too much and think too little, and electronic access to journals and online journals is exacerbating this problem.

And there are other problems as well. The most serious is access. Access is a problem because there is no industry standard for search engines, processing packages, or downloading protocols. The technology is advancing so quickly that there is a constant problem of updating to the most recent technology or losing the knowledge. Many of us have cassette tapes we can no longer play, and some of you may have the old 'floppy disks.' But a book (journal), is a book, is a book. It will still be readable many years from now.

Also, we too easily assume that online access is readily available. It is not. Over the past two years I have been a visiting scholar at universities in Botswana, France, Ghana, and Mauritius, and at only two of these did I have reasonable Internet access from on campus, and in none of those places was there any off-campus access. When only online resources are available, they are limited to those who have online access. This is not yet a valid assumption even for academics and practitioners. Is travelling miles to get online access an improvement on travelling the same distance to a library? Also, during my travels, access tended to be restricted to journals to which the university library subscribed – very few in most cases.

One possible solution would be to have hierarchies of journals, with the highly specialized and very long versions of articles available online but the 'best' articles still being produced as hardcopy. There already is a hierarchy of journals, and some, the 'c' journals, may eventually migrate to an electronic format (much like what happened with archaic 'mimeo' citation). Another solution might be to produce electronic abstracts; this would simplify searches while pointing the researcher to either the full version in a print journal or an even longer version on someone's webpage. *Canadian Public Administration* already does the latter, allowing readers to access a longer version than the published one on a website. On that more positive note, I will conclude this section – albeit with one last caution: until the technical and access problems can be resolved (which is unlikely to happen within my

active academic lifetime), I would be wary of putting too many eggs in
the electronic basket.

Conclusion

I leave the last word on the relationship between academics and practitioners, or theory and practice, to Ken Kernaghan, who twenty-five
years ago wrote that a

> defence of public administration scholars does not change the fact that
> their research and publications are widely viewed as irrelevant to the
> requirements of the profession ... The discipline is not the handmaiden of
> the profession, but reality demands that academics be sensitive to the
> needs of practitioners. If academics want their research and ideas to affect
> practice, they must write on matters of current or perennial concern to the
> profession. Moreover, they must use a vocabulary that is easily compre-
> hensible to the non-academic. The development of a common language
> for communication between the discipline and the profession is especially
> important for articulating shared values and assumptions. Those who
> share a common language are more likely to find common ground.[30]

These words were prescient; it seems that the situation has not
changed since they were written. It may in fact have grown worse,
because there is now a distinct bureaucratic language, and another language of management consultants and business, and neither of these is
the language of public administration academics – though 'accountability' and 'values' seem to be making a comeback.

I am not sanguine about the future. For understandable reasons, the
academic journals have migrated to the academic side so that there is
little contribution by, or relevance to, practitioners. As one person put
it, the 'nature of scholarly publication these days would seem to make it
improbable that this trend can be reversed.' And this trend is only
being strengthened by large funding engines such as the SSHRC, which
direct funding to issues of importance to politicians or academics but
not necessarily to practitioners. The nature of academia makes it difficult for young academics to ignore this pressure. Nevertheless, I think
we should continue to strive to produce academic research that discusses those timeless topics – responsibility, legitimacy, discretion,
(de)centralization, and accountability to name only a few – which are of
enduring relevance for practitioners; and we should encourage reports

by practitioners that are informative for academics and practitioners alike.

Something positive may come out of present-day efforts to repair aspects of our political system. For example, in one book on 'reinventing a new liberalism in Canada,'[31] both academics and practitioners try to apply theories to problems. The book is a refreshing throwback to the 'glory days' of rational policy making in the 1970s; it is also an excellent attempt to apply theory to practice.

In closing, I quote one former editor, who offered what I think was an elegant tribute to Ken's contribution to this field. Colin Campbell remarked: 'Guy Peters and I tried to follow the example set out by Ken in developing *Governance* ... The continuing commitment of *Canadian Public Administration* to bridge the two worlds certainly grounds itself substantially in the example set by Ken.' I return, finally, to the questions asked in the title of this chapter: Is there a gap between theory and practice? Yes, and it is widening. Can it be closed? Maybe, if academic journals can meld theory and practice by requiring that articles be written in accessible language and by applying rigorous analysis to their laboratories – the offices of government.

NOTES

1 Sten A. Jonsson and Rolf A. Lundin, 'Myths and Wishful Thinking as Management Tools,' *Academy of Management Journal* 12 (1969): 157–70. See Daniel Cohen, 'Jumping into the Political Fray: Academics and Policy-Making,' *IRPP Policy Matters* 7, no. 2 (2006); Carol H. Weiss, 'The Uneasy Partnership Endures: Social Science and Government,' in Stephen Brook and Alain G. Gagnon, eds., *Social Scientists, Policy, and the State* (New York: Praeger, 1990).

2 Ian Clark and Harry Swain, 'Surreal Management,' *Canadian Public Administration* 48, no. 4 (2005): 453–76.

3 Chester Barnard, *The Functions of the Executive* (Cambridge, MA: Harvard University Press, 1938).

4 I would like to thank the ten former and current journal editors and associate editors who answered my plea for help in writing this chapter. Some, such as Gilles Paquette, Audrey Doerr, and Colin Campbell, were willing to be quoted; most, however, chose not to be, so I have used their words without attribution. I would also like to thank Peter Aucoin and Ian Clark for their comments on an earlier draft.

5 Luther Gulick and L. Urwick, eds., *Papers on the Science of Administration* (New York: Institute of Public Administration, 1937).

6 Woodrow Wilson, 'The Study of Administration,' *Political Science Quarterly* 2 (1887): 197–222.

7 Carbone, Robert, and J. Scott Armstrong, 'Note: Evaluation of Extrapolative Forecasting Methods: Results of a Survey of Academicians and Practitioners,' *Journal of Forecasting* 1, no. 2 (1982): 215–17.

8 Simon Hix, 'A Global Ranking of Political Science Departments,' *Political Studies Review* 2 (2004): 293–313.

9 Rosalie L. Tung, 'Reflections on Engendering a Sustainable Community within the Academy,' *Academy of Management Review* 30, no. 2 (2005): 239–45.

10 Mary Timney Bailey, 'Do Physicists Use Case Studies? Thoughts on Public Administration Research,' *Public Administration Review* 52, no. 1 (1992): 47–54.

11 I should note that I was taught by both these individuals and graduated from American University, where they both taught. I was also taught by Peta Sherif, cited later.

12 Nick Baxter-Moore, Terry Carroll, and Rod Church, *Studying Politics: Introduction to Analysis and Argument* (Toronto: Copp-Clark, 1994), 379.

13 Jay D. White, 'On the Growth of Knowledge in Public Administration,' *Public Administration Review* 46, no. 1 (1986): 22.

14 David J. Houston and Sybil M. Delevan, 'Public Administration Research: An Assessment of Journal Publications,' *Public Administration Review* 50, no. 6 (1990): 678.

15 Ibid., 679.

16 Ibid.

17 Ibid., 53.

18 V. Seymour Wilson, *Value for Many: The Institute of Public Administration of Canada, 1947–1997* (Toronto: IPAC, 1997).

19 Gregory Streib, Bert J. Slotkin, and Mark Rivera, 'Public Administration Research from a Practitioner Perspective,' *Public Administration Review* 61, no 5 (2001): 515–25.

20 Michael J. Bolton and Gregory B. Stolcis, 'Ties That Do Not Bind: Musings on the Specious Relevance of Academic Research,' *Public Administration Review* 63, no. 5 (2003): 626–30.

21 Jennifer Dodge, Sonia M. Ospina, and Erica Gabrielle Foldy, 'Integrating Rigor and Relevance in Public Administration Scholarship: The Contribution of Narrative Inquiry,' *Public Administration Review* 65, no. 3 (2005): 286–300; Sonia A. Ospina and Jennifer Dodge, 'Narrative Inquiry and the Search

for Connectedness: Practitioners and Academic Developing Public Administration Scholarship,' *Public Administration Review* 65, no. 4 (2005): 409–23.

22 Kenneth Kernaghan, 'Canadian Public Administration: Progress and Prospects,' *Canadian Public Administration* 25, no. 4 (1982): 144–56.

23 Ibid.

24 Ibid., 449.

25 Barbara W. Carroll, 'The Relevance of Academic Journals to Practitioners,' paper presented at Panel on Practitioners and Academics, Canadian Political Science Association meetings, Charlottetown, 1996.

26 Ibid.

27 Weiss, *The Uneasy Partnership Endures*, 102.

28 *Howard Business Review*, 'Editorial Guidelines.'

29 Herbert M. Blalock Jr, *Social Statistics*, 2nd ed. (New York: McGraw-Hill, 1979).

30 Kernaghan, 'Canadian Public Administration,' 454.

31 Howard Aster and Thomas Axworthy, eds., *Searching for the New Liberalism: Perspectives, Policies, Prospects* (Oakville: Mosaic, 2003).

13 Case Studies and the Case Study Method in Canadian Public Administration

CAROLYN JOHNS

For many academics and practitioners, case studies and the case study method are an important part of public administration research, teaching, and professional development. Case research involves both a type of literature (a case) and a pedagogical technique (the case method).[1] Many who research and teach in public administration consciously or unconsciously conduct case research, use cases, and employ the case method in a variety of ways. The case method is a learning process in which individuals and groups learn by analysing a description of actual administrative situations and decisions. In their analysis and discussion of a case, students and practitioners are expected to apply ideas and insights from theoretical materials presented in scholarly writings to the issues and problems contained in the case. In this way, abstract models and theories can be related to concrete situations and practical experience.[2] Cases allow learners to explore the nexus between theory and practice; that is this aspect of the case study method that makes case studies a powerful research and learning tool. Though now viewed as an important part of learning in Canadian public administration, case studies and the case method continue to face challenges unique to the discipline in Canada.

This chapter focuses on the evolution of case studies and the case study method in Canadian public administration since the 1970s. Following the structure of an article written by Ken Kernaghan thirty years ago, the first section begins with a general overview of case research and different types of case studies in public administration. The second section focuses on how case studies are employed in different learning contexts through the case method and the advantages of using the case method in public administration. The third section focuses on the evolution of case research, writing, and use over the past three decades. It is argued in this section that despite significant progress, the evolution of case research and the case method reflects broader developmental issues of the discipline and profession in Canada. The final section discusses the current place of case research, case studies, and the case method in Canadian public administration and highlights some outstanding challenges and potential opportunities for further integrating case research and the case method into the discipline and profession.

Case Research and Case Studies

There is a well-developed interdisciplinary literature on case research, writing, and teaching. Simply defined, a case is a description of a situation in which one or more administrators made, influenced, or implemented a decision. A case is a narrative of an actual (i.e., real) problem that portrays actors (typically historical or fictional) confronted with the need to make a decision. Cases and simulations, if not absolutely factual, are 'more or less' factual in that they typically are based on situations that real public administrators have faced. They may duplicate the circumstances of a real situation; or those circumstances may have been altered in order to incorporate additional actors, contextual factors, and interpersonal dynamics, and/or additional legal, organizational, and ethical complexities, to allow learners to explore the interface of politics and administration. Cases and simulations are designed to be interactive, experiential, and learner-centred.

Research for cases typically involves examining published materials available inside or outside government, reading unpublished materials available only within government departments or agencies, and interviewing individuals who were involved in, or who are knowledgeable about, specific administrative situations. Some cases are based on interviews with the decision makers themselves and then written up by skilled and experienced case writers.[3] It is the research element of writing case studies that injects realism into cases and that has the potential to link theory and practice.

Many cases are written by teachers of public policy or public administration who have learned about particularly interesting administrative happenings based on research, personal experience, or the experiences of friends and contacts in government. Political and administrative scandals and crises often stimulate case writers to research the events and to write a case on the basis of that research. Many other cases are written by public servants who have actually been involved in or have observed first hand the administrative situations on which the cases are based. Practitioners have an advantage as case researchers in that they are 'participant observers' who can easily recall situations that were especially instructive in terms of their implications and lessons for the theory and practice of public administration. Indeed, public administrators from all levels of government, all ranks, and all professional areas are potential authors of case studies if provided with some guidance on the case writing process and the case method. A common approach is for practitioners to team up with academics to conduct case research and write cases that link theory and practice. Retired academics and practitioners are also a potential source of rich cases.[4] Another source of case research has been students in senior public administration courses and graduate programs. This form of research and writing can also be an excellent assignment for in-service and continuing education students.

Public administration cases can be broadly classified according to their general emphasis on policy or management concerns.[5] *Policy* cases focus mainly on policy formulation – the development, weighing, and choice of policy options. These cases tend to emphasize the historical, legal, and institutional aspects of political and administrative decisions. The emphasis is on policy considerations, but many management issues are raised. *Policy management* cases contain a more even mix of policy and management concerns. These cases usually involve significant elements of both policy formation and policy execution. The authors of these cases do not distinguish sharply between 'policy' and 'administration'; rather, they attempt to emphasize the limitations of the politics–administration dichotomy. Finally, *management* cases focus on one or more of the great assortment of management problems that arise when public policies and programs are implemented at various levels of bureaucratic organizations. These cases tend to focus on skills development and preparation for management and are written mainly for pre-career or mid-career public administrators.[6]

A typology of five basic types of public administration case studies was developed by Ken Kernaghan more than thirty years ago and is still applicable today.[7] A *descriptive* case provides a record of an administrative situation, including an account of the problem involved and the decision taken. The case study group is expected to analyse critically both the decision-making process and the decision itself. An *issue* case describes the situation only up to the point where a decision must be made. The group is required not only to analyse the situation but also to explore the implications of possible solutions. A *puzzle* case is more demanding than an issue case in that the group must begin by determining what problem exists and then analyse the problem and suggest solutions. A *comprehensive* case is characterized by the existence of a number of interrelated issues and problems. The group is required to single out the problems to be resolved, analyse their interrelationships and comparative importance, and suggest a series of decisions that, taken together, constitute a coherent solution to several related problems. Finally, a case may be *participative*. This form is directly related to the pedagogical technique known as role-playing or simulation. A participative case normally includes written roles for the main actors in the case.[8] Each type of case requires a slight variation in terms of the case method.

The Case Method

The case method can be distinguished from other teaching methods such as lectures and seminars.[9] It differs in some important ways from conventional post-secondary classroom learning, and like other learning methods it has advantages and disadvantages. It is particularly valuable in public policy and administration, yet it is generally regarded as a complement to other learning approaches, not a superior substitute.

Generally the case method is a student-centred group learning process.[10] Traditional case analysis typically includes two analytical stages: individual preparation and group discussion. The steps in individual preparation and group discussion are still highly relevant when the case method is used in public administration.[11] Indeed, many instructors who use the case method in their teaching include 'how to' instructions in their courses and take time to teach the method itself before employing it.

By far the most prevalent version of the case method involves reading, analysing, and discussing a description of an administrative situation. Students are required to read and ponder the case on their own; they then meet with a case study group or in class to identify the problems, to discuss the nature and implications of those problems, to set out the points of policy and management raised by the case, to debate possible solutions, and to make a decision or outline a plan of action. This general approach can be utilized in a variety of courses and can be modified for different types of learners. Some institutions and programs, such as the Kennedy School of Government at Harvard, have adopted the case method at an institutional and program level and allocated significant resources to allow instructors and students to use the method effectively. Indeed, the Harvard case method is a distinct method.[12] There are, however, many variations.

Given the different types of cases, it is not surprising that each type requires a different approach and that approaches have evolved in the context of learning theories and technologies.[13] Though traditionally a group learning approach, the method can be modified for individual analysis and assignments. More recently the method has been developed in self-directed and online learning contexts and has incorporated multimedia features such as guest speakers and video clips.[14] Like all learning methods, the case method has advantages and disadvantages. There are some particular advantages to using the case method in public policy and public administration learning contexts.

The case method is basically a problem-solving method that is inductive and experiential. Case learning develops tolerance for ambiguity and fosters the ability to make timely decisions and take effective action despite incomplete information, unclear problems, and uncertain consequences. The ability of case studies to mirror the dynamic, complex, and uncertain reality of public administration has made them a valuable part of research and teaching in the discipline. By challenging students and practitioners to adopt an action perspective and by engaging them in relatively unstructured but interesting case discussion, the case method allows for interactive debate, analysis, and learning. The differing views of those involved in a case discussion can produce a creative process of hypothesizing and problem solving.

The participants are active learners and active listeners; they offer interpretations, raise questions, build on one another's statements, construct a collective analysis, reframe the discussion, apply theory, challenge the instructor and literature, and learn from one another. The emphasis is on the students' or practitioners' reasoning, interpretation, and capacity to 'unpack' problems – on restructuring the problem and working out one or more solutions. Case discussion is an exercise in building analytical bridges between theory and actual historical and contemporary situations. The method itself is a learning process beyond the substance of the inquiry; thus a case discussion often ends up with questions as well as conclusions.[15] The many purposes of a case discussion and analysis include these: fostering critical and analytical thinking; encouraging student responsibility for learning; and developing applied knowledge and collaborative problem solving skills.

The case method is consistent with a certain philosophy and style of teaching that assumes a major goal of higher education and professional learning is to empower learners to think critically in their various roles and in their communities. It asserts that learners need to take responsibility for their learning, be able to apply concepts and theories to complex situations, and integrate knowledge from other contexts and life experiences. As the case method encourages active learning, it requires a different instructional approach.[16] As an active facilitator, the instructor highlights opposing views; pulls contributions together; ties the discussion to course themes, literature, and theories (instead of delivering information); highlights alternative explanations; and provides answers. Teachers need to be aware of how to modify the case method for different groups of learners. For example, a different approach is required for pre-career and mid-career learners.[17] One notable difference is that pre-career learners require more structured guidance, whereas mid-career users of the method benefit from more free-flowing exchange and intergroup, experiential learning. Teachers, students, and practitioners therefore need to understand case research, the type of case, the case method, and the type of learner before employing cases effectively. Instructors have to be comfortable using the method and shifting from an instructor-centred to a learner-centred approach.

The case method can be used to teach almost any topic in public administration. The method is particularly well suited for topics that are sometimes difficult to teach using traditional Socratic methods. Skills-based topics like decision making, time management, communications, public consultation, stakeholder management, and crisis management are ideal candidates for the case method. Topics such as discrimination, defining the public interest, and values and ethics allow learners to apply knowledge and discuss their own attitudes and the perspectives of others. Indeed, some topics are taught mainly with the case method. For example, the case method is a common and enriching tool for teaching public service ethics.[18] These cases can take the form of short, dialogue-type cases[19] or longer, more complex cases and can be used as the basis for drawing on personal experiences from those learners who have themselves faced various ethical dilemmas. In many instances cases can also be customized to suit the style of the instructor and for the level and type of learner.

From the learners' perspective, preparing for case discussions may seem frustrating as most cases (like the situations faced by most policy analysts and public administrators) are written with a strong emphasis on context. First, they are often missing information and the problems are presented as both ambiguous and complex. However, lack of information and complexity are features of case studies that add realism, given that public administrators are often required to make decisions under conditions of uncertainty and with less than complete information.[20] That cases can tap into the 'grey areas' is one of the primary values of the case method. Second, case discussion can be intimidating at the outset as users must work collectively to solve unfamiliar problems. Third, some students are uncomfortable in the beginning when they are required to role play, express their opinions, and make decisions. Again, this is another skill-building aspect of the case method.

From the instructor's perspective the case method in public policy and administration learning also has disadvantages. The difficulty finding current cases on relevant topics, the limited class time for discussing cases,[21] and the need for students to prepare are often cited as reasons why instructors do not use the case method in their classes. The case method also requires a certain style that may not suit the style of the instructor. It requires group facilitation skills and a certain comfort level with a learner-centred approach. There is also some debate about the degree to which case studies allow students to apply theory and critically analyse complex topics, particularly if the learning objective is to more narrowly teach management concepts and skills in a training context.

Despite these disadvantages, instructors and learners who have used the method contend that case studies offer public policy and administration learners rich, applied learning outcomes when the cases are well researched and well written and when the method is used effectively. Those who have experienced these positive outcomes as learners are often those who employ the case method when they become teachers. Indeed, this may explain why the case method has become increasingly popular over the past few decades. However, case research and the use of cases and the case study method were not always a significant part of research and teaching in Canadian public administration, and the use of case studies remains limited.

The Evolution of Case Research and Case Studies in Canadian Public Administration

Many disciplines such as law and business administration have been employing case research and the case method for decades.[22] Case research and case studies have long been central to learning and teaching public administration in countries like the United States. In the postwar years the use of case studies burgeoned in that country and became a key element of American public administration's intellectual history.[23] Harvard University's decision in the mid-1960s to develop its public policy program around cases was important to the American public administration case study movement. By the 1970s the use of cases in many public policy and public administration programs had fostered a well-developed tradition of case research and the case method in the growing number of American education programs.[24]

In the 1970s the discipline of Canadian public administration was just beginning to develop. There was by then a small but growing literature on public policy, government decision making, and public sector administration. The lack of progress in case research was attributed to the long neglect of the study of Canadian public administration in general, and to the neglect of case research in particular.[25] Because of this neglect, and the scarcity of published materials, university faculty and public servants responsible for in-service training and development came to rely on American and British case studies.[26] Those who wanted to use cases in their teaching had to rely on external sources or write their own. According to Kenneth Kernaghan, the scene was characterized by 'the absence of a sustained, systematic and coordinated effort to produce case study literature on problems of public policy and management.'[27] Even more salient, 'university teachers and public administrators, through their neglect of case research, had failed to exploit an opportunity to advance the study and practice of public administration in Canada.'[28] He concluded at the time that 'the use and writing of cases are much more advanced in business administration than in public administration, especially in Canada.'[29]

The divide in Canada between the disciplines of public administration and business administration was cited as an important reason why case studies were not being written and used to the same degree they were in business administration programs. Business schools across Canada were launching efforts to produce Canadian business case materials. Public administration programs were not keeping pace, and the writing and use of case studies remained connected to individuals rather than institutions or disciplines.

Kernaghan went further, arguing that case studies were being written and used less than they ought to be because of the reliance on traditional pedagogical techniques (i.e., lectures and seminars in political science departments). He observed that 'political scientists teaching public administration seemed to be unaware of the case method or unwilling to use it.'[30] Moreover, those few who were writing and using cases tended to emphasize the political, policy, and institutional aspects of public bureaucracy rather than the organizational, procedural, and technical concerns of public management. He was not surprised that the focus was on policy formation rather than policy implementation, given that most training and teaching occurred in political science departments.[31]

The other important factor that Kernaghan pointed to in the late 1970s was the lack of interaction in Canada between academic instructors and public administration practitioners. He observed that few university faculty had public sector experience or were involved in mid-career training programs for public servants. Thus it was 'not surprising that the case method which relies on narrative and actual administrative situations has not taken root in the academic community.'[32] Though not required, the relationship between academics and practitioners is an important part of the case research and writing process. He argued that the fault for this situation had to be shared by both sides and that the public service itself was not demanding case studies from the academic community or their own personnel.

Kernaghan also pointed to the general secrecy in government – a reality of the Canadian parliamentary system – as a reason why case studies were so difficult to research and write for both academics and practitioners. But there were, he noted, creative ways that case studies could be researched and written, ways that would preserve confidentiality and disguise the people and administrative units involved. Finally, he noted one more reason for the poor state of case research in Canada: there was no distribution outlet for written cases.

He was painting a grim picture of the state of case studies in the discipline. But he also noted some promising developments relating to case research. There were increasing numbers of scholars, courses, and programs in public administration, and the public service itself was growing. These two developments were creating an environment more conducive to the writing and use of cases. In addition to this, institutional changes were happening: schools of public administration were being founded, with more interdisciplinary programs; business programs were beginning to offer public administration courses; public administration programs were taking a more professional orientation; and there was a general strengthening of the intellectual status of public administration within political science departments. All of these developments were having a positive impact on the state of case research and writing in Canada.[33] He also observed that intellectual ties and personal contacts between university teachers and administrative practitioners seemed to be developing. Exchange programs between universities and the public service seemed to be fostering more interaction and more open access to government documents, and IPAC was facilitating more interaction between the two communities.

Despite all these developments, in the mid-1970s the case method barely existed in Canada. Early in his career, Kernaghan understood the importance of case studies and the case study method for public administration education. While on the federal government's Executive Interchange Program in 1974–5, as the Director of Educational Research with the Executive Education Division of the Public Service Commission (PSC), he was instrumental in establishing a national case study program. The PSC, several government departments, and some academics were by then writing cases to meet their own course needs; however, except for L'École nationale d'administration publique, Canadian universities were neglecting case research and writing.[34] Under Kernaghan's leadership, and with the commitment of several other key individuals, the PSC agreed to fund a joint venture with IPAC to establish a national case program. The program's objectives were two: stimulate the writing of cases and simulations in public policy and administration; and to distribute these widely in university and college courses and in training programs at all levels of government.

Kernaghan was appointed the director of the program, a post he held from 1975 to 1979. He was supported by an advisory board that commissioned the writing of cases and that evaluated, peer reviewed, and distributed them. In his annual report to IPAC and the PSC, Kernaghan reported that six cases had been published in 1976 and six more in 1977, generating sales of 2,700 copies. Many of these cases went on to become best sellers; some, including Kernaghan's own 'Conflict of Loyalties,' continue to generate sales thirty years later.

There was by then a perceived need for more management cases. To address that need, and realizing that the IPAC case program was focusing more broadly on policy and policy management, in 1977 Kernaghan published his own *Canadian Cases in Public Administration*. Again, it is noteworthy that many of the cases in this book – with some alterations to dates and details – are timeless classics. Some, such as 'Foot and Mouth Disease Epidemic,' remind us how many issues in public administration are enduring; how crises, scandals, and various current events continue to form the basis of engaging case research and writing; and why lessons from administrative history are so important.

By the early 1980s all types of cases were being published through the IPAC case program. By 1982 the program was publishing between ten and fifteen cases a year; in the first seven years of the program, from 1976 to 1982, 14,000 cases were sold,[35] generating an average of $6,000 in sales per year. Major strides were being made in generating case studies on a wide range of topics that were central to the discipline and profession such as representative bureaucracy, personnel management, public sector labour relations, accountability, Crown corporations, and values and ethics. By the mid-1980s the IPAC case collection also included cases on financial management, budgeting, human resource management, federal–provincial relations, policy analysis, cabinet decision making, briefing notes, and time management. A review of the case list from thirty years ago tells us which research and professional topics were central to the discipline and profession at the time; many of those topics are still important thirty years later.

Ten years after the case program was established, the number of cases sold had almost doubled. The lengthening topic list reflected the development of Canadian public administration as a discipline and the growing number of cases being authored by practitioners and practitioner–academic teams. Case topics reflected key issues in the discipline and profession, including policy analysis, regulation, leadership, strategic planning, program evaluation, and human resource management. Public administration courses were by then being offered at most universities and colleges across Canada, and undergraduate and graduate degree programs were well established. The growth of the public service and the financial support for internal and external training and development encouraged the use of case studies in the post-secondary and in-service contexts.

In the early 1990s the case program was still growing. Public service was still viewed as an attractive employment option for many post-secondary students, and public administration courses and graduate programs in public administration were enjoying increased enrolments. Governments continued to support the internal and external continuing education of their employees. By 1991 the Canadian Centre for Management Development (CCMD) was developing its own cases for teaching public administration to senior managers in the federal public service. That year, IPAC and the CCMD entered into a partnership with the goal of cross-promoting cases and distributing them more broadly. By then, the IPAC catalogue included cases on most topics in public administration and concerted efforts were being made to support case research and publications in specific topic areas. For example, an editor of the case program, Lloyd Brown-John, organized a round table for municipal administrators in 1992 to generate much-needed cases on municipal administration. Annual sales of IPAC cases peaked in 1995, with almost 7,000 copies sold.[36] Some instructors began designing entire courses around cases, and IPAC began to sell case packages to students and bookstores.

By the mid-1990s the case study program was beginning to reflect the significant changes that were taking place in the public sector. Sandford Borins argued that the new public sector agenda of the 1990s was making the 'policy analyst' model of MPA education increasingly irrelevant and that schools of public administration needed to place greater emphasis on the teaching of management skills through simulations and the case method.[37] There were renewed calls for more management cases and for more of a business school approach to case study use; according to some analysts, however, in the mid-1990s 'the road to the top of the federal public service was far easier for the policy specialist.'[38] Most programs and schools in public administration continued to be housed in political science departments and continued to focus more on policy than administration.[39] For many cultural and institutional reasons, the discipline was not finding a home in business and management schools.[40] The case program reflected these realities and debates in the discipline; both policy and management cases were still being written by academics and practitioners.

By that time the public sector was beginning to embrace the principles, practices, and values of New Public Management (NPM) and to grapple with significant changes and reforms. This meant that students and practitioners needed a wide range of cases to learn about and critique those changes. Unfortunately, the case study program witnessed a decline around that time, as did public service training and development more generally. The case study program faced an uncertain future.[41] By the late 1990s no new cases were being written and published, and the marketing and sales of existing cases reflected these changes (see figure 13.1).

As budgets were cut, and as downsizing and restructuring became commonplace at all levels of government, opportunities and support for in-service training and development declined, especially for those

Figure 13.1. IPAC cases sold, 1977–2004

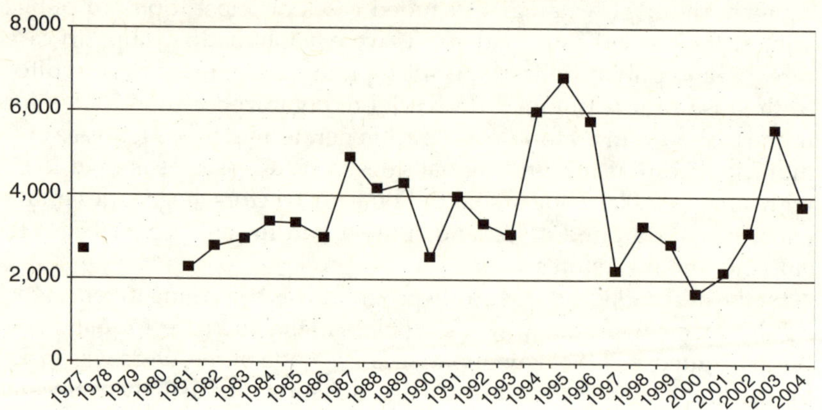

Source: Annual Reports of the IPAC Case Program Director, 1977–1997. IPAC Case Sales database 1998–2004.

below the senior management ranks. With the decline in the employment prospects in the public service came a corresponding loss of interest in public administration courses and programs. Public service as an employment option was losing its appeal to young Canadians,[42] and post-secondary students were increasingly looking to studies and employment in the private and not-for-profit sectors. Few new faculty were being hired to teach public administration courses, and retiring public administration faculty were not being replaced.[43] General declines in enrolment in political science were felt in public administration courses and programs. In addition, enrolments were drifting away from Canadian politics programs towards international relations.

The demand for case studies from the traditional student and practitioner user groups seemed to be declining. Faithful instructors continued to purchase the timeless best sellers; even so, a gap seemed to be developing between the learning needs of public administration students and practitioners and the ability of the case program to keep pace with the demand for cases on new topics such as privatization, contracting out, alternative service delivery, e-government, labour relations, and organizational change in the public sector.

Public sector reforms like the federal Program Review had created a 'quiet crisis' in terms of human resources and the subsequent federal 'la Relève' initiative proclaiming the importance of 'Valuing Our People.'[44]

That much was recognized; even so, there was a period during which learning opportunities remained limited in the federal public service. In the post-deficit context the federal government began slowly to reinvest in human resource development, recognizing the significance of knowledge assets and knowledge management.[45] However, the provinces and municipalities were facing different realities in terms of public sector reform as a result of reductions in federal transfers and their own public sector reform initiatives.

Though the IPAC case study program had generated 116 cases and/ or simulations by the year 2000, that program needed to be reassessed in light of the changes in the discipline and in the public sector. The value of cases and the case method was still recognized, but the context in which case studies were written and used had changed significantly. Strategies for rejuvenating the case program would have to reflect these new realities.[46] The editors of the case program arrived at various new strategies as the learning context and realities of the discipline changed over time. For example, in the late 1980s David Siegel realized the need for shorter cases. The annual reports of IPAC Case Program Directors typically alluded to the need to revise many existing cases, to market cases beyond public administration courses, and to increase the number of practitioner-authors.

Between 2001 and 2004, IPAC made an effort to revitalize the case program. One noticeable change was in the format of the cases. Cases are now much shorter than the typical ten to twenty pages of thirty years ago.[47] Also, the expansion of public sector information available on the Internet has had a positive impact on case research and writing. Since 2002, forty-four new cases have been published on a wide range of topics and several of the best-selling classics have been updated and revised. Winners and finalists in the IPAC Innovation Awards program have been encouraged to transform their submissions into case studies. Calls from IPAC for new case studies are being heard by practitioners, who in recent years have been the majority of new authors. As in earlier decades, the topics reflect changes in the public service and the discipline. Many reflect new issues such as partnerships, service delivery, technology, and accountability. Others clearly indicate the impact of NPM in Canada at all levels of government and provide opportunities for learners to unpack, debate, and critically discuss the new lexicon and approaches in Canadian public administration.

Thirty years ago, cases were needed for all topics in Canadian public administration. There has been much progress on this front, and there are now case studies covering all aspects of public policy and all functional management areas in public administration. The IPAC case program contains cases from all levels of government, the broader public sector, and the not-for-profit sector. More of these cases are policy management cases – a reflection of the increasingly complex realities of partnerships, horizontal management, intergovernmental relations, e-government, performance management, the changing nature of accountability, and public service values and ethics. The editor of the case program, members of the Canadian Association of Programs in Public Administration (CAPPA), the IPAC Research Committee, post-secondary instructors, and practitioners continue to identify topics that require case research and writing. Currently, the IPAC case program publishes five to ten cases a year. Despite this progress, many of Kernaghan's observations relating to case research and the use of case studies in Canadian public administration continue to apply.

Enduring Challenges and Potential Opportunities

Ken Kernaghan argued thirty years ago that the state of case research and the case method in Canadian public administration could be explained by the slow development of public administration as a discipline; by the institutional location of public administration within departments of political science; by the minimal contact between teachers of public administration and business administration; by the limited exchange of information and personnel between the public service and universities; and by administrative secrecy in government.[48] Though the discipline has developed quite significantly over the past thirty years, and though case research and the case method have been important components of this development, case research and the use of case studies in Canadian public administration continue to reflect broader developments in the discipline. A combination of factors then and now help explain the status of case research and the case method in Canada. Many of those factors relate to the status of, and changes in, the discipline more broadly.

The prevalence of case research and the case method is partly a function of the size of the scholarly and practitioner community in Canada, which obviously impacts the number of public administration programs and courses. The United States has 155 Master's-level programs accredited by the National Association of Schools of Public Affairs and

Administration;[49] leading American case programs include the Electronic Hallway at the University of Washington[50] and the Case Program (containing more than two thousand cases) at Harvard's Kennedy School of Government.[51] Contrast this with Canada. CAPPA reports nine doctoral programs and eighteen Master's-level programs in public policy and administration,[52] and the case study method is not a key component at any of them. There are no program 'champions' of the case method in Canada, as there are in the United States. Some Canadian programs, such as the one at L'École nationale d'administration publique, have used case studies and the case study method quite extensively. There is of course an additional challenge that is uniquely Canadian: the need to publish cases in both French and English.

Case research and case writing efforts continue to encompass policy, policy management, and management cases, reflecting the broader research and teaching realities of the discipline. A recent study of Master's programs in public administration, public management, and public policy found that most programs are still located in political science departments (or faculties of social science more broadly) and that Canadian programs tend to emphasize policy over management (especially compared to accredited American programs).[53] American programs in public administration generally have more management content; that said, the success of the Kennedy School and the University of Washington case programs suggests that an emphasis on management cases is not a precondition for a well-developed case study tradition, and that neither is locating public administration programs in business schools.

A related challenge is to redefine the discipline's boundaries so as to reflect its interdisciplinary realities. Potential case researchers, writers, and users can be found in a wide range of related fields such as urban planning, social work, education, health administration, justice studies, public health, and voluntary sector management. There is a need for case research, writing, and distribution to better reflect the broader public service and the quasi–public sector character of public administration. In the future, case research, writing, and use may require a broadening of the definition of public service research, education, and training; it may also require reaching out to other disciplines. The discipline and profession of public administration will need to consider this, through organizations such as IPAC.

Over the years, post-secondary teachers have been crucial to the sustainability of case research and writing in terms of case research, writing, and sales. Cases are purchased mainly by post-secondary instructors and their students. There are many good reasons why: it is those people who can afford them; they are the market that IPAC has identified; they are the ones who see the cases as relevant; and they are the ones who use cases for training purposes (i.e., rather than for education purposes). As part of its renewed case program, IPAC has established a new editorial board comprising academic *and* practitioner peer reviewers; the goal in this is to produce relevant, high-quality cases with broad appeal. Sessions on the case method at Canadian Political Science Association meetings, and on case writing at the IPAC annual conference, have been designed to recruit new case researchers, writers, and users. However, in Canada there are no institutional leaders or formalized forums like the annual case writing and teaching workshop offered by the University of Washington. Kernaghan's observation from thirty years ago – that case research in Canadian public administration is characterized by sporadic, piecemeal contributions from a few university faculty and civil servants acting in relative isolation from one another and pursuing specific, limited objectives[54] – still applies today.

How to encourage practitioners to write and use case studies has been a pertinent question ever since the inception of the case study program. Though the interactions between university faculty and the public service through interchange programs, IPAC, and in-service teaching opportunities for university faculty looked promising thirty years ago, the state of these relations remains an issue when it comes to case research, writing, and use. Though the cohort of public administration teachers and researchers is small, there has definitely been more interaction through IPAC and, at the federal level, through CCMD (now CSPS; the Canada School of Public Service) as well as a concerted effort over the past few years to strengthen this teaching and research relationship through CAPPA. In the post-deficit context, the federal government seems to have recognized the value of 'learning organizations.' Yet despite the recent support for in-service learning and post-secondary studies, the implications for case research are an open question.

The new IPAC case series is targeting practitioner-authors with some success. It is interesting that most of the cases written by practitioners in the past few years have been of the descriptive type described by Kernaghan. Many are cases about success stories. Perhaps this is a form of pride and recognition; perhaps it is related to the desire to share innovations after a period of experimentation and significant change. However, CSPS reports that for many of its courses, it is consultants rather than academics who are commissioned to research and write most cases. The limited use of cases in in-service teaching may reflect a broader cultural shift in the public service away from a questioning culture that values debate, discussion, and questioning in favour of a more deferential, technical, skills-focused culture.[55] The general decline of research capacity in the public service remains an important factor; so does the issue of secrecy that Kernaghan identified thirty years ago.

Despite these enduring challenges, a number of opportunities remain for improving the state of case research, writing, and use in Canadian public administration. When the IPAC case program was in its infancy there was an established fund, as well as a practice of commissioning case studies on specific topics. To sustain and develop the discipline in the future, this type of pooled effort may be needed to solicit case research on specific topics. Perhaps that effort will be tied more directly to the IPAC research agenda and study teams or to the recent partnership initiatives between CAPPA and CSPS.

Throughout the history of the IPAC case program, the approach of teaming academics with practitioners to conduct case research and write cases has been a productive one. Efforts to recruit retired academics and practitioners as well as graduate students in public administration have been somewhat less successful, but the potential is there.[56] Also, there are some instructors who write and use their own cases without making them part of the IPAC national program. Though this is difficult to quantify, new public administration educators, programs, and practitioner needs seem to be emerging. These are potential sources of cases and users of the case method.

Many post-secondary institutions with public administration programs have developed partnerships with public service organizations at the provincial and municipal levels to provide customized learning opportunities. Ryerson University, for example, has two partnership programs with First Nations administrators and fire service professionals in Ontario. These partnerships have generated public administration case studies that have been incorporated into the IPAC series for others to use in a variety of learning contexts. Other universities and colleges have developed similar partnership programs. There seems to be some recognition that post-secondary programs are best suited to provide broader educational programs and that public service organizations are best suited for shorter (e.g., in-service) training courses. However, partnerships between universities, colleges, the Canada School of Public Service, and various organizations at the provincial and municipal levels remain underdeveloped. There is much potential here for enhancing case research, writing, and teaching. There is a need for stronger relations among academics, universities, IPAC, CAPPA, CSPS, and lead agencies involved in education and professional training and development in the provinces, municipalities, and First Nations. These organizations have a key role to play in identifying the new cohort of public administration academics and practitioners who are potential authors and users of case studies. For example, IPAC could act as a clearing house – that is, as a place where learning agencies in the public service could go to solicit case research to meet specific learning needs by linking expertise from the IPAC researcher and practitioner database.

Integrating cases into course materials and public administration textbooks is another important strategy. It has been almost thirty years since Kernaghan's *Canadian Cases in Public Administration* was published as a supplementary text. Other important approaches might include incorporating case studies into texts and instructor's guides, as Kernaghan and Siegel have done,[57] and producing customized collections of cases, as IPAC currently does for instructors who wish to use multiple cases in their courses. Full integration of IPAC cases into public administration textbooks, Canadian politics textbooks, and other related course texts, along with online access links, would be a way to reach learners beyond public administration courses. In the United States, cases are published in scholarly journals;[58] perhaps there is scope for *Canadian Public Administration* to feature peer-reviewed case studies from the IPAC case program.

The use of case studies and the case method in in-service education and training is also fertile ground for research in that little is known about the degree to which practitioners value and use case studies in their learning, especially in provincial, municipal, and First Nations learning programs. In the 1990s, CCMD had a strong case research and case method presence as well as an agreement to broaden access and distribute those cases through IPAC. Though this relationship had waned by the late 1990s, the new Canada School of Public Service – which has a broader mandate to provide learning for all federal public servants from entry to executive level across all regions – reports that

65 to 75 per cent of classroom-based courses use case studies.[59] Given the increasing number of courses delivered via distance learning technologies like the Internet, and given reports from the CSPS that case studies are not used in this predominantly individual learning context, this raises another issue related to the use of cases and the case method with emergent learning technologies.

It is possible that case studies and the case method could be used beyond the traditional classroom and group analysis context. For example, case studies could be used in distance education courses or online courses for individual or group learning. While some of the interactive, deliberative discussion might be lost in an online or independent learning environment, there would still be plenty of scope for learners to critically evaluate and apply their knowledge to cases. This is particularly important now that post-secondary certificate, diploma, and degree programs in public administration are available at many institutions in both traditional print-based formats and online formats. It is not clear whether new online programs at the Master's level at Dalhousie University and the University of Victoria are utilizing the case method.

Online access to case studies is crucial for a new generation of learners who are accessing all of their course materials and research sources from the Internet. Downloading a case study for a small fee is the preferred mode of access. Although the case catalogue is now available and searchable on IPAC's website; being able to download review copies for free (for IPAC members) or for a nominal fee (for non-members) would also be beneficial to instructors who are considering using cases and the case method. Many instructors now use the Internet for their courses, so fully integrating links to case studies would benefit them and their students. In-service users would benefit as well from online access. New multimedia and in-person conceptualizations of case studies are becoming popular in other disciplines.[60] Video recordings and in-person narratives of real or fictionalized public policy and public administration situations can be very effective ways to engage learners and allow them to use the case method in new ways.

There is also a general need for more comparative public administration cases and for Canadian cases to be distributed internationally. While this was frowned on thirty years ago, using public administration case studies from other countries such as the United States, other Commonwealth countries, and developing countries can be a rewarding experience. For example, case studies on public service ethics and corruption in other countries offer learners interesting insights into a wide range of related topics such as professionalism, accountability, career public service, and the political–administrative interface. Partnering with organizations like the Commonwealth Association for Public Administration and Management (CAPAM) and the International Institute of Administrative Sciences (IIAS) could produce some very valuable cases and expand the use of Canadian cases in other jurisdictions.

Conclusion

In the past thirty years there has clearly been significant progress made in terms of case research and the case method in Canadian public administration. Paralleling the development and current state of public policy and administration as a discipline and profession in Canada, many challenges endure, yet there are also many opportunities to ensure the sustainability of this importance part of research, teaching, learning, and professional development.

Early in his career Ken Kernaghan realized the significance of case studies and the case study method in public administration research and education. He was indeed a pioneer in this area. Many of his writings on this topic, and many of the case studies he authored, remain relevant and indeed set standards for those writing and using cases today. Many students of public administration, such as myself, benefited from this pioneering work and have become faithful writers and users of case studies and the case method in public administration. Owing to the foresight of Ken Kernaghan and the other academics and practitioners who continue to see cases as a valuable part of the discipline and profession, case research and the case method have become important components of public policy and administration teaching and learning in Canada. The remaining challenge is to ensure that case studies remain a vibrant part of the discipline and profession.

NOTES

1   Kenneth Kernaghan, 'Case Research in Canadian Public Administration,' *Optimum* 6, no. 2 (1975): 6.
2   Kenneth Kernaghan, *The Use and Writing of Cases in Public Administration: Guidelines for Instructors and Case Writers* (Toronto: IPAC, 1976).

3 Kennedy School of Government, 2005, www.ksgcase.harvard.edu/ index.asp.

4 Lloyd Brown-John, 'Rejuvenating the IPAC Case Programme,' Report to IPAC, 2000.

5 Kernaghan, *The Use and Writing of Cases in Public Administration.*

6 Ibid.

7 Kernaghan, 'Case Research in Canadian Public Administration,' 5–20; idem, *Canadian Cases in Public Administration* (Toronto: Methuen, 1977).

8 Kernaghan, *Canadian Cases in Public Administration*, 4.

9 Kernaghan, *The Use and Writing of Cases in Public Administration.*

10 Kernaghan, 'Case Research in Canadian Public Administration,' 6.

11 See Kernaghan, *The Use and Writing of Cases in Public Administration.*

12 Sandford Borins, 'Simulation, the Case Method, and Case Studies,' *Canadian Public Administration* 33, no. 2 (1990): 221.

13 Louise A. Mauffette-Leenders, James Erskine, and Lichiel R. Leenders, *Learning with Cases*, 2nd ed. (London: University of Western Ontario, 2001).

14 Max B.E. Clarkson, 'Ethics Education: How to Do It,' *Canadian Public Administration* 34, no. 1 (1991): 192–5.

15 John Boehrer and Marty Linsky, 'Teaching with Cases: Learning to Question,' in M.D. Svinicki, ed., *The Changing Face of College Teaching* (San Francisco: Jossey-Bass, 1990).

16 Vicki Golich, Mark Boyer, Patrice Franko, and Steve Lamy, 'The ABCs of Case Teaching,' Pew Case Studies in International Affairs, Georgetown University, 2000, www.usc.edu/programs/cet/private/pdfs/abcs.pdf.

17 Borins, 'Simulation, the Case Method, and Case Studies.'

18 Kernaghan and Shirley Mancino, 'Approaches to Ethics Education,' *Canadian Public Administration* 34, no. 1 (1991): 184–91.

19 Kenneth Kernaghan and John Langford, *The Responsible Public Servant* (Halifax: IRPP and Toronto: IPAC, 1990).

20 Kernaghan, *The Use and Writing of Cases in Public Administration.*

21 Brown-John, *Rejuvenating the IPAC Case Programme.*

22 David A. Garvin, 'Making the Case: Casing the Future,' *Harvard Magazine*, September–October 2003.

23 David H. Rosenbloom, 'The Use of Case Studies in Public Administration Education in the USA,' *Journal of Management History* 1, no. 1 (1995): 33–46.

24 Ibid., 43.

25 Kernaghan, 'Case Research in Canadian Public Administration,' 9.

26 Ibid., 12.

27 Ibid., 9.

28 Ibid., 5.

29 Kernaghan, *The Use and Writing of Cases in Public Administration*.
30 Kernaghan, *Canadian Cases in Public Administration*, 11.
31 Ibid.
32 Ibid., 12.
33 Ibid., 14.
34 Kernaghan, 'Case Research in Canadian Public Administration,' 16.
35 IPAC, *Case Program Director Annual Reports*, 1976–2005.
36 IPAC, 'Case Program Annual Report to the Research Committee,' July 1997.
37 Borins, 'Simulation, the Case Method, and Case Studies.'
38 Donald Savoie, 'Public Administration: A Profession Looking for a Home,' in Laurent Dobuzinkis, Michael Howlett, and David Laycock, *Policy Studies in Canada: The State of the Art* (Toronto: University of Toronto Press, 1996), 171.
39 Ibid., 132.
40 Ibid., 131.
41 Brown-John, *Rejuvenating the IPAC Case Programme*.
42 Jennifer L. Smith and Susan Snider, *Facing the Challenge: Recruiting the Next Generation of University Graduates to the Public Service* (Ottawa: Public Policy Forum and Public Service Commission of Canada, 1998).
43 Evert Lindquist, 'Presentation of Survey Findings on the State of Public Administration Teaching and Research,' CCMD University Seminars, Ottawa, 2001; David Good, 'Report on the Session on the Future of Research in Public Administration,' prepared for CCMD's Annual University Seminar, CCMD, 2001.
44 Canada, *Fourth Annual Report to the Prime Minister on the Public Service of Canada* (Ottawa, 1996); *La Relève – Valuing Our People*, Report of the Advisory Committee on the Workforce of the Future (Ottawa, 1997).
45 CCMD, *A Primer of Knowledge Management in the Public Service* (Ottawa, 1999).
46 Brown-John, *Rejuvenating the IPAC Case Programme*.
47 Kernaghan, *The Use and Writing of Cases in Public Administration*.
48 Kernaghan, *Canadian Cases in Public Administration*, 8.
49 National Association of Schools of Public Affairs and Administration (NASPAA), 'Roster of Accredited Programs' (2005), www.naspaa.org/ accreditation/news/news.asp.
50 University of Washington, School of Public Affairs 'Electronic Hallway,' hallway.org.
51 Kennedy School of Government Case Study Program, www.ksgcase. harvard.edu/index.asp.

52 Canadian Association of Programs in Public Administration (CAPPA), www.cappa.ca/programs.html.

53 James Iain Gow and Sharon Sutherland, 'Comparison of Canadian Master's Programs in Public Administration, Public Management, and Public Policy,' *Canadian Public Administration* 47, no. 3 (2004): 379–405.

54 Kernaghan, 'Case Research in Canadian Public Administration,' 10.

55 Bryan Evans, 'Conquering the Traditional Public Service: The Transformation of Managerial Culture within the Ontario Public Service,' *Philosophy of Management* 5, no. 2 (2006): 47–68.

56 Brown-John, *Rejuvenating the IPAC Case Programme*.

57 Kenneth Kernaghan and David Siegel, *Public Administration in Canada*, 4th ed. (Toronto: Nelson Education, 1999). Instructor's Guide prepared by Jennifer Berardi and Jacqueline Dix.

58 David H. Rosenbloom, 'The Use of Case Studies in Public Administration Education in the USA,' *Journal of Management History* 1, no. 1 (1995): 33–46.

59 Telephone interview with Louis Valois, Canada School of Public Service, October 2005.

60 Garvin, 'Making the Case.'

Short Biography and Selected Publications of Kenneth Kernaghan

Born: Hamilton, Ontario, 18 December 1940
Married: Helgi, 1963, three sons (Kevin, Scott, and Kris)

Education

Honours BA, Economics and Politics, McMaster University (1962; Chancellor's Gold Medal and Student Council President)
MA, Political Science, Duke University (1964; James B. Duke Commonwealth Fellowship)
PhD, Political Science, Duke University (1966; James B. Duke Fellowship)

Selected Awards and Distinctions

Brock University Award for Distinguished Teaching (2004)
Brock University Faculty of Social Sciences Award for Excellence in Teaching (2004)
Pierre De Celles/IPAC Award for Excellence in the Teaching of Public Administration (2003)
Fellow of the Royal Society of Canada (1997)
Vanier Gold Medal for Excellence in Public Administration, Institute of Public Administration of Canada (1996)
Brock University Award for Distinguished Research and Creative Activity (1996)
McMaster University Alumni Gallery (1997)
J.E. Hodgetts Prize for best English-language article published in the quarterly learned journal *Canadian Public Administration* (1992; first recipient)
Senior Research Fellow, Canadian Centre for Management Development (from 1995)

Fellow, Institute for Citizen-Centred Service (from 1999)

Professional Employment Record

Assistant Professor, Department of Political Science, University of Waterloo (1965–67)

Assistant Professor, Department of Political Science and School of Public Administration, Carleton University (1967–68)

Assistant–Associate Professor, Department of Political Science, Brock University (1968–73)

Visiting Professor, Department of Political Science, McMaster University (1969–70, 1973–74)

Chairman, Department of Political Science, Brock University (1970–72)

Professor, Department of Political Science, Brock University (from 1973; joint appointment with Faculty of Business)

Director of Educational Research, Bureau of Executive Education, Public Service Commission (1974–75; via the federal government's Executive Interchange Program)

Founding Director, School of Administrative Studies (now the Faculty of Business), Brock University (1974–79)

Professional Activities

Editor, *International Review of Administrative Sciences* (1989–2005; quarterly journal published in separate English, French, and Arabic editions.)

President, Institute of Public Administration of Canada (1987–88)

Vice President and Chair of the Planning and Priorities Committee, IPAC (1986–87)

Vice President (for Program), International Association of Schools and Institutes of Administration (1986–89). Chair of the Program Committee (1986–89). Member (1989–92)

Member of the Scientific Committee of the International Institute of Administrative Sciences (1986–2005)

Member of the Executive Committee of the International Institute of Administrative Sciences (1989–2005)

Editor, *Canadian Public Administration* (1979–87)

Member, Academic Advisory Committee, Ontario Council on University Affairs (1981–90). Chair (1988–90)

Founding Director, Case Program in Canadian Public Administration (1975–79)

Associate Editor, Canadian Public Administration (1973–79)

Assistant to Editor, Canadian Public Administration (1972–73)
Book Review Editor, *Canadian Public Administration* (1969–79)
Editorial Board Member, *Canadian Public Administration* (1969–87)
Editorial Board Member, *Canadian Public Policy* (1979–87)
Editorial Board Member, *Public Administration Review* (U.S.) (1992–99)
Editorial Board Member, Public Administration Theory and Praxis (1994–2003)
Editorial Board Member, International Review of Public Administration (from 1997)
Editorial Board Member, *Innovation Journal* (from 1998)
Editorial Board Member, Corporate Governance (from 2002)
Editorial Board Member, International Journal of Management Concepts and Philosophy (from 2003)
Research Committee, IPAC (from 1968) (Vice Chair, 1971–73; Chair, 1973–75).
Executive Committee, IPAC, 1970–72 (elected), 1973–75 (ex officio), 1976–79 (elected), 1979–89 (ex officio).
Member, International Public Administration Committee, IPAC (1981–90)
Canadian representative on the Board of Management of the International Association of Schools and Institutes of Administration (1980–89)
Canadian representative on the North American section of the International Association of Schools and Institutes of Administration (1984–89)
Member, Canadian Association of Programs in Public Administration (from 1974)
Member, Vanier Medal Selection Committee (1988–93)
Chair, Selection Committee, Amethyst Awards for Excellence in the Ontario Public Service (1999–2002)
Chair, Task Force on the Disclosure of Wrongdoing, Government of Canada, 2004.

Selected Publications

Books, Monographs, and Reports

Public Administration in Canada: Selected Readings (ed., five editions, 1968–85). Toronto: Methuen.
Bureaucracy in Canadian Government (ed., two editions, 1969 and 1973). Toronto: Methuen.

Ethical Conduct: Guidelines for Government Employees. Toronto: IPAC, 1975.

Executive Manpower in the Public Service (ed.). Toronto: IPAC, 1976.

Canadian Cases in Public Administration. Toronto: Methuen, 1977.

Freedom of Information and Ministerial Responsibility. Toronto: Ontario Commission on Freedom of Information and Individual Privacy, 1978.

The Accountability of Universities to Society. A Study for the Quebec Commission d'étude sur les universités. Québec: Gouvernement du Québec, 1981.

Canadian Public Administration: Discipline and Profession (ed.). Toronto: Butterworths, 1983.

Coordination in Canadian Governments: A Case Study of Aging Policy (coauthored with Olivia Kuper). Toronto: IPAC, 1983.

Ethics in the Public Service: Comparative Perspectives (coedited with O.P. Dwivedi). Brussels: International Institute of Administrative Sciences, 1983. Translated into Arabic and published by the Arab Organization of Administrative Sciences, 1985.

Public Administration in Canada (coauthored with David Siegel; four editions, 1987–99). Toronto: Nelson Education.

The Changing Nature of the Public Service (ed.). Brussels: International Institute of Administrative Sciences, 1987.

Social Change as a Source of Competing Values in Public Administration (ed.). Brussels: International Institute of Administrative Sciences, 1988.

The Responsible Public Servant (coauthored with John Langford). Toronto: IPAC and Halifax: IRPP, 1990.

Development Policy: Implications for Public Administration (ed.). Brussels: International Institute of Administrative Sciences, 1990.

Do Unto Others: Ethics in Government and Business (ed.). Consists of thirty papers initially presented at a conference on government and business ethics. Published as a symposium issue (guest editor) of *Canadian Public Administration* and as a separate publication in Spring 1991.

Research in Public Administration: An Agenda for the Year 2000 (with M. Charih). Ottawa: IPAC, 1996. Section reprinted under title of 'La recherche en administration publique. Etat de la situation,' in M. Charih and R. Landry, eds., *La Gestion Publique Sous Le Microscope*, 7–23. Quebec: Presses de l'Universite du Quebec, 1997.

Innovations and Good Practices in Single-Window Service (with S. Bent

and Brian Marson). Ottawa: Canadian Centre for Management
  Development, 1999.
The New Public Organization (with Brian Marson and Sandford Borins).
  Toronto: IPAC, 2000.
Digital State at the Leading Edge (ed., with Borins et al.). Toronto: University of Toronto Press, 2007.

Articles and Book Chapters

'An Overview of Public Administration in Canada Today.' *Canadian Public Administration* 11 (1968): 291–308.
'Civil Liberties in the Canadian Community.' In Carl Beck, ed., *Law and Justice*, 323–45. Durham: Duke University Press, 1970.
'Civil Liberties and a Constitutional Bill of Rights.' In F. Vaughn et al., eds., *Contemporary Issues in Canadian Politics*, 68–82. Toronto: Prentice Hall, 1970.
'The Political Rights and Activities of Canadian Public Servants.' In Kenneth Kernaghan and A.M. Willms, eds., *Public Administration in Canada*, 383–90. Toronto: Methuen, 1971.
'The Role of the Public Service in the Canadian Democratic System.' *Quarterly of Canadian Studies* 2 (1972): 184–97.
'The Ethical Conduct of Canadian Public Servants.' *Optimum* 2 (1973): 5–18. Reprinted in K. Gibbons and D.C. Rowat, eds., *Political Corruption in Canada*, 274–277. Ottawa: Carleton University Press, 1976.
'Identity, Pedagogy, and Public Administration: The Canadian Experience.' *Public Administration* (Australia) 32 (1973): 286–96.
'Responsible Public Bureaucracy: A Rationale and a Framework for Analysis.' *Canadian Public Administration* 16 (1973): 572–603.
'Codes of Ethics and Administrative Responsibility.' *Canadian Public Administration* 17 (1974): 527–41.
'Case Research in Canadian Public Administration.' *Optimum* 6, no. 4 (1975): 5–20.
'Management Development for Canada's Public Services.' *Executive Manpower in the Public Service* (1976): 1–18.
'Ethics and Public Servants.' In D. Bellamy et al., eds., *The Provincial Political Systems*, 357–68. Toronto: Methuen, 1976.
'Politics, Policy, and Public Servants: Political Neutrality Revisited.' *Canadian Public Administration* 19, no. 3 (1976): 432–56. Reprinted in updated and expanded form in R.S. Blair and J.T. McLeod, eds., *The Canadian Political Tradition*, 398–423. Toronto: Methuen, 1987.

'Political Control of Administrative Action.' *Cahiers de Droit* 17, no. 4 (1976): 927–34.

'Changing Concepts of Power and Responsibility in the Canadian Public Service.' *Canadian Public Administration* 21, no. 3 (1978): 389–406. Reprinted in Barbara W. Carroll, David Siegel, and Mark Sproule Jones, eds., *Classic Readings in Canadian Public Administration*, 166–81. Toronto: Oxford University Press, 2005.

'Representative Bureaucracy: The Canadian Perspective.' *Canadian Public Administration* 21, no. 4 (1978): 489–512.

'The Use and Writing of Cases in Public Administration: Guidelines for Instructors and Case Writers.' In *Case Program in Canadian Public Administration*. Toronto: IPAC, 1978.

'Power, Politics, and Public Servants: Ministerial Responsibility Revisited.' *Canadian Public Policy* 3 (1979): 383–96. Reprinted in expanded form in H.D. Clarke et al., *Parliament, Policy and Representation*, 124–43. Toronto: Methuen, 1980.

'Codes of Ethics and Public Administration: Progress, Problems and Prospects.' *Public Administration* (United Kingdom) 58 (1980): 207–24. Reprinted in Barbara W. Carroll, David Siegel, and Mark Sproule Jones, eds., *Classic Readings in Canadian Public Administration*, 182–96. Toronto: Oxford University Press, 2005.

'Politics, Public Administration, and Canada's Aging Population.' *Canadian Public Policy* 5 (1981): 68–82.

'Universities and Government: Accountability Re-examined. *Optimum* 12 (1981): 29–41.

'Ministers and Mandarins in the Canadian Administrative State' (with T.H. McLeod). In O.P. Dwivedi, ed., *The Administrative State*, 17–30. Toronto: University of Toronto Press, 1982.

'Intergovernmental Administrative Relations in Canada.' In Kenneth Kernaghan, ed., *Public Administration in Canada*, 4th ed., 80–93. Toronto: Methuen, 1982.

'Canadian Public Administration: Problems and Prospects.' *Canadian Public Administration* 25 (1982): 444–56 (in English) and 457–70 (in French).

'Merit and Motivation: Public Personnel Management in Canada' (with P.K. Kuruvilla). *Canadian Public Administration* 25 (1982): 696–712.

'Public Service Ethics in Canada.' In Kernaghan and O.P. Dwivedi, eds., *Ethics in the Public Service: Comparative Perspectives*, 37–48. Brussels: International Institute of Administrative Sciences, 1983.

'Public Service Ethics: Issues and Ideas' (with Dwivedi). In Kernaghan and O.P. Dwivedi, eds., *Ethics in the Public Service: Comparative Perspectives*, 1–11. Brussels: International Institute of Administration Sciences, 1983.

'Public Service Accountability Re-examined.' *Débats sur l'imputabilité*, Centre d'études politiques et administratives au Québec, ENAP, 1984.

'The Hired Help.' *Policy Options* 5 (1984): 45–8.

'The Conscience of the Bureaucrat: Accomplice or Constraint?' *Canadian Public Administration* 27 (1984): 576–91.

'Pressure Groups and Public Servants in Canada.' In Kernaghan, ed., *Public Administration in Canada: Selected Readings*, 5th ed., 308–22. Toronto: Methuen, 1985.

'The Public and Public Servants in Canada.' In Kernaghan, ed., *Public Administration in Canada: Selected Readings*, 5th ed., 323–30. Toronto: Methuen, 1985.

'Judicial Review of Administrative Action.' In Kernaghan, ed., *Public Administration in Canada: Selected Readings*, 5th ed., 358–73. Toronto: Methuen, 1985.

'The Ethics of Public Men.' *Policy Options* 6 (1985): 31–4.

'Representative and Responsive Bureaucracy: Implications for Canadian Regionalism.' In *Regional Responsiveness and the National Administrative State*, vol. 37 of the Research Studies for the Royal Commission on the Economy. Toronto: University of Toronto Press, 1985.

'Evolving Patterns of Administrative Responsiveness to the Public.' *International Review of Administrative Sciences* 52 (1986): 7–16.

'Political Rights for Public Servants: Finding the Balance Point.' *Canadian Public Administration* 29 (1986): 639–52.

'The Statement of Principles of the Institute of Public Administration of Canada: The Rationale for Its Development and Content.' *Canadian Public Administration* 30 (1987): 331–51 (in English) and 352–75 (in French).

'The Evolution of the Concept of Merit in the Canadian Bureaucracy.' In *The Merit System, Cahiers Histoire de l'Administration*, no. 2, 47–58. Brussels: International Institute of Administrative Sciences, 1987.

'Managing with Integrity.' *Public Sector Management* 2 (1991): 28–31.

'Approaches to Ethics Education: A Public Service Perspective' (with S. Mancino). *Canadian Public Administration* 34 (1991): 184–91.

'Managing Ethics: Complementary Approaches.' *Canadian Public Administration* 34 (1991): 132–45.

'The Evolution of Representative Bureaucracy in Canada.' In V. Wright, ed., *The Representativity of Administration*. Brussels: International Institute of Administrative Sciences, 1991.

'Whistle Blowing in Canadian Government: Ethical, Political, and
   Managerial Considerations.' *Optimum* 22 (1991): 34–43.
'Career Public Service 2000: Road to Renewal or Impractical Vision?'
   Canadian Public Administration 35 (1991): 551–72.
'Empowerment and Public Administration: Revolutionary Advance or
   Passing Fancy?' *Canadian Public Administration* 35 (1992): 194–214.
   (Winner of J.E. Hodgetts award for best article of the year.)
'The Political Rights of Canada's Federal Public Servants.' In Michael
   Cassidy, ed., *Democratic Rights and Electoral Reform*, Royal Commis-
   sion on Electoral Reform and Party Financing, vol. 10, 213–67. Tor-
   onto: Dundurn, 1991.
'Promoting Ethical Behaviour: The Codification Option.' In Richard
   Chapman, ed., *Ethics in Public Service*, 15–30. Edinburgh: University
   of Edinburgh Press, 1993. This essay was translated into Italian and
   published in *Il nuovo governo locale* (1995).
'Partnership and Public Administration: Conceptual and Practical
   Considerations.' *Canadian Public Administration* 36 (1993): 57–76.
'Reshaping Government: The Post-Bureaucratic Paradigm.' *Canadian
   Public Administration* 36 (1993): 636–44.
'Rules Are Not Enough: Ethics, Politics, and Public Service in Ontario.'
   In John Langford and Allan Tupper, eds., *Corruption, Character, and
   Conduct: Essays on Canadian Government Ethics*, 174–96. Toronto:
   Oxford University Press, 1994.
'The Emerging Public Service Culture: Values, Ethics, and Reforms.'
   Canadian Public Administration 37 (1994): 614–30.
'The Ethics Era in Canadian Public Administration.' Research Paper
   Series. Ottawa: CCMD, 1996.
'Towards a Public Service Code of Conduct – and Beyond.' *Canadian
   Public Administration* 40 (1997): 40–54.
'Values, Ethics, and Public Service.' In Jacques Bourgault et al., eds.,
   Public Administration and Public Management: Experiences in Canada,
   101–11. Québec: Les Publications du Québec, 1997.
'The Challenges of Change: Emerging Issues in Contemporary Public
   Administration.' *Canadian Public Administration* 40 (1997): 218–33.
'Shaking the Foundations: Traditional versus New Public Service Val-
   ues.' In M. Charih and A. Daniels, eds., *New Public Administration
   and New Public Management in Canada*, 47–65. Toronto: IPAC, 1997.
Editor, symposium on 'Values, Ethics and Professionalism in the Public
   Service.' *International Review of Administrative Sciences* 63 (1997).
'Administering the Canadian Summit: Politics and Bureaucracy at the
   Apex of Power.' In F.M. van der Meer and J.C.N. Raadschelders,

eds., *Administering the Summit: Comparative Perspectives*, 97–115. Brussels: International Institute of Administrative Sciences, 1998.

'Is the Doctrine of Ministerial Responsibility Workable?' In M. Charlton and P. Barker, eds., *Contemporary Political Issues*, 3rd ed., 220–31. Toronto: Nelson Education, 1998.

'The Post-Bureaucratic Organization and Public Service Values.' *International Review of Administrative Sciences* 66 (2000): 91–104.

'Rediscovering Public Service: Recognizing the Value of An Essential Institution.' Toronto, IPAC, April 2000.

Editor (and initiator of project), '"Pride And Performance In Public Service" – Seven Papers on Eleven Countries.' *International Review of Administrative Sciences* 67 (2001).

'Governance for the Twenty-First Century: Joining Up Accountability.' Report of the Conference of the Commonwealth Association of Public Administration and Management, Birmingham, April 2001.

'An Honour to Be Coveted: Pride, Recognition, and Public Service.' *Canadian Public Administration* 44 (2001): 67–83.

'Bricks, Clicks, and Calls: Clustering Services for Citizen-Centred Service' (with J. Berardi). *Canadian Public Administration* 44 (2001): 417–40.

'East Block and Westminster: Conventions, Values, and Public Service.' In C. Dunn, ed., *Handbook of Canadian Public Administration*. Toronto: Oxford University Press, 2002.

'Corruption and Public Service in Canada: Conceptual and Practical Dimensions.' In Seppo Tihonen, ed., *The History of Corruption in Central Government*, 83–98. Brussels: International Institute of Administrative Sciences, 2003.

'Integrating Values into Public Service: The Values Statement as Centerpiece.' *Public Administration Review* (US) 64 (2003): 711–19.

'The Future of a Non-Partisan Professional Public Service in Ontario.' Premier's Panel on Future Governance of Ontario, May 2003. 60 pp.

'Beyond the Barriers: Integrated Service Delivery.' Paper for Canada's Chief Information Officer, July 2003. 107 pp.

'Integrating Information Technology into Public Administration: Conceptual and Practical Considerations,' *Canadian Public Administration* 47 (2004): 525–46.

'Moving toward the Virtual State: Integrating Services and Service Channels for Citizen-Centred Service.' *International Review of Administrative Sciences* 71 (2005): 119–31.

'Encouraging "Rightdoing" and Discouraging Wrongdoing: The Case for a Public Service Charter and Disclosure Legislation.' Study for

the Gomery Commission of Inquiry into the Sponsorship Program
and Advertising Activities: *Restoring Accountability.* Research Studies, vol. 2: 71–114.

'Building a Better Whistle.' *Public Sector Management* 16, no. 4 (2005):
1–7.

'Public Integrity and Post-Public Employment: Issues, Remedies, and
Benchmarks.' OECD, May 2007. ww.olis.oecd.org/olis/
2007doc.nsf/3dce6d82b533cf6ec125685d005300b4/094bd5b8e58
d381bc12572d4004ee488/$FILE/JT03226639.pdf.

'Transforming Service to Canadians: The Service Canada Model.' *International Review of Administrative Sciences* 73 (2007): 583–96.

On the Internet

'Milestones to the Millennium: In Pursuit of the Public Good. History
of the Federal Public Service – Millennium Project for the Treasury
Board Secretariat.'

'Perceived Corruption and Low Public Respect' www.worldbank.org.

World Bank webpage on *Topical Debates* – Every Three Months – New
Contribution on current debates in Public Administration And Management (2000-2005). http://go.worldbank.org/KZFYZJHPD1.

'Ministerial Responsibility: Interpretations, Implications, and Information.' Study for federal Access to Information Task Force Review,
2001. http://www.atirtf-geai.gc.ca/paper-ministerial-e.html.

'International Comparison in Human Resource Management Reform.'
Canadian Centre for Management Development, 2002, pp. 40.
www.ccmd-ccg.gc.ca.

Contributors

Peter Aucoin is Eric Dennis Memorial Professor of Government and Political Science and Professor of Public Administration at Dalhousie University. He was the 2005 recipient of the Vanier Medal, awarded by IPAC. He is a Fellow of the Royal Society of Canada and a member of the Order of Canada.

Jennifer Berardi is a faculty member at Brock University, where she teaches courses in public administration and public policy. Kenneth Kernaghan served as the supervisor for her MA thesis and continues to mentor her as she develops her research and teaching interests.

Sandford Borins is Professor of Public Management at the University of Toronto. He is the coauthor of 'Digital State at the Leading Edge' (www.digitalstate.ca) and does research on information technology and narrative. He was President of the Canadian Association of Programs in Public Administration from 2003 to 2007.

Jacques Bourgault holds a State PhD in Political Science from La Sorbonne (Public Administration). He is a lawyer and a member of the Quebec Bar. He has taught at Université du Québec à Montréal since 1973 (Full Professor) and has been an adjunct professor at l' École nationale d'administration publique since 1989. Mr Bourgault is a Fellow researcher at CSPS. He has served as President of the Institute of Public Administration of Canada.

David Brown is Senior Associate at the Public Policy Forum in Ottawa and a doctoral candidate in political science at Carleton University. He was previously a federal public servant, managing the information, communications, and security policy unit in the Treasury Board Secretariat. He is a former president of the International Institute of Administrative Sciences.

Barbara Wake Carroll is a Professor of Political Science at McMaster University and editor of the journal *Canadian Public Administration*. She has taught at the University of Waterloo, Waikato University (Hamilton, New Zealand), the University of Guelph, and Carleton University and has had visiting appointments as the University of Mauritius, the University of Technology (Mauritius), the University of Ghana, the University of Botswana, and the CEAN (Bordeaux, France). She is the author of some sixty articles, papers, and books on the subject of public administration, organization theory, and public policy. She has worked as a policy analyst/manager for the governments of Canada, Alberta, Manitoba, and New Brunswick.

Michael Duggett is a British career civil servant. He has worked in various ministries in Whitehall but also in the European Parliament in Luxembourg and Brussels, where he also served on secondment (from the Cabinet Office) as the Director General of the International Institute of Administrative Sciences from 2001 to 2007. He has published widely on public service and management and is currently a consultant with the National School of Government in London.

Patrice Dutil is Associate Professor of Politics and Public Administration at Ryerson University. He was Director of Research at IPAC from 1999 to 2006. He was the founder, and editor for five years, of the *Literary Review of Canada*. He is also the author of *Devil's Advocate: Godfroy Langlois and the Politics of Liberal Progressivism in Laurier's Quebec* (R. Davies Publishing) and the editor of *Searching For Leadership: Secretaries of Cabinet in Canada* (University of Toronto Press).

David A. Good is a Professor of Public Administration at the University of Victoria and a former federal assistant deputy minister. His most recent book is *The Politics of Public Money: Spenders, Guardians, Priority Setters, and Financial Watchdogs inside the Canadian Government*. He is the author of the prize-winning book *The Politics of Public Management: The HRDC Audit of Grants and Contributions*.

J.I. Gow is Emeritus Professor of Political Science at l'Université de Montréal. After five years as a foreign service officer (1957–62), he took a doctorate in Political Science at l'Université Laval before joining the Department of Political Science at l'Université de Montréal. His main research interests are administrative history, the Quebec public service, administrative innovation, culture and ethics, and politics and administration. His principal publications are *Histoire de l'administration publique québécoise, 1867–1970; Learning from Others: Diffusion of Administrative Innovations in Canada; From Bureaucracy to Public Management: The Administrative Culture of the Government of Canada* (with O.P. Dwivedi); and *A Canadian Model of Public Administration?*

Carolyn Johns is Associate Professor in the Department of Politics and Public Administration at Ryerson University. She teaches courses in Public Policy and Public Administration at the undergraduate and graduate levels and in Ryerson's partnerships programs with Fire Services and First Nations in Ontario. She was editor of IPAC's Case Study Program from 2001 to 2004.

Evert Lindquist is Professor and Director of the School of Public Administration, University of Victoria. He has served as Visiting Fellow, Treasury Board of Canada Secretariat; President of the Canadian Association of Programs of Public Administration (for three years); and Chair of the Research Committee for the Institute of Public Administration of Canada. He is currently Senior Academic Visiting Fellow with the Canada School of Public Service.

Brian Marson, the Senior Adviser, Policy and Service Transformation, Treasury Board Secretariat of Canada, has become well known across the public sector in Canada and internationally for his advocacy of excellence in public service and for his leadership in cofounding the Institute for Citizen Centred Service (www.iccs-isac.org). He is coauthor of *The Well-Performing Government Organization* and *The New Public Organization*. A former National President of IPAC and Vice President of the CCMD, he has taught graduate courses in public policy, economics, and public management at Queen's University, Harvard University, and the University of Victoria.

Michael McConkey is a freelance writer in Vancouver. He was Research Officer at IPAC from 2003 to 2006.

Esther Parent obtained an undergraduate degree with distinction in history from Concordia University in 2002. She has since completed studies in Administration of Public Services at the Université du Québec à Montréal, where she worked with Jacques Bourgault. She is presently pursuing an MA in history at Concordia University. She has been working in the field of public heritage presentation at Parks Canada Agency since 2003 and is an active member of a joint union–management committee on recognition practices.

Ken Rasmussen is Director of the Johnson-Shoyama Graduate School of Public Policy at the University of Regina and a Professor in the Department of Political Science. He has written numerous articles on public administration reform, provincial politics, and public policy and has served on the national board of IPAC.

David Siegel is Dean of the Faculty of Social Sciences and Professor of Political Science at Brock University.

Paul G. Thomas is the Duff Roblin Professor of Government at the University of Manitoba where he has taught for more than thirty years. He is the author of more than one hundred articles and chapters in books. Earlier in his career he coauthored a best-selling textbook in Canadian public administration. He has been a frequent consultant to governments at all levels. In 2003 he won the Vanier Medal for Excellence in Public Administration awarded by the Institute of Public Administration of Canada.

**The Institute of Public Administration of Canada Series in
Public Management and Governance**